# The History of the
# GREAT WESTERN A.E.C. DIESEL RAILCARS

*Frontispiece:* New diesel railcars for the Great Western Railway. With the order for ten new steamlined railcars, three railcars, Nos. 10, 11, and 12, pose in the A.E.C. Southall (Middlesex) works before leaving for GWR metals, on 13th January 1936. Note the white panelled livery on the roofs.
*The BBC Hulton Picture Library*

# The History of the
# GREAT WESTERN A.E.C. DIESEL RAILCARS

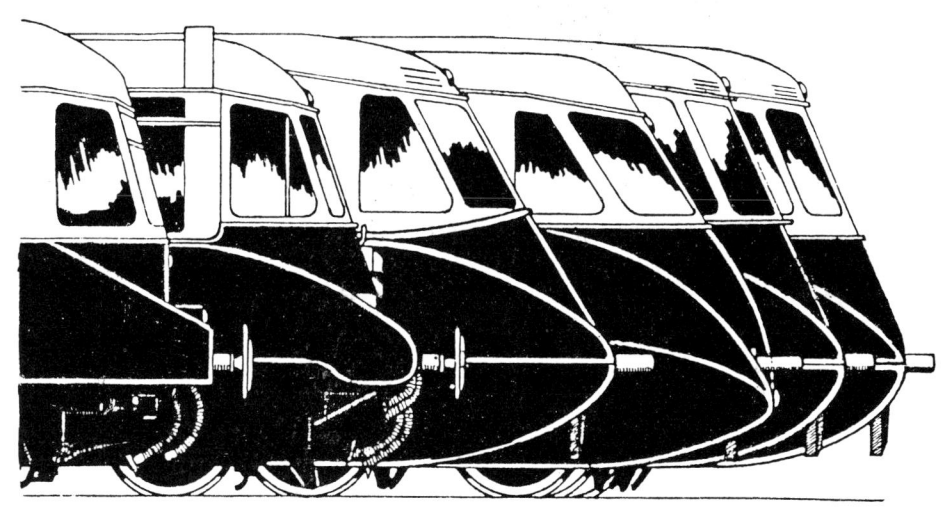

Compiled by
C. W. Judge

**Oxford Publishing Co.**

Copyright © 1986 C. W. Judge and Oxford Publishing Co.

ISBN 0-86093-139-0

All rights reserved. No part of this book may be reproduced or transmitted in any form or by any means, electronic or mechanical, including photocopying, recording or any information storage and retrieval system, without permission in writing from the Publisher.

## ACKNOWLEDGEMENTS

I wish to thank the following for their help in the preparation of this book. David Allan, Dick Blenkinsop, Gordon Baron, Neville Bridger, Colour-Rail, John Coiley, Colin Caddy, H. C. Casserley, Peter Durrack, Ron Drummond, the late Maurice Earley, John Edgington, Chris Gammell, Derek George, Michael Hale, Joe House, Bill Jardine, Ian Kennedy, Rex Kennedy, Philip Kelley, Roger Kidner, Doug Lindsay, Brian Morrison, Norman Preedy, Alan Peck, Kevin Robertson, Dick Riley, John Smith, John Senior, Ray Simpson, Ken Smith, Grahame Wareham, Peter Webber. Also the staff of the following companies, organisations and institutions for their help: Bodleian Library, Oxford, Radio Times Hulton Library, Public Record Office, Kew, Leyland Vehicles Ltd., Leyland, Ian Allan Ltd., Leyland Museum, Gloucester Carriage & Wagon Co., British Rail (Western Region), National Railway Museum, York, British Rail Engineering, Swindon, and Oxford Publishing Co. Ltd. Finally, thanks go to typists Christine, Jill and Wendy for 'de-ciphering' the handwriting, and to Christopher Potts for his meticulous checking of the final manuscript.

The extracts from the magazine *Locomotive* are reproduced by kind permission of Ian Allan Ltd., Shepperton.

The extracts from *The Railway Gazette* and *Diesel Railway Traction* are reproduced by kind permission of the editor.

The extracts from the *A.E.C. Gazette* are reproduced by kind permission of Leyland Vehicles Ltd.

The extracts from *The Engineer* are reproduced by kind permission of the editor.

The quotation from the *Railway Magazine* is reproduced by kind permission of the editor.

The extracts from the *Great Western Railway Magazine* are reproduced by kind permission of the Public Relations Office of British Rail (Western Region).

Typesetting by:
Aquarius Typesetting Services, New Milton, Hants.

Printed in Great Britain by:
Netherwood, Dalton & Co. Ltd., Huddersfield, Yorks.

Published by:
Oxford Publishing Co.
Link House
West Street
POOLE, Dorset

## BIBLIOGRAPHY

Many books, pamphlets, articles and papers were consulted, and the major works are listed below:

*Great Western Railway General Appendix 1936*
*Great Western Railway Magazine*
*Great Western Railway Working and Public Timetables*
*Great Western Echo* (Great Western Society)
*Meccano Magazine*
*Oil Engine*
*The Locomotives of the GWR (Part 11)*: RCTS
*A.E.C. Gazette*
*The Engineer*
*The Railway Engineer*
*The Railway Gazette*
*Railway Magazine*
*The Locomotive*
*Railway Wonders of the World*
*Hardy Motor Company Journals*
*Diesel Railway Traction Gazette*
*SLS Journals*
British Railways documents
*Railway Observer*
*County Donegal Railway* (David & Charles)
The many Oakwood Press Railway Histories and Light Railway Handbooks

# CONTENTS

Acknowledgements ... iv
Bibliography ... v
Foreword ... vi
Publisher's Note ... vi
Chapter One: Setting the Scene ... 1
Chapter Two: Early Development of the Prototype ... 29
Chapter Three: No. 1 into Great Western Service ... 49
Chapter Four: The Next Three Cars (Nos. 2, 3 and 4) ... 57
Chapter Five: Nos. 5, 6 and 7 (The Gloucester Bodies) Enter Service ... 77
Chapter Six: Ten More Ordered ... 85
Chapter Seven: No. 18 – A Radical Departure fom the Original Design ... 107
Chapter Eight: Swindon-Built – Nos. 19 to 34 – The New Design ... 135
Chapter Nine: The Twin-Coupled Units – Nos. 35 to 38 ... 179
Chapter Ten: The Power Plant and its Construction ... 191
Chapter Eleven: Three are still Preserved ... 197
Chapter Twelve: Railcar Workings, Timetables and a Pictorial Tribute ... 205
Appendix One: Shed Allocations and Changes ... 227
Appendix Two: Lot Numbers, Miles and Hours, Dates into Service, Mileage and Costs ... 230
Appendix Three: Lubrication ... 231
Appendix Four: Wheel Profiles ... 231
Appendix Five: Railcar Driving Instructions for GWR Cars Nos. 19 to 38 ... 232
Appendix Six: Heating of Railcars ... 233
Appendix Seven: General Appendix to the Rule Books Extracts ... 234

# INTRODUCTION

During the early part of the 20th century, the challenge and competition from road transport was growing. This was not only beginning to affect the local branch line services, but also many main line services. One reason for this was that the petrol and diesel-engined type of road vehicle could be made much lighter and be operated much more economically than the relatively heavy, and cumbersome, steam train or steam railmotor. Moreover the road vehicle could be arranged to work a more frequent and efficient service than the steam train.

The road vehicle was usually designed to be as light as possible, whereas the steam vehicle, owing to the type of construction employed, was considerably heavier for the same number of passengers carried. One particular road vehicle, for example, worked out at 300lb. for every passenger carried against a particular railway coach which, by comparison, weighed 1,100lb. per passenger carried. It was also becoming obvious to engineers (at this time) that the steam locomotive was far less efficient than the petrol engine, for it would generate about one fifth of the useful horsepower from the same weight of fuel used. If the performance of the steam locomotive was compared with the diesel engine, then the discrepancy in the power output was even greater. Although, during this period of time, coal was cheaper per pound weight than diesel or petrol fuel, the fuel cost of the steam locomotive was appreciably higher amounting from two to three times that of the petrol engine developing the same power.

Further disadvantages of steam locomotives were that they needed a longer period of time in which to raise steam, and also that the level of steam pressure needed had to be maintained whether the locomotive was moving or stationary. On the other hand, the diesel or petrol engine could be started from cold and then operated within a few minutes of warming up. Experimental operation of converted road vehicles on the railways revealed that the substitution of plain flanged wheels and smooth straight railway track, for the bad road conditions, (then prevailing) could result in a marked reduction in the driving effort required to haul such vehicles on the rails. Thus was made the case for the small diesel or petrol-driven coach, which was to prove more economical than any form of electric traction, because the latter involved a high capital outlay.

In view of all the new-found advantages of the internal combustion engine, it was not surprising that several companies and railway authorities concentrated their attention on the possibility of adapting road passenger vehicles for use on the railway network. Their prime objective was to improve rail vehicles sufficiently to enable them to compete on level or even better terms with their new up-and-coming road rivals.

In this study, one particular set of railway vehicles is fully considered, namely the A.E.C. Great Western Railway diesel railcars which, in my opinion, set the standards for the present day diesel multiple units and diesel passenger transport schemes.

*C. W. Judge*
*Oxford*

# FOREWORD

An extract from the *Railway Magazine* of 1935 summed up contemporary feeling about the introduction of diesel railcars to the Great Western Railway:

**GWR Diesel Railcars**
With the exception of the express buffet railcars on the Birmingham-Cardiff service, which were instituted to provide faster transit between these cities on a route whose traffic would not have justified additional steam services, the GWR diesel railcars have all been built in order to fill up gaps in the ordinary services in the economic way which is best provided by a railcar service. You need have no fear of any general displacement of steam by diesel propulsion in this country.

One can only say that because of the success of the GWR/A.E.C. diesel railcars, the Great Western Railway Company paved the way for the introduction of diesel traction into all the railway systems of what is now British Railways. If these vehicles had not been successful one wonders how the railway system would have looked today, and if the above statement might not have been more accurate.

# PUBLISHER'S NOTE

Both the Publisher and Author would like to bring to the attention of the reader that this comprehensive volume on The Great Western Diesel Railcars was compiled, using information from the official files in Swindon Works and in production with the Publisher before any similar work was published. All the information from the companies mentioned in the acknowledgements and involved in the production of these vehicles was cleared for inclusion in this book. The Special Reports prepared for British Railways and clearly marked "Private and not for Publication" were included by the kind permission of British Rail, Western Region.

# Chapter One: Setting the Scene

In setting the scene for the history of the Great Western Railway railcars, there would not be room to discuss all the many early design attempts at this form of transport, so the choice of vehicles reviewed had to be those which, in my opinion, influenced the design, development, and service running of the diesel railcars. Therefore, if a certain design has been missed in this highly active period of development, I hope the reader will accept my apologies.

In a effort to provide a cleaner, more flexible and economical type of rail traction, investigations were made early in the 1900s into using petrol engines and electro-transmissions. One of the first comprehensive designs recorded seems to be this drawing *(see Figure 1)* by the LNWR dated 3rd March 1904, Wolverton. Driven by a 40hp 4-cylinder petrol engine, and designed to carry 36 passengers, with a drivers cab at either end, it was a very advanced design, but there is no evidence that this vehicle was ever built or ran any trials. The similarity of this vehicle to the LB&SC vehicle of 1905 is very evident and one wonders if the design was sold or acquired and used for these vehicles *(see Plates 4 & 5)*. The British Thomson-Houston Co. Ltd. of London was much in evidence among the early equipment and railcar manufacturers.

In 1905, Maudslay Motor Co. Ltd. of Coventry were building two railmotor coaches for the Cape Government Railway *(see Plate 1)*. The body of the coach was carried on a Brill standard 21E truck, with wheels and axles specially adapted to the railway's requirements. There were three compartments: first class to seat seven passengers, third class to seat four passengers, and a large luggage locker in the centre. The motor consisted of a Maudslay 3-cylinder engine of 27b.h.p., with high tension ignition. The drive from the gearbox to the back axle was through a universally jointed shaft to a bevel box on the axle, and the reverse was operated by ordinary Panhard-type sliding bevels. There were three speeds in each direction, the top speed at a normal number of revolutions being about 18m.p.h., but the car was capable of acceleration to about 20 per cent above that figure. A special design of epicyclic gearing was used, the various speeds being always in mesh, and being brought into operation by means of metal-to-metal clutches running in an oil bath, thus allowing a considerable amount of slip without heating. The control gear was duplicated throughout, so that the car could be driven from either end if desired.

Also, during 1904 and 1905, the Great Northern Railway experimented with two vehicles *(Plates 2 & 3)* which were propelled by a petrol engine. One of them had, for some time, been running trial trips between Hatfield and Hertford. The cars, built by Dick, Kerr and Co., had seating accommodation for 32 passengers, and were propelled by two 4-cylinder petrol engines which drove both axles; the wheels were 3ft. 6in. in diameter; the length of the car was 34ft. 6in., with a width of 8ft. 6in., and it weighed 11 tons. There was a roomy platform at each end forming the driver's compartment. Handbrakes only were used, which must have been quite inadequate when trying to stop in the wet or on a falling gradient. These vehicles, although painted in GNR livery, were not accepted, and the Company equipped themselves with the fashionable steam railcars of the time.

Further experimentation by the London Brighton & South Coast Railway *(see Plates 4, 5, & 6)* took place in 1905 with a similar petrol railcar to that of the Great Northern. These two petrol railcars (Nos. 3 and 4) were also built by Dick, Kerr and Co. and although having novel reversible seating for 'which way' travel, as it was recorded, they did not impress the railway, and were again superseded by steam railmotor coaches. One worked the Brighton to Dyke branch for some time, but was reported 'not to be popular'. Little or no development of petrol railcars seems to have taken place between 1905 and 1912, with the exception of a series of petrol-driven inspection cars for the North Eastern Railway, one of which is shown in *Figure 2*, and an interesting railcar for the County Donegal Railway of Ireland, shown in *Plate 7*.

During 1912, the Great Western Railway Company introduced its first serious petrol railbus. This particular railcar carried out most of its trials on the Windsor branch. The vehicle was designed by the British Thomson-Houston Co. Ltd., having a matchboard wooden body, as can be seen from the accompanying *Plate 8*, and was numbered 100 by the Great Western Railway. It was powered by a 40hp Maudslay petrol engine, having a bore and stroke of about 5in., which drove a dynamo which in turn powered two tram-like electric motors on the axles. Two carburettors were fitted, although only one was in use at any one time, the second being a standby in case a malfuction occurred. A similar precaution was taken in regard to the ignition system, for which there were two entirely separate systems — namely, a coil and accumu-

*Plate 1:* The Maudslay petrol rail motor coach, built for the Cape Government Railways in 1905.
*Railway Gazette*

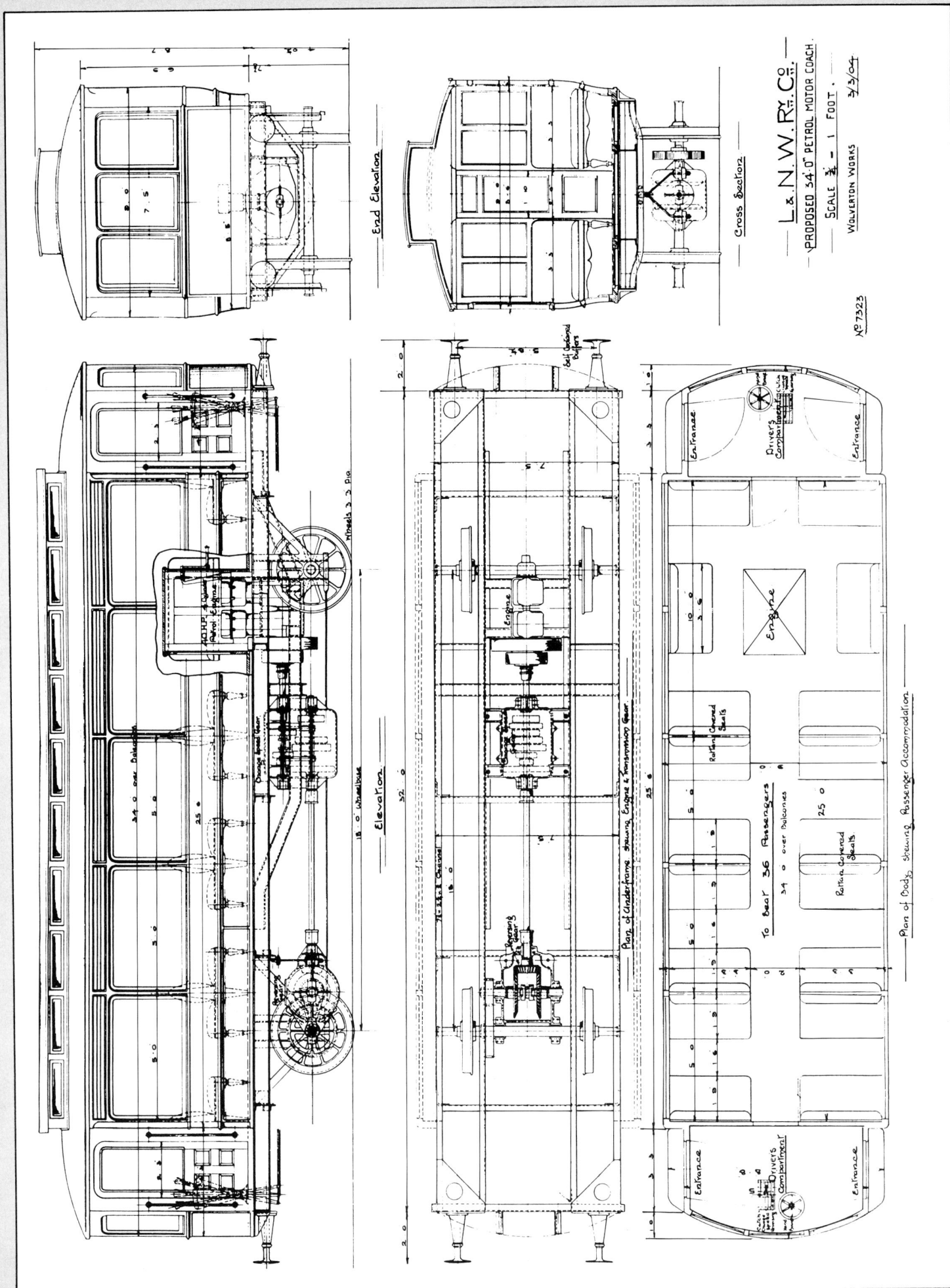

Figure 1

# SETTING THE SCENE

*Plate 2:* One of the Great Northern railcars of 1905, seen here without a livery.
*Lens of Sutton*

*Plate 3 (below):* A further look at the 1906 Dick, Kerr, Great Northern railcar, this time fully lined-out, and in the Company's livery, being numbered 3.
*National Railway Museum*

*Plate 4:* London, Brighton & South Coast Railway's railcar No. 3, showing the central door and larger passenger area than the Great Northern car seen in *Plate 3*.
*Lens of Sutton*

*Plate 5:* With the crew strategically placed, is petrol railcar No. 4 of the London, Brighton & South Coast Railway. This car has the window layout changed to that of No. 3, and is more in line with the GNR railcar, except that this vehicle has a centre door. It is seen standing at Kemp Town Station.
*Lens of Sutton*

*Plate 6:* The interior of the LB&SCR railcar No. 4, showing the spaciousness, and its light and well-designed layout.
*Railway Gazette*

*Figure 2:* A petrol motor inspection vehicle.

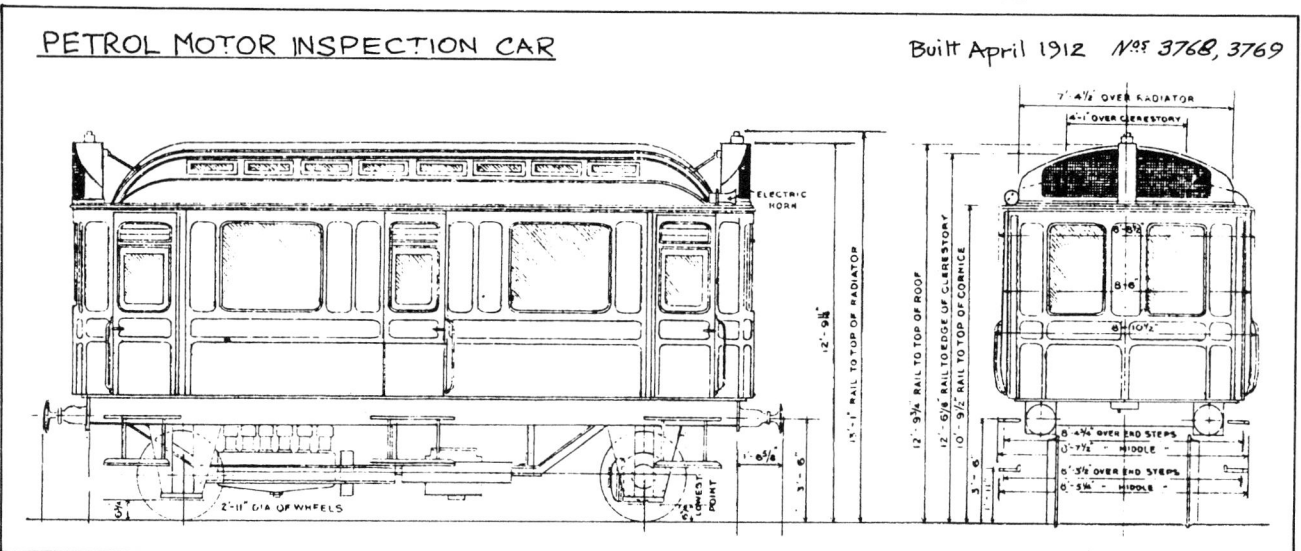

*Plate 7:* Railcar No. 1 of the County Donegal Railway of Ireland, which started its life in 1906 with a petrol 10hp engine, and cost £237 from Allday & Onions, the builders.
*Lens of Sutton*

*Plates 8a, b & c:* The Great Western Railway petrol railcar No. 100. It was built by British Thomson-Houston Co. and *Plate 8a* clearly shows the radiator fitment, with further details in *Plates 8b & 8c*.
*British Rail*

ulator, the other being a high-tension Bosch dual magneto. The radiator was placed on the roof (a board was bolted over the front of it to render part of it inactive during the winter). By virtue of the radiator's position, thermo-siphon circulation was employed, to cool the engine. There were two independent sets of brakes; one set was controlled by hand and the other by means of compressed air provided by a pump, driven by the engine. The compressor was placed in and out of gear automatically.

A trip in this vehicle, which appears to have been satisfactory, was recorded at the time and is reproduced below:

The journey between Slough and Windsor was about 2½ miles in length; the timetable allowed 9 minutes and no difficulty was experienced in adhering to it, despite fairly heavy gradients. A maximum speed of 32 miles per hour was obtained. On petrol, the consumption worked out at about 8 miles per gallon with a range of 240 miles, a creditable performance, bearing in mind that the vehicle weighed 14 tons 9 cwts. The overall length was 33 feet 3 inches, which allowed seating accommodation for up to 46 persons. Two staff only were required to run the vehicle — a driver and a guard.

The Great Western Railway withdrew this vehicle in October 1919, after a relatively short-lived career, and sold it to the soap giants, Lever Brothers Ltd. at Port Sunlight, Cheshire, for use on their private railway system.

*Plate 9:* The twelve seat railmotor of the Midland Great Western Railway, looking quite fragile around the chassis and wheels.
*Railway Gazette*

The Midland Great Western Railway, during this period of time, were also experimenting with a petrol-driven car for passengers and mail *(Plate 9),* which was constructed by Messrs. Chas. Price & Son, of Broadheath, near Manchester, to the specification of Mr E. Cusack, Locomotive Superintendent of the MGWR. It was designed to carry 12 persons, including the driver, and about ¼ ton of mails in the lockers at each end. The engine was of the 4-cylinder water-cooled vertical type, having cylinders 4in. in diameter, by 5in. stroke, developing 26b.h.p. at 1,000 revolutions per minute. The cylinders were cast in pairs and the crankshaft was supported on three white metal bearings. A centrifugal water circulating pump and the high tension magneto for ignition were located at the front of the engine and driven from the crankshaft by helical gear wheels, to ensure silent working. The crankcase was made in halves, and the bottom part was detachable, so that the main bearings were accessible without disturbing the engine. The 'Claudel Hobson' carburettor was controlled by 'Bowden' wire mechanism from either end of the car. The gear was arranged for three speed ratios in either direction, the sliding gear wheels travelling on castellated shafts, mounted on ball bearings. The transmission from the last shaft in the gearbox to the driving axle was by a silent chain, a spring-loaded adjustable leather-faced roller being fitted for taking up the adjustment. The clutch was of the leather-faced cone type, arranged so that when it was engaged there was no end-thrust when running.

Lubrication of the journals was by slip rings, the bottom half of the axle box forming an oil reservoir, and the wheels were of crucible cast steel, of 30in. diameter, pressed on to taper axles and secured by nuts.

The driving control was arranged to be worked from both ends of the car, and the forward and reverse rods were arranged so that no two sets of gears could be put into mesh simultaneously, by an interlocking device at either end of the car. Accelerator pedals at each end were fitted. Two braking systems were employed, one operated by foot pedal, and the other by a hand lever, acting on both pairs of wheels. The radiators located on each side of the engine were of the spiral tube pattern. The pressed-steel underframe was 20ft. long, and the wheels spaced 8ft. centre to centre. Duplicate water and fuel tanks were provided, the latter being under the seats, and fed the carburettor by gravity. Seats were upholstered in leather, with reversible backs, and the weight was 3 tons, with a maximum speed stated as 33m.p.h.

From 1912 onwards many novel designs were put forward, and *Figure 3* shows a drawing of a 1922 North Eastern Railway design for an omnibus-style motor railbus. In 1921 some of the smaller companies invested in railcars, one such company being the Weston, Clevedon and Portishead Light Railway *(see Plate 10).* Their railcar was constructed by the Drewry Car Co. Ltd. (Works No. 1252), to the instructions of Lt.-Col. H.F. Stephens, Engineer and General Manager of the light railway and was delivered in October 1921. The car was worked by a 4-cylinder petrol engine of 25/35b.h.p., the consumption on easy grades averaging 16 miles to the gallon. The overall length was 19ft., height 8ft. 3in. from rail level to roof, and extreme width 8ft. It was driven in either direction by chain transmission, and was fitted with handbrakes worked from either end. The wheels were 2ft. in diameter, and the vehicle was fitted with windows at the ends as well as at the sides, and all the side windows opened for ventilation. Thin steel panels were used on the sides and ends of the coach.

Lighting was by means of acetylene lamps (replaced later by an electric system) and the railcar was designed to convey a staggering 42 passengers on slatted wooden seats. A further feature was the fact that light rails were placed around the roof to allow luggage and market produce to be carried. One point of importance is that Lt.-Col. Stephens, in 1890, is reported to have arranged for an old Priestman oil engine to drive a tramcar bogie, thus claiming to be the pioneer of the use of the internal combustion engine for use in traction on the railway, and also of the motor car, as there were certainly none on the road until after this date.

The weight of the railcar was only 6 tons, and it had a maximum speed of around 25m.p.h. It was recorded that it ran for about 6d. per train mile, which allowed the makers to claim that, 'we think it has been a source of considerable profit to the railway'. On busy days and when necessary, a trailer car was

# SETTING THE SCENE

*Plate 10:* The Drewry railmotor car of the Weston, Clevedon & Portishead Railway.

*Lens of Sutton*

*Figure 3:* The North Eastern Railway design for a rail motor bus.

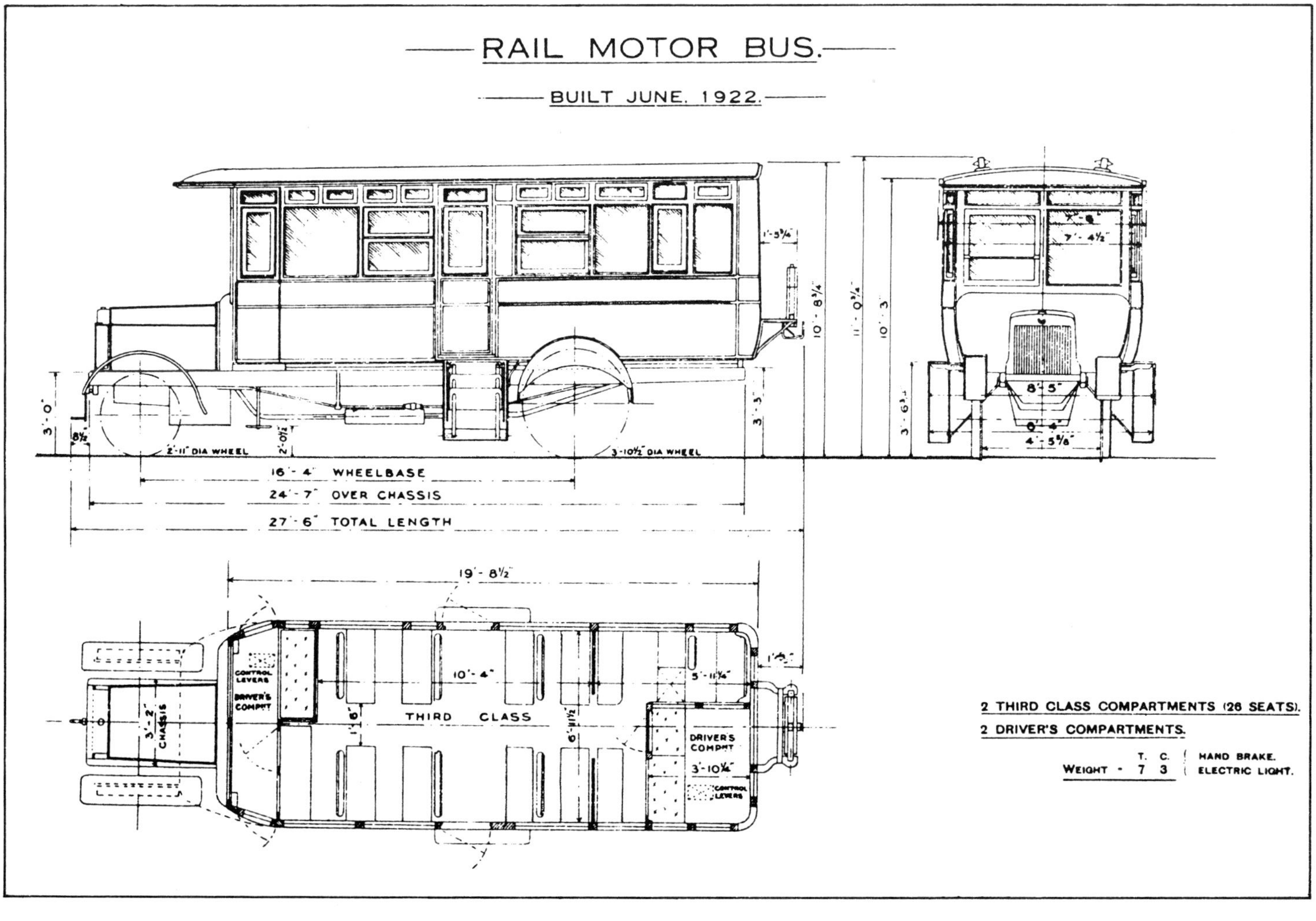

*Plate 11:* The 'back to back' petrol railmotors of the Kent & East Sussex Railway.
*Author's Collection*

*Plate 12:* The three-car petrol railmotor train of the Shropshire & Montgomeryshire Railway, when delivered in 1923.
*Railway Gazette*

*Plate 13:* Another experimental railcar again on the Kent and East Sussex Railway. Built by the Wolseley–Siddley Company and seen here at Rolvenden. Note the chain drive to rear axle.
*R. Kidner*

hauled in the rear of the railmotor; this was a four-wheeled vehicle, supplied in March 1923 by the same firm, with seats for 24 passengers and a weight of only 3 tons 5cwt. It was fitted with a handbrake and was similar to the motor car, but waterproof curtains were provided instead of the drop side windows.

Both the railmotor and trailer car were reportedly painted in smart dark green livery. A further railcar (built in 1928) was also purchased in 1934, from the Southern Railway, and was numbered 5 in the WC&P stock fleet.

Two other light railway companies were experimenting around this time with railmotors, the first being the Kent & East Sussex Railway. They purchased, in 1923, a set of Ford 'back to back' units from Edmonds of Thetford (with bodywork carried out by Eton Coachworks of Cringleford). These operated between Robertsbridge and Headcorn and were reported to have a petrol consumption of 1¾ gallons (with a full load) for the 24 miles (up gradients of 1 in 50) — *see Plate 11*. With the success of this vehicle, another set of units, of a similar design, was purchased in 1924. Secondly, the Shropshire & Montgomeryshire Railway (Shrewsbury to Llanymynech) put into service a three-car railmotor train in 1923 under the supervision of Lt.-Col. H. F. Stephens. These interesting adaptations of road motors for rail service were arranged back to back, with an intermediate dummy car in the centre, giving accommodation in all for 60 passengers *(see Plate 12)*. Light passenger bodies were fitted on the motor car frames (the usual steering gear dismantled), and flanged wheels were fitted to solid axles. A sliding door at the rear of each body provided ready access to the centre car. Centre draw-pin connections were used for coupling the cars.

The train maintained a good average speed; the economical rate being about 25m.p.h., but it was capable of running faster. It climbed gradients of 1 in 50 with curves of 9 chains radius quite easily, and managed long stretches of 1 in 130 and 1 in 150 without overheating. On trial, the train ran 50 miles on 7 gallons of petrol with three cars, or working as a two-car unit just over 1½ gallons of petrol for 18 miles, the load being made up with bags of coal, etc. to compensate for the weight of a full complement of passengers. This, again, was a pioneering effort into trailer car operation, as used today on the British Rail fleet.

As already recorded, the Great Western Railway were experimenting in petrol-driven vehicles and, although not railcars as such, they are worthy of mention. Although Drewry petrol shunting locomotives and inspection trolleys were in use on the GWR around 1910, and a Simplex petrol locomotive around 1921, it was not until 1923 that several new petrol-driven shunters were purchased *(Plate 14)*. These were numbered 15, 23, 24, 26 and 27, and they proved very useful, as they were the type for one-man-operation. All the vehicles were completed at the works of the Motor Rail & Tram Car Co. Ltd. Bedford, to the order of the Great Western Railway, for use on the standard gauge, and had a weight of 10 tons in running order.

The leading dimensions were: overall length, 13ft. 4in.; overall width, 7ft. 7in.; height 10ft. 7in.; wheelbase, 5ft. 6in. and the wheel diameter 3ft. 1in.

The internal combustion engine fitted, as seen in *Plate 15*, was made by Messrs W. H. Dorman & Co., Ltd., Stafford, and was of the 4-cycle type having four cylinders, water-cooled, each of 120mm. bore and 140mm. stroke, and developing 40b.h.p. at 1,000r.p.m. All the bearings were force-fed lubrica-

*Plate 14:* The new petrol shunting locomotive of the Great Western Railway.
*Railway Gazette*

ted, the oil being constantly filtered. Ignition was by high-tension magneto, provided with an advance and retard lever. The valves were of the poppet type, with means of adjustment, and both inlet and exhaust valves, springs, etc., were interchangeable. The engine was cooled by means of a radiator situated longitudinally on the locomotive, through which the water from the water jacket of the cylinders was forced by a direct-coupled pump, and cooled by means of a fan, the cooling effect being equally effective whichever way the locomotive was travelling.

The drive was through a patent change speed gearbox, providing two speeds in either direction. From the gearbox, heavy roller chains took the drive to each axle, simple provision being made for adjustment. The clutch was of the inverted cone type, situated in a large diameter flywheel, and was provided with the necessary means of adjustment. With the engine running normally at 1,000r.p.m., there were two speeds in either direction, 3m.p.h. in low gear, and 7m.p.h. in top gear. These speeds could be increased by 25 per cent by accelerating the engine. On the level, the tractive effort in low gear was 3,750lb. and in top gear it was 1,540lb., and it could haul 159 tons in low gear and 60 tons in top gear. On a 1 in 20 gradient, 17¾ tons could be hauled in low gear and 1½ tons in top gear.

The petrol consumption was 0.7 pints per b.h.p. hour, which worked out at about 50 gallons per working week. When working on paraffin, the haulage capacity was reduced by about 20 per cent. Petrol or paraffin fuel tanks were fitted with large capacity and gravity feed. As is seen in *Plate 16*, the control levers were conveniently arranged for the use of the driver, for running in either direction. The engine could be arranged for either hand or electric starting.

The locomotive was fitted with standard-type side buffers and central spring drawgear. Spoke-type wheels with steel

*Plate 15:* The Dorman 40hp 4-cylinder petrol engine, as fitted in the petrol locomotive of the Great Western Railway.

*Railway Gazette*

*Plate 16:* The engine of the GWR shunting engine, showing the flywheel end of the engine and also the control levers, etc.
*Railway Gazette*

tyres were hydraulically pressed on to the steel axles and axleboxes, having removable gunmetal bearings. Lubrication was effected by a wick-type feeder, lightly pressed against the lower half of the journal. Laminated springs of standard railway design were fitted. The framework was made of built-up channel steel, and the power unit had a sheet metal casing which was readily removable for inspection. Many railway companies, including the LMS and LNER, purchased these vehicles, and the type illustrated was the fifth built for the Great Western Railway and numbered 27 *(Plates 14, 15 & 16).*

These locomotives were employed variously at Bridgwater Docks, Taunton Engineering Sidings, Stafford Road Depot, Wolverhampton, Didcot Horse Provender Sidings, and Reading Signal Works. The two remaining petrol engines on the GWR register were of narrow gauge design, and numbered 22 and 25, again being built by the Simplex Company for use in the special departmental sidings of the GWR, at Banbury and St. Austell. These particular engines had a 2-cylinder petrol engine developing 20b.h.p. at 1,000r.p.m., with a weight of 7½ tons.

In early 1921 the Four Wheel Drive Lorry Company Ltd (FWD) was formed to construct and convert lorries left over (surplus) from World War I. Discovering that the 'gauge' of these lorries was almost 4ft. 8½in., a certain Major General L. Holden realised the potential of this coincidence and contacted the Four Wheel Drive Company.

His idea was to have a standard wheel with solid rubber tyres for running on the road, and to make them adaptable by

## SETTING THE SCENE

fitting interchangeable steel railway tyres for running on the railway tracks. Basically, the wheel centre was turned on its outside diameter to suit a taper wedge ring, which was split and fitted to the inside diameter of either the rubber tyre or the steel railway tyre, the whole being locked in position by suitable bolts. Difficulties arose, and regrettably the idea was dropped. Although this particular idea did not progress, the inventor worked hard at the problem and finally designed the first four wheel drive locomotive. It was decided to sell these locomotives under a separate company, and it is reported that, while trying to register a name for the company, the proposer was looking out of the office window in Trafalgar Square, London, and seeing Nelson's Column, he exclaimed 'got it!', and that was how Hardy Motors Ltd. (relevant in later chapters), obtained its name.

The 'standard' FWD (Hardy) locomotive had a 65hp engine with two radiators, only the one at the engine end having a fan (*see Figure 4*). Situated between the main gearbox and clutch was a reverse gearbox. On the road vehicle application, this box could be used as an alternative high gear, and thus be used as a power take-off for driving ancillary equipment, such as fire-water pumps or early hydraulic pumps. The drive from the main input shaft to the secondary driving axles was by means of chains, but this method was only used on the tail locomotive version. Other driving controls consisted of a conventional gate-type gear change, clutch, and foot brake, with a supplementary hand 'screw' brake. There was also a throttle pedal as well as a mixture and ignition lever.

Axles were of the lorry-type, but the steering arrangements were dropped, although conventional springing was retained. A drum-type brake was attached to the rear of the gearbox input shaft and became a four wheel brake, as also did the compensated brakes acting on the rims of the four wheels. A heavy frame was used to attach the buffers and drawgear. To save cost, the body was constructed of wood, with sheet metal covering, leaving a large space available for any required ballast.

This new development in railmotor transport and the development of Hardy Motors is very relevant to the final GWR railcar design, and so the technical aspects of these vehicles is dealt with in full within the following paragraphs. Contemporary reports called this invention 'very useful'.

The four wheel drive vehicle was either used as a commercial road or railway vehicle, especially in countries where roads were very rough and in bad condition, and also on branch lines where trains were infrequent and where it was not a paying proposition to keep an engine in steam. As the lorry was not of special design, spare parts were available from any dealer. The chassis was built for commerical work, and, on account of the four wheel drive which placed it on the same plane as a four-coupled locomotive, and its narrow tread, it was eminently suitable for railway work. Since, as was stated before, all four wheels drive, the strain was equally taken and distributed throughout the chassis. The engine was a 4-cylinder of 36hp, developing 56hp. The clutch was the 'Hele Shaw' multi-disc type, consisting of steel and copper plates, and ran in oil.

The standard lorry had three speeds forward and one reverse, with standard chain reduction giving speeds of 2.6, 4, 8 and 16m.p.h. respectively, but for passenger work, a special gearbox was fitted, having four speeds forward and four reverse — equal ratio — giving higher speeds in either direction. For tilting purposes, a small ram was fitted under the body of the lorry, two small pins were removed from one side, oil was

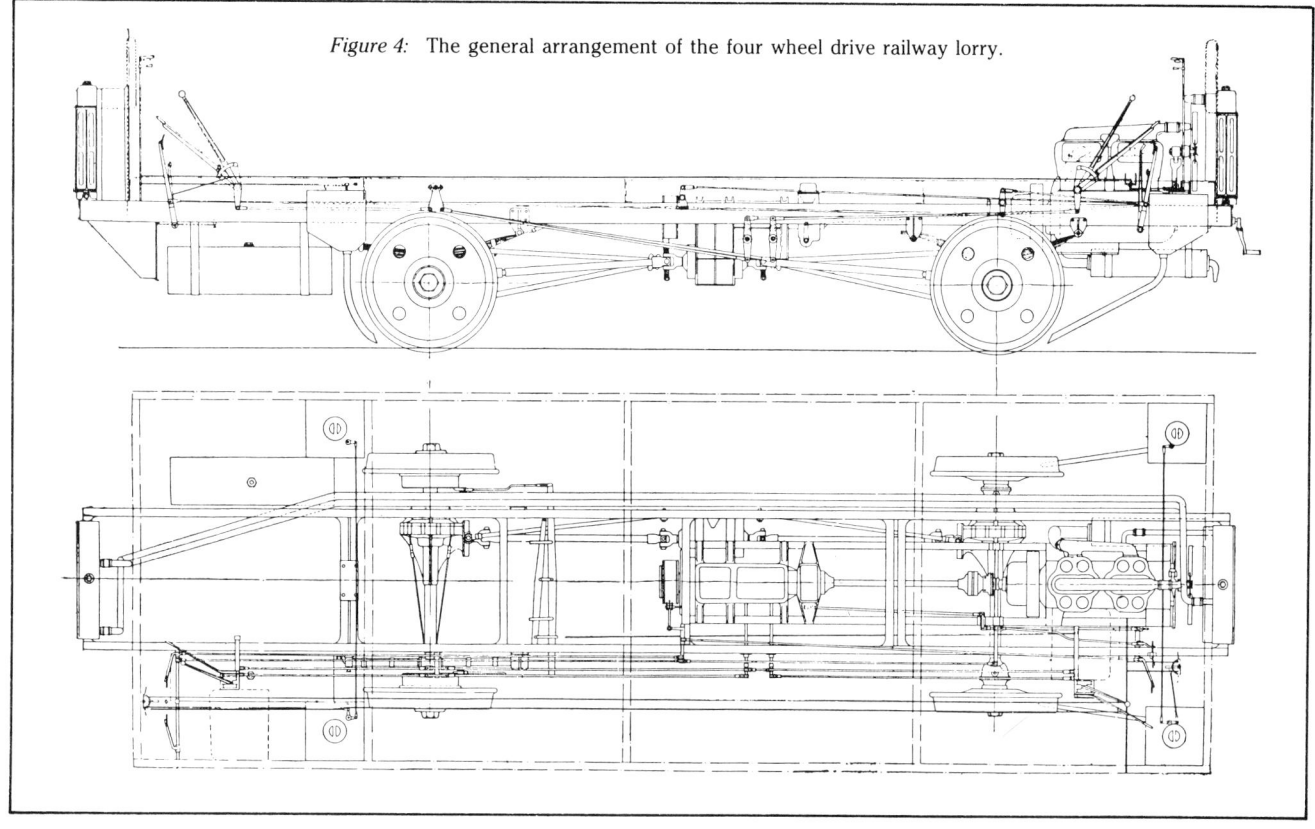

*Figure 4:* The general arrangement of the four wheel drive railway lorry.

*Plate 17:* The four wheel drive lorry version showing the 'oil' rams lifting the tilting bodies.
*Railway Gazette*

pumped into the ram, and the ram pushed the body over to the side required. When the oil was released, the ram slowly descended and the body returned to its normal position. *Plate 17* illustrates a lorry and trailer showing the bodies tilted.

For railway service, the four road wheels with solid rubber or pneumatic tyres were removed, and flanged wheels were substituted; a simple operation requiring, reputedly, a few minutes. The transmission was of the sliding dog-jaw clutch type, making it very easy to change speed. Braking was effected by an external foot brake on the transmission shaft, and there was also an emergency brake. *Plates 18 & 19* show the lorry adapted for running on rails and fitted with 'Newlay' rolled-steel wheels.

One vehicle was constructed for the Derwent Valley Light Railway, a 16 mile standard gauge agricultural line, running from York to Cliff Common on the North Eastern section of the LNER. The Four Wheel Drive Co. designed a very neat locomotive as illustrated in *Plates 20 & 21*.

Further development of these vehicles took place, and early uses of these FWD (Hardy) four wheel drive locomotives included supplying the Spurn Head Fort and South American Tramways. Others were constructed for the Swansea & Mumbles Railway and the Port Dinorwic Quarry in North Wales. The North Wales locomotive was different, as it had a 260ft. cable winch mounted under the rear buffer beam which was used for hauling wagons up from the steep quarry lines *(Plate 22).* Another locomotive was built, which required the driver to sit sideways so that the vehicle could have low headroom into the quarries.

The development work in 'motor' rail transport was now growing at a fast pace and so the Four Wheel Drive Motors Ltd.* (FWD/Hardy Motor Company) became allied with the Associated Equipment Co. Ltd., in November 1929 and between them decided to design and build an entirely new range of four and six-wheeled drive vehicles, incorporating the units (engines, gearboxes, axles, etc.) which had proved so successful in the A.E.C. road vehicle range.

So that these new vehicle types would not be confused with the old FWD products, the models incorporating the 'British' A.E.C. units were to be marketed purely under the name

*Plate 18:* A four wheel drive lorry converted for rail use.
*Railway Gazette*

'Hardy'. This name had previously been used to market vehicles produced for shunting, and lightweight locomotives, etc.

The further development of Hardy Motors was now taking on a new identity and beginning to shape around the larger bus-style vehicle and, following further research, a new Hardy chassis appeared in September 1931.

*Plate 19:* A useful load of wagons being hauled by the four wheel drive lorry vehicle.
*Railway Gazette*

*\*Footnote: The Four Wheel Drive Motors Ltd., was registered in October 1929, absorbing the Four Wheel Drive Lorry Co.*

# SETTING THE SCENE

*Plate 20:* The chassis of the four wheel drive petrol locomotive for the Derwent Valley Light Railway.

*Railway Gazette*

*Plate 21:* The completed locomotive for the Derwent Valley Light Railway.

*Railway Gazette*

*Plate 22:* A front end view of the petrol locomotive for quarry use, showing the winch and winding drum.

*Railway Gazette*

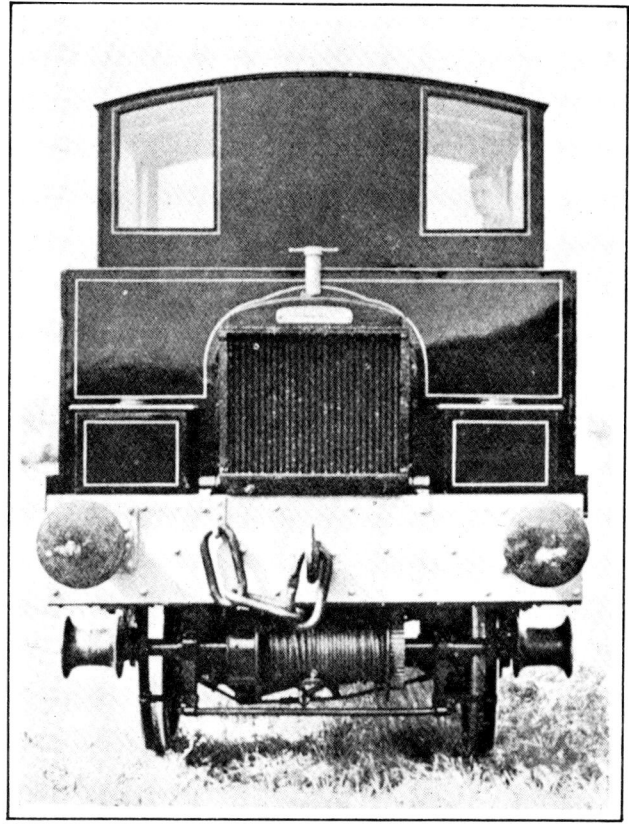

The two-page *A.E.C. Bulletin* article *(overleaf)* sums up the final, four-wheeled Hardy motor vehicle, before development of the bogie version used in the GWR railcar of 1933.

# NEW BRITISH RAIL CHASSIS FOR ABROAD

## A.E.C. 110 H.P. ENGINE IN HARDY MOTORS' NEWEST PRODUCT.

A DEMONSTRATION which aroused considerable interest among representatives of British and foreign railway interests was given at the works of Hardy Motors, Ltd., Slough, last month, when a new metre gauge rail coach chassis designed for service on the Argentine Transandine Railway was operated along the above Company's private test track.

The chassis—illustrated below—incorporates an A.E.C. 6-cylinder 110 h.p. engine similar to the power unit which is now giving such meritorious service in the latest type A.E.C. passenger and goods vehicles. This engine has a bore of 110 mm. and a stroke of 130 mm.: it develops 56 b.h.p. at 1,000 r.p.m. and 110 b.h.p. at 2,500 r.p.m.

The clutch is of the single plate type with a total wearing surface of 280 sq. inches, and with the gearbox is of unit construction with the engine. Exceptionally wide gears and large diameter shafts are features of the gearbox, which is of the four-speed type. In the reverse box the drive is taken from the driving to the driven shaft, either through a pair of gears, or a train of three gears, thus giving forward and reverse drive.

Double reduction type axles are used, designed so that any wearing parts may be easily replaced without removing the wheels. The drive is by a pair of spiral bevels to a countershaft which drives the main axle through wide double helical gears. These gears are carried in a cast steel casing, which is mounted on the axle on large diameter roller bearings, the torque being taken from the casing to the frame by means of ball-jointed tubular torque rods. Bevels and countershafts are carried on adjustable ball and roller bearings. The final driven double helical gear is pressed and keyed to an axle of 6¾in. maximum diameter on to

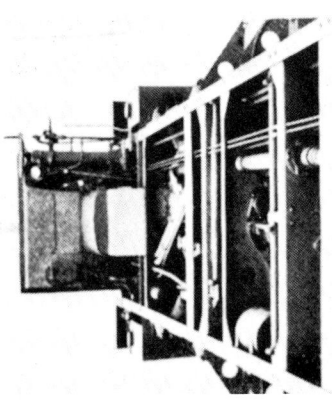

Top view of new rail chassis. Petrol tank is on left, water tank on right, and sanding boxes are in front.

which the wheels are pressed, these wheels having cast steel centres with rolled steel tyres pressed on, and are 2ft. 6 in. diameter on tread. The axle boxes which are outside the wheels are fitted with Timken roller bearings.

The brakes, operated by a 6in. by 8in. Westinghouse brake cylinder, are applied to all wheels through cast-iron shoes and all brake rigging is fully compensated. The brakes can also be applied from either end of the chassis by a screw down hand wheel. Sanding is carried out from sand boxes fitted with Westinghouse Air Sanding Valves.

All controls are duplicated, and included among these is the A.E.C. standard change speed gear, consisting of a change speed box mounted on the side of the crankcase and operating all gears through a single shaft. This is extended through the gearbox and connected up to the opposite end of the chassis where a corresponding change speed box is provided.

Circulation of the cooling system is by centrifugal pump on the engine through two "Still" tube radiators mounted at each end of the chassis, the water being forced through the radiators in series. The radiators are connected together and to the engine by 2in. diameter pipes, and a 45 gallon auxiliary tank is incorporated on the frame to which the water may be by-passed if required. The frame itself, of carbon steel, is of exceptionally stiff section and has side members 12in. deep and 3½in. wide.

Spring suspension, outside axle bearings and brake blocks. Brakes are Westinghouse operated.

Control levers at rear of chassis. Only the clutch pedal and sanding device are foot-operated.

Petrol is obtained from a 45-gallon tank, mounted on the side of the chassis, and a large dynamo, battery, self-starter and Henricot automatic couplers are included among the equipment.

# SETTING THE SCENE

During the period 1928-1933, before the introduction of the A.E.C./GWR railcar, other railway companies were progressing in the design of diesel and petrol railcars, and several are worthy of mention.

Firstly, the LMS Railway was experimenting with the use of the diesel engine for traction purposes, but their ideas were somewhat different. In the first place, a gear drive was considered, but the difficulties of providing a suitable gear change and transmission was such that electric transmission seemed to be the more favourable method, and therefore details of this vehicle have been included in this chapter to give some comparison between pure petrol/diesel traction and these other forms of power plants.

A four-coach electric train off the Manchester to Bury line was converted into a diesel oil/electric train at the LMS Railway works at Horwich, and was tried out by the railway company between Blackpool (Central), Lytham and Preston. As reconstructed, the train weighed 144 tons, and accommodated 32 first class and 255 third class passengers. The power unit, consisting of the oil engine and electric generator, was arranged at one end of the train, but it could be operated or controlled from either end (by electrical means) through a master switch. It is estimated that the power output was equivalent to that of a tank engine used for five or six coach trains up to 175 tons. At low speeds, the tractive effort was greater than the steam locomotive, but possibly less at the higher speeds.

The power equipment consisted of a 500hp 8-cylinder Beardmore crude oil engine, coupled to a 340kW, 600 volt direct current English Electric traction type, and an 8kW exciter. The engine cylinders were 8¼in. in diameter with a stroke of 12in. The engine and generator were coupled together with one intermediate bearing, and the frames were rigidly connected by a common bedplate. The exciter was of the overhung type, at the generator end of the set. The engine had four speeds, an idling speed of 350r.p.m., intermediate speeds of 600 and 750r.p.m., and a full load of 900r.p.m. The generator supplied power to two traction motors, each rated at 280hp, mounted on one of the motor coach bogies, with a gear ratio of 18/60.

The control apparatus was mounted on a self-contained framework, fixed over the generator, and was entirely electrical. The master controllers (which were provided with 'dead man's' handles) were similar in design to those used on electric stock, with the usual vacuum brake controls. The engine speed was determined by solenoid-operated valves, energised from the master controllers. The motor coach was designed to operate with three trailer coaches, so it was provided with a driving compartment at one end, and another driving compartment was located on the third trailer at the other end of the train.

A 120 volt battery, consisting of sixty cells, made by the D. P. Battery Co., was provided for starting the engine. When the battery was connected by means of a change-over switch to the generator, the latter acted as a motor, and rotated the set until the engine commenced to fire. The battery was then disconnected from the generator. In addition to this, the battery (at engine speeds under 600r.p.m.) supplied the lighting and control current and the power for driving the exhauster motors. Normally, these supplies were provided by the exciter, but as the exciter was driven by a variable speed engine, arrangements had to be made to provide them from the battery when the speed dropped. At engine speeds of over 700r.p.m., the exciter — which was self-excited, as well as energising the main field of the generator — supplied current for the various auxiliaries, i.e., lighting, control operation, driving the brake exhausters, and also for battery charging. To give a further range of speed than that given by the various speeds of the engine, there were two additional notches on the master controller, which brought about weakening of the fields of the traction motors. Sufficient fuel was carried to work one day's full service.

In Ireland, amongst mounting activity in the railmotor field, two railcars were supplied to the Great Southern Railway, being built in 1927 by the Drewry Car Co. Ltd., of London. The 75hp four-wheeled rail coaches were constructed to suit 5ft. 3in. gauge track, and were designed to give speed of 40m.p.h. on the level, and a speed of 20m.p.h. up a gradient of 1 in 75. Two of these cars were delivered in January 1928, and were put into service on the Goolds Cross-Cashel section. Having accommodation for thirty passengers, the estimated running costs were under 1/- per mile, including fuel oil, interest, depreciation, maintenance and wages for one driver, based on an annual mileage of 40,000 miles.

These two cars were fitted with 6-cylinder water-cooled engines, having cylinders 5in., in diameter by 6in. stroke, and developing 75b.h.p. at 1,000 revolutions per minute. Controls, mounted at each end of the car so that the vehicle could be driven equally well in either direction, consisted of reverse and change-speed levers, foot accelerator, foot brake acting on the drum on the reverse shaft, and a hand lever brake working direct on to the carrying wheels.

The main frame was of steel channel, provided with an inner frame to carry the engine and gearbox. The light enclosed-type body was of teak, with steel panels outside and 'Venesta' plywood inside, up to the waistline. The side lights were arranged to drop for ventilation, and the reversible seats were covered in 'rattan' material. The roof frame was of ash, covered with matchboarding, canvas and white lead. Dynamo, electric lighting and self-starter sets were fitted, including head and tail lights and interior roof lights. The steel petrol and water tanks carried 40 and 20 gallons respectively. The rail wheels were of 30in. diameter, and of rolled-steel disc pattern. The design was similar to the car in *Plate 23*, but obviously a larger vehicle.

The above general description also applied to the two 40/45hp cars constructed to suit the 3ft. gauge track, except that they were lighter and smaller *(Plate 24)*. These narrow gauge cars were in service between Kilrush and Kilkee in County Clare, on the former West Clare Railway. The running cost was under 9d. per mile. They would negotiate a gradient of 1 in 75 at from 23 to 25m.p.h. in top gear, and one of 1 in 20 in low gear at from 6 to 7m.p.h. They were provided with 4-cylinder engines, having cylinders 4¾in. in diameter by 6in. stroke; the running wheels were 24in. in diameter over treads. Fifteen gallons of petrol and twelve gallons of water were carried in the tanks, and like the 'broad gauge' cars they each carried thirty passengers.

During 1928, Lt.-Col. H. F. Stephens acquired a set of 'Shefflex' railcars for the West Sussex Railway. Satisfactory results had been recorded at the trials of a new railcar which had been introduced on the passenger service of the West Sussex Railway (Chichester to Selsey) — formerly the Hundred of Manhood & Selsey Tramway. These cars were built by the Shefflex Motor Co. of Tinsley, Sheffield.

As will be seen from the accompanying illustration *(Plate 25)*, there were two cars, each seating 23 passengers, which usually ran coupled together. The wheelbase was 11ft., and the overall length of the frame 16ft. 8in., plus front and rear

*Plate 23:* Railcar No. 2 of the Great Southern Railway of Ireland. Note the starting handle at the front.
*Lens of Sutton*

*Plate 24:* The Drewry railcar for the 3ft. gauge of the Great Southern Railway of Ireland.
*Railway Gazette*

*Plate 25:* The 'back to back' coupled Shefflex railmotor cars of the West Sussex Railway.
*Railway Gazette*

*Plate 26:* The radiator, and 4-cylinder petrol engine for the Shefflex railcar of the West Sussex Railway.
*Railway Gazette*

*Plate 27:* A scene on the West Sussex Railway at Chichester, showing the sparse facilities and the driver carrying out maintenance on the engine of one of the railcar units.
*Lens of Sutton*

buffers. Ball and roller bearings were used in practically every part of the chassis, while, in keeping with its place of origin, special steels were used where ordinarily mild steel would normally have been employed.

With dimensions of 100mm. bore ($3^{15}/_{16}$) and 120mm. stroke (nearly $4\frac{3}{4}$in.), the engine's four cylinders were cast in pairs. All three of the crankshaft bearings were ball bearings, which also carried the skew-gear driven camshaft, although, on this component, a split bronze centre bearing was also used as a steady *(see Plate 26)*.

Oil was delivered to the big-end troughs by a submerged pump, and arrangements were made whereby all oilways could be cleaned from the exterior of the engine. Petrol was gravity-fed to the Claudel carburettor from a 14 gallon tank under the seat, and a hot air intake was led from an exhaust muff to the carburettor.

Ample cooling was afforded by thermo-syphon action, which was assisted by the large pipe from the cylinder heads to the three-piece cast aluminium and Dreadnought tube radiator, which was trunnion-mounted above the front dumb irons.

The engine was mounted at three points; the rear bearer actually forming the back, and bearing housing of the crankcase, whilst the front chassis cross-member carried the front trunnion mounting through which the starting handle passed.

The Ferodo-faced cone clutch was kept in contact with the flywheel by a single control spring, while the clutch shaft was capable of universal movement, thanks to a laminated-steel disc joint at the gearbox, and a ball spigot in the flywheel. In the clutch withdrawal fork, the ball-bearing principle was also introduced, and an adequate clutch stop was incorporated in the design.

The patent gearbox included three forward speeds and reverse, and here the construction was unusual in that the changes were effected by a combination of sliding gears and dog clutches, the former engaging before the latter took up the drive. By such an arrangement, damage to the gear teeth became practically impossible. Behind the gearbox was a fabric-to-metal transmission brake, and at the front end of the propellor shaft to the over-worm rear axle was an enclosed star joint, whilst the rear joint was of the sliding block type. Wear and chatter were eliminated from the latter by combining the radiused steel blocks with bronze pads, which prevented backlash and play.

The casing, or body, of the rear axle, was a one-piece steel pot construction, with the worm carried by the lid. Taper roller bearings carried the back wheel hubs on their axle tubs (the front wheels also ran on similar bearings), and the axle shafts were 3 per cent nickel steel.

Fabric-faced expanding brakes acted in open drums bolted to the rear wheel spokes, each shoe working on its own fulcrum pin, and the end of the cam spindle arm carried a loaded wing nut adjustment.

Supported on semi-elliptic springs, fore and aft, (with the rear springs taking torque and drive reactions), the channel section frame was strengthened with ample cross members in addition to diagonal bracing at the back corners.

Running empty, a steady speed of about 30m.p.h. could be maintained, and the ability to pick up from very low speeds in top gear was excellent. Gear changing, due to the dog clutches, required a little practice, but actually became easier than with the conventional type, apart from the fact that little damage could be done by mere clumsiness. The gear ratios of $6\frac{2}{3}$ to 1, $13\frac{1}{5}$ to 1, and 24 to 1 for the vehicle, was adequate for service under all normal conditions.

A particularly noticeable feature of the engine was its quietness when idling. Although the valve tappets were not enclosed, there was no clatter. The lighting system was CAV with head and rear light and also interior lights.

The bodies were built by Messrs W. J. Flear Ltd. of Burton Road, Sheffield, with luggage rails fitted on the tops. Large plate-glass windows were provided above elbow level, ventilators being fitted above to admit air without draught. Throw-over spring seats were arranged across the car with a gangway down the centre. The carriages were warmed by hot-air pipes, heated by the exhaust gases, which were easily disconnected in warm weather. Exhaust whistles were fitted and operated by the driver. A 'Tecalemit' high-pressure greasing system was fitted throughout, and a gear and handbrake locking device

*Plate 28:* No. 8 of the County Donegal Railway's railcar fleet. An interesting design, with its long nose, it looked very powerful. Note the mail bags on the roof.

*Lens of Sutton*

was fitted to prevent passengers accidently putting these into action. The cars were combined with a 2 ton open truck, which was easily dealt with over gradients as steep as 1 in 50; the sharpest curve negotiated was of 6 chains radius. The gauge of the vehicle was 4ft. 8½in.

A further development took place in 1931 on the County Donegal Railway in Ireland, who had used railcars in service from 1906 and had progressed into the 1920s with several designs within their fleet. One railcar, No. 8, is pictured in *Plate 28* and was built by G. N. and O'Doherty at a cost of £2,086, entering into service in 1931 on the Ballyshannon branch. These were powered by a GL diesel engine, and could carry 32 passengers in the coach which weighed 7 tons. This particular vehicle was scrapped in 1949.

In 1932, a really novel design of diesel railcar appeared on the LMS *(see Plate 29)* and the trials were carried out early in the year by the LMS Railway in conjunction with the Michelin Tyre Co. on the Bletchley to Oxford branch *(see Plate 30)*.

The car used for the demonstration was the first vehicle in this country to run on rails with pneumatic tyres, having a light metal-framed body, and was of the same pattern as several supplied to the Eastern Railway of France for use on its branch lines. It would carry twenty four persons, plus the driver, and had a passenger compartment 21ft. long by 8ft. wide, with luggage compartments at either end. The overall length of the vehicle was 44ft. 9in. The vehicle was carried on ten wheels, on bogies of six and four wheels, the main 'drivers' being the middle pair of wheels, which were connected to the front axle by roller chains. The remaining pair of wheels of this bogie, as well as those of the rear bogie, acted purely as carriers.

The car was fitted with a 27hp Panhard & Levassor sleeve-valve engine, driving through a clutch and a four-speed unit-mounted gearbox. A separate reverse gear allowed four speeds to be used in either direction. The engine was water-cooled by means of aeroplane type radiators attached to the sides of the roof. Control was similar to road vehicle practice, with the exception that steering was obviously not necessary.

Braking was also similar to that used on road vehicles and was Lockheed hydraulic-operated, controlling the shoes on the drums, on all the wheels. Electric lighting and starting were provided, and heating of the passenger compartment was effected by air passing over the exhaust. The car could cover twelve miles on one gallon of petrol. It weighed about 5 tons empty, so that the dead weight per passenger was slightly over 4cwt.

The tyres, illustrated in *Plate 31*, were of the straight-side type, 910mm. by 125mm., with a split detachable metal tyre flange on the wheel rim. The wheel was removable from the hub in the ordinary way, the change taking about five minutes. On each wheel was a pressure gauge; should this record a drop of more than 14lb. below the normal 85p.s.i., an automatic audible warning signal was brought into action. This obviated all risk of running with a deflated tyre, even in the case of an instantaneous burst. In the event of sudden deflation there was a wooden hoop inside the tyre which took the load, so that there was no loss of stability to the vehicle. Behind the metal guiding flanges were rubber inserts, which effectually deadened noise arising from lateral motion of the car. The life of these tyres had been found to be about 20,000 miles, and the permissible load per wheel, 12½cwt.

The trial run was made under normal conditions, with a full load, from Bletchley to Oxford and back, 31 miles each way. The acceleration was excellent; a speed of 50m.p.h. was attained in one minute from the start, and 60m.p.h. in two minutes, but as the car ran almost noiselessly, there was little impression of the high speed to the passenger. The braking was very efficient, the car being pulled-up dead from a speed of 55m.p.h. in 45yds.

The railcar travelled under its own power from the Michelin Works at Chateau-Ferrand to Dunkirk, whence it was shipped to Tilbury, and then taken on a special machinery wagon to the LMS works at Derby for inspection; it afterwards ran to Bletchley for the tests. Truly a remarkable vehicle.

During this highly active development period, many further

*Plate 29:* The Michelin pneumatic-tyred railcar, showing clearly its novel 'aircraft-type' radiators, each side of the driving cab.
*Lens of Sutton*

*Plate 30:* Outside the LMS shed at Oxford (Rewley Road), poses the Michelin pneumatic-tyred railcar, in 1932.
*Railway Gazette*

*Plate 31:* A poor reproduction, but the only one available of the pneumatic tyre of the Michelin railcar.

*Railway Gazette*

novel ideas were being put forward, and one particular brainchild of the Chairman of A.E.C. (the late Lord Ashfield) was to use a normal A.E.C. 'Regal' single-deck bus and convert it for railway operation. This project was earmarked for the United Railways of Havana and Reglee Warehouses, and the Hardy Motor Division of A.E.C. were confident that it could redesign and build the vehicle. The A.E.C. 'Regal', chosen for the experiment, was fitted with a new front axle (without steering connections) to the gauge of the railway. It was reported that sand boxes were also fitted but were never used. The first outing was from Slough to Reading, on the Great Western main line, one Sunday morning in 1932. Apparently, there was anxiety during the trials about the 1 in 70 gradient down to one of the reversing turntables, as no high speed reverse was available.

The next tests were carried out by kind permission of the late Sir Nigel Gresley, as he provided a line near Hatfield *(see Plate 32)*, where a clear run was allowed, and also the use of some siding facilities. The vehicle was moved by road by replacing its front axle by a steerable one and rubber tyres replacing the rail tyres on all wheels. While being towed to Hatfield, the lorry driver relayed messages to the 'locomotive bus' by means of suitable bell connections.

When the trials were being carried out, an ingenious turntable was used, as shown in *Plate 33*. There was a siding at each end of the branch line on which the tests were carried out, and it was only necessary to run to this siding and on to a very crude small turntable on which the rear axle only just fitted. This was made out of a sheet of plate, with longitudinal

*Plate 32:* A fine view of the A.E.C. 'Regal' bus at Stapleford, near Hatfield, during trials.

*(A.E.C. Ltd.) Leyland Vehicles Ltd.*

*Plate 33:* The turntable (as described in the text) being used during the trials on the LNER.

*A.E.C. Ltd. Leyland Vehicles Ltd.*

tracks just high enough to clear the wheel flanges, and being well-greased and fitted with rollers, it was easily turned. A semi-circular turntable or track about 2ft. wide was built at rail level, with its radius equal to the wheelbase of the bus, and was lined with sheet metal. It was then only necessary to raise the front axle on an ordinary garage jack a few inches, and pull it round on the semi-circular track until it was standing facing in the reverse direction. The jack was removed and the front axle was lowered on to the rails. The bus ran forward and the turntable was removed. One man, it was reported, could handle the whole job, but the photograph *(Plate 33)* seems to tell a different story. After a series of trials, where it was found that the springs at high speeds (55m.p.h.) were 'sloppy', and that in general the axles were not suitable, the trials were dropped. The *A.E.C. Magazine* again recorded the trials and the following extract is worthy of inclusion:

**THE 'REGAL' ON THE RAILS**

Will the 'Regal' which has already won renown on the road, become, in time, an equally reliable railmotor for handling light passenger traffic on branch lines where it is no longer economic to run steam trains made up of several coaches? This question rises to the mind after witnessing a demonstration run made recently by a 120hp Hardy-A.E.C. 'Regal' rail-coach, destined for work with the United Havana Railways *(see Plate 34).*

The vehicle making the run was a standard type 32 seater 'Regal' coach, with the exception of the front axle which had been replaced by built-up rail wheels with wooden inserts. The axle ratio was 5¾ : 1.

On the outward journey the average speed was 22.2m.p.h. and on the return journey, including one official and one involuntary stop, 28.6m.p.h. Both these figures could be considerably improved upon. They are due to the caution of the driver, who was unfamiliar with the 'road', and not to the inability of the engine to put up higher speeds. This is substantiated by the fact that the log of the run reveals speeds over certain clear sections on the line ranging from 30m.p.h. to 49.5m.p.h. Even at the last speed, there was ample power in the A.E.C. 120hp engine to add many more miles to the maximum actually attained.

In tests taken for acceleration from rest, the following figures were obtained:

| | |
|---|---|
| 0 to 12.5m.p.h. in 7sec. | 0 to 37m.p.h. in 72sec. |
| 0 to 25m.p.h. in 28sec. | 0 to 41m.p.h. in 88sec. |
| 0 to 29m.p.h. in 50sec. | 0 to 45.5m.p.h. in 113sec. |
| 0 to 33m.p.h. in 58sec. | |

The petrol consumption of 6m.p.g. does not truly reflect the engine's capabilities in this direction, because, again owing to the driver's

*Plate 34:* The rail-going 'Regal' differs only from the road vehicle in its built up wheels with wooden inserts.
*(A.E.C. Ltd.) Leyland Vehicles Ltd.*

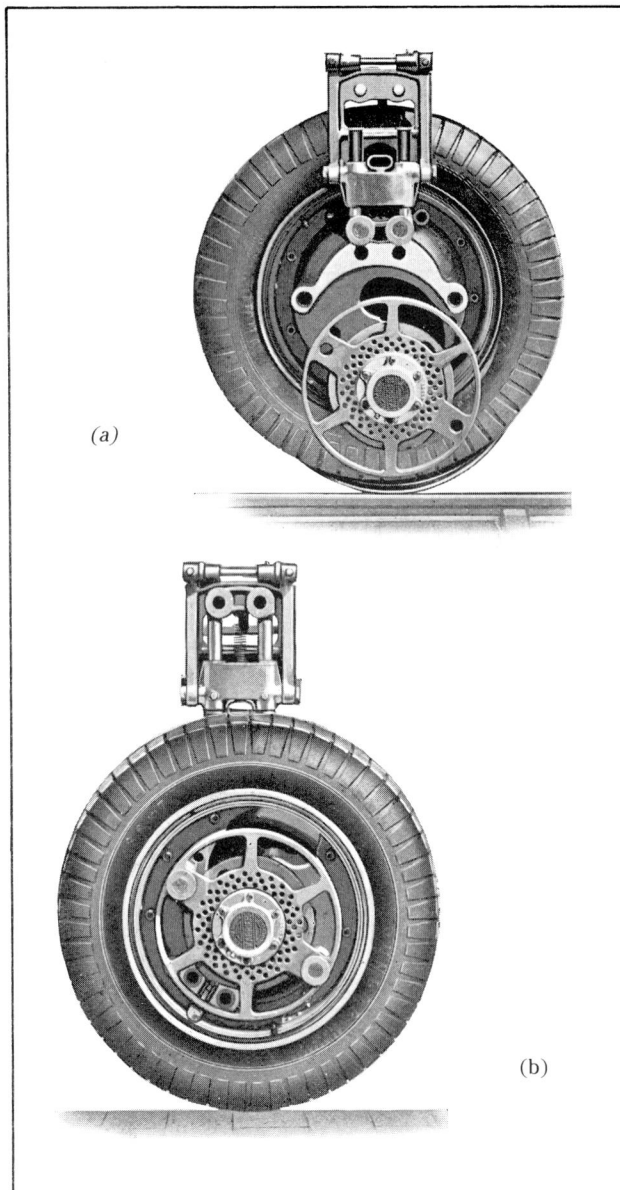

*Plate 35:* This shows the two positions of the wheel:

(a) On the rail — The road wheel in its raised position, with the steel-tyred rail wheel carrying the load.
(b) On the road — The road and rail wheels concentrically locked with the pneumatic-tyred road wheel carrying the load.

*Author's Collection*

caution on a strange 'road', the vehicle was run in low gear for far longer distances than would normally be the case.

There are undoubted possibilities for this class of rail coach on light passenger lines, and the run made with the 'Regal', while by no means conclusive in its results, has shown that this class of vehicle is well adapted for certain forms of rail service.

It remains for subsequent trials to show what the rail-'Regal' can do in the hands of a driver familiar with running conditions over a given stretch of line, such as would be the case in actual practice.

While all the trials and 'seed sowing' was taking place at the A.E.C. Company, further experiements were being carried out by Karrier Motors Ltd., of Luton. As early as 1928 the General Superintendent of the LMS Railway had commented that he would like to see such a vehicle as being able to load and unload passengers from both road and station platform levels, and that any wheel changing mechanism should be carried out in around 2½ minutes. The sales brochure of the day described such a vehicle and how the wheel arrangement worked:

**ROAD TO RAIL TRANSFER OPERATIONS**
On arriving at the railway, the vehicle is driven on to the permanent way at any place where the road level has been made up level with the rail tops. Then when its rail wheels are directly over the lines, the vehicle is driven slowly forward for a few yards to a point where the road level declines gently. Here the rail wheels gradually make contact with the rails to support the entire weight of the vehicle. It remains only for the driver to raise the road wheels above rail level by rotating them on lifting sleeves and inserting the locking pins to secure each wheel in the raised position *(see Plate 35).* The average time taken for the complete change-over for a four-wheeled 'Road-Railer' is approximately four minutes. The road wheels do not rotate when the vehicle is proceeding along the railway lines and the change-over operation is, of course, reversed at the point where road travel is to be resumed.

The specially prepared brochure went on to show the operation of the vehicles in some detail and is reproduced in full *(see the next four pages, 23–26).*

When the bus-designed 'Road-Railer' vehicle was delivered to the LMS Railway, it ran an extensive series of trials during the latter part of 1930 on the Redbourn to Hemel Hempstead branch line, going daily from Watford road motor depot to Redbourn by road, then to Hemel Hempstead by rail, off on to the road, round the houses and back on rail to Redbourn, and then home by road to Watford.

After several weeks of this routine, and after many railway men had been given 'rides', the vehicle showed no bad defects or serious faults. Several trials took place on the Huddersfield to Mirfield line, and here small changes were made to the wheel changing mechanisms and then an official order was placed. On 22nd January 1931, a special train was run from St. Pancras to Redbourn to 'sample' the 'Road-Railer' and the following was quoted by the local newspaper:

On arrival at Redbourn, the special drew up beside the 'Road-Railer' which, to the relief, it may be supposed, of the road motor engineer, had arrived safely by road and, looking rather insignificant beside the main line locomotive, was standing on the right spot straddling the rails ready to show off its tricks and capabilities. Well, indeed, it did show off in the capable hands of Messrs Messeter & Burchell of the RME Department, and a regular guard from the traffic department, doing several round trips until the many interested guests had tested it fully-laden over many miles by road and rail.

The demonstration attracted literally world-wide attention, and requests for further information were received from all quarters, including many railways in the USA. The reception by the popular press was almost embarrassing. *The Times*, cautiously said, 'Railwaymen regard favourably the prospects of the new type of vehicle'. *The Morning Post* said, 'The search for the 'missing link' in transport . . . has at last met with success'. *The Yorkshire Telegraph* reported 'An invention which may well effect a revolution in transport development'; and one of our more exuberant dailies headed its report, 'The 9.15 is at the door, sir.'

The various important members of the railway fraternity

# The potentialities of the
# Karrier "Road-Railer"
## in relation to the
### ECONOMICAL CO-ORDINATION OF ROAD AND RAILWAY TRANSPORT

The idea of increasing the scope of existing transport facilities by the aid of vehicles that can travel with equal ease over permanent ways and roads has long appealed to the imagination of railway and road transport engineers. Until about seven years ago, however, little was done in the way of developing the idea as a commercial proposition, but in 1930 widespread interest was aroused both at home and abroad by the introduction of the Karrier "Road-Railer." Produced in the form of an omnibus, capable of successful operation on road and rail, the original vehicle was acquired by the London Midland & Scottish Railway Co., Ltd., and used experimentally for two or three years in various places. During that time, the machine attracted world-wide attention and enquiries were received by its originators not only from railway engineers in both hemispheres but also from people interested in all classes of industrial transport. This volume of enquiries, when subjected to careful analysis, revealed the enormous possibilities of further "Road-Railer" developments which should satisfy the main demands outlined briefly in the following paragraphs.

*Above illustrations depict (top) Karrier "Road-Railer" approaching rails by means of built-up track, and (bottom) the vehicle on rails after running down ramp.*

*The original Karrier "Road-Railer" undergoing tests on a branch line of the L.M.S.R.*

Page 23

# THE PRINCIPLE OF THE "ROAD-RAILER"

Notwithstanding the varied requirements laid down by engineers and others who have investigated all possibilities of a vehicle capable of working on road as well as rail, experience in operating the Karrier "Road-Railer" has proved that all such requirements can be amply fulfilled.

In fact, it has now become quite evident that its designers have anticipated the full needs of all potential operators with remarkable foresight. Among the numerous outstanding features incorporated in the design of the Karrier "Road-Railer"; which, from every other point of view, is an orthodox motor vehicle, the principle upon which the wheels of the vehicle become operative on the rail is of particular interest.

Flanged rail wheels are fitted to the chassis axles and to the outside of the flanged wheels are attached pneumatic-tyred road wheels. Each pair of wheels are mounted on a separate hub, those carrying the road wheels incorporating a "C" shaped slot disposed from the centre to its periphery. The centre of the "C" is formed into a boss carrying a fulcrum pin pivoted to a sleeve with cranked ends.

When travelling on the road, the pneumatic-tyred wheels are locked concentrically with the axles carrying the flanged rail wheels which, being of lesser diameter, run clear of the road surface.

*Goods type "Road-Railer" operating on the road.*

The mechanism for effecting the lifting of the road wheel is very simple, consisting essentially of an inner hub assembly carrying the rail wheel and an outer assembly embodying the special wheel rotating and locking devices. On the road both road and rail wheels are concentric and revolve as one. In the rail position, the road wheels are lifted about their special fulcrum pins to a position in which locking devices are introduced, an arrangement which allows free movement in a vertical direction only and avoids interference due to the action of the chassis suspension, while still retaining the wheels securely.

The principle is applicable to practically any size of motor vehicle, whether for carrying passengers or goods. It can be adapted with equal efficiency to tractors and trailers. Another highly important feature of the mechanism refers to its overall width. A rail track of 4 ft. 8½ in., and a maximum width of 7 ft. 6 in., suit this type of machine, these dimensions allowing ample room for fitting the road wheel outside its flanged fellow. Standard railway platform dimensions leave ample space for unloading the vehicle in stations and give the necessary clearance for the road wheel when locked to the chassis frame.

Apart from regulations affecting the weight and dimensions of road motor vehicles, there is no limit to the carrying capacity of the "Road-Railer" which can be produced in four, six or eight-wheeler form, and vehicles can be so constructed as to be operated on lines of varying gauges.

There is nothing in the construction of the outer hub assembly to interfere with any type of bodywork, ranging from the ordinary flat platform truck to the most advanced type of luxury coach. In the production of such a vehicle embodying standard motor vehicle chassis units and components, the only increase in manufacturing cost is that of providing the additional hub assemblies. The latter lend themselves admirably to jig and repetition manufacture and involve no production complications of any kind, either as components of a complete "Road-Railer" or for supply as separate assemblies for converting existing vehicles to operate on rail as well as road.

*Goods type "Road-Railer" on rail, towing a brake van.*

## OPERATING COSTS AND OTHER FACTS

Compared with the cheapest branch line train or railcar, the costs of the "Road-Railer" are very favourable. Since the tractive effort on the rails is small, the running costs show a considerable reduction on those of road buses, more particularly in respect of fuel consumption, mechanical maintenance and tyre wear.

Contrary to an early supposition, there is no tendency for the "Road-Railer" to develop steering wander when travelling at low speed on the permanent way. The vehicle sacrifices nothing in the way of road performance when the usual overall gear ratios are in action, but for rail use it is advantageous to embody an auxiliary "overspeed" gear to permit of lower engine speed whilst a high rail speed can be maintained with definite economy in fuel consumption together with reductions of normal transmission stresses. There is no difficulty in ensuring adequate tractive effort when other vehicles are being hauled by the "Road-Railer" although, as in the case of rail locomotives, provision for sanding gear is necessary to serve the driving wheels. It should be specially noted that either the passenger or goods carrying types of "Road-Railer" can, if necessary, be attached to the rear of an ordinary goods or passenger train, being detached from the train to work forward as a road vehicle under its own power to any destination.

This remarkable dual-purpose vehicle presents outstanding advantages for maintaining transport services in countries where, during certain periods of the year, the roads are rendered impassable by heavy rains. At such times, the permanent way can be used to bridge the impassable areas so that travel facilities can be continued, and vice versa if the railway should be cut by land slides, etc. In like manner the "Road-Railer" offers a useful solution to the problem of maintaining the lines of communication in the event of hostilities, for should a portion of a railway line be destroyed, the dual-purpose vehicle or a train of such vehicles could travel across country to unaffected permanent way. Again the "Road-Railer" provides an efficient means of transport for working in conjunction with Airports. For normal service, however, it will be seen that the "Road-Railer" vehicle combines the many advantages given separately by the motor bus or lorry with regard to mobility, picking up and setting down passengers or goods without geographical restriction, comfort, safety and low operating costs.

# "ROAD-RAILER"

**KARRIER MOTORS LTD., LUTON, BEDS.**

World Exporters: Rootes Ltd., Devonshire House, Piccadilly, W.1

# SETTING THE SCENE

*Plate 36:* The road-railer bus in LMS service between Stratford-upon-Avon and Blisworth, in April 1932. Railway buffing and coupling gear, used in the 1931 Harpenden line demonstration, were at this time removed. It entered service on 1st April 1932, and was withdrawn on 2nd July 1932.
*Railway Gazette*

*Plate 37:* A fine study of the Karrier railcoach No. UR 7924, with the driver and guard ready for duty.
*Lens of Sutton*

present were handed the specially-prepared brochure that has been reproduced earlier in this chapter. From the brochure's contents it was clear that 'a revolution was going to take place', with the railways turning to the road and road vehicles turning to the rail, but luckily this 'revolution' did not come to fruition.

The LMS 'Road-Railer' did appear in regular service between Blisworth Station and Stratford-upon-Avon for some months *(see Plates 36 & 37)* but was withdrawn after front wheel wobble was experienced. At night, the vehicle left the rails at Stratford-upon-Avon and ran on the roads to the Welcombe Hotel, being garaged there for the night, and then returning to the railway in the morning. It can fairly be claimed that the LMS 'Road-Railer' was successful mechanically, although, no doubt, better machines would have evolved from it. It was too heavy for its power and seating capacity, but the wheel-changing system met all requirements. The LNER acquired one such vehicle for permanent way work, as did the Liverpool Tramways. Two were sold to Holland for use on a narrow gauge railway there. Working drawings were also prepared for a 'Road-Railer' goods truck or trailer, but were not used.

Returning to the Hardy Motor Co., we find that with the A.E.C. amalgamation truly established, this company was moving forward with chassis designs. Being well-placed alongside the Great Western main line, it was not long before both A.E.C./Hardy Motors and the GWR were collaborating and combining resources. Our A.E.C./GWR diesel railcar story now begins to unfold. Perhaps the reader will feel that many other designs and experiments in railcar design could have been included, but I felt that the most important developments, especially in the GWR, A.E.C. (Hardy) Light Railways, Irish Railways and LMS companies that have been recorded, were all that was needed to 'set the scene' for this fascinating development and revolution in rail travel.

# Chapter Two: Early development of the Prototype

*Plate 38:* The official A.E.C./Hardy heavily-retouched and airbrushed photograph of the prototype, with various livery details and lettering painted in on the photograph.

*(A.E.C. Ltd.) Leyland Vehicles Ltd.*

In July 1933, Hardy Motors Ltd., of Southall were completing the final stages to their new experimental oil engine driven railcar chassis. This chassis then had to be transported in mid-1933 from Southall (by road) to the Park Royal factory, as there was no convenient route* it could have taken by rail. It was carried on an MRS 110hp 14-wheeled road transporter, which was 68ft. 8in. long, and was fitted with double steering. This vehicle (in its simplest form a series of wheeled girders), could be raised and lowered by 50 ton hydraulic rams. The journey was accomplished at a rate of 2m.p.h., between 12.30 a.m. and 1.30a.m., when the roads were clear of traffic. The whole vehicle was being completed to be shown at the Commercial Motor Transport Exhibition at Olympia in October 1933. It was reported at this exhibition that the Great Western Railway Company had purchased this experimental vehicle and would put it into service between Slough and Reading at the close of the exhibition.

The coach body was built and fitted by the Park Royal Coachworks Ltd. of Abbey Road, Park Royal, London, and can be seen in *Plate 38*. This heavily retouched publicity photograph was specially prepared by A.E.C. Ltd., for their brochures. *The Engineer* magazine included its own photograph of the prototype seen in *Plate 39*. It is interesting to compare *Plate 38* with *Plate 40* which is an official photograph of No. 1, standing at Southall Station, taken by the Great Western Railway during the acceptance trials.

The difficulty of transporting the complete vehicle from the A.E.C. sidings to Olympia and back involved one or two ingenious movements, and again magazine articles of the day recorded this event. Here is included the September report of 1933 from the *A.E.C. Gazette*.

> Many visitors to Olympia inquired as to the transportation of this heavy and large vehicle through London. This was achieved by MRS Ltd. with their 100 ton Scammell articulated vehicle. The overall length of railcar and transporter was around 104ft. and therefore, pillar boxes, gateposts, railings, lamp posts, etc. were vulnerable. An advanced survey of the route was carried out to work out clearances for the trip. The Scammell had only a 43ft. carrying capacity, so the rear four-doubled tyres were detached and strapped to the railcar by a carrier unit, which consisted of 30ft. timbers, (12in. × 12in.) lashed to girders of the chassis to support the whole vehicle.
>
> The loading for the return journey was carried out by six men on the Friday and, at around midnight, commenced the return journey. This was made easier by the fact that the rear of the Scammell was steerable. The overall height was around 16ft. which, although clear of all the tram wires, did cause problems at some bridges. By 4a.m., the complete convoy had arrived at Brentford, where the railcar was jacked up and the Scammell driven away. The railcar was then lowered on jacks to the track beneath, which had been carefully sleepered previously to allow the Scammell to drive over.

The design of this vehicle was revolutionary for its time and very many new features were incorporated. Firstly the design afforded a reduction in wind resistance, and thus allowed a saving in weight, making it possible for the standard A.E.C. 130hp diesel engine to be fitted, providing enough power for a satisfactory performance. Fitted with two four-wheeled bogies, the vehicle was 62ft. long by 9ft. overall width, but weighed less than 20 tons, giving it a higher power/weight

*Footnote: The siding available had a curve too tight for the vehicle.*

30 THE HISTORY OF THE GREAT WESTERN A.E.C. DIESEL RAILCARS

130 H.P. RAILCAR FOR GREAT WESTERN RAILWAY

HARDY MOTORS, LTD., SOUTHALL, MIDDLESEX, ENGINEERS

*Plate 39:* The Engineer's official picture, again with a crude number 1, and 'Great Western' retouched on to the photograph.
*The Engineer*

*Plate 40:* The first Great Western railcar, No. 1, showing the full GWR livery and primitive buffers or buffing gear. It is pictured at Southall Station on 28th October 1933, during the acceptance trials. Note the smaller window ventilators and 'outward' central doors.
*(A.E.C. Ltd.) Leyland Vehicles Ltd.*

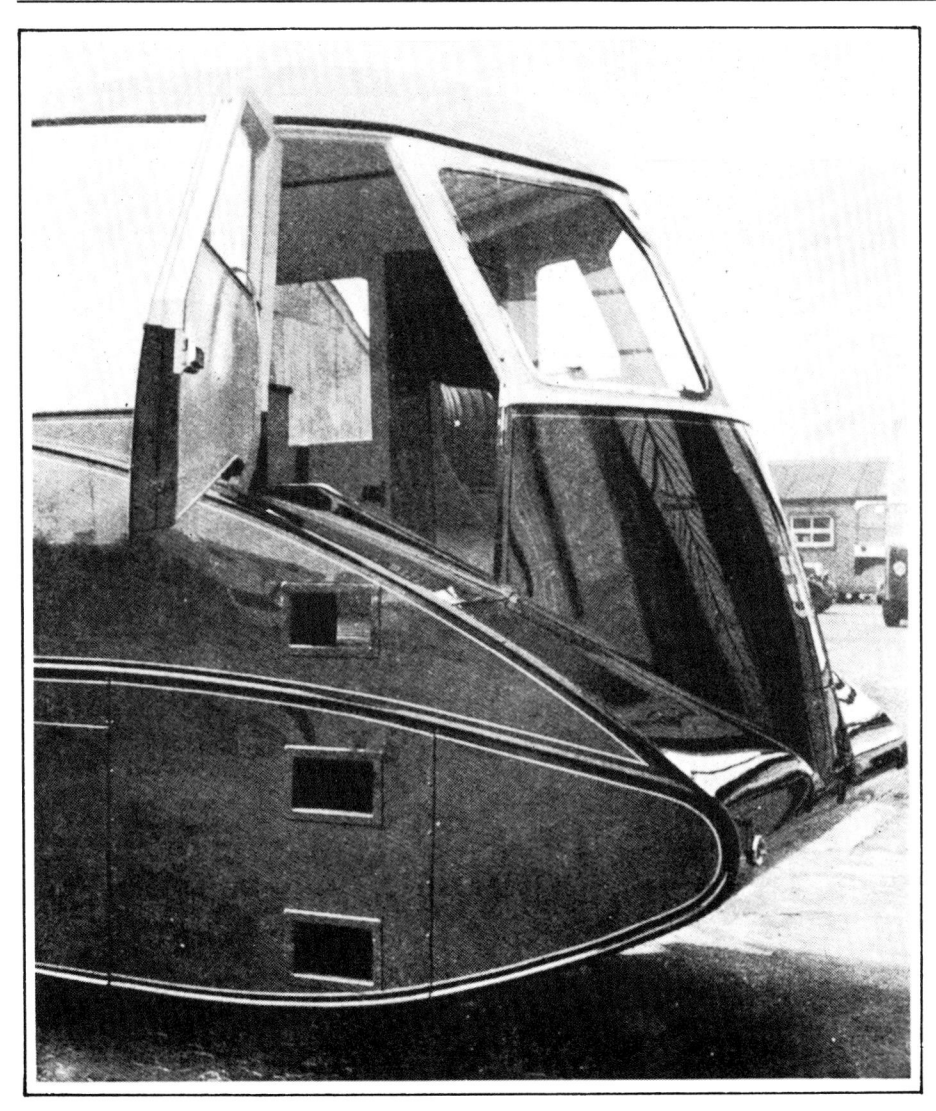

*Plate 41:* The streamlined nose of Great Western railcar, showing the retractable steps and entrance to the driver's cabin. The driver's seat is partly visible. This photograph was taken of the prototype before the 'buffers' were added.
*(A.E.C. Ltd.) Leyland Vehicles Ltd.*

ratio than most steam locomotives of its time.

Accommodation was provided for sixty nine passengers with a luggage compartment at one end, and in the Company sales brochure it stated that eight passengers could be carried if the luggage compartment was not provided. The aerodynamic design was revolutionary for its day, and even the steps to the driver's cab (from rail level) were covered with flaps, when the door was closed, *(Plate 41)*. The hinges were also reported as being designed to a streamlined profile.

The whole concept was designed from the results of wind tunnel tests, carried out at the Chiswick Laboratory of the London Passenger Transport Board on a few models, some of which are included in *Plates 42 & 43*. A graph corresponding to the various tests is also shown in *Figure 5*, which plots 'wind resistance' in pounds against 'speed'. Projected speeds and results were shown by dotted lines. Curve 'F' showed a very high resistance, which applied to the coach with very flat ends. The bests results obviously came from model 'A' (curve 'A') but the Company decided that this design was ugly and used a design based on models 'B' and 'C' as a compromise. It is worthy of note that British Railways (Western Region) 'Warship' class diesel locomotives (built in the 1950s) looked very similar to Model 'A'! The two models, 'B' and 'C', appear identical, but note that the shape of the roofs differ, and 'B' is curved upwards at the centre by 6in. relative to model 'C'. This surprisingly had a large influence on the design as can be seen in the graph results.

The chassis, portrayed in *Figure 6 and Plates 44 & 45*, was again very unusual as the engine was situated in the body, and offset near the centre. Both axles of the rear bogie were driven, and the whole of the transmission was outside the main frames on the left-hand side of the vehicle. The designs also incorporated valances right down to the rail level to enclose the mechanism. Considerable design and trial work was carried out on bogie design and, as can be seen from the drawings, the bogie was of a swing-link bolster type, with laminated springs over the axleboxes with an auxiliary rubber suspension block. The design of the main frame allowed the main engine and transmission units to be arranged on cantilevered arms from it. Access from inside the vehicle was made by means of a trap door system, to allow inspection to the underframe from inside the vehicle. The channelling used in the construction of the main frames was reported to be 10in. x 3½in. channel, trussed with 4in. x 4in. x ½in. angle.

As previously stated, because of the sensible tests carried out and the modern aerodynamic design used, the available 130hp

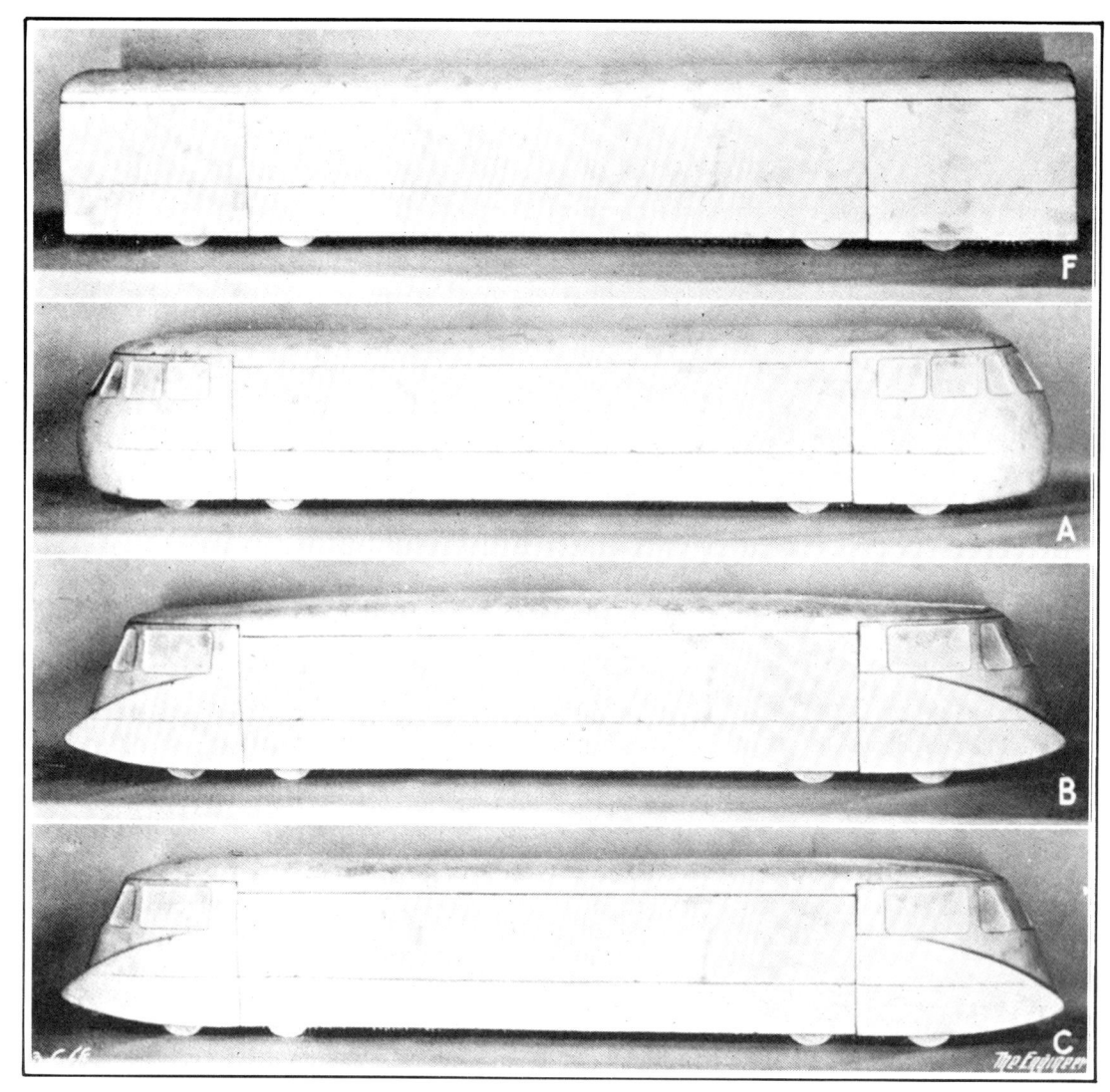

32 THE HISTORY OF THE GREAT WESTERN A.E.C. DIESEL RAILCARS

*Plate 42:* Early models used in the wind tunnel tests. The letters at the side correspond to the graph results in *Figure 5*.
*The Engineer*

*Plate 43:* The more advanced models used in the final wind tunnel tests.

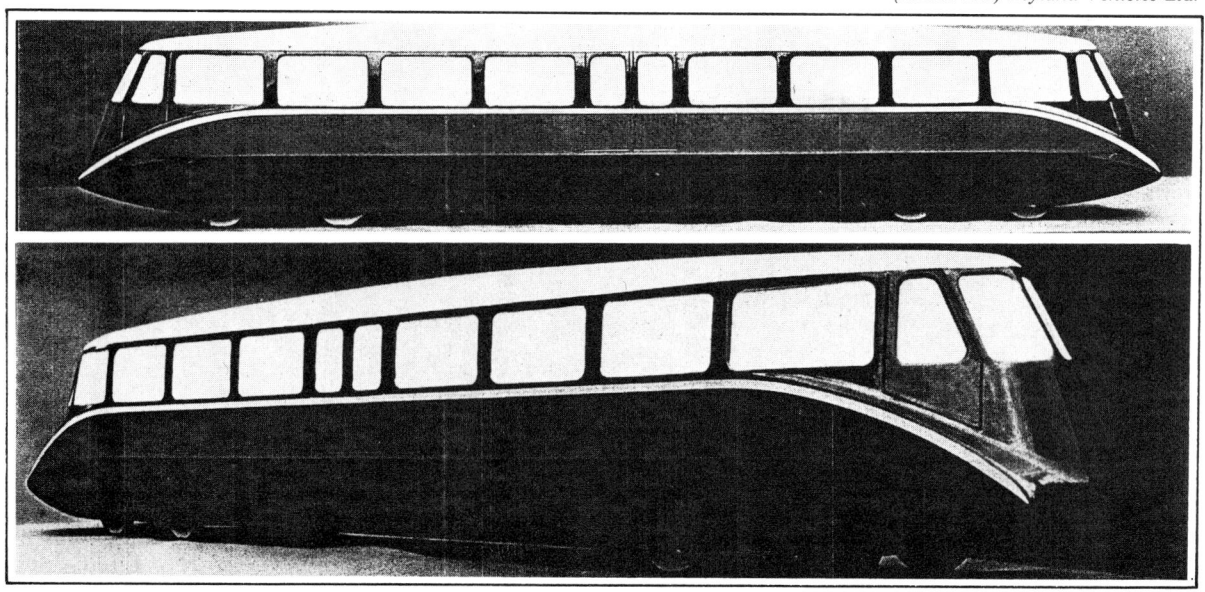

*(A.E.C. Ltd.) Leyland Vehicles Ltd.*

# EARLY DEVELOPMENT OF THE PROTOTYPE

*Plate 44:* The side view of the prototype chassis showing the general arrangement of the A.E.C. power unit and transmission.
*The Engineer*

*Plate 45:* The complete prototype chassis.
*(A.E.C. Ltd.) Leyland Vehicles Ltd.*

*Figure 5:* Results of the wind tunnel tests on the models shown in *Plate 42*.
*The Engineer*

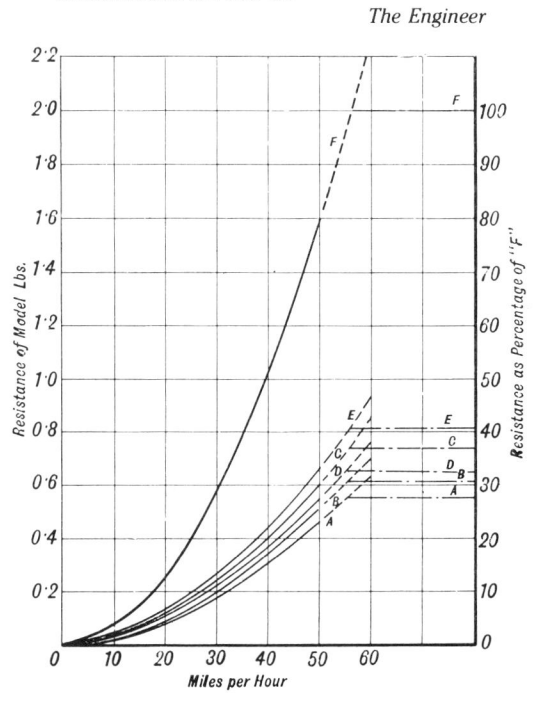

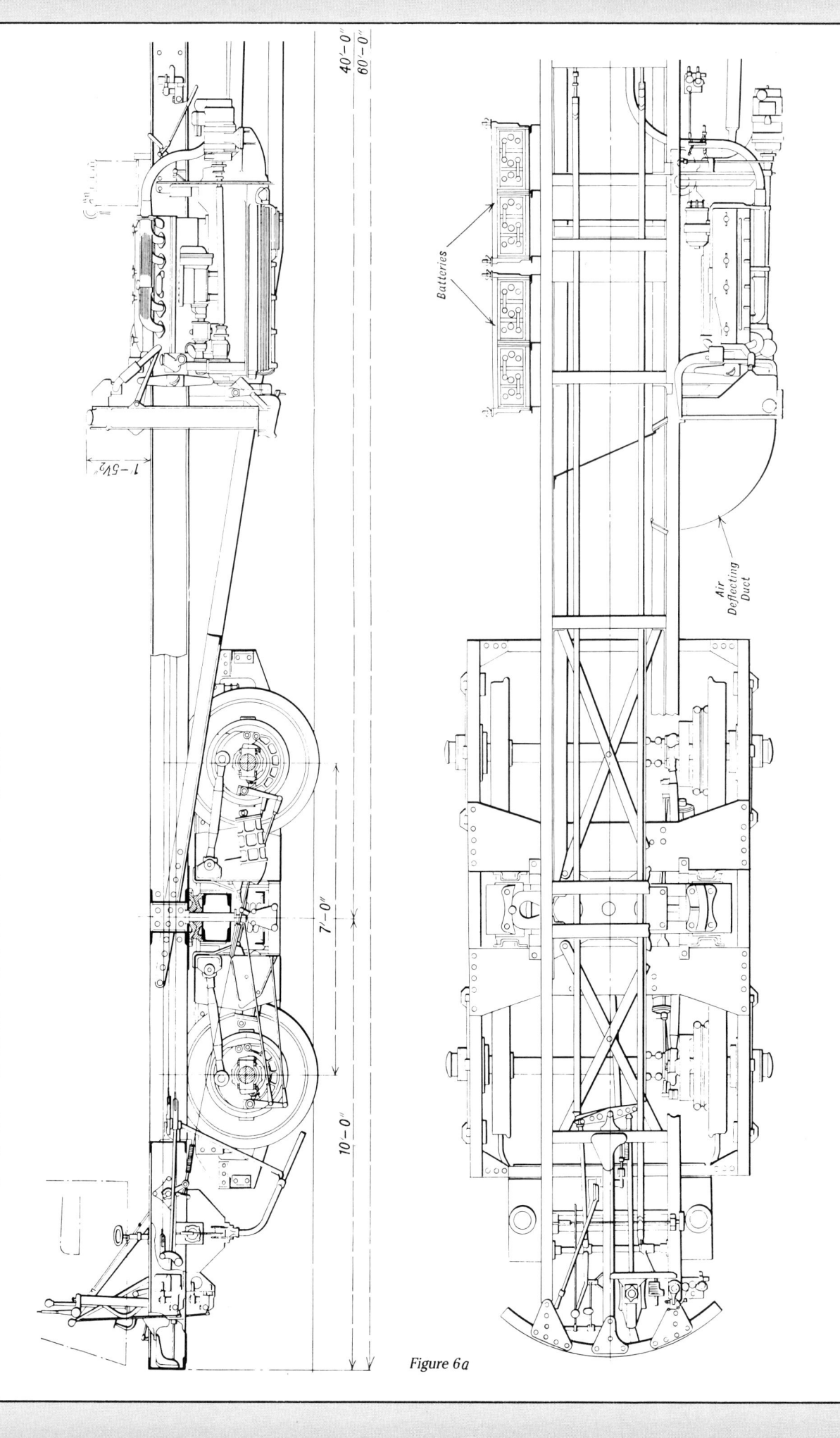

CHASSIS OF 130 H.P. OIL ENGINE-DRIVEN RAILCAR FOR SERVICE ON GREAT WESTERN RAILWAY

*Figure 6a*

Batteries

Air Deflecting Duct

HARDY MOTORS, LTD., SOUTHALL, ENGINEERS

*Figure 6b*

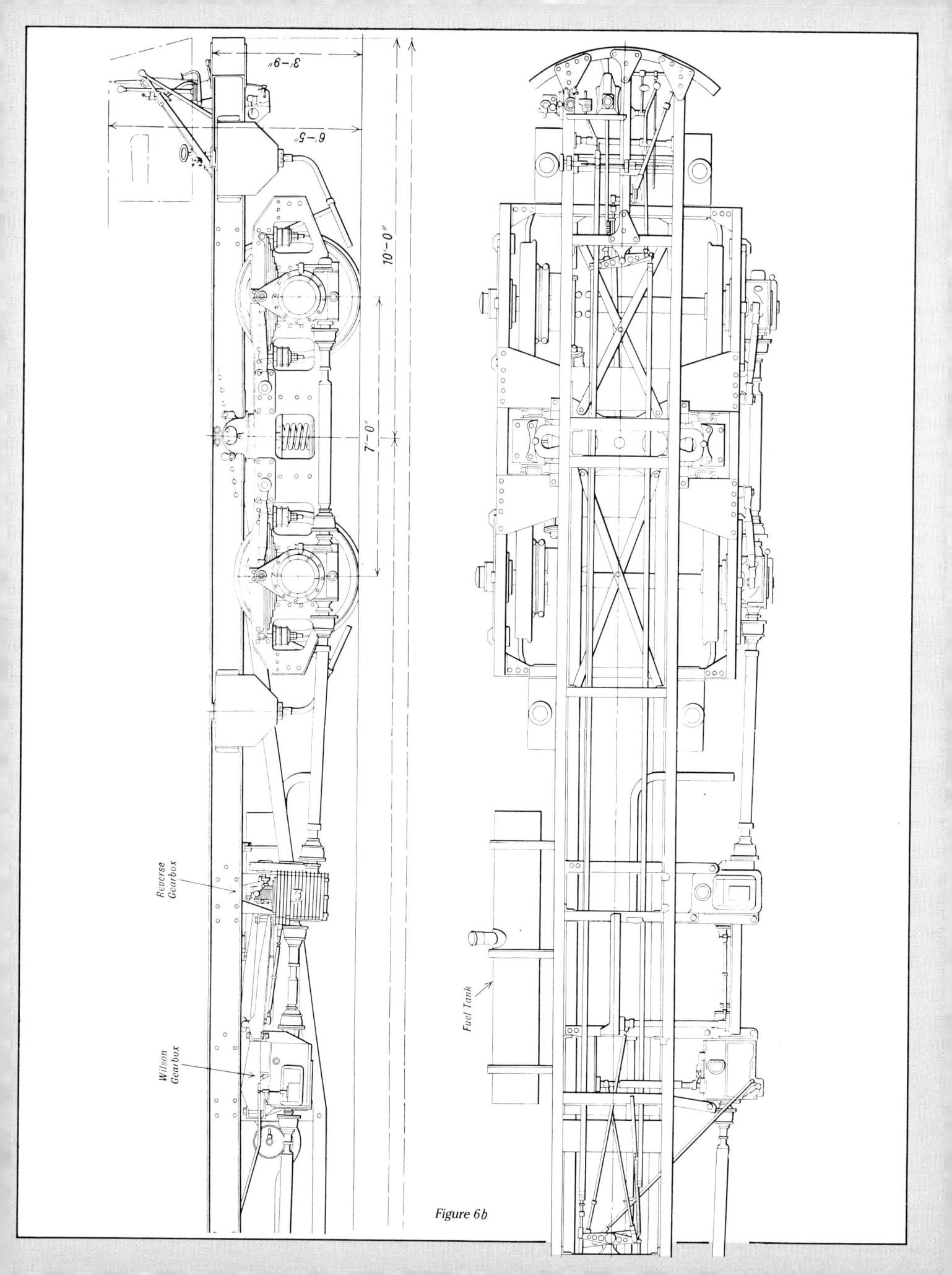

Figure 7: Hardy Motors' original drawing of the prototype.

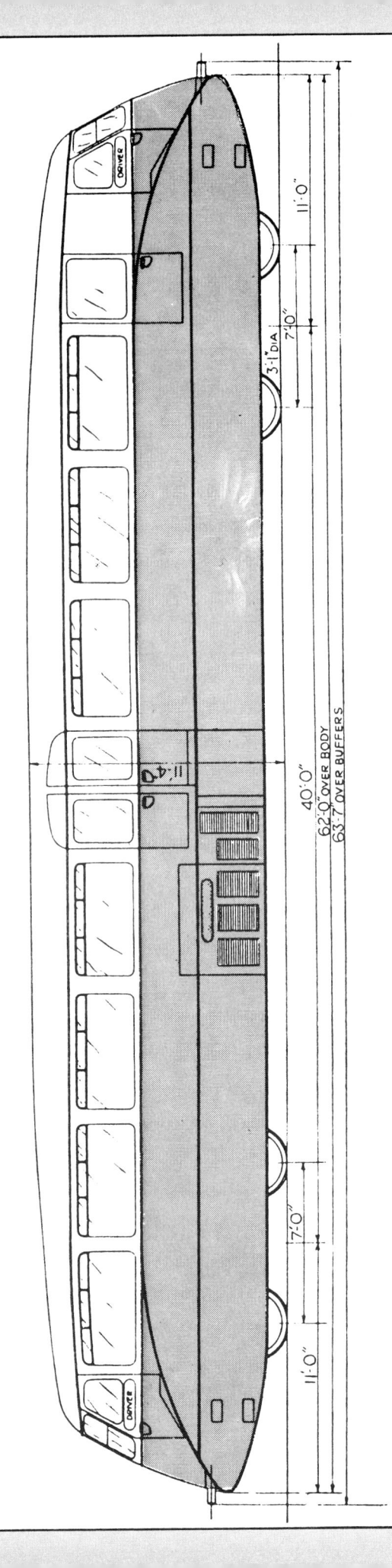

# A NEW STREAMLINED RAIL CAR

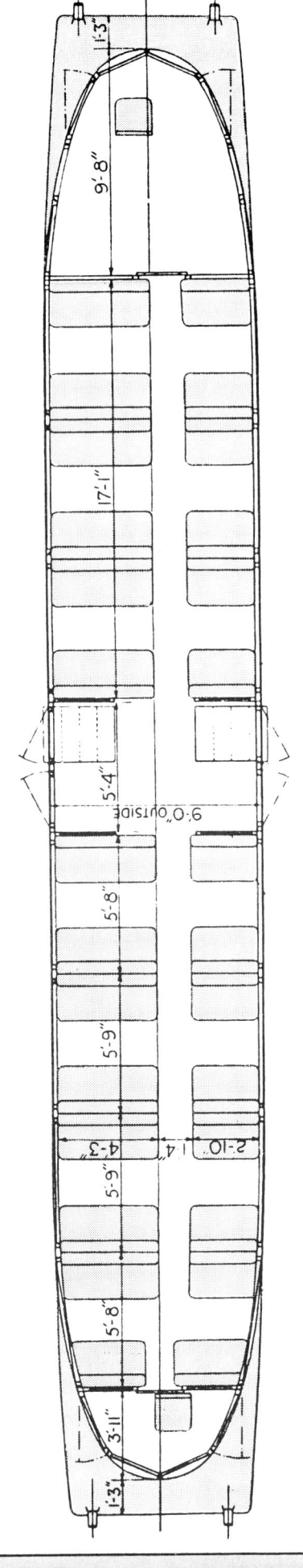

Designed and Manufactured by

**HARDY MOTORS LTD.**

(a Company allied to)

**THE ASSOCIATED EQUIPMENT CO. LTD.**

SOUTHALL, MIDDLESEX.

FITTED WITH THE

130 H.P. 6-CYLINDER OIL ENGINE

EARLY DEVELOPMENT OF THE PROTOTYPE 37

*Plate 46:* The radiator and engine of the prototype chassis. *(A.E.C. Ltd.) Leyland Vehicles Ltd.*

*Plate 47:* This view shows the engine (left) driving the gearbox and bogie.
*The Engineer*

*Plate 48:* This view of the prototype chassis shows the gearbox and reverse gearbox (with the chain-driven exhauster on top). Note the load on the chassis to simulate body weight.

*(A.E.C. Ltd.) Leyland Vehicles Ltd.*

A.E.C. oil engine could be used and, as this was the standard engine being produced for the A.E.C. road vehicles, very little development work was needed on the engine employed. The conventional radiator was mounted in front of the engine unit and, as this was enclosed, special measures were employed to ensure ample air flow through the radiator. Beneath the vehicle, a swinging metal sheet flap hung on a vertical axis. The free end projected into the mouth of a metal duct which was across the frame of the vehicle. As the vehicle moved forward, the flap swung backward and the air was deflected into the duct and so into the radiator. Rubber buffers stopped the flap from hitting the duct and, after the air had passed into the radiator, the conventional fan passed the air over the engine and it was then discharged through louvres in the side walls of the vehicle. This simple but ingenious device ensured ample cool air to the engine.

The accompanying two photographs *(Plates 46 & 47)* show the radiator and engine layout on the first prototype vehicle and also the driving bogie. Immediately behind the engine was situated the fluid flywheel, which replaced the standard clutch. From this box, a shaft, with two universal joints, took the drive to a pre-selective gearbox of the Wilson type. The gearbox gave four forward speeds and a reverse, and at 2,260r.p.m. the following speeds were quoted:

    1st    14.45m.p.h.
    2nd  25.04m.p.h.
    3rd   40.25m.p.h.
    4th   60.00m.p.h.

The reverse gearbox was an ingenious device *(see Figure 8 & Plate 48)* and in whichever direction the vehicle was travelling, there was no conventional direct drive. This design allowed the reduction from five gears within a conventional gearbox, to just three. The whole of this gearbox was enclosed in an aluminium-ribbed gear casing, to allow for better oil cooling, as overheating had been experienced in earlier trials with cast-iron casings. Also, a chain drive was taken from this shaft to a rolling drum exhauster *(see Figure 8)* mounted on top of the gearbox. This particular exhauster helped maintain the vacuum in the brake reservoirs, and supplemented the other exhauster driven by the engine. This would be used when the vehicle was coasting down a long gradient with gears in neutral; the engine-driven exhauster was more or less out of action due to the engine's idling speed.

Up to the point of the gearbox, the shafts transmitting the power only had to allow for differences in angularity, but for the final drive to the axle gearboxes, a further degree of flexibility was needed in order to allow for bogie rotation and springing. The telescopic design of the coupling shaft can be seen in *Figure 9*, and employed running splines and ingenious retaining covers, which were screwed on to the ends of the tubes to prevent complete withdrawal of the shafts from the tubes.

A further unusual feature was the fact that both axles of the rear bogie were driven through a worm and wheel mechanism *(see Figure 10)* and if any differences in the diameters of the wheels occurred, this would set up stress in between the shafts.

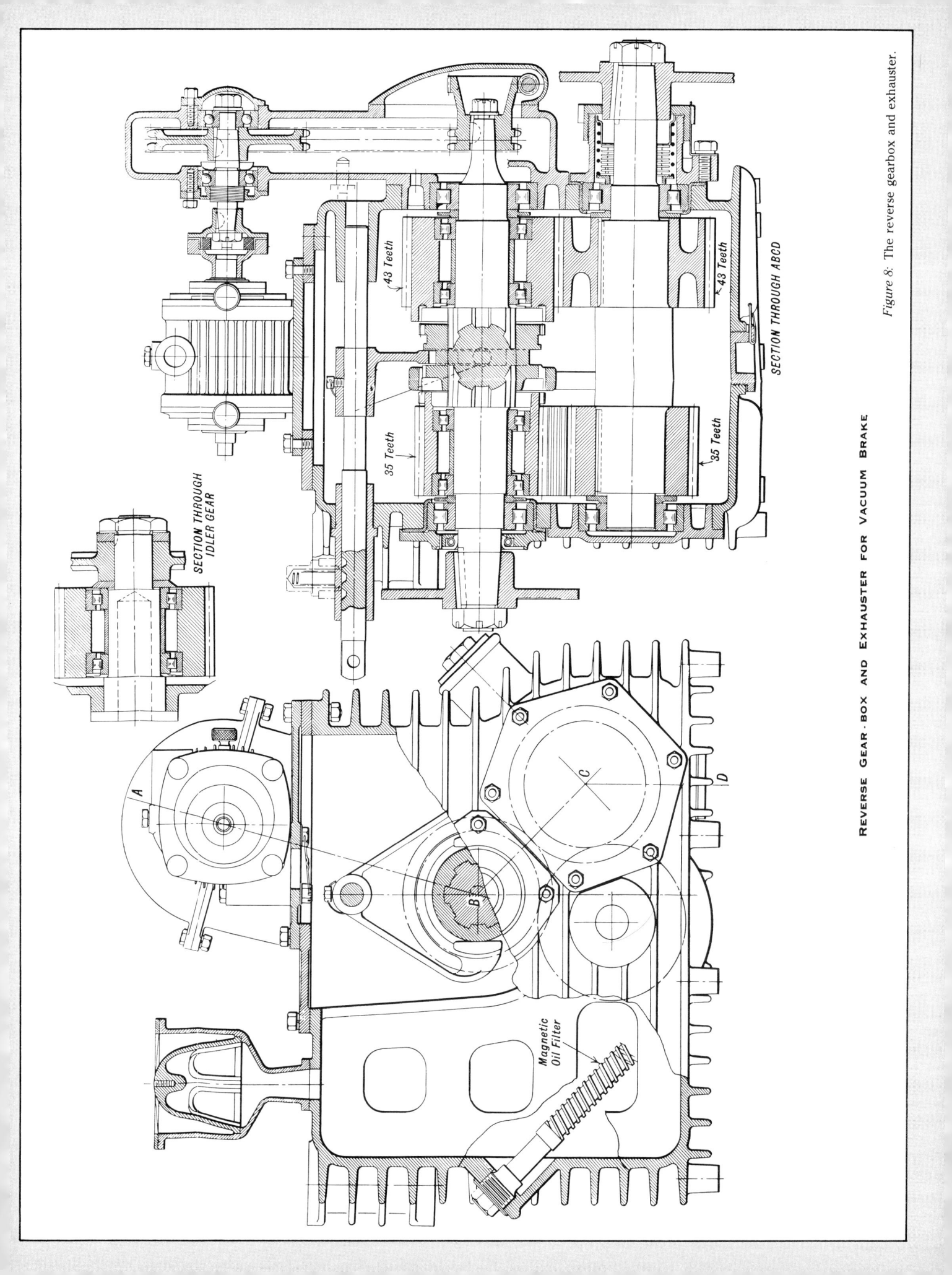

REVERSE GEAR-BOX AND EXHAUSTER FOR VACUUM BRAKE

*Figure 8:* The reverse gearbox and exhauster.

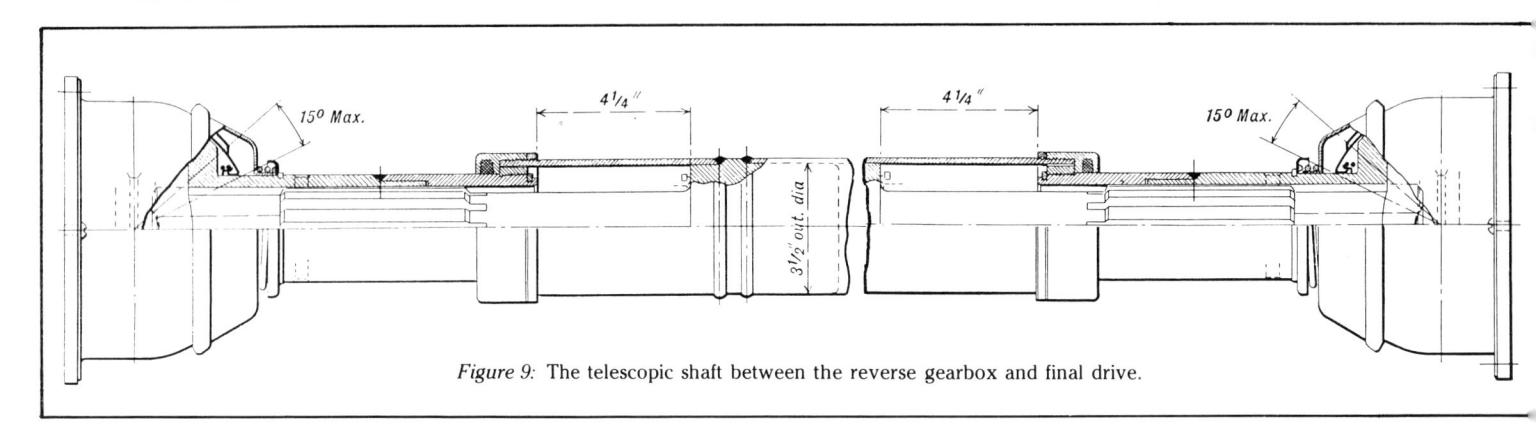

*Figure 9:* The telescopic shaft between the reverse gearbox and final drive.

*Plate 49:* The driving bogie and non-driving bogie showing the comparison. Note the torque arms and telescopic shafts, as discussed in the text. The driving bogie has both wheels fitted with sanding gear, but the other bogie has only one wheel so fitted,

*(A.E.C. Ltd.) Leyland Vehicles Ltd.*

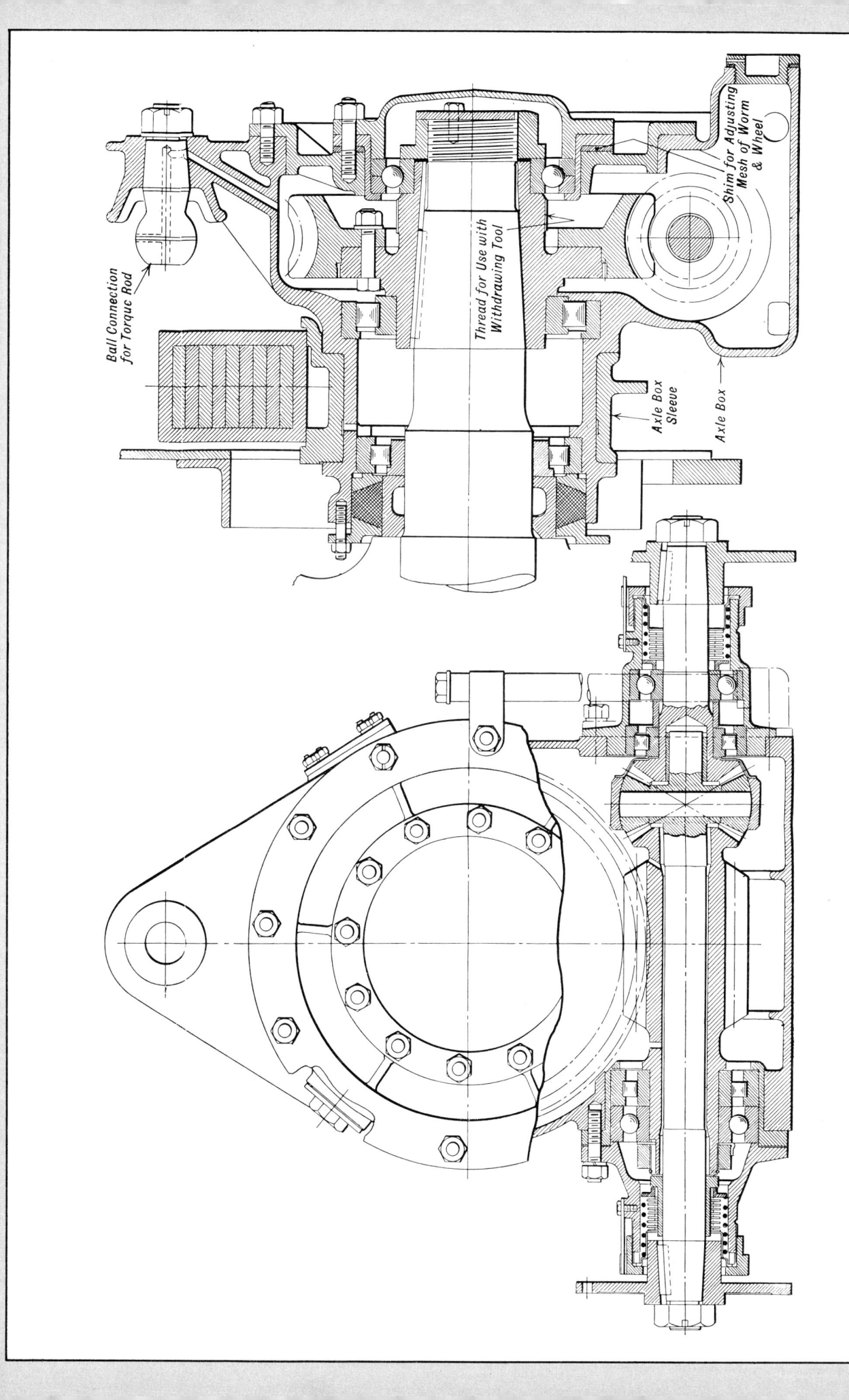

*Figure 10:* The worm drive and axlebox assembly.

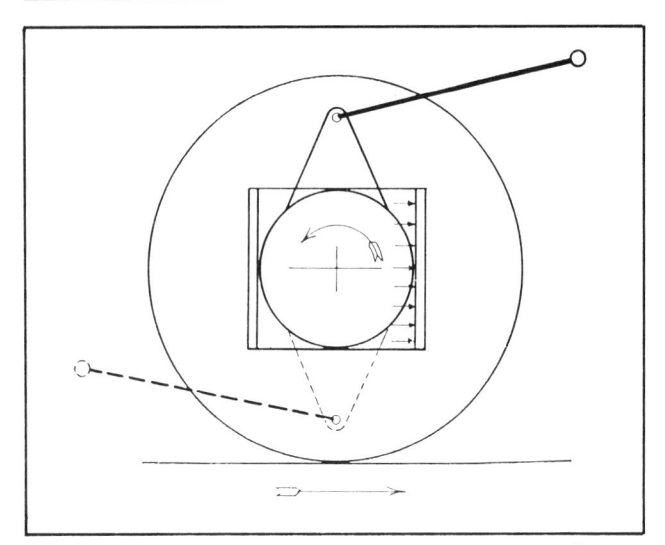

*Figure 11:* A diagrammatic drawing of the torque rod connections on the railcar bogie.

*The Engineer*

By this type of drive and use of shims, the position of the worm wheel relative to the worm could be adjusted. Another feature of the whole design that becomes apparent from the drawing, is that the complete worm and wheel mechanism could be dismantled for repair or replacement without touching the axle or removing it from the vehicle. This work could then be carried out from the trackside rather than from underneath the coach. The early use of torque rods are shown in *Figure 11 and Plate 49* and this is reported to have eliminated 'chatter' and wheel judder under acceleration and braking.

As regards brakes, again the introduction of conventional drum brakes (as used on road vehicles) was employed. Modifications were carried out so that the 5in. wide, ¾in. thick

*Figure 12:* The brake gear assembly.

*The Engineer*

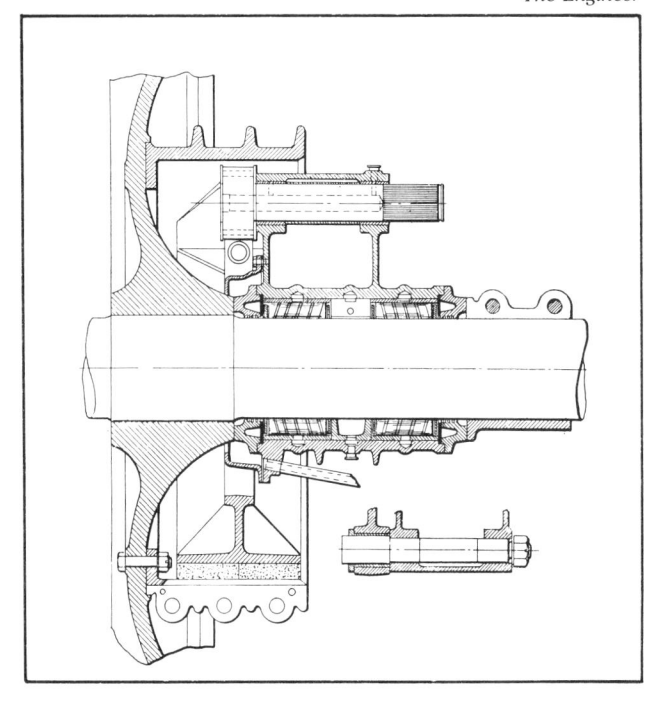

shoes, operating cams and the pivot pins, could be removed without the removal of the drum or wheels. An assembly drawing in *Figure 12* shows how this arrangement was achieved. The 20in. drums were split and could be removed for truing and replacement, and the whole assembly could be inspected by simply slackening the retaining collar, detaching one end of the torque rod, disconnecting the brake rod, and then sliding the whole assembly along the axle *(see Plate 50)*. The brakes had two individual vacuum cylinders on each bogie, one to each axle, thus ensuring fully compensated braking. The hand parking brake was coupled from the driver's cab to the cam levers by means of rodding.

The main vacuum for the brake and sanding gear was held in three reservoirs under the chassis, and was monitored by two gauges in the driver's cab, showing cylinder vacuum and brake-pipe vacuum. The main electrical supply came from a large capacity accumulator, mounted on the frame just opposite the engine, while the fuel tank was on the same side as the accumulator, but situated further back.

*Plate 50:* A photograph showing the brake shoes extracted from the brake drums, allowing replacement and ease of servicing.

*(A.E.C. Ltd.) Leyland Vehicles Ltd.*

The driver control cabins at either end *(Plates 51 & 52)* of the vehicle were identically arranged, with an accelerator pedal, a pre-selector gear lever, a reverse gear lever, a ratchet handbrake, a finger control lever for the vacuum brake, and another for the sanding gear. A further pedal was incorporated for changing the gears in the Wilson box. The handbrake at each end only controlled the handbrake on the bogie wheels at that end, and these two levers were not inter-connected. The connection of the controls was cleverly joined by means of steel ribbons. A problem that might have arisen in the 'gated' gear change was overcome by allowing only one gear selector available to the vehicle. *Figure 13* shows that the lever could be lifted out of its socket when the direction of motion of the vehicle was reversed, and be carried from one end of the coach to the other by the driver. The toe of this detachable lever engaged with the gate, so that when it was removed, no interference was possible from that end.

Finally, the prototype vehicle was reported to be very simple to drive, and the following sequence was used to control it.

An electric starter initiated the engine and the reverse lever was next pushed in the direction in which the vehicle was to travel. The pre-selector gear lever was brought through the 'gate' into the first gear position. After this, the gear change pedal (clutch), was pressed down and, releasing the air brake and handbrake, the vehicle would then move. To change gear, the pre-selector lever was moved once more, and the gear change pedal depressed when the gear change was needed. A

# EARLY DEVELOPMENT OF THE PROTOTYPE

*Plate 51:* Spaciousness and comfort are the keynote of the driver's compartment in the A.E.C. diesel railcar. As the engine is placed within the chassis, the view through the wide glass windows is uninterrupted.

*(A.E.C. Ltd.) Leyland Vehicles Ltd.*

*Plate 52:* The controls (somewhat sparse) on the prototype chassis.

*(A.E.C. Ltd.) Leyland Vehicles Ltd.*

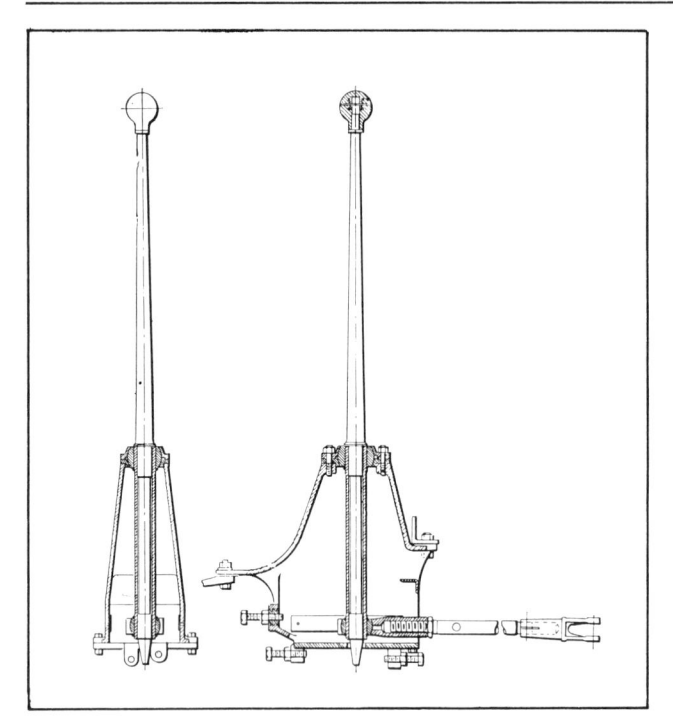

*Figure 13:* The arrangement of the gear selector lever.
*The Engineer*

full driving sequence applicable to these early vehicles is incorporated in the next chapter.

To sum up the prototype, several extracts from one of the Hardy Motors/A.E.C. sales brochures does give some idea of the market aimed at, how the Company felt about the future of diesel railcars, and how they tried to sell the vehicle. An extract follows:

> This railcar, although its body is of streamlined form, has not been designed to travel at very high speeds, but to give economical services at speeds up to 60m.p.h. It is, in fact, intended for suburban rather than express long-distance service. In order that its maintenance costs may be small, as many parts standard to Hardy road vehicles have been used as the design will permit, while the various units have been placed in accessible positions so that the replacement of worn parts may be carried out easily and quickly. As to the interior of the body, a photograph of the prototype interior is seen in *Plate 53*. It is particularly luxuriously furnished in a colour scheme of brown and green; the seats are upholstered in leather, and the passengers sit back to back. At one end, a door leads into the luggage compartment but, at the other, glass panels are interposed between the driver and the interior of the coach. As long windows are arranged on each side, the coach has a visibility as good as that of an 'inspection' car. Deep luggage racks are provided and lights, mounted beneath them, are arranged above the heads of seated passengers in just that position most suitable for reading. A total of forty lights is incorporated. A recording speedometer is open for inspection by the passengers; there is a clock, and in case of emergency a handle may be depressed to apply the brakes and stop the flow of fuel to the engine.

Further extracts in *Figure 14* include drawings, cover and specification from this first sales brochure by Hardy Motors.

The prototype now born and with trials complete, it was not surprising that the Great Western Railway Company, whose rails ran alongside the A.E.C. Works, concluded a deal to purchase No. 1 for the fair price of £3,249 *(see Appendix Two)*, and with the full GWR crest on each of the 'noses' of the railcar, it is reported to have been delivered to Southall Depot on 24th November 1933. It is seen in the official photograph in *Plate 54*, ready for its inaugural run in December 1933. The next chapter will discuss No. 1 in Great Western service — 'a new era was dawning'.

*Plate 53:* The interior of the prototype, No. 1, showing the leather seats, luggage racks and the overall spacious appearance of the vehicle.
*(A.E.C. Ltd.) Leyland Vehicles Ltd.*

# The HARDY RAIL CAR

## THE "HARDY" RAIL CAR

### Foreword

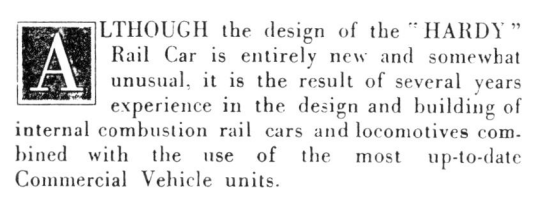

ALTHOUGH the design of the "HARDY" Rail Car is entirely new and somewhat unusual, it is the result of several years experience in the design and building of internal combustion rail cars and locomotives combined with the use of the most up-to-date Commercial Vehicle units.

To reduce cost of construction and to give efficient service, standard road chassis units have been used wherever possible. These have all been thoroughly proved by actual use, and being manufactured in quantity can be produced relatively cheaply and replacements quickly supplied from stock.

For the essentially "railway" details such as bogies, etc., railway practice has been followed and the very useful advice of Railway engineers adopted.

**HARDY MOTORS LIMITED**

SOUTHALL, MIDDLESEX, ENGLAND

*Allied to The Associated Equipment Co. Ltd.*

Telephone: SOUthall 2424 (12 lines)

Telegrams and Cables: "VANGASTOW" SOUTHALL

*Figure 14*

# THE HARDY

## PETROL OR OIL DRIVEN MODEL TO SEAT 65-90 PASSENGERS
### Absolute accessibility to all Power Parts

The Rail Car has been designed for economical running at speeds up to 60 miles per hour, rather than for exceptional speeds above this figure, which can only be attained with very high running and maintenance costs.

With this in view, special attention has been paid to :—

(a) Low first cost.
(b) Low weight per passenger.
(c) Careful streamlining of the body.
(d) Accessibility.

(a) Modern practice in railway carriage construction has been followed for the framing and bogies, in other words, for the carrying portion of the car, while the most up-to-date commercial motor vehicle units are used for the driving parts. In this way most of the components are stock units, and being manufactured in quantity for road vehicles, they can be produced at low cost.

Incidentally, this means that spare parts are readily obtainable from stock.

(b) The weight of the chassis is only 13 tons 10 cwt., and a complete coach seating 80 to 90 passengers will weigh between 19 and 20 tons. This gives a coach weight of approximately 5 cwt. per passenger, or about half the weight per passenger of a suburban train, or about one quarter the weight for an express train.

(c) As the result of wind tunnel experiments with models of various designs of bodies, one has been designed which, at 60 miles per hour, will require only about one-fifth the power to overcome head wind resistance that a square ended body of the same cross-sectional area would require.

The consideration of head wind resistance, and hence streamlining, is of far greater importance on a rail car than on a train. On the latter the frontal area is only about one per cent. of the side area, and therefore head wind resistance is negligible compared with side thrust. On the former, however, it is about 15 per cent., and the proportion of frontal area to power is far higher.

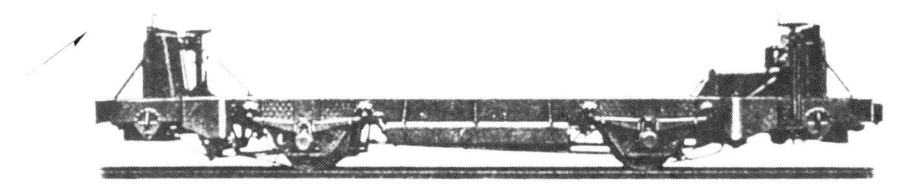

## RAIL CAR

By taking full advantage of the saving in power which results from low weight and streamlining, as indicated above, a comparatively small engine (130 h.p.) is employed, with considerable saving in first cost and running expenses. Even so, the ratio of about 5 h.p. per ton (laden) compares most favourably with, say, an express train weighing from 500 to 600 tons and hauled by a 1500 h.p. locomotive.

(d) A most important factor in low maintenance cost is accessibility, and the chassis is so designed that practically every working part may be removed for examination or renewal without disturbing the body or taking the bogies out of the car.

The chassis, which is carried on two four-wheeled bogies, has an overall length over headstocks of 60 feet, and an overall width of 8 ft. 1 in.

All driving units are mounted on the outside of the frame on the left hand side. The engine, of the compression ignition type, is just ahead of the centre of the coach, and the drive is taken from a fluid flywheel by means of a propeller shaft to a pre-selective type gearbox, and thence by another shaft to a reverse box. †

Thence the final drive is to two pairs of worms and wheels, contained in the two axle boxes on one side of the rear bogie, these two drives being coupled together by a propeller shaft.

A feature of this construction is that, as all units are outside the wheels, the design can be altered to suit various gauges with the least possible modifications.

All controls are duplicated, so that the car may be driven at the same speeds from either end.

The fuel tank and batteries are carried on the outside of the frame also, but on the right hand side.

Brakes are of the drum type, mounted inside the wheels, and sand is provided for braking as well as starting in both directions.

All driving and other units are placed below floor level, they do not occupy any body space, and the sides of the body are extended down as far as possible in the form of valances and provide protection for the driving units as well as maintaining a smooth exterior surface which is essential to efficient streamlining.

† NOTE.— The car being double ended, there is no "front" or "rear," and therefore the non-driving end is referred to as the front and the driving end as the rear. The left hand side is on one's left as one sits in the car facing the front.

# THE HARDY

## GENERAL DATA

| | |
|---|---|
| OVERALL WIDTH OF CHASSIS | |
|    at bogies | 8 ft. 1 in. |
|    between bogies | 7 ft. 10 in. |
| HEIGHT OF FRAME | 3 ft. 9 in. |
| OVERALL WIDTH OF BODY | |
|    above floor level | 9 ft. 0 in. |
| FLOOR HEIGHT | 4 ft. 3 in. |
| MAXIMUM HEIGHT at centre | 11 ft. 4 in. |
| WHEEL DIAMETER | 3 ft. 1 in. |
| HORSE POWER OF ENGINE at 2000 revs. | 130 |

EPICYCLIC GEARBOX RATIOS AND SPEEDS

| | Ratio | Speeds at 2000 r.p.m. | at 2260 r.p.m. |
|---|---|---|---|
| Top | 1.0 : 1 | 53.0 m.p.h. | 60 m.p.h. |
| 3rd | 1.49 : 1 | 35.5 ,, | 40.25 ,, |
| 2nd | 2.36 : 1 | 22.4 ,, | 25.4 ,, |
| 1st | 4.15 : 1 | 12.7 ,, | 14.5 ,, |
| Reverse box ratio | 1 : 1 | | |
| Axle ratio | 4.16 : 1 | | |

CHASSIS WEIGHT. Leading bogie 6 tons 10 cwts. 2 qrs.
                      Driving bogie 6 tons 19 cwts. 2 qrs.

                                  13 tons 10 cwts. 0 qrs.

*Guarantee.* Comprehensive guarantees are given with all HARDY products, full particulars of which are stated in the Company's current Conditions of Business.

*Important.* We strongly advise customers operating our vehicles to refrain from carrying more than the scheduled load, as we cannot accept responsibility for faults arising out of excessive strain due to overloading.

*Whilst every endeavour has been made to ensure the correctness of this specification its absolute accuracy cannot be guaranteed, and it is liable to alteration without notice.*

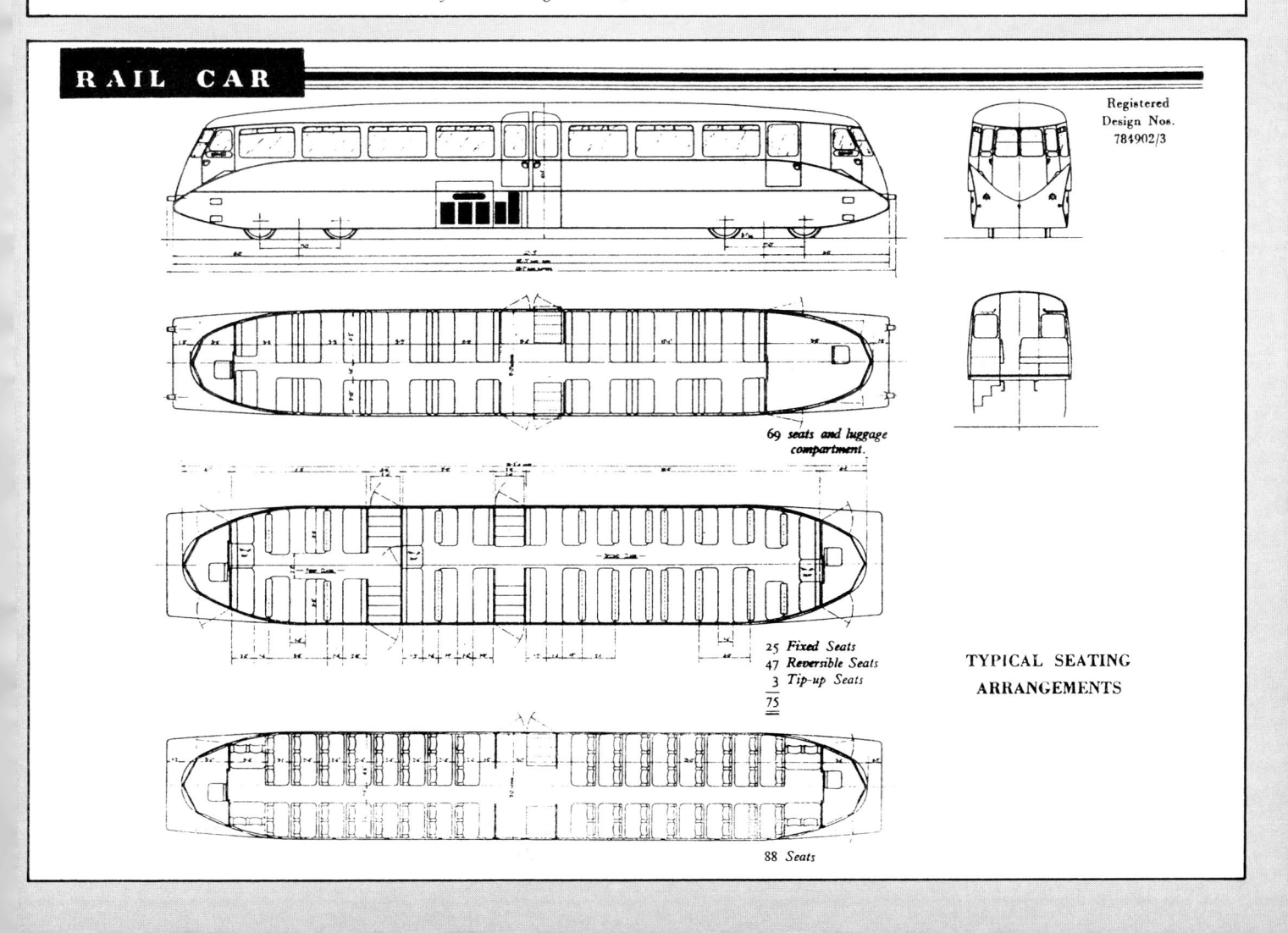

## RAIL CAR

Registered Design Nos. 784902/3

69 seats and luggage compartment.

25 Fixed Seats
47 Reversible Seats
3 Tip-up Seats
—
75

TYPICAL SEATING ARRANGEMENTS

88 Seats

*Plate 54:* An official Great Western Railway photograph of No. 1, taken at Didcot on 25th November 1933, the day after delivery from the makers. The streamlined hinges show up well on this photograph.

*British Rail*

# Chapter Three: No. 1 into Great Western Service

The Great Western Railway introduced the new streamlined heavy oil railcar to its railway employees in the following article, published in the 1933 staff magazine:

**EXPERIMENTAL STREAM-LINED HEAVY OIL RAIL CAR**

As was briefly recorded previously, a heavy oil rail car has been purchased by the Great Western Railway Company for experimental use, and will be brought into service trials on Monday, December 4, 1933, between Southall, Slough, Windsor, Reading, Henley-on-Thames and Didcot (a total of 218 miles) where it will supplement the existing local services *(Plate 55)*. It was built for the Company by Hardy Motors at the Associated Equipment Company's works at Southall, and in the early part of this year the chassis underwent exhaustive running tests on the Southall-Brentford branch line before the body was fitted

The car has been designed for economical running at speeds up to 60m.p.h., and with this in view, special attention has been paid to low original costs, weight per passenger, streamlining to reduce wind resistance, accessibility of all mechanical parts, and the use of standard road chassis parts wherever possible. Modern practice in railway carriage construction has been followed for the framing and bogies, and the most up-to-date commercial motor vehicle units are used for the driving parts.

The stream-lining has been carried out to a far greater extent than on any other railway vehicle in the country, the reason being that for a vehicle of this size the head-wind resistance is equal to 15 per cent of the side thrust, whereas with an ordinary train it is only about 1 per cent.

In appearance, the car is not unlike a huge seaplane float surmounted by a series of flush-fitting observation windows which merge at each end into a control cabin. The sides are carried down to within a foot of the track level, so that practically the whole of the vehicle, including the wheels, is enclosed. The design is the outcome of wind tunnel tests, and it is claimed, reduces wind resistance to a fifth of that which would be encountered by a similar flat-ended car.

The weight of the vehicle is less than 20 tons, or under 6cwt. per passenger. This feature, and the stream-lining have enabled a comparatively low horse-powered engine to be employed.

A speed of thirty miles per hour can be reached in one minute, and forty miles per hour in two minutes.

**THE CHASSIS**

The underframe is 60ft. long overall, and has a width outside its main members, of 3ft. 2in. It is carried on two four wheel bogies. These are of the swing link bolster type, having laminated springs over the axle boxes, with auxiliary rubber suspension blocks and nests of coil springs between the bolster and the spring plank. The frame, side, and cross members of the bogies are of pressed steel, lightened in their design wherever possible, and riveted together. All axle boxes are fitted with roller bearings.

The car is driven by a 130hp heavy oil engine, using non-inflammable fuel, and is almost identical with the engines used in some of the London omnibuses. Fuel consumption is about a gallon to ten miles.

The transmission of power from the engine to the wheels is by means of a fluid flywheel in conjunction with a pre-selective type of epicyclic gearbox, exactly similar to that employed in pleasure cars. Gear changes can at all times be made silently and without shock. The drive to the wheels is similar to that used on an omnibus, but is enclosed in the axle boxes on the ends of the axle, and is easily accessible.

An electric dynamo fitted near, and driven from, the engine, is employed for lighting purposes. This is capable of supplying 40 lamps, in addition to headlamps and lights in the driver's compartment.

All the driving mechanism is mounted below the floor, on the outside of one of the underframes near the middle of the car, the 45 gallon fuel tank and batteries being on the opposite side.

Protection from weather is afforded the mechanism by the casing, but any of the units can be inspected, repaired, or taken out by the removal of inspection covers, which form part of the casing.

The radiator is not in the conventional position it occupies on a car. It is just in front of the engine, and the air which passes under the front of the car is deflected sideways and drawn through it by a fan, afterwards passing out through vents in the casing.

**BODY AND SEATING ARRANGEMENTS**

The design of the body follows omnibus practice. The main frame construction is built up in ash, covered outside in aluminium and inside with plywood panelling faced with rexine.

The car has a seating capacity for 69 third class passengers. It has an overall length of 63ft. 7in. Entrance is through double doors in the middle of the car. These open into a vestibule 5ft. wide. Two compartments, one on each side, open out from the vestibule, the seats being placed back-to-back on each side of centre gangways. The smaller compartment, which is divided by a sliding wooden door from a combined luggage compartment and control cabin, has a seating capacity for 30 passengers. The larger compartment accommodates 39 passengers; access to the control cabin is by a glazed doorway. Along one side of the car each seat accommodates two passengers; on the opposite side each seat accommodates three passengers.

The windows are each five feet long and so arranged that no pillars obstruct the passengers' view. Provision is made in the vestibule so that passengers may enter or leave the car from the track level. This is by means of built-in steps, covered (when not in use) by a hinged flap which, when lifted, opens a door in the outside casing.

**INTERIOR DECORATIONS AND FITTINGS**

The interior decorations have been carried out in green and brown. The seats are covered in pleated brown leather and fitted with cellular rubber cushions *(see Plate 57)*. The sides of the coach, as well as the undersides of the luggage racks (which run practically the whole length of both sides of the car) are covered in mottled green rexine, and the ceiling is covered in cream rexine.

The floors are covered first with insulboard to deaden noise and to ensure silent running, then with green linoleum and mottled green carpet to match the sides. Interior woodwork is walnut, and all interior fittings, including hand rails, flush fitting electric ceiling lights, and lights on the underside of the luggage racks, are chromium-plated.

Sepia views of some of the beauty spots on the Great Western Railway system are framed in walnut.

Hot water heaters are fitted in both compartments and fed from the radiator.

A clock is provided in each compartment, and a speedometer in the smaller compartment as well as in the control cabins. An unusual feature is the provision of a microphone and loudspeaker, which enables the guard to communicate to passengers in either compartment, or to the driver.

To stop the car, in case of emergency, a lever is provided which, when pulled down, stops the engine by cutting off the fuel and applying the brakes.

### PRINCIPAL DETAILS OF THE RAIL CAR

| | |
|---|---|
| Length over buffers | 63ft. 7in. |
| Length of frame | 60ft. 0in. |
| Bogie centres | 40ft. 0in. |
| Overall width of body | 9ft. 0in. |
| Height from ground level | 11ft. 4in. |
| Height from ground to floor | 4ft. 3in. |
| Wheel diameter | 3ft. in. |
| Horsepower of engine | 130 |
| Seating capacity | 69 |
| Weight, empty | 20 tons |
| Weight per passenger (approx.) | 6 cwt. |
| Maximum speed | 60m.p.h. |
| Fuel consumption (approx.) | 10m.p.g. |

*Plate 55:* The poster advertising the original trial service of railcar No. 1.

*Plate 56:* The Great Western Railway's streamlined railcar running alongside a West of England express, as they speed across Maidenhead Bridge on 12th February 1934. This photograph is, in fact, a publicity mock-up, as the railcar and West of England express were recorded on film at different times. They were joined together, as can be seen, down the middle of the photograph, alongside the railcar.

*The BBC Hulton Picture Library*

*Plate 57:* A view similar to that in *Plate 53*, but showing just one vestibule. Notice the pictures on each pillar, the clock, the lighting arrangement and the two/three seating arrangement.

*(A.E.C. Ltd.) Leyland Vehicles Ltd.*

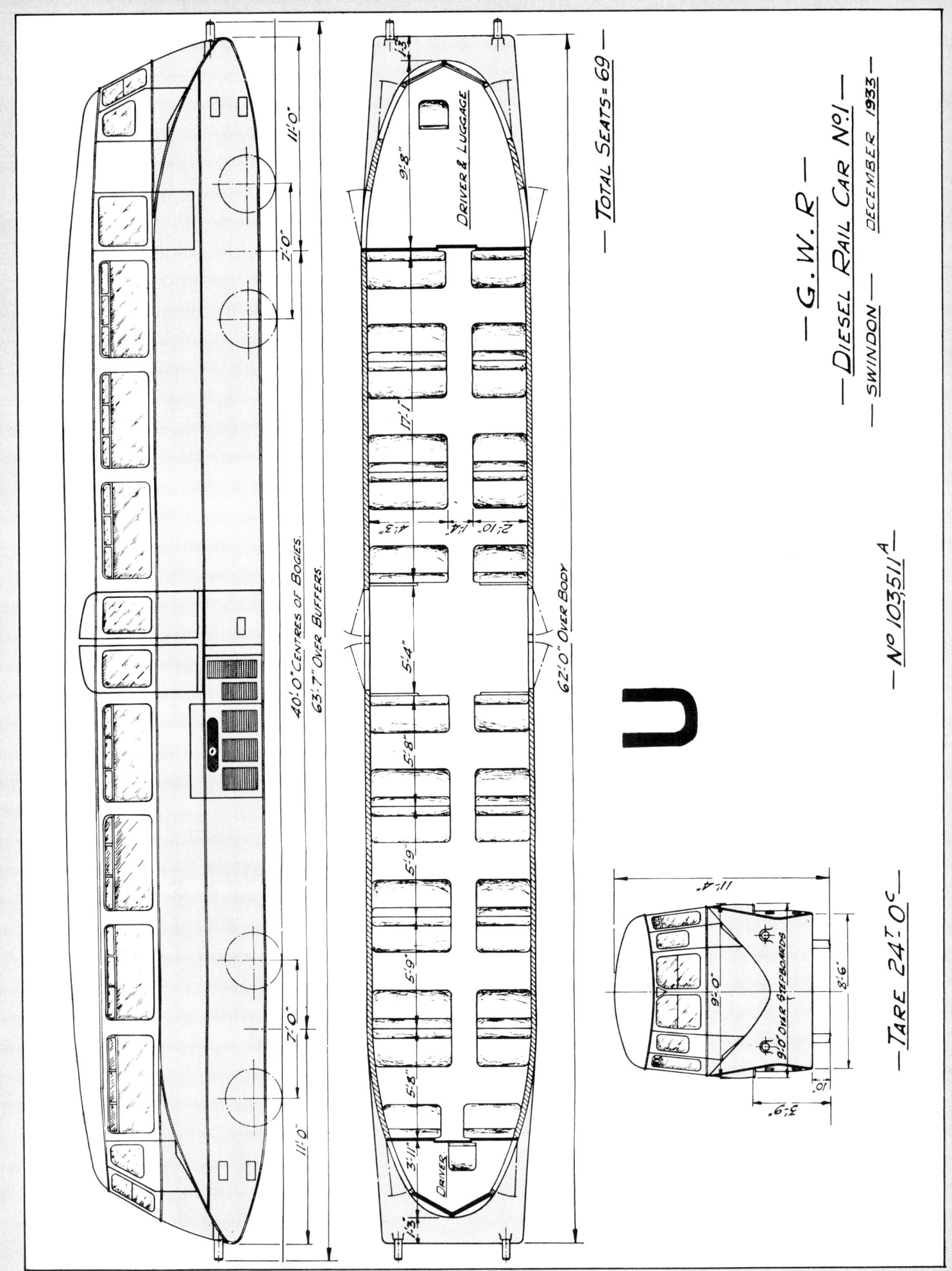

Figure 15

## THE CONTROL CABINS

All the driver's control equipment is duplicated so that the car may be driven from either end. It comprises an accelerator pedal, a pre-selective gear lever, a reverse gear lever, a ratchet handbrake, a finger control lever for the vacuum brake, and another for the sanding gear. The handbrake only applies the brake on the wheels of the bogie immediately beneath the end from which the car is being driven.

Head and tail lights, which are fitted flush with the casing, and all interior lighting, are under the direct control of the driver, who can switch any of them on or off without leaving his seat.

In front of the driver is a dashboard on which is mounted a speedometer, electric starter, heater button, two vacuum gauges, and a pilot light to indicate whether the engine and oil pump are operating.

## EXTERIOR DECORATIONS

The exterior decorations are carried out in the Company's Great Western Railway standard colours, chocolate and cream, with black and gold lining, and the Company's crest appears at each end of the car.

The car was on view at the Commercial Motor Show at Olympia, London, last month, and created considerable interest. It was inspected by more than 35,000 visitors. A model of the car was also exhibited on the 'Lawn' at Paddington Station.

So the first diesel railcar of the Great Western Railway entered service. It was brought into the Lot register at Swindon Works as Lot 1516 to diagram 'U', and officially placed into passenger service trials on 4th December 1933. The official drawing is shown in *Figure 15*, issued under Swindon No. 103511A.

The first official photograph taken by A.E.C. Ltd. for publicity purposes *(see Plate 38)*, showed no buffers, windscreen wipers or the word 'No.' in front of the figure one. Although this photograph was used on posters *(Plate 55)* and in the first publicity brochure, it was soon evident that No. 1, when arriving for duty with the GWR, had steel buffers, windscreen wipers and 'No.' added. In the early *Great Western Magazine* article, the A.E.C. photograph, again used, was of the early prototype.

Most major railway journals of the time recorded the event in some detail. The *Locomotive Magazine* was one of them and most of what it printed was a repeat of the A.E.C./Hardy Motor Co. Ltd. publicity brochure and followed closely the technical description given in *Chapter Two*. Some differences and alterations had however already taken place in No. 1, from its prototypical state, to its 'passenger-carrying' configuration on the GWR.

Firstly, the leading dimensions and gearbox speeds vary slightly and the table below is worth comparison with the quoted Hardy specification dimensions, etc. They also vary with the *GWR Magazine* report. After further research and checking, the figures in *Table One* are compiled from the records held in Swindon Works.

### TABLE ONE

| | |
|---|---|
| Gauge | 4ft. 8½in. |
| Overall length, frame | 60ft. 0in. |
| Overall length, body | 62ft. 0in. |
| Bogie centres | 40ft. 0in. |
| Bogie wheelbase | 7ft. 0in. |
| Overall width of chassis at bogies | 8ft. 1in. |
| Overall width of chassis between bogies | 7ft. 10in. |
| Overall width of body above floor level | 9ft. 0in. |
| Floor height | 4ft. 3in. |
| Maximum height at centre | 11ft. 3in. |
| Wheel diameter | 3ft. 1in. |

**Epicyclic gearbox ratios and speeds:**

*Ratio*          *Speeds*

| | @ 2,000 r.p.m. | @ 2,750 r.p.m |
|---|---|---|
| Top — 1.0 : 1 | 43.6 m.p.h. | 60 m.p.h. |
| 3rd — 1.49 : 1 | 35.5 m.p.h. | 48.75 m.p.h. |
| 2nd — 2.36 : 1 | 22.2 m.p.h. | 30.5 m.p.h. |
| 1st — 4.15 : 1 | 12.7 m.p.h. | 17.5 m.p.h. |

Reverse box ratio 1 : 1
Axle ratio 4.16 : 1
Chassis weight: Leading bogie, 6 tons, 10cwt. 2qr.
                Driving bogie, 6 tons 19cwt. 2qr.

Various additional interesting data was released when the GWR purchased the vehicle, and the following extract contains several of these features:

The speed of the engine is controlled by an accelerator pedal, which is connected by light rods and bell cranks to the fuel pump. A feature of this accelerator pedal is that it is fitted with a ratchet and pawl, which latter may be engaged by a small hand lever, but the position of the pawl is such that, when the accelerator is again depressed, it automatically disconnects from the ratchet. Thus, if the driver wishes to leave his seat when the coach is running to pick up a staff, or for any other similar reason, he may engage the ratchet and pawl and thus hold the accelerator pedal down in any desired position, but immediately he sits down and puts his foot on the accelerator pedal, the ratchet is thrown out of action. A small lever for operating sanding gear is placed near the driver, as well as a button for operating an electric horn. An instrument board is provided which carries the speedometer, starter and heater button, two vacuum gauges, and a pilot light to indicate whether the engine and oil pump are operating, and in convenient reach are switches for the interior lamps.

A 24 volt dynamo of 1,200 watts capacity is mounted on a bracket at the rear of the engine and driven from it by a small propeller shaft, while batteries of 220 amp hour capacity are carried on the opposite side of the frame, but close to the engine, to ensure the leads being as short as possible. Starting is by an electric starter having a solenoid switch, connected to a button on the instrument board in both driver's compartments. Pre-heating plugs, also controlled from the driver's compartment, are fitted to the engine. The capacity of the dynamo is such that 40 lamps may be fitted inside the body, in addition to headlamps and the lights in the driver's compartment. A 45 gallon tank is mounted on the right-hand side of the frame and feeds the engine oil pump by means of an autovac, with a Bosch filter inserted between tank and the autovac.

As regards the actual performance of this vehicle, one reporter, riding a trials train before it entered service, recorded that the highest maximum speed of 60 m.p.h. was obtained and the running was very smooth, even though the floor area was loaded with wooden weights and temporary seating of wooden planks (unpadded). The ride was smooth and comfortable over the points. Noiseless and quick gear changes were in evidence, but the acceleration was not of the highest order, being comparable with the equivalent light steam trains.

When the railcar entered service, it was worked hard and performed up to sixteen workings daily in the Slough to Reading and Didcot areas, including the Henley-on-Thames and Windsor branches. All these services were additional to the normal service, and the idea behind this was that the railcar would attract would-be passengers away from bus services during off-peak times. It covered 218 miles each day, with the

*Plate 58:* Railcar No. 1 at Paddington's No. 2 platform on 1st December 1933, awaiting its Press run to Reading, with locomotive No. 6001 *King Edward VII* waiting at No. 1 platform, alongside.
*British Rail*

*Plate 59:* The interior of the railcar on Press run day, 1st December 1933.
*British Rail*

*Plate 60:* Railcar No. 1, at speed, passing a 'steamer' on its Press run on 1st December 1933. It does look as if this is an official 'posed' photograph, for Press release.
*British Rail*

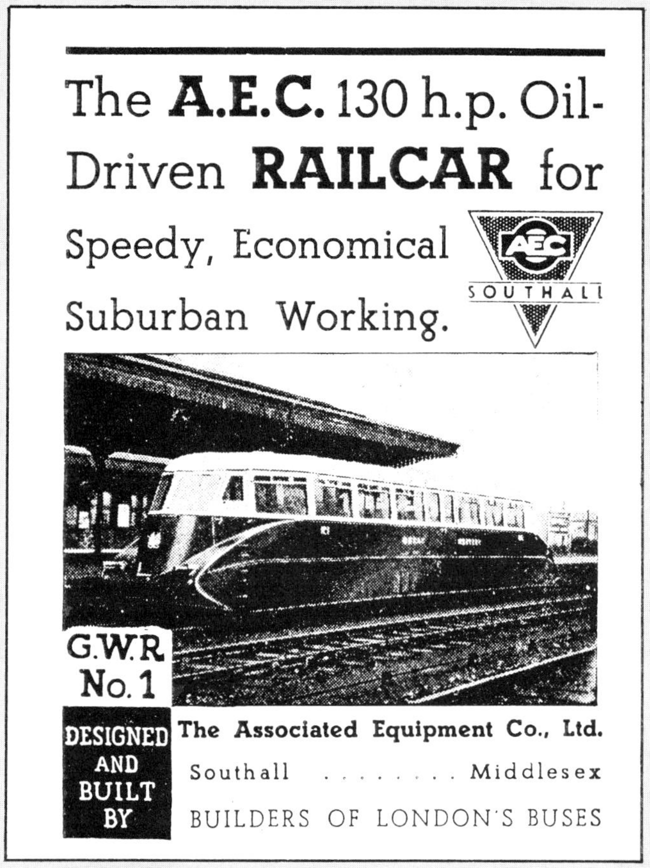

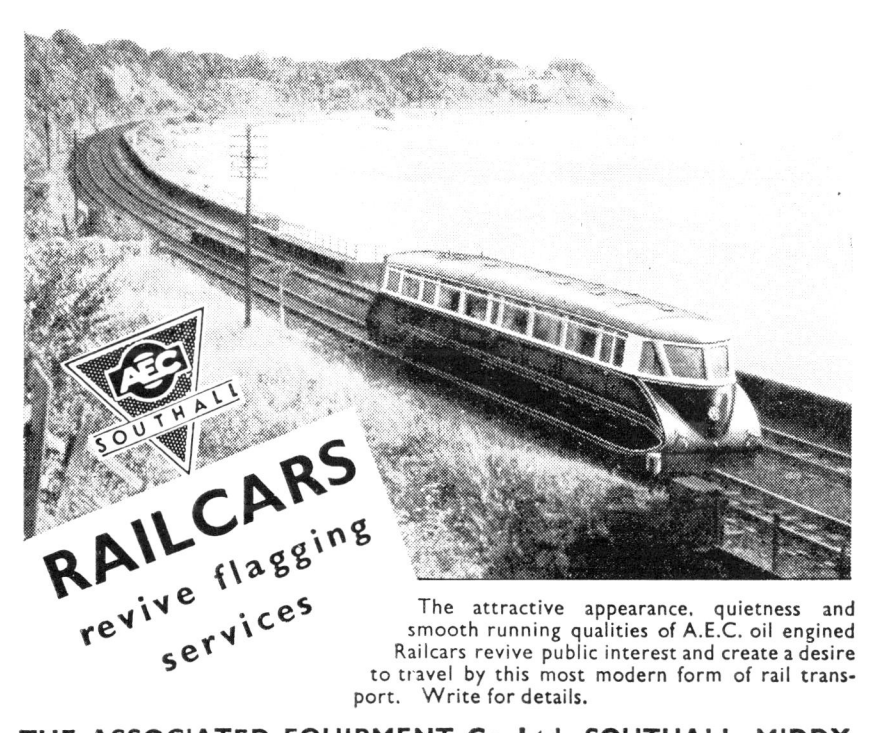

## G.W.R. No.1

Note the scientific streamlining of the A.E.C. 130 h.p. oil-driven Railcar — the latest achievement for the working of suburban traffic. Apply for details

*Designed & Built by*
**The Associated Equipment Co., Ltd.**
Southall, Middlesex
BUILDERS OF LONDON'S BUSES

---

## The A.E.C. 130 h.p. Oil-Driven RAILCAR for Speedy, Economical Suburban Working.

G.W.R. No. 1

DESIGNED AND BUILT BY **The Associated Equipment Co., Ltd.**
Southall ........ Middlesex
BUILDERS OF LONDON'S BUSES

---

## RAILCARS revive flagging services

The attractive appearance, quietness and smooth running qualities of A.E.C. oil engined Railcars revive public interest and create a desire to travel by this most modern form of rail transport. Write for details.

**THE ASSOCIATED EQUIPMENT Co. Ltd., SOUTHALL, MIDDX.**

*Please say you saw the advertisement in the " A.E.C. Gazette."*

---

Some of the advertisements from A.E.C. Ltd., selling their new product.

duties mapped out for the railcar spread out over a period of twelve hours, and comprised two services between Southall and Slough, four between Reading and Didcot, two between Reading and Henley-on-Thames and two between Slough and Windsor *(see Chapter Twelve)*.

Stops were made at all the intermediate stations, and early results showed an overall fuel consumption of 7½m.p.g. Before the use of No. 1 on these services, a special trip was organised for the Press and GWR Company representatives, on 1st December 1933, from Paddington to Reading. *Plates 58, 59 & 60* show the railcar waiting to leave Paddington, assembled passengers, and passing a 'steamer' near Maidenhead.

It was reported that the car ran with notable steadiness and silence, even at a speed of 61m.p.h., which was maintained between Taplow and Maidenhead on the outward journey; this took 39min. 50sec. for the 36 miles. The return journey (against a fairly stiff wind) took 42min. 20sec.

The Great Western also publicised the new roomy interior of the railcar with a statement that:

Upon entering through the large double doors in the saloon's centre, you were to find an interior contemporary to the omnibus, with notices requesting, 'smokers to occupy the rear seats'.

A further report from *The Railway Gazette* also informs us of the other improvements to passengers' comfort that No. 1 had brought, and the extract is included in full:

During a trial trip of the A.E.C.-Hardy streamlined diesel railcar on the GWR, we were much struck by the fact that, although there were about 30 passengers (mostly smoking intensively) on board, and that, the day being cold and the heating apparatus in full and effective operation and no window open, yet the car never became stuffy. The reason for this happy state of affairs must, it seems, be attributed to the Colt patent ventilator, a product of G. D. Peters & Co. Ltd., of Slough, with which this vehicle was fitted. The type of ventilator used is shown in the accompanying illustration and indicates the principle upon which it works. It is of simple and robust construction and has no moving parts to get out of order or require lubrication. It is made in two types, the 'BS' type for road vehicles and the 'P' type for railway coaches. The former is the simpler of the two, is made in six sizes, and ensures almost equally efficient ventilation whatever the direction of the wind. As the largest size has a height of only 2½in., it projects little from the roof of the vehicle. Entry of water, dust, or exhaust gases is completely excluded. The type 'P' projects from 3in. to 7in., according to which of its three sizes is used, the largest size being mainly for perishable traffic vans; it too, excludes all water and cinders, and is very efficient both in providing fresh air and in extracting the vitiated air.

Other than a slight hiccup in late December 1933, when the railcar was withdrawn for modifications to the braking system, and also for the fitting of Automatic Train Control apparatus,

*Figure 16:* The type BS colt ventilator, showing the air flow.
*Railway Gazette*

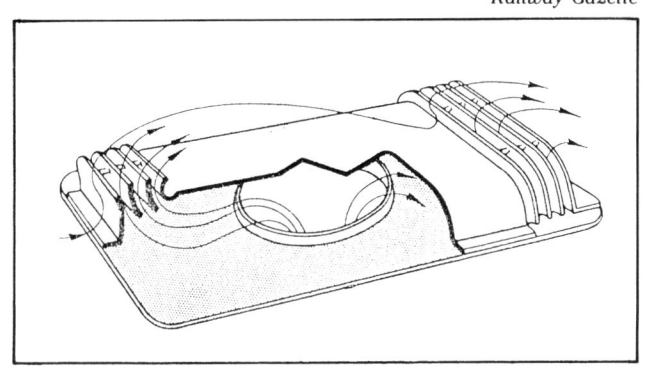

the vehicle performed superbly, from its reintroduction to service on 5th February 1934, until its condemnation at Oxford in August 1955. During its first year of service, it carried 136,000 passengers and ran over 60,000 miles. It was stated by a railway official that the railcar proved second only in popularity to the famous 'Cheltenham Flyer', and that many people took trips on the GWR main line for the sole purpose of riding in the car and watching the track ahead, for the first time.

A final note regarding No. 1 was published in the February 1942 edition of the *A.E.C. Gazette*, and read:

### A.E.C.'s FIRST RAILCAR
*Completes 8 Years Service.*

This month, A.E.C. railcar No. 1 completes eight years' service on the GWR. It has now run 360,500 miles. This mileage would be greater but for the fact that, at the beginning of the war, many of the A.E.C. railcars were temporarily withdrawn from service. Nearly all are now at work again.

Exhibited at the 1933 Commercial Show, No. 1 was visited by 35,000 people, who were attracted by its revolutionary streamline design. Described and illustrated in the world's press, it quickly became known as 'the car that's shaped like a seaplane float.'

After an inaugural run between London and Reading, when it attained 63m.p.h., No. 1 was put into regular service in February 1934, and in its first month's running, carried some 10,300 people and only lost time twice, due to trivial mechanical troubles (once for 4 minutes and once for 19 minutes) which were soon rectified. As well as providing a new standard of travel comfort, No. 1 had the added novelty that its front seat passengers could — for the first time on any railway in Great Britain — see the line ahead.

Today, this veteran streamliner — as popular as ever — is working local services in the Reading area. Of the 38 A.E.C. railcars ordered by the GWR, it is still the only single-engined model.

Big advances in design have been made since No. 1 first challenged the steam locomotive on local and semi-main line routes.

**Railcars were here to stay!**

# Chapter Four: The Next Three Cars (Nos. 2, 3 and 4)

With the great success of the diesel railcar in 1934, the Great Western Railway decided to order three more, Nos. 2, 3 and 4. The purchase of these vehicles was agreed by exchange of letters, in April 1934. Costing £6,541 each, the cars were built to a specification worked out jointly between A.E.C. and the GWR, to the drawing dated July 1934 under Lot 1522, Diagram 'V'. The main differences in chassis arrangements between No. 1 and these three railcars is graphically shown in a diagrammatic layout in *Figure 17*.

The new design was for a much more ambitious type of railcar *(see Figure 18)*, designed for high speed cross-country routes, and incorporated lavatories and a small buffet section, to attract customers. The staff magazine of the Great Western Railway reported the introduction of a service using these new railcars in an article in July 1934, which is reproduced below:

### GREAT WESTERN RAILWAY STREAM-LINED RAIL CARS FOR THROUGH EXPRESS SERVICES

The pronounced success of the Great Western Railway Company's experimental use of a heavy oil stream-lined rail car on passenger services in the London Division has led to a further striking development in the use of this class of vehicle.

Commencing on July 9, cars of a similar character to the original GWR No. 1, but capable of considerably higher speeds, are to be run on express services between Birmingham, Gloucester, Newport and Cardiff.

This new development gives an accelerated passenger service (one class only) in which the 117½ miles between Birmingham and Cardiff will be covered at an average speed of nearly 50 miles per hour, including the intermediate stops *(see Plates 61, 62, 63 & 64)*.

The two services to be operated by the new cars are the 9.05a.m. and 3.40p.m. Birmingham to Cardiff, and the 9.10a.m. and 4.50p.m. from Cardiff in the reverse direction. The detailed time table is as follows:

|  |  | a.m. | p.m. | Miles |
|---|---|---|---|---|
| Birmingham (Snow Hill) | dep. | 9.05 | 3.40 | — |
| Gloucester | arr. | 10.17 | 4.52 | 60¾ |
|  | dep. | 10.19 | 4.54 |  |
| Newport | arr. | 11.10 | 5.52 | 105 |
| Cardiff (General) | arr. | 11.27 | 6.10 | 116¾ |

|  |  | a.m. | p.m. |  |
|---|---|---|---|---|
| Cardiff (General) | dep. | 9.10 | 4.50 | — |
| Newport | dep. | 9.27 | 5.06 | 11¾ |
| Gloucester | arr. | 10.21 | 5.55 | 56 |
|  | dep. | 10.23 | 5.56 |  |
| Birmingham (Snow Hill) | arr. | 11.35 | 7.15 | 116¾ |

Standard third class fares will be charged on the services, with a flat-rate supplement of 2/6.

Not only will travelling speeds be enhanced by these new cars, but the standard of comfort will also be much improved, no effort having been spared to make the journey an entirely pleasant experience for passengers.

This will be appreciated from the following description of the coachwork and interior fittings of the cars.

### ACCOMMODATION AND INTERIOR FITTINGS

Each car has seating accommodation for forty passengers, and is provided with a central entrance. This seating is arranged in sections of four on either side of the gangway, in a similar way to the arrangement of a dining car; that is to say, the body is divided up into five 8-passenger compartments, which, however, are not divided off from one another, and have an open centre gangway.

Travel amenities are enhanced by the provision of removable tables between each pair of seats; these, when not in use, may be stored under the seats. Only part of the space under the seats is, however, reserved for the tables and the rest is available for hand luggage.

The ends and framing of the seats are in weathered oak, while the upholstery is in a pleasing shade of green horsehair, the upholstery being supported on tension springs. The tables are also in weathered oak. The luggage racks are of chromium plated steel netting, with a light oak rail on the outside edge, and the same wood is used for the curtain pelmet rail as well as for the waist rail and other mouldings *(see Plates 65, 66, 67 & 68)*.

A golden brown 'Rexine' is used for covering the walls, while the floors are covered in green linoleum, which is carried up the sides of the car for about nine inches, the sides and floor of the car being merged into one another by the radius which is covered by this linoleum. Both longitudinal and cross gangways are provided with a fine quality brown carpet.

All the windows are fitted with tussore silk curtains, and roller blinds.

Special attention has been paid to the lighting, to give a well diffused effect without glare, and for this purpose tubular lights are mounted on the window pillars opposite each seat back, these being placed horizontally. Similar fittings, placed vertically, are mounted in each corner of the compartment with further similar fittings along the centre line of the ceiling.

### THE CAFETERIA, KITCHEN, ETC.

Next to the passenger compartment, and connecting with it by a short central passage way, is the cafeteria. This feature, which is expected to add much to the popularity of the cars, consists of a compartment about 12ft. long, divided across the centre by a counter, on

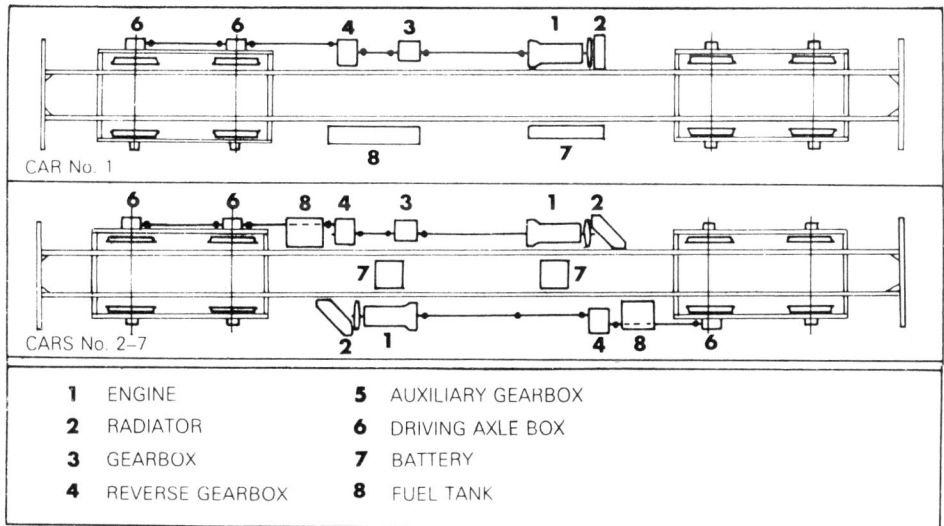

| 1 | ENGINE | 5 | AUXILIARY GEARBOX |
| 2 | RADIATOR | 6 | DRIVING AXLE BOX |
| 3 | GEARBOX | 7 | BATTERY |
| 4 | REVERSE GEARBOX | 8 | FUEL TANK |

*Figure 17:*
Schematic comparison of railcar chassis, etc.

*Plate 61:* Railcar No. 4, posed for publicity photographs at Cardiff in 1934. The photographer is up the signal gantry, as can be seen in the reflection on the nose of the railcar. This view shows up the 'all white' roof detail nicely.

*British Rail*

*Plate 62:* Railcar No. 2 at Cardiff (General), with its white-uniformed driver.

*British Rail*

*Plate 63:* An A.E.C. official photograph of No. 3 on acceptance trials in 1934.

*(A.E.C. Ltd.) Leyland Vehicles Ltd.*

*Plate 64:* Cardiff (General) again, with further publicity photographs of No. 4 before the inauguration of the Birmingham to Cardiff service.

*British Rail*

*Plate 65:* The saloon of diesel railcar No. 2, photographed on 25th April 1934, showing the 2 x 2 seating which is different to the offset seating of No. 1. This view is looking away from the buffet section.

*British Rail*

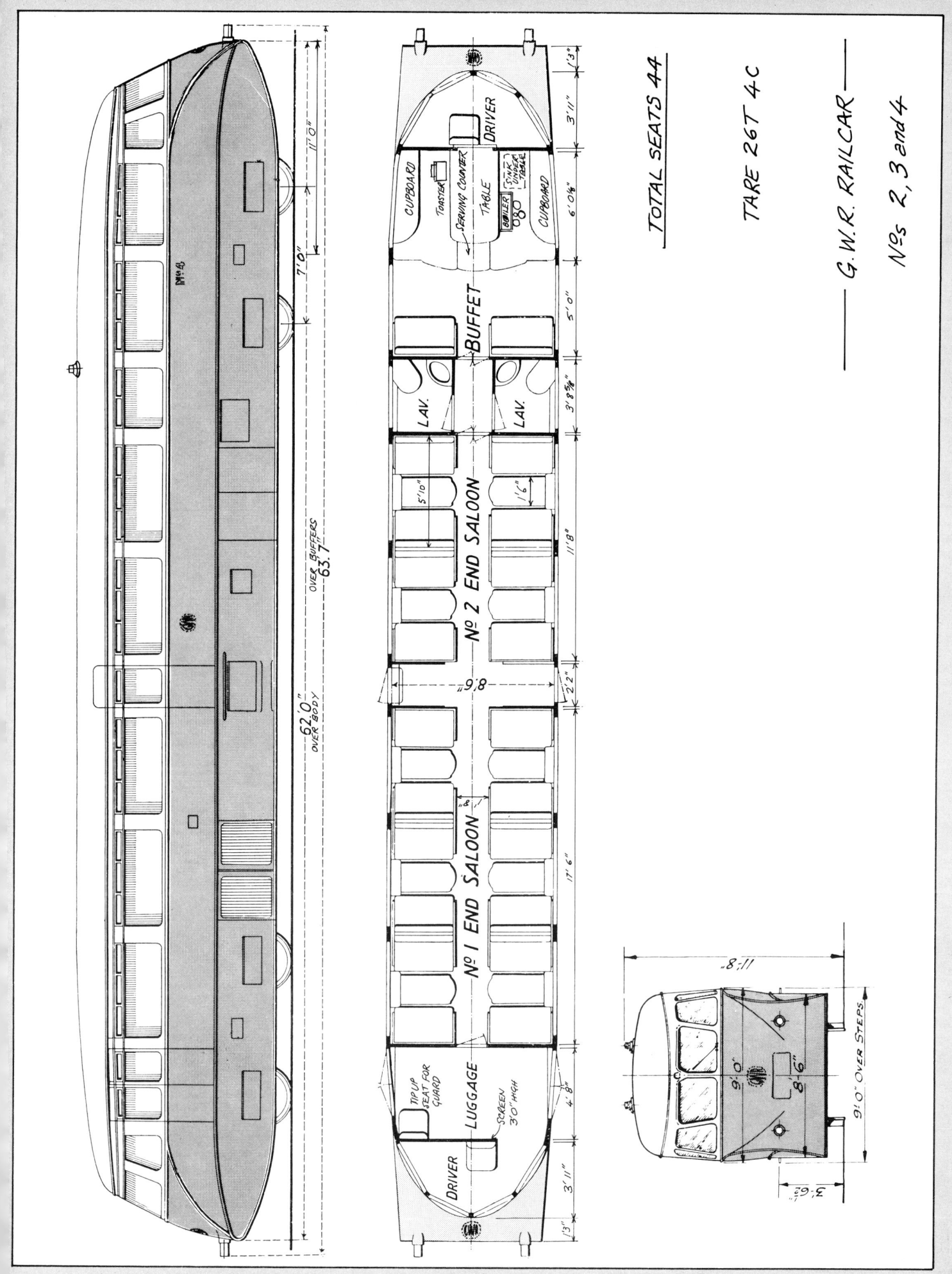

Figure 18

*Plate 66:* This photograph of No. 2, taken on the same day, shows the view from the driver's cab, looking, this time, towards the buffet counter. Note the guard's tip-up seat is in a different position from that on the drawing.
*British Rail*

*Plate 67:* An interior view of No. 3, showing the totally different covering material as installed during a refit, and photographed on 27th October 1938.
*British Rail*

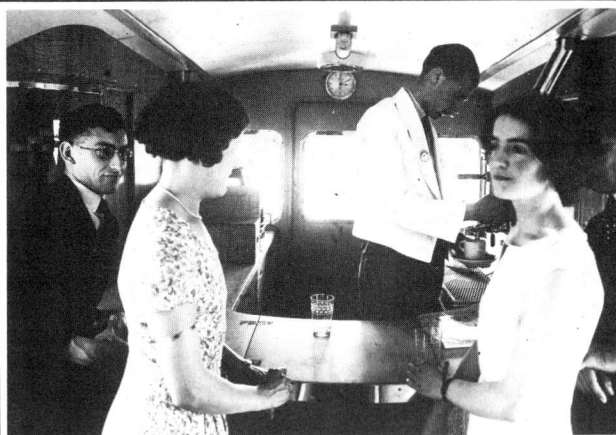

*Figure 19:* The interior of the buffet, drawn by a GWR staff artist, showing the glass panelled door into the driving compartment, the foot rest bars, and the glass cabinets, etc.
*Railway Gazette*

*Plate 68:* A view looking the other way to that in *Plate 67*. Note the different light fittings from those seen in *Plate 65*.
*British Rail*

# THE NEXT THREE CARS (NOS. 2, 3 AND 4)

one side of which are placed the necessary tables and cupboards for the kitchen, and on the other side are four seats, facing the counter, for the use of the passengers *(see Plates 69 & 70)*.

Provision is made in the cupboards for the storage of wines and other drinks, as well as food, glass, cutlery, etc. A small gas-heated boiler and toaster are provided, the former being connected to a nickel-plated coffee and milk boiler. At the ends of the counter, against the sides of the car, are rounded glass showcases for carrying chocolates and cigarettes *(Figure 19)*.

The whole of this kitchen equipment is carried out in weathered oak, with chromium-plated fittings, to match with the passenger compartments, while the seats facing the counter are of similar design to those in the main passenger compartment.

On either side of the gangway, connecting these two compartments, is a small lavatory, fitted with a water heater providing a constant supply of water for washing. This water is heated by the exhaust of the engines which passes up through the roof of the car.

At one end of the car is a combined driver's and luggage compartment, and at the other a driver's compartment. An interesting feature of the design is that passengers both in the cafeteria and in the main compartment can see through the glass screens of the driver's compartment and so obtain a good view of the line ahead of or behind the coach.

Ventilation is by sliding ventilators above all the windows and by Colt extractors fitted in the roof. For use in winter, heaters are provided throughout the car, which employ the heat from the engine cooling water; this heat being distributed through the car by electric fans. In summer weather, when this hot water is turned off, the same fans may be used for circulating cold air through the car.

July 1934 saw the start of the first fast long-distance regular service of diesel railcars in Great Britain — between Birmingham and Cardiff on the Great Western Railway. The service, which provided facilities additional to those existing, operated from Monday to Friday only on the timetables given on *page 57*, and during the week, each car covered 234 miles daily. Local passengers were not conveyed between Cardiff and Newport, or vice versa, and a supplementary fee of 2s. 6d. was charged in addition to the ordinary third class fare.

The week before going into regular operation, the first of the three cars which were maintaining this service (one being held in reserve) made some extremely interesting trial trips. On 3rd July 1934, a return trip was made between Paddington and Oxford, in the course of which eight consecutive miles were covered at a speed of 70-72m.p.h., and 44 miles were run in 40 minutes, or an average speed of 66m.p.h. On the following day, a trip was made over the much more difficult line from Paddington to Birmingham and return, and speeds up to 76m.p.h. were attained. A reporter privileged to be on board for the trip obtained the speed record shown in the accompanying diagram *(Figure 20)*. From Widney Manor, on into Birmingham (Snow Hill), numerous delays were encountered. Before this trip, the railcar was inspected by several Directors of the GWR, including Sir Robert Horne, Lord Palmer, Sir James Milne, and C. B. Collett, Chief Mechanical Engineer. On 6th July 1934, a trip was made from Birmingham to Cardiff. The party on board included the Lord Mayors of Birmingham and Cardiff, the Mayors of Gloucester and Newport, Mr C. W. Reeve, Managing Director of A.E.C., Mr G. E. Orton, Publicity Agent, GWR, and a number of Press representatives *(see Plate 71)* The run was made in 130½ minutes, with a top speed of 72.3m.p.h., but the first 57.5 miles to Churchdown were covered in an hour, after which the car was eased to prevent further gain of time and embarrassing signal stops.

The three cars had been designed and constructed by A.E.C., under the direction of Mr C. F. Cleaver, to the requirements of Mr C. B. Collett, the Chief Mechanical Engineer of the Great Western Railway. The design had been developed from that of the 130b.h.p. car (diesel railcar No. 1) which had been working since February 1934 on the Thames Valley lines, but in view of the required higher speeds, two engines had been fitted instead of one.

Streamlining of the body had again been carried out to a contour envolved from new wind tunnel tests made at the Chiswick Laboratory of the London Passenger Transport Board. These tests showed that the air resistance of the adopted form was only one-third that of a square-ended car at a speed of

*Plate 69 (top left):* A view of the buffet counter of railcar No. 2, photographed on 25th April 1934. Note, '10 for 6d., 20 for 1/-', presumably for cigarettes or cigars. The crockery is all crested, and note the Bulmer's bottle on the left counter.
*British Rail*

*Plate 70 (centre left):* An A.E.C. officially posed photograph of the buffet in use on railcar No. 2.
*(A.E.C. Ltd.) Leyland Vehicles Ltd.*

*Plate 71:* The trial run on 6th July 1934 in railcar No. 2., with the two mayors and mayoresses posed for the official A.E.C. photographer.
*(A.E.C. Ltd.) Leyland Vehicles Ltd.*

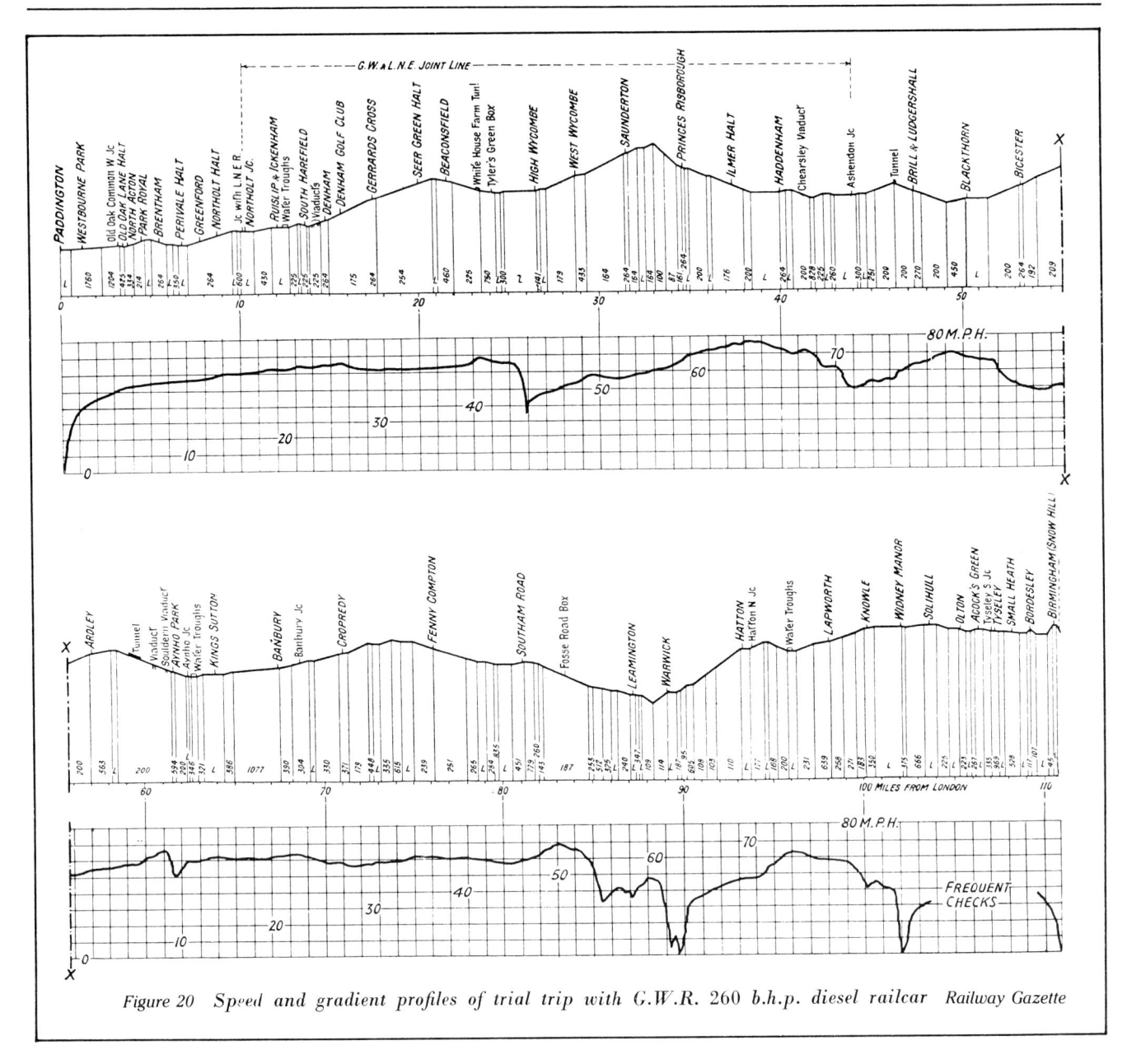

Figure 20 Speed and gradient profiles of trial trip with G.W.R. 260 b.h.p. diesel railcar  *Railway Gazette*

50m.p.h. Another feature of these three new railcars was the accessibility of the working parts, which had been obtained without the power or transmission units encroaching upon the revenue-earning space. These three new vehicles were similar to the prototype No. 1, but the following technical specifications show the comparison and changes that were incorporated.

**THE CHASSIS**
The chassis of these cars was a development of the GWR diesel railcar No. 1, which was a single engine vehicle designed for a maximum speed of 60m.p.h.

In the design of these new cars, a maximum speed of from 75 to 80m.p.h. had been aimed at, and therefore two engines were fitted in place of one, to provide the extra speed and overcome additional wind resistance.

The designers had also two major objectives well in mind; firstly, accessibility, so that any part which might fail or wear out could be quickly replaced and, secondly, floor space. In respect of the first feature, it will be seen *(in Figure 21 & Plate 72)* that all the driving units were mounted on the outside of the frame, and were readily inspected by removing the valance panels on the side of the body, while the power units were mounted below floor level, so that the whole floor space of the car was available for passengers or luggage.

**POWER EQUIPMENT**
Two A.E.C. 130b.h.p. diesel engines were used as the propulsive units, and they differed only slightly from the standard model as used in the London buses. The main difference was in the sump, which had been increased in capacity and provided with cooling fins, thus raising the weight of the engine from 1,414lb. to just under 1,500lb. A section through the engine is shown in *Figure 22*. There were six cylinders with a

Figure 21

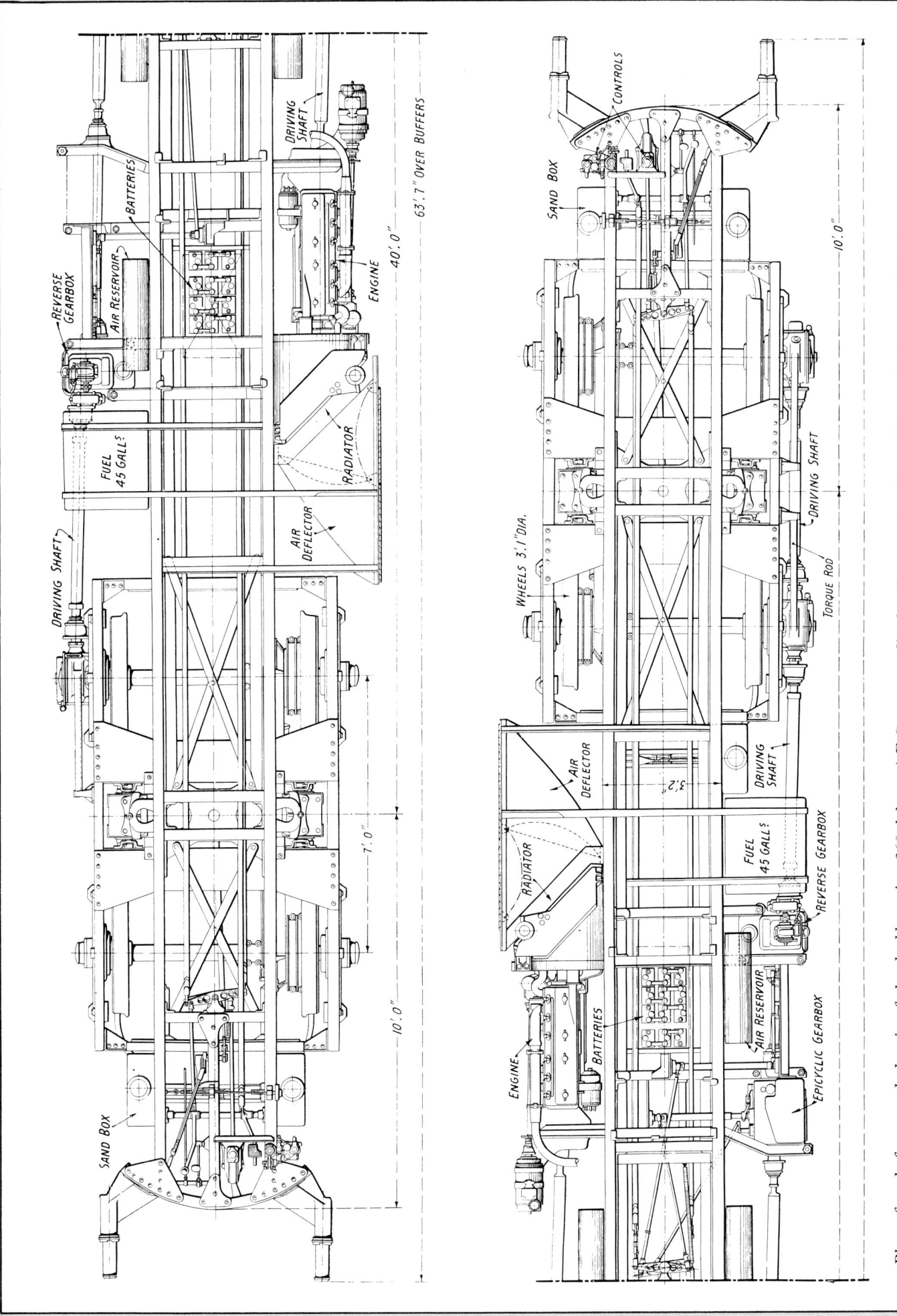

*Plan of underframe and chassis of the double-engine 260 b.h.p. A.E.C. express diesel railcar on the Great Western Railway. This drawing shows the layout of the direct and geared drive engines and their transmission systems, and also the interconnections between the various controls at each end of the railcar*

*Plate 72:* A general view of the chassis of the new A.E.C.-engined railcar Nos. 2, 3, and 4 on the GWR.

*The Engineer*

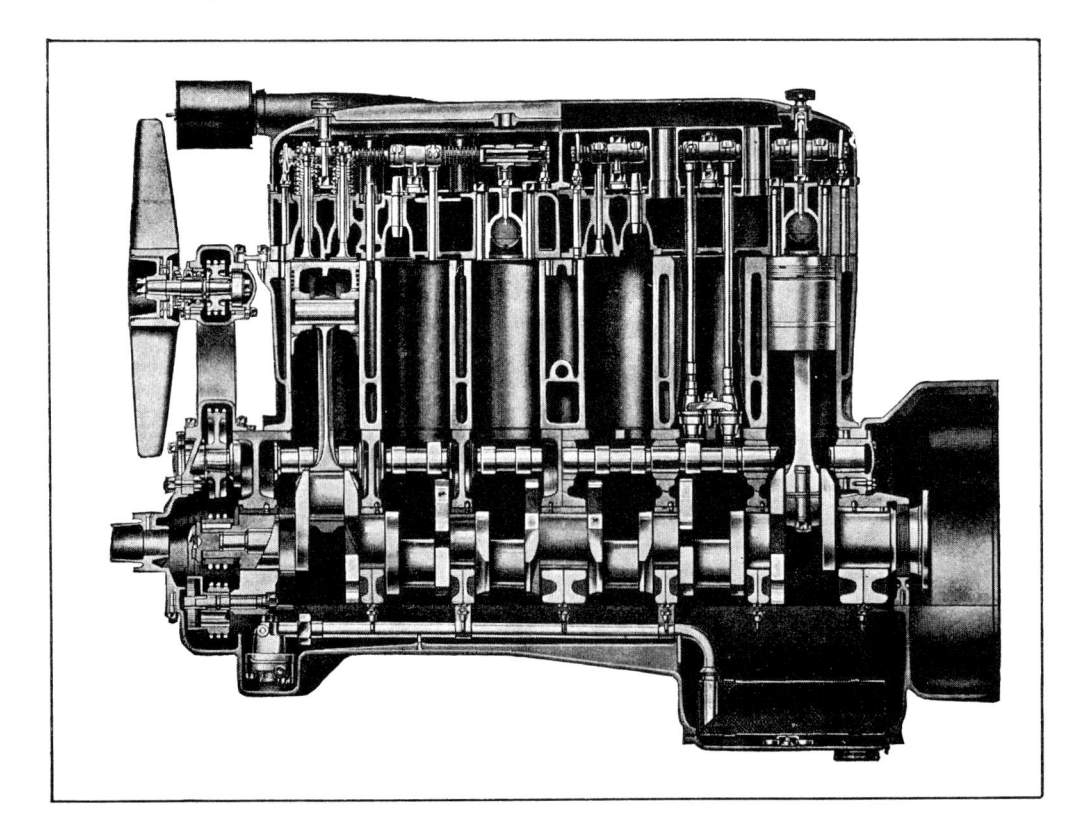

*Figure 22:* A section of the 130 b.h.p. A.E.C. engine as used in the GWR railcars.

*Railway Gazette*

*Plate 73:* This view shows the radiator, louvres, engine and auxiliary units. Note the sump cooling fins.

*(A.E.C. Ltd.) Leyland Vehicles Ltd.*

bore of 4.53in. and a stroke of 5.59in. The normal rated speed was 2,000r.p.m., giving a piston speed of 1,865ft. per min., and a brake m.e.p. of 95p.s.i., but in the present case the speed was limited to 2,400r.p.m., which corresponded to a road speed of 80m.p.h. Idling took place at 350 to 400r.p.m. C.A.V.-Bosch fuel injection equipment was fitted, and injected the fuel into a Ricardo spherical combustion chamber, which gave a high rotational swirl to the air swept up by the rising piston. Extensive use was made of aluminium and light alloys in the engine parts.

A novel method of suspension was employed for the engines, one of which was located down each side of the chassis in the manner of the well-known A.E.C. 'Q' type bus. The engine was hung at the rear through a Silentbloc rubber bush, and the front-end foot was supported on a rubber pad, so that the engine was free to move about the line joining the bush and pad, which passed through the centre of gravity of the engine. Rotation of the engine about this line was prevented by a torque arm at the rear, which was restrained by rubber blocks.

In order to obtain the necessary frontal area for the radiator, without making it so high that it would project through the body floor, a location at 45 degrees to the longitudinal centre line of the car was necessary. An engine-driven fan was mounted between the radiator back and the engine, and a good flow of air through the cooling elements was therefore ensured by two means.

Firstly, the lower panels of the body, which form the outside of the deflector box, were fitted with two sets of louvres which pointed in opposite directions. Should the car be travelling with the engine leading, the air was drawn in through the louvres nearest the engine, and these were shaped in such a way as to deflect the air towards the radiator. When travelling in the opposite direction, air was taken in through another set of louvres which were straight.

Secondly, inside the aluminium deflector box was a curved flap-plate, hinged at the joint between the two sets of panels, which took up a position according to the direction of motion. When the engine was leading, this plate was blown back by the air pressure in such a manner as to shut off that half of the box away from the engine, and when running in the other direction it shut off the louvres nearest the engine. The two positions of the curved deflector plate can be seen in *Figure 21*, showing the general arrangement drawing of the chassis.

The relation of the deflector box and fan to the engine is well-shown in *Plate 73*, which also gives a good idea of the layout of the engine auxiliaries. The C.A.V.-Bosch fuel pump is at the mid-length of the engine, with the exhaust manifold above it, and a vacuum brake exhauster to the left. At the right, a dynamo, for one of the two electric systems, is mounted on bearings supported by the fluid flywheel casing. A long shaft transmitted the drive from the gearing at the other end of the engine, and alongside this is situated the centrifugal water pump. Attached to the cylinder head casing at the far end is the air filter leading to the induction manifold, and above the radiator is the filling cap for the cooling water system. Between the dynamo and the underframe, the tubular driving shaft leads to the wheels.

**TRANSMISSION**

The transmission system was probably unique among railcars of any type, in that both geared and direct drives were fitted. When it was found that the propulsion of the car, at the proposed speed, required two engines, it was decided that in order to simplify the mechanism and reduce the cost, a gearbox would be fitted to one engine only, the remaining unit driving directly to the bogie.

This at once gave rise to several interesting engineering problems. In the first place, as the two engines would be working at the same time (although driving separate bogies) it was necessary that the speed of the driving shafts should be the same. This would not be possible if it were not for the 'slip' in the fluid flywheel, but to reduce the amount of slippage, and thus the heating of the oil, a device was incorporated in the throttle connection between the two engines so that the direct drive engine was given a full throttle only when in top gear, the opening for starting being approximately one-quarter of the setting. A small length of roller chain was interposed in the throttle rod connecting the two engines, and a cam-operated device connected with the change-speed gear allowed slack in this chain in all gear positions except top, when the chain was taut. When in an intermediate gear, the chain slack had to be taken up before the throttle of the direct drive engine opened.

Another difference in the drives, resulting from the elimination of the gearbox on one side, was that only one axle was driven by the direct-coupled engine against the two driven by the geared unit, as the reduced torque was taken up adequately by the adhesion of one pair of wheels. On the geared side, they comprised a fluid flywheel, a driving shaft with flexible couplings, a four speed Wilson epicyclic gearbox *(Figure 23)*, a short driving shaft with flexible couplings, a reverse gearbox *(Figure 24)*, another driving shaft leading to a worm drive incorporated in the roller bearing axlebox, a coupling shaft leading to the second axle of the bogie and, finally, two torque rods. On the direct drive side, the epicyclic gearbox and coupling shaft were eliminated, and there was only one torque rod; the place of the epicyclic gearbox being taken by an intermediate bearing between the first and second driving shafts.

The epicyclic gearbox had wide teeth of the constant mesh type, and planet wheels mounted on double-row roller bearings. The ratios of the four speeds were 4.5, 2.53, 1.64 and 1.0 to 1, but the worm drive on the axle was 3.12 to 1, giving a maximum normal wheel speed of 720r.p.m. The road speeds were 18, 32, 50 and 75m.p.h., with the engine running at 2,250r.p.m. Fabric-lined brake bands encircling large diameter drums actuated the first, second, and third gears, and the top gear was controlled through a cone clutch. The whole actuating mechanism was adjusted automatically, and the gear was enclosed in a casing having a large oil capacity.

To give an equal number of speeds in both directions, the

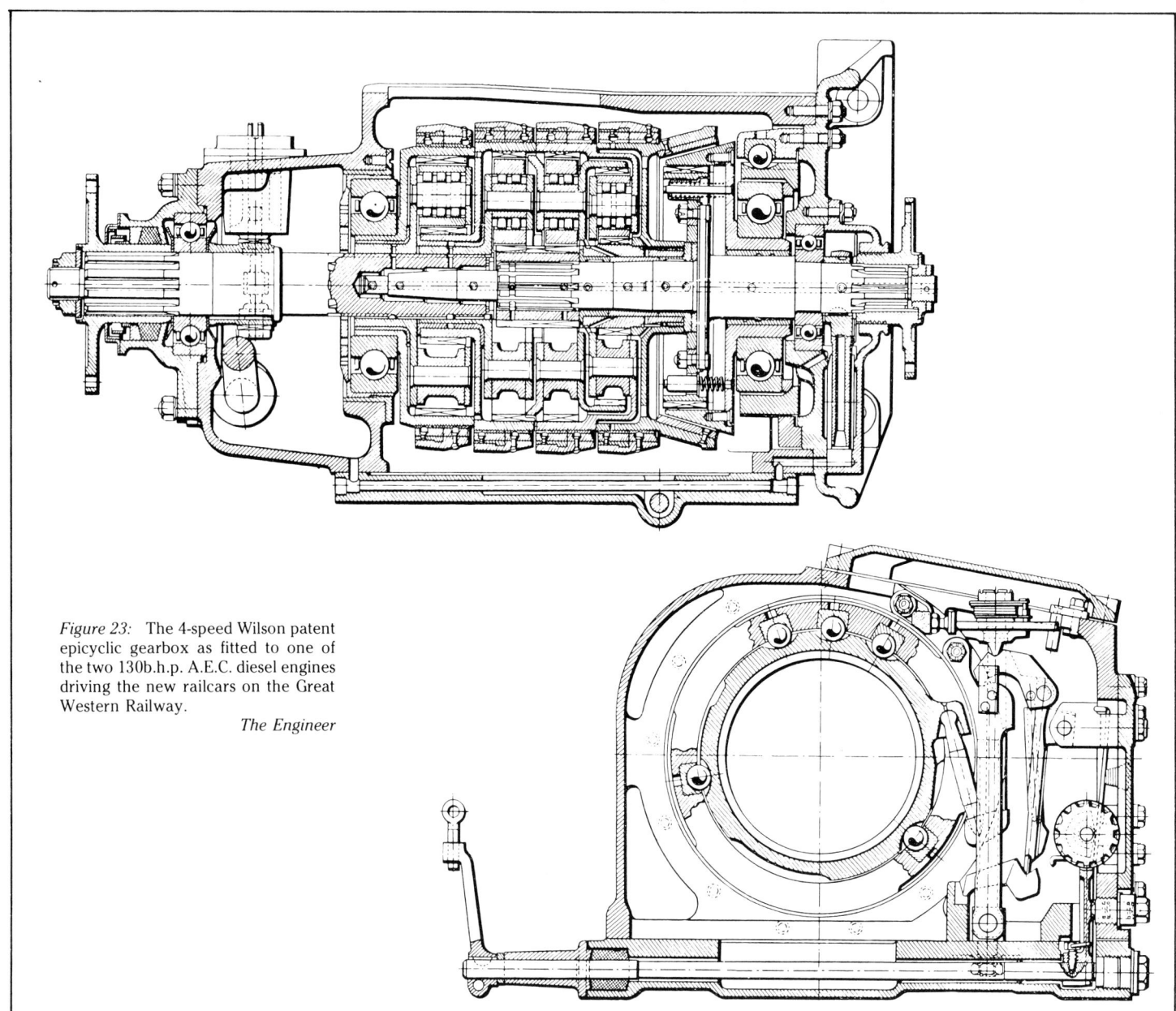

*Figure 23:* The 4-speed Wilson patent epicyclic gearbox as fitted to one of the two 130b.h.p. A.E.C. diesel engines driving the new railcars on the Great Western Railway.
*The Engineer*

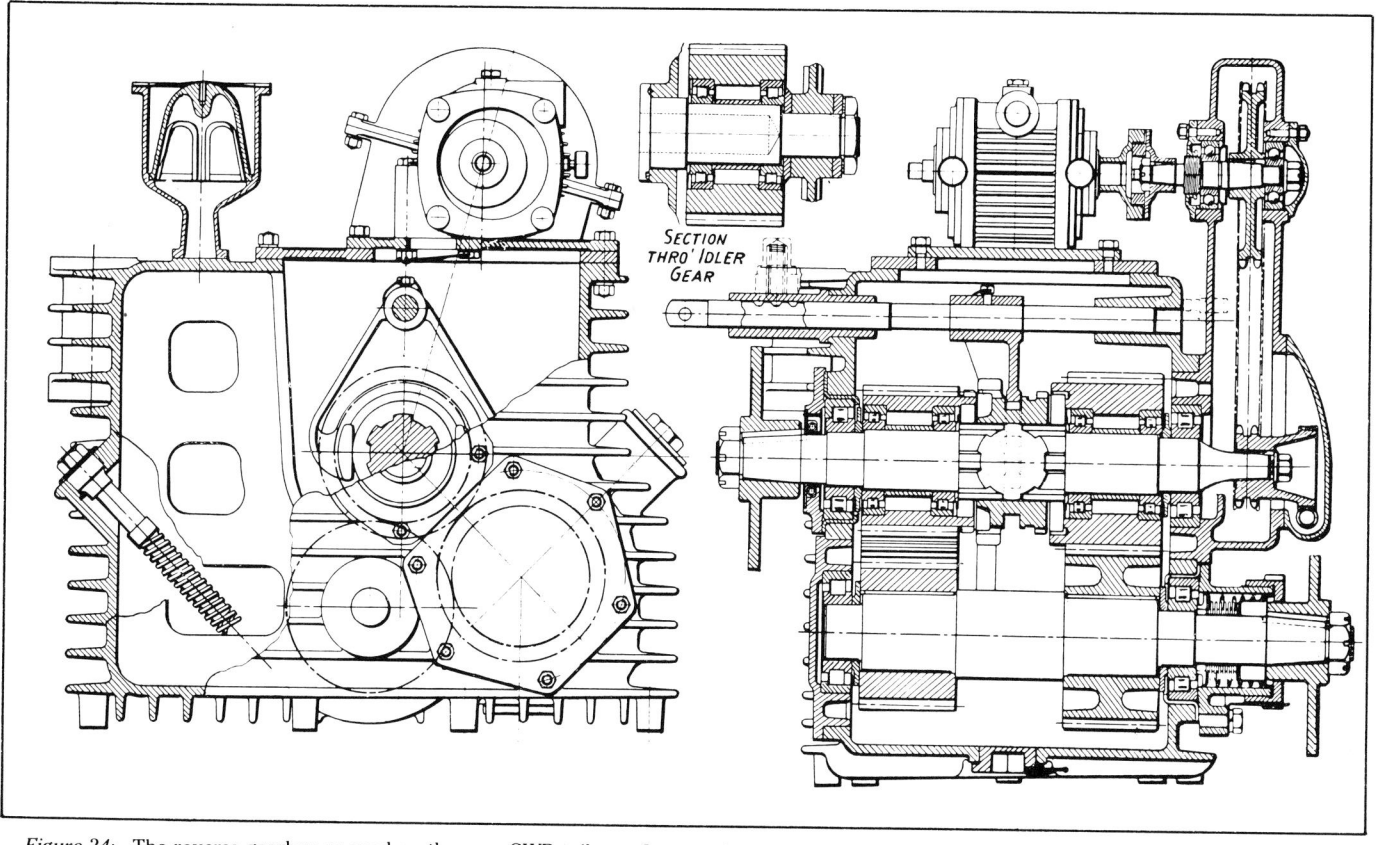

*Figure 24:* The reverse gearbox as used on the new GWR railcars. One supplementary exhauster is mounted on top of the box and driven by a chain.

*The Engineer*

drive passed through the reverse gearbox. The two shafts in this box were parallel, the driven member being the lower, and further away from the underframe, thus enabling the drive to be lined up between the engine and the axle. The aluminium box had a large oil capacity, and as a further cooling medium, ribs were cast on the outside. The final worm drive on the axles was housed in the roller bearing axleboxes which also carried the weight of the vehicle. As may be seen from the three views of the axlebox in *Figure 25*, the worm drive was of the underslung type; the steel worm was carried in bearings in the axlebox casing, and the phosphor-bronze worm wheel was bolted and splined to a flange carried on the axle. On the gear-driven side of the vehicle came another problem in this novel system of drive, and that was the possibility of the wheels on the two driven axles being of slightly different diameters. To prevent the resulting excessive stress on the driving gear, a small differential was incorporated in the leading worm drive, and its construction may be seen in *Figure 25*.

Both axleboxes and the brake carriers were controlled by pressed-steel torque arms, attached to the bogie framing by shackles, fitted with graphite-loaded bushes (Silentbloc) to take up the torque reaction and to ensure that this force was taken squarely on the axlebox guides.

On the first car, No. 1, these arms were horizontal and were ball-jointed at the ends. Considerable chatter was experienced when the brakes were applied, and eventually one of these arms failed. Investigation pointed to the fact that the reaction was transmitted horizontally on the horn cheeks, thus causing this to chatter, and the trouble was cured by bolting the arms rigidly to the brake carriers and applying the reaction to the framing, vertically.

## UNDERFRAME AND BOGIES

Compared with normal carriage construction, the underframe was unusual in that only two main longitudinals were used *(see Figure 21)*. The transverse spacing over the outside of these members had been restricted to 3ft. 2in. in order that the complete power plant could be mounted on the outside without encroaching upon the loading gauge, and without any detail being hidden by the frame structure. This spacing also permitted the mounting, inside the body, of any steps down to rail level which might be required. The main longitudinals were 10in. x 3½in. channel sections, trussed with 4in. x 4in. angles, and fitted with cantilever brackets for carrying the driving gear.

Swing-link bogies *(see Plate 74)* of a type which did not differ greatly from normal practice, were used, fitted with 3ft. 1in. wheels spread over a base of 7ft. The bolsters were supported by helical springs, and the weight of the body and underframe was taken through the pivot and two side bearers secured to the underframe longitudinals and bearing on the bolster. The side frames and cross members were of pressed steel, riveted together. Roller bearings were fitted to all axleboxes, those of the driving boxes being of the Hoffmann type, and those incorporated in the carrying boxes, Timken.

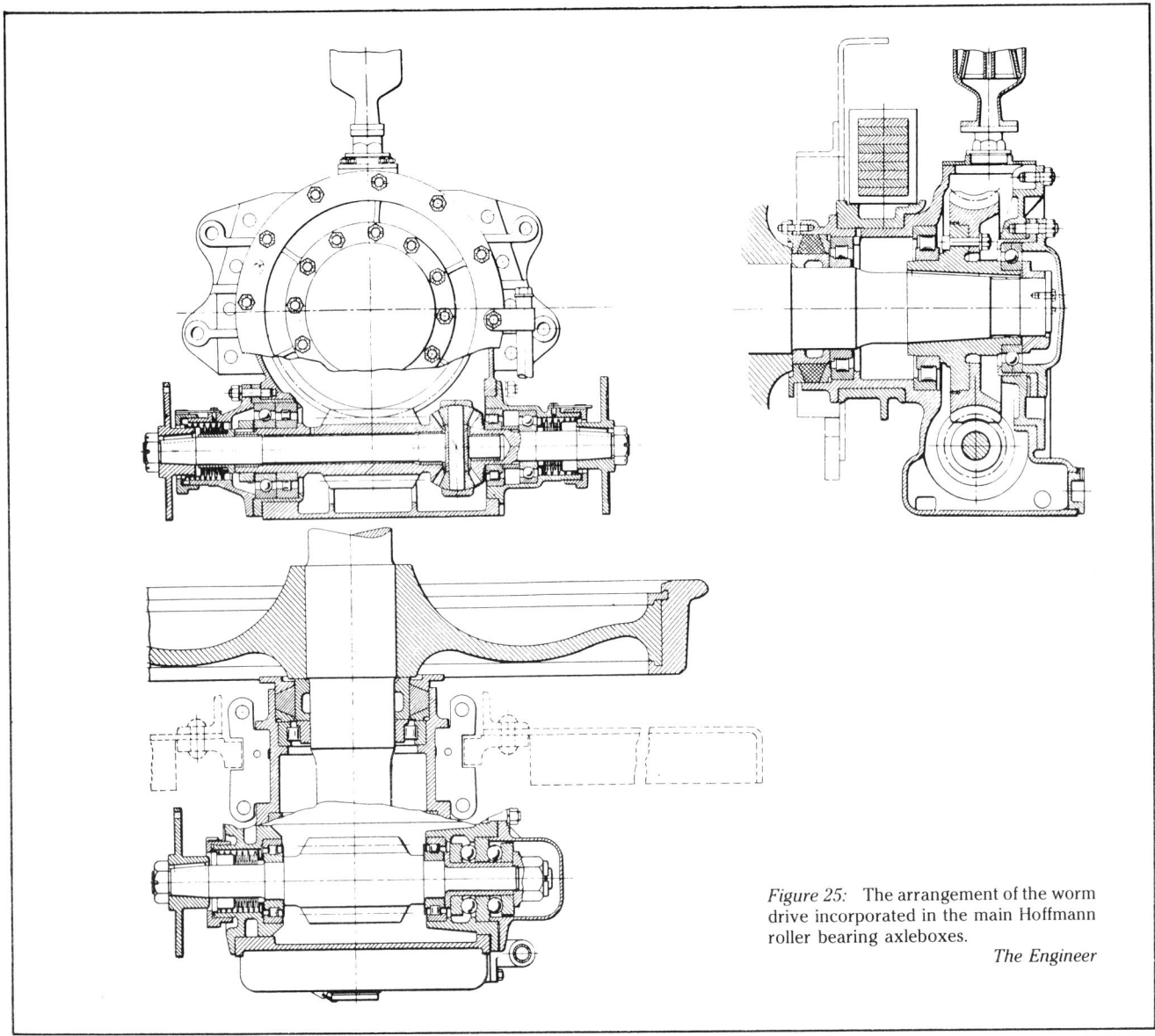

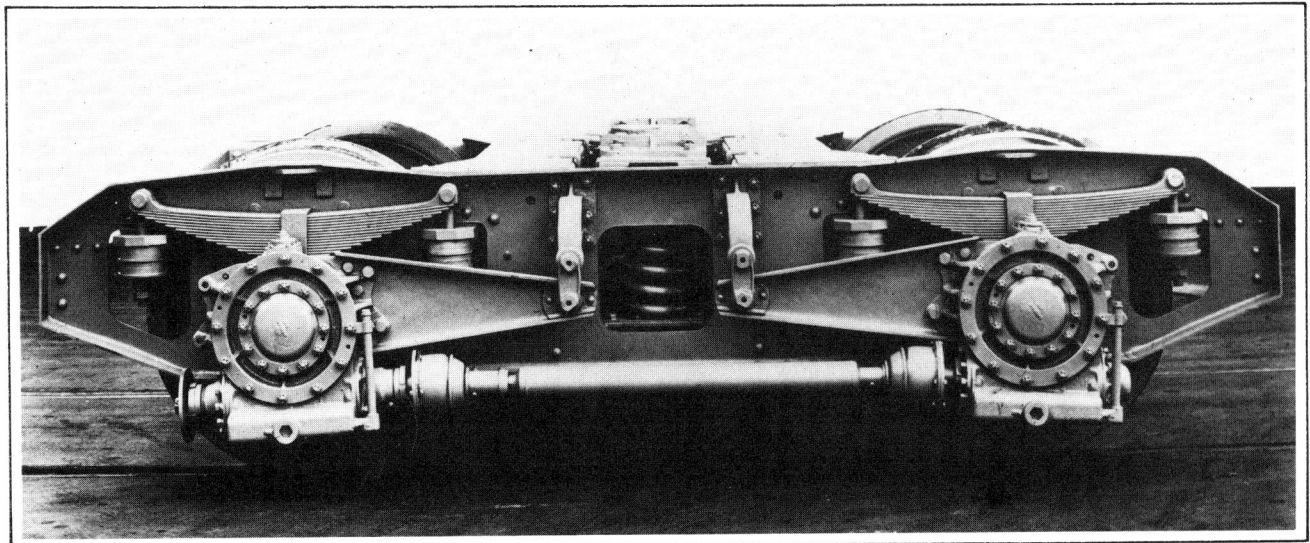

*Figure 25:* The arrangement of the worm drive incorporated in the main Hoffmann roller bearing axleboxes.

*The Engineer*

*Plate 74:* The bogies for railcars Nos. 2, 3, and 4.

*(A.E.C. Ltd.) Leyland Vehicles Ltd.*

## THE NEXT THREE CARS (NOS. 2, 3 AND 4)

**BRAKES**

Automobile practice had been followed in the design of the braking system, which was of the vacuum-hydraulic type. On each bogie was mounted a vaccum cylinder, connected to the master cylinder of a Lockheed hydraulic brake, and as the operating cylinders of this sytem were mounted directly on the torque arms, all the reactions were self-contained, and there was no relative displacement due to axle movement. *Plates 75 & 76* show this layout well. In the centre foreground of *Plate 75* is the vacuum cylinder operating the hydraulic master cylinder situated on the right-hand side of the vertical gusset. The master cylinder was connected by two flexible pipes to the operating cylinder mounted on the torque arm at the left-hand side, and to the immediate right of this was the split collar, holding the brake carrier in position.

Cast-steel drums of 20in. internal diameter were bolted to the inside of one wheel on each axle; the drums were split, bolted together in halves, and registered into the wheels *(see Figure 26)* so that they could be removed for truing-up or replacement without disturbing the wheels. The shoes were of the internal expanding type with Ferodo liners 5in. wide and 0.75in. thick and, along with their operating cams and pivot pins, were mounted in a carrier supported on the axle by roller bearings, and prevented from turning by a torque rod. The carrier was held endwise by the split collar, and by slackening this off, detaching one end of the torque arm, and disconnecting the brake rod, it could be withdrawn, complete with shoes, from the drum. It can be seen in this position in *Plate 76*.

Three exhausters were used on these vehicles to produce the necessary vacuum. Two were mounted directly, one on each engine, and the third (which ensured a continous vacuum during coasting periods when the engines were not running) was mounted on top of one of the reverse gearboxes and driven by a chain from the final driving shaft *(see Figure 24)*. Four cylindrical reservoirs were secured to the underframe and, as far as possible, the pipes between the exhausters, reservoirs, and valves were arranged down one side of the underframe, and the delivery pipes from the valves to the cylinders down the other. The usual gauges were provided in both driving compartment ends.

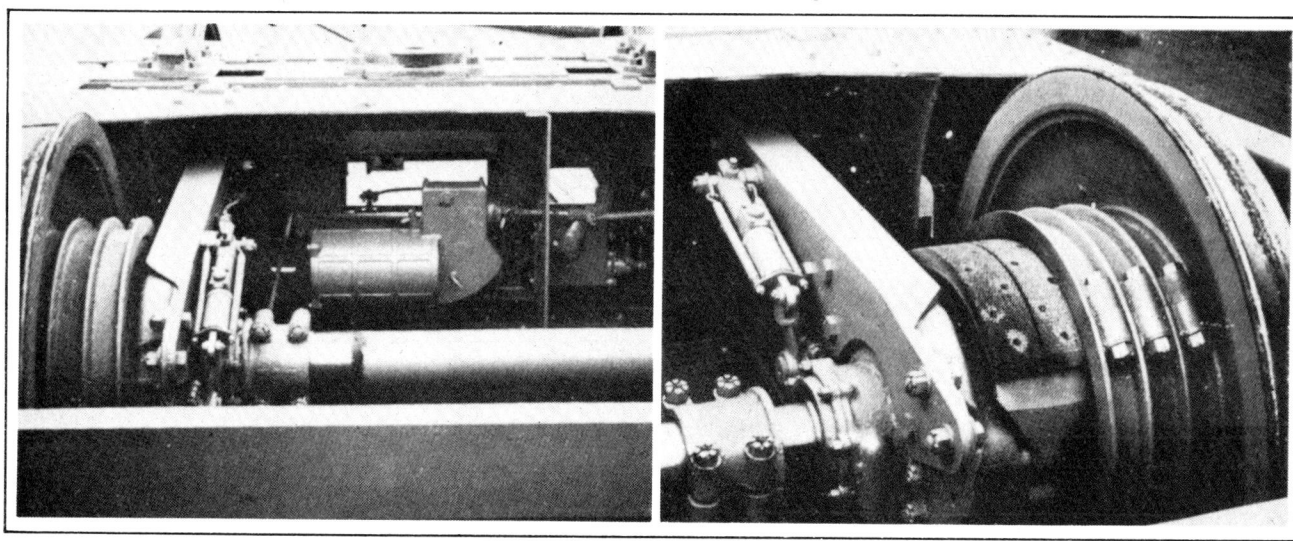

*Plate 75:* The vacuum-operated Lockheed brake in position on the bogie.

*Railway Gazette*

*Plate 76:* Ferodo brake linings withdrawn from the drum for examination.

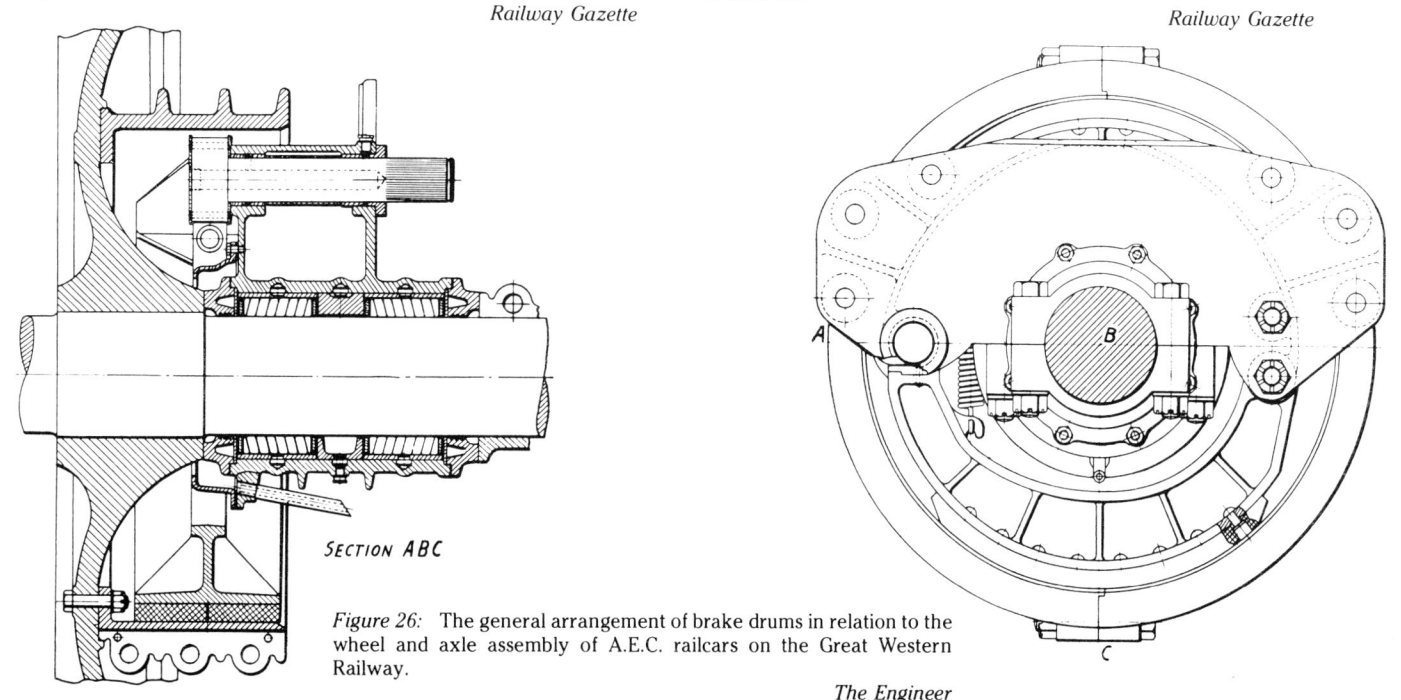

*Railway Gazette*

*Figure 26:* The general arrangement of brake drums in relation to the wheel and axle assembly of A.E.C. railcars on the Great Western Railway.

*The Engineer*

*Plate 77:* Although this view shows the bodywork of railcar No. 1 being built at the Park Royal Coachworks, it also shows the type of wood and metal construction incorporated in these early vehicles.

*(A.E.C. Ltd.) Leyland Vehicles Ltd.*

**THE DRIVING CONTROLS**

Compared with a steam locomotive, the controls were naturally rather unusual and were very similar to those on a bus, except for the lack of a steering wheel. Centrally, in front of the driver, was the lever for pre-selecting the required gear, this being more like an aeroplane joystick than the usual lever mounted on the steering column of cars fitted with this type of gearbox. This lever was fitted into a 'gate' on the floor. By removing it from one end of the coach to the other, the gate was rendered inoperative, and did not interfere with the driver's movements at the other end. To obtain a push and pull connection to the gearbox, three horizontal levers were mounted on cross members, and the ends connected by steel ribbons, as shown in the general arrangement drawing *(Figure 21)*. Whatever the direction of the end lever, one of these ribbons was in tension, and thus moved the centre lever.

Reversing was effected by a hand lever in each cab, the centre of the above three balance levers being connected by rods and cross shafts to the reverse boxes. The driver's hand lever was moved in the direction of travel. The speed of the engine was controlled by an accelerator pedal, which was connected by light-rods and bell-cranks, to the fuel pump. The engine 'stop' apparatus was applied only to the engine which drove through the epicyclic gearbox, so that when the driver's foot was taken off the accelerator pedal, the gear-drive engine came down to idling speed and the direct-drive engine to the stop position. Actually, in such a position, the road wheels drove the direct engine until the vehicle stopped. In practice, the car started moving with one engine.

A series of coloured lights was mounted on the dashboard, and included a green light, coupled electrically, to each engine, to show whether it was running, and a blue light for the water level in the radiator. The starter and heater switches for the two engines, the speedometer, and vacuum gauges were also mounted on the dashboard, and the vacuum sanding lever was close to the driver's hand. An emergency control gear was fitted, to enable the car to be stopped from the passenger compartment. Two separate electric systems were incorporated, each receiving its current from a 24 volt, 800 watt dynamo driven by the oil engines, so that if either system failed, half the lights in the railcar would still be available. Two Exide batteries of 130amp. hr. capacity were carried below the underframe.

**BODY**

The car bodies were again built by Park Royal Coachworks Limited, and the interior decoration by Heal & Son. All the body panelling was of aluminium sheets, supplied by the British Aluminium Co. Ltd., and the side panels were brought down in the form of a valance to within 10in. of the rail level, thus covering the driving units and providing a smooth exterior. Inspection covers were fitted opposite the various units; they were unlocked with a standard carriage key, and were easily taken down. The whole of the panelling was in commercially pure aluminium, the side valances and lower panels being 18SWG thick and the upper panels 14SWG. All external woodwork, not covered by panelling, was sheeted in 20SWG aluminium sheet. The streamlined nose and cowling of the car ends form a good example of aluminium sheet work, for several complicated curves were involved, *(see Plate 77)* and the covering was made up of a number of sheets beaten and welded together. The end pieces of the roof were also made of aluminium, beaten to the required profile.

*Plate 78:* Another posed A.E.C. publicity photograph, showing the spaciousness of the vehicle. The 'alarm signal' lever is above the door, to the left. The passengers seemed to have appeared in several previous photographs.
*(A.E.C. Ltd.) Leyland Vehicles Ltd.*

*Plate 79:* This 'posed' view shows the buffet counter and carriage fitments. The two toilets are on each side of the coach through the centre door.
*(A.E.C. Ltd.) Leyland Vehicles Ltd.*

*Plate 80 (left):* 'Water Sir?' Table service on the new buffet service. He probably deserved this drink, having been a passenger in all the official photographs.
*(A.E.C. Ltd.) Leyland Vehicles Ltd.*

*Plate 81 (below):* Railcar No. 2 at Cardiff, showing the new GWR monogram on the nose.
*(A.E.C. Ltd.) Leyland Vehicles Ltd.*

*Figure 27 (above):* The new GWR monogram that was to become internationally famous.

*Figure 28:* One of the submitted slogans for GWR that did not catch on!

Although the *Great Western Railway Magazine* article, at the beginning of this chapter incorporated a description of the interior of these railcars, a further look at the interior specification in more detail is of interest.

Third class accommodation only was provided, and the seating was arranged as shown in *Figure 18*. The two passenger saloons were divided by the gangway connecting the two central doors, and were fitted with 40 fixed seats with removable tables as shown in *Plates 78, 79 & 80*. The seats were upholstered in light green horsehair, and the tables were in oak, with a top of gold-brown Rexine to match the same material lining the interior. The panels, pelmets, and woodwork generally were in weathered oak. Green linoleum covered the floor with the addition of a heavy brown carpet covering the gangway, cross-gangway, and buffet floor.

Special attention was paid to the lighting to give a soft diffused effect. Tubular lights with two bulbs were fitted on the side panels above each seat, and the same type of lamp was fitted down the centre of the roof, where it was interspersed with the Colt ventilators. Additional ventilation was provided by Beresford extractors above the windows. Electric fans were provided in the buffet compartment, and Clayton-Dewandre heaters were installed in the passenger saloons, buffet, and both driving compartments.

The passenger saloon was connected at one end with the buffet, by means of a short gangway, with a lavatory on each side. Each lavatory had a water heater, which consisted of the silencer surrounded by a water jacket, the engine exhaust gases passing through on their way to the exhaust pipe in the roof. The buffet was divided across its centre by a counter, with four seats facing it. There was ample room for passengers to stand at the counter, and on the other side were arranged tables and cupboards for the stocking of light refreshments, and also a gas-heated toaster, boiler-connected to a nickel-plated coffee and separate milk boiler. Crockery and cutlery were also stored in the cupboards, and the water tanks were built into the bulkhead between the lavatories and the buffet, with reserve tanks beneath the tables in the kitchen.

### AUTOMATIC TRAIN CONTROL

The railcars were equipped with the Great Western Railway Company's Automatic Train Control, whereby distant signal indications were communicated to the driver, and brakes were automatically applied on passing a distant signal at caution.

### GENERAL DIMENSIONS, ETC.

A table of general dimensions, etc., for Nos. 2, 3 and 4 follows:

| | |
|---|---|
| Overall length of frame | 60ft. 0in. |
| Length over buffers | 63ft. 7in. |
| Overall width of chassis | 8ft. 1in. |
| Height to top of frame | 3ft. 9in. |
| Distance between bogie centres | 40ft. 0in. |
| Bogie wheelbase | 7ft. 0in. |
| Horsepower of each engine at 2,000r.p.m., total | 260hp |
| Number of cylinders | 6 |
| Wheel diameter | 3ft. 1in. |
| Chassis weight in running order | 16 tons 9cwt. |

Two fuel tanks, each of 45 gallons capacity, were provided. This was sufficient to run the car for approximately 450 to 500 miles without refuelling, so allowing a full day's work.

One important feature of 1934 was that the Great Western Railway adopted a new monogram; namely the initials 'GWR' in a circle *(see Figure 27)*. This was to take the place of the words 'Great Western Railway', the Company's crest, and the various other combinations and abbreviations that had been used over the years. The idea was to use this monogram on such diverse articles as antimacassars, cutlery, posters, handbills, stationery, cups and saucers, road motor vehicles, and uniform badges. Every department of the GWR was to use the monogram, in order to give uniformity and provide a distinctive Great Western Railway badge, which was soon to become familiar to the trading and travelling public.

Such was the success of the idea, that it was immediately used on the 'nose' of vehicles Nos. 2, 3 and 4. Also, a marvellous Great Western publication appeared on the new diesel railcar service which the three new cars were operating, called *The Streamline Way*. Parts of this publication are reproduced to demonstrate the enthusiasm with which the GWR launched its new streamlined railcar service.

It is also interesting to report that several 'slogans' were submitted to the advertising department in 1934, to include in the publicity for this new service. The one that seems most appropriate, but did not become adopted, is seen in *Figure 28*.

*Plate 82:* Railcar No. 2, photographed in pristine condition before delivery to the Great Western Railway.

*(A.E.C. Ltd.) Leyland Vehicles Ltd.*

The success of diesel railcars Nos. 2, 3 and 4 was now beginning to be noticed, and in 1937, the *A.E.C. Gazette* recorded:

> Since being introduced in July 1934, the railcars have maintained express services between Birmingham and Cardiff to the tune of 100,000 miles on each car.

Such also was the novelty and popularity of the railcars that groups were beginning to hire the vehicles for special trips, and several are worthy of mention.

One, in 1934, was of an excursion over GWR rails in connection with the Birmingham Junior Chamber of Commerce, which utilised one of the railcars for a trip to Avonmouth. The party had thirty members, which proved about the right number for a 'comfortable' journey. A time of 165 minutes had been allocated in each direction for the 141 miles via Oxford and Bristol, including one stop. On the return trip, due to traffic congestion in the Bristol area, they left 17 minutes late, but thanks to the high speed performance of the railcar, this had been regained by Oxford. The 74½ miles between Bristol and Oxford had been covered in 68 minutes instead of the 85 minutes allowed. An average speed of 70m.p.h. was maintained for nearly 30 minutes and a maximum of over 80m.p.h. was recorded.

The initial run of the 'new' railcar No. 2 *(see Plate 82)* was also recorded by Mr Humphrey Baker on the Press trip of 6th July 1934, and the following were recorded; probably the fastest ever recorded times for a railcar between Birmingham, Newport and Cardiff.

An easy start was made to Tyseley, the 3.3 miles taking 5min. 46sec. from Snow Hill, but speed was maintained at 60m.p.h. up the 1 in 230 past Earlswood Lakes; the latter station, 10.2 miles from the start, was passed in 14min. Down the 1 in 150 past Danzey, the maximum rate was 73m.p.h. and Henley-in-Arden, 17.0 miles, was cleared in 19min. 49sec. A slack of 50m.p.h. was made over Bearley West Junction (21.3 miles in 23min. 56sec.) and the generous working allowance of 6½min. over the 5.7 miles thence to Stratford-on-Avon was cut to just under 4min. making 27min. 49sec. from the start (25.0 miles). On rising grades from here to Honeybourne, speed was maintained at 62½m.p.h., Honeybourne East Junction, 33.0 miles, being cleared in 35min. 49sec. After that, the minimum up the 1 in 200 past Broadway was 54m.p.h., and no higher speed than 67½m.p.h. was attempted on the falling grades from Winchcombe to Gloucester. Broadway, 38.0 miles, was passed in 41min. 3sec., Toddington, 42.5 miles, in 45min. 33sec., Gotherington, 48.5 miles, in 51min. 7sec., and milepost 20, 53.1 miles, in 55min. 31sec., speed being then reduced to 45m.p.h. through Malvern Road Station at Cheltenham. To Malvern Road, the time was 56min. 51sec. for the 54.1 miles, and Churchdown, 57.5 miles, was passed in 36sec. over the hour, but the car was now before time, and severe signal checks were experienced outside Gloucester. To Gloucester Station, passed dead slow, the time was 65min. 49sec. for the 60.9 miles.

Speed was again reduced to 35m.p.h. at Over Junction, but after that was maintained at or just above the mile-a-minute along the level stretch bordering the Severn. Grange Court, 68.4 miles, was cleared in 75min. 45sec., Awre, 75.1 miles, in 82min. 20sec., and Lydney, 80.3 miles, in 87min. 25sec. A p.w. slack occurred 1½ miles beyond Lydney and, after that, a service slack to 40m.p.h. before Chepstow, with a maximum of 61½m.p.h. intermediately; after this the power output was reduced, to avoid running too far ahead of time. Chepstow, 88.2 miles, was passed in 96min. 47sec., Severn Tunnel Junction, 95.6 miles, in 104min. 58sec, and Llanwern, 101.6 miles, in 109min. 24sec., Newport being reached, after an actual non-stop run of over a hundred miles — 105.4 miles to be precise — in 115min. 16sec. This was about 8min. less than the time allowed, but there was a very easy booking of 52min. for the final 44½ miles. A run of 15min. 19sec. from Newport to Cardiff completed the journey.

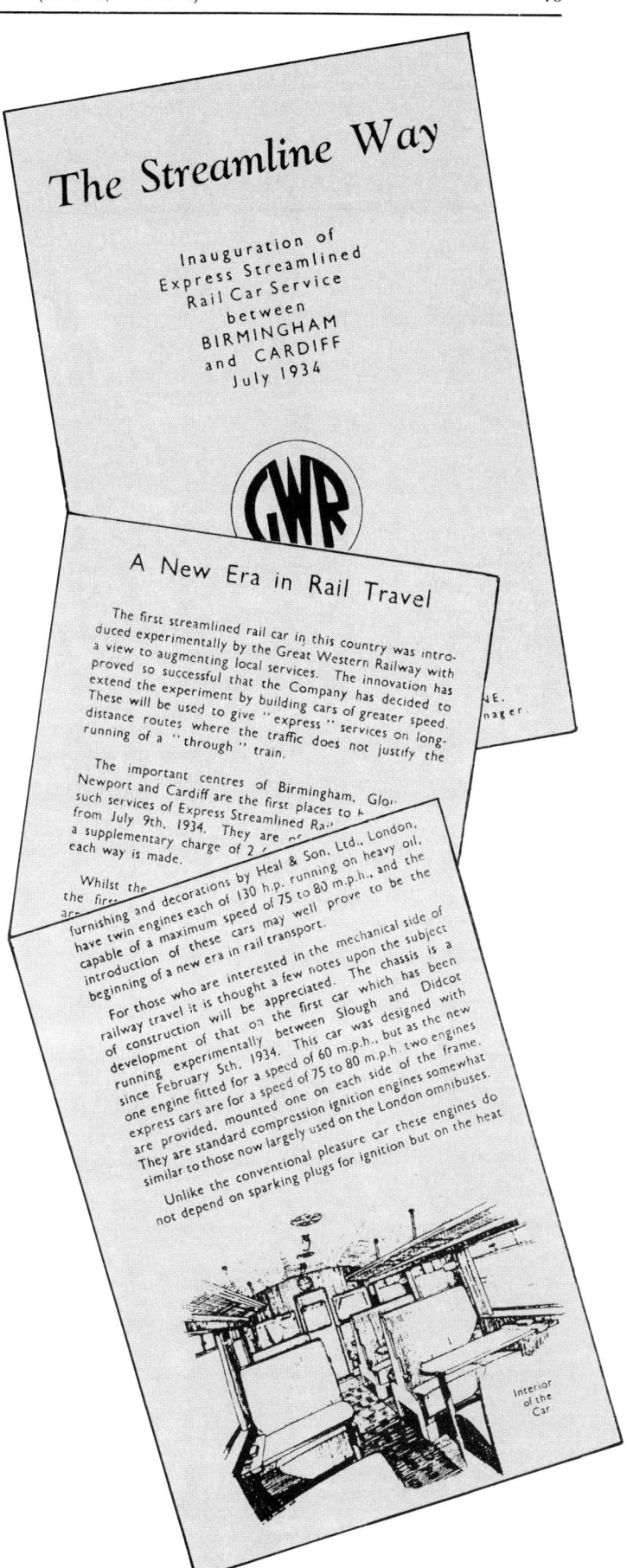

A further railtour organised was reported in *The A.E.C. Gazette* of 1935, and again an extract has been included to illustrate the GWR's ingenuity in the use of these railcars. The newsline read:

## Novel Use For A.E.C. Railcar
### SUNDAY EVENING MYSTERY TRIPS
### Also Carries Wedding Guests

*... and then went on to report:*

Mystery trips were, until the Licensing Authorities compelled their restrictions, a general feature of road travel at seaside resorts and holiday centres. But they have only figured occasionally in the summer programmes of the railways.

Special interest was accordingly aroused by the announcement of the GWR that on Sunday, August 18th, a five hours' mystery trip would be run from Worcester, using one of the company's new A.E.C. twin-engined, streamlined railcars. This was certainly the first occasion upon which a railcar had been employed for an excursion of this nature. Accommodation was limited and a fare of 2s. 6d. was charged for the run. To maintain the mystery nature of the trip, sealed orders were handed to the driver and guard only a moment before departure.

According to a *Worcester Evening News* correspondent, seventy-five people took part in this 'Cruise of Adventure'. Many more would have taken tickets if room had been available.

'We drove out of Worcester', related this correspondent, 'in brilliant sunshine. Away to the right we saw the Malverns, and passing through the market garden country, we later had the magnificent Bredon Hills on our right. Through Evesham, and then the guard hands out printed slips telling us that the mystery train leaves here for another destination at 7p.m.

'Here' proved to be Stratford-on-Avon, where a stop of one and a half hours enabled us to visit the Shakespeare Memorial Theatre.

Back to our Magic Carpet... we could see we were going westwards... away in the distance someone espied the tower of Gloucester's Cathedral. But our destination was not Gloucester. It was Cheltenham, where we had another hour and a half of leisure.

The trip back in the glowing dusk was really enchanting. At one point the car was travelling at 72 miles an hour but we were always comfortable. Dead on time we ran into Foregate Street Station (Worcester) at five minutes to ten'.

There seems no doubt that the trip, which was in the nature of an experiment, was an unqualified success, and that the mode of travel provided by the railcar won the instant approval of passengers. The necessary restriction in the number of people travelling gave a private party 'air' to the journey and a degree of quick friendliness — unattainable in a bigger excursion — was one of the most noticeable features of the trip.

Encouraged by the success of the first 'Mystery Tour', the GWR ran another the following Sunday, and it is understood that similar runs will be made during the remainder of the season.

The foregoing suggests that there are many uses to which the A.E.C. streamlined railcar can be put when not engaged in scheduled services. As an example of this, *The A.E.C. Gazette* understands that recently one of these units was employed to take a number of wedding guests from London to a small station in Berkshire, and back.

Perhaps it is only a question of time before newly married couples will engage a railcar for their honeymoon trips! Such a vehicle would at least provide a degree of privacy unknown in the otherwise estimable steam trains, by which the twin slaves of Hymen normally travel.

Diesel railcar No. 4 was used in more publicity when the railcar featured in the film-making industry, and this was well documented in *The A.E.C. Gazette* and summed up the popularity of these railcars, in the mid-1930s.

*Plate 83:* This shows a fine *Times* photograph of an A.E.C. streamlined twin-engined railcar, crossing Brunel's eighty three year old bridge over the River Wye, at Chepstow. This again was a GWR 'first' in April 1935, and a unique event in railway history, as it was one of the first recorded football supporters' specials.

*A.E.C. Gazette*

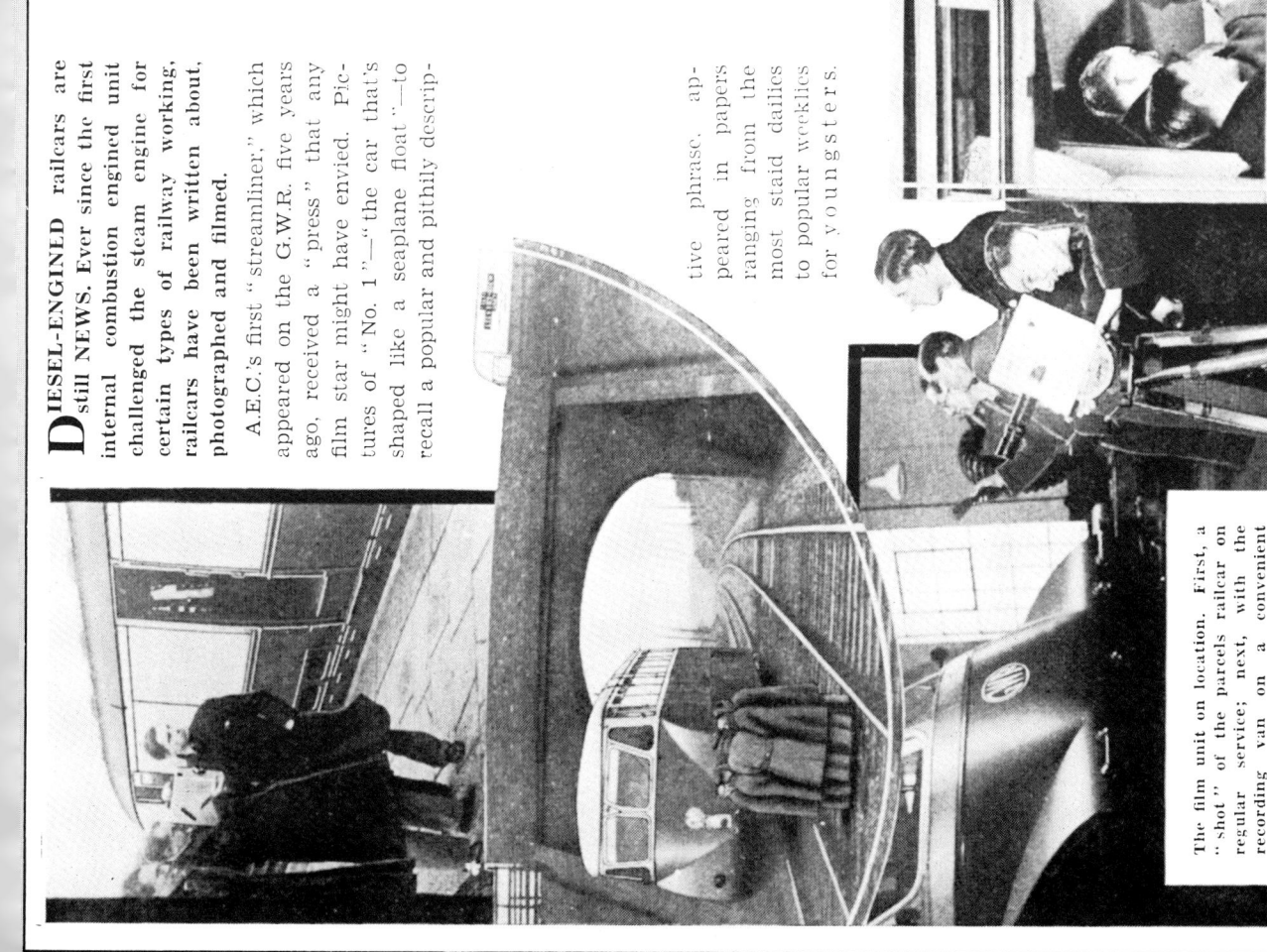

# MOVIE MAKING AT SOUTHALL
## Diesel Railcar In Another Film
### "STREAMLINERS" STILL NEWS

DIESEL-ENGINED railcars are still NEWS. Ever since the first internal combustion engined unit challenged the steam engine for certain types of railway working, railcars have been written about, photographed and filmed.

A.E.C.'s first "streamliner," which appeared on the G.W.R. five years ago, received a "press" that any film star might have envied. Pictures of "No. 1"—"the car that's shaped like a seaplane float"—to recall a popular and pithily descriptive phrase, appeared in papers ranging from the most staid dailies to popular weeklies for youngsters.

Long before it made its first journey, over 1,500 column inches had been devoted to descriptions of the most revolutionary railcar ever seen in this country.

Since then every diesel railcar development on the G.W.R. has brought to Southall press photographers, journalists, news-reel cameramen—once even a B.B.C. commentator. Many hours have been expended in filming A.E.C. "streamliners" on service so that a vast cinema public could learn something about this new type of rail travel.

Last month camera and sound men again visited Southall for pictures of "No. 4," one of the Birmingham-Cardiff express cars, to include in a film "Romance of the Railways," shortly to be released for general exhibition.

A.E.C. staff once more co-operated, acted as passengers, entering and leaving the "streamliner," taking a meal in the buffet compartment, and giving realism to the "shots."

A recording van linked to microphones on a branch line embankment picked up sounds of "No. 4" starting, stopping, and at speed, as well as the distinctive notes of its two electric horns.

As often on location, grey skies and rain curtailed exterior sequences and the railcar was run into its own shop at the Southall Factory, for the occasion, turned into a miniature studio. Here powerful electric lamps flooded the saloon with dazzling light while the camera recorded "passengers" at tea.

There's still a story in the Great Western's fleet of diesels. And as oil gives way to steam on local lines, signifying changing conditions, marking a new era in railway service, A.E.C. "streamliners" will continue to be news in the Press, on the radio and on the cinema screen.

The film unit on location. First, a "shot" of the parcels railcar on regular service; next, with the recording van on a convenient bridge, a sound track of "No. 4" at speed; then a glimpse of the driver at his controls, and finally, a close up, under powerful lights, of passengers in the buffet compartment.

*Plate 84:* Railcar No. 5 at Gloucester Railway Carriage & Wagon Works, in July 1935.
*Gloucester Railway Carriage & Wagon Co. Ltd.*

# Chapter Five: Nos. 5, 6 and 7 (The Gloucester Bodies) Enter Service

The four diesel railcars with which the Great Western Railway were now experimenting, were proving so satisfactory that the Company placed an order for a further three (to be numbered 5, 6 and 7) — *see Plates 84, 85, 86 & 87*. This order was made by exchange of letters under Lot 15221, and the cars were built in 1935 and entered GWR service as follows: Nos. 5 and 7 both came into service in July 1935, and No. 6 in August 1935. The cost of each of these three vehicles came to a total of £5,031, of which A.E.C.'s part amounted to £4,766 and the GWR cost, £265.

It is of interest to the reader that the original 20th December 1934 specification from the A.E.C. factory to the Gloucester Carriage & Wagon Company (who built the bodies) still exists, and is reproduced in full as it supplies a good insight into the detailed body construction *(Figure 29)* of Nos. 5, 6 and 7.

**THE ASSOCIATED EQUIPMENT COMPANY LTD.
SPECIFICATION
OF
BODIES FOR RAIL CARS
NOS. 5, 6 AND 7 FOR
GWR**

*DESIGN* — To be generally in accordance with our drawing No. U.64400.

*CONSTRUCTION* — All materials to be of best quality and subject to approval where necessary.
All timbers to be well-seasoned and free from knots and shakes, sapwood and other defects.
Quotation may be for either composites or all-metal construction.
Consideration to be given to the mounting of crossbearers on the chassis frame by rubber pads.

*PANELS* — External panels to be in aluminium, but reduction in price, if steel panels fitted, to be quoted, and increase in weight by so doing to be specified.
Lower edge to be turned under body framing, or similarly treated to give smooth finish.
Detachable cowls to be fitted over buffers.
Special consideration to be given to reduction of drumming and similar noises in panels by spraying with asbestos or by similar means; such treatment to be quoted as an extra.

*ROOF* — To be tongued and grooved spruce boards covered with canvas, well-bedded in white lead paint or similar material.
Interior to be lined with 3mm. plywood covered with 'Rexine' to suit general colour scheme.
Front and rear ends of roof to be of aluminium beaten to shape, or alternatively, of sheet steel. Alteration in price for the latter to be quoted.
Guttering to be fitted round roof, with concealed down pipes.

*DRIVER'S COMPARTMENT* — Accommodation to be provided for driver at both ends of the car, floor being slotted where necessary to suit control pedals and levers.
Boarded partition 3ft. high to be provided at back of driver's seat in luggage compartment, as indicated, and glazed partition with sliding door to be provided at other end.
Driver's seat to be of the 'bucket' type trimmed in leather to suit general colour scheme and fitted with 'Dunlop' rubber cushions, to be arranged to tilt forward and to be adjustable both vertically and horizontally by 'Leverex' or similar fitting.
Tip-up seat to be provided at each end on right of driver.
Full drop windows to be fitted on either side of driver in each compartment, fitted with straps, and to lift over fence. Straps to have metal eyelets.
Horizontal protecting bar to be fitted across window, level with top of drop window when dropped.
Two one-piece fixed screens to be fitted to the front of each compartment. Frames to be in brass, chromium-plated and glazed with 3/16in. 'Triplex' or similar glass.

*INSTRUMENT BOARD* — In stove enamel aluminium to be fitted in each driver's compartment to accommodate instruments supplied by A.E.C.

*INTERIOR FINISH AND FITTINGS* — Interior of passengers' compartment below garnish rail to be covered with 'Rexine' to match general colour scheme. Lower parts below seat rails to be in steel panels covered with lino to match floor *(Plates 88 & 89)*.
Two 8 day clocks to be fitted, one on each bulkhead.
Ash trays to be fitted between all seats; these to be of a type which will not rattle.
Electric screen wiper to be fitted at each end capable of hand operation also. Special consideration to be given to an extra heavy type of screen wiper which will act on both inside and outside of windscreen.
One Pyrene Fire Extinguisher to be fitted in luggage compartment.
First-aid outfit (supplied by GWR) to be fitted in luggage compartment.
All metal fittings to be chromium-plated finish.
Care to be taken that condensation vents in interior panels will not cause inconvenience to passengers.
Emergency stop lever (provided by A.E.C.) to be fitted and suitable notice painted on panel.

*HEATING* — Four large type 'Clayton Dewandre' heaters to be supplied and fitted in passengers' saloon and one small type to be fitted in each driver's compartment.
Care to be taken by means of restriction in pipe to outer heater in passenger compartment, or by similar means, to ensure circulation through heaters in driver's compartment.
Shut-off cocks to be so arranged that they may be operated from the inside of coach either by means of extended spindles or by long keys, with suitably covered openings in the floor.
Drain cocks to be provided, and piping arranged to completely drain system.

*LIGHTING* — Interior lighting of saloons, luggage compartments to be wired and suitable light fittings supplied and fitted.
Illustration of type of light fitting proposed to be submitted with tender.
As two separate lighting systems are provided for on the car, preference will be given to light fittings containing two bulbs, wired up separately to the two distinct systems.
Sockets for inspection lamps to be provided in each engine casing.
Two bulkhead lamps with wire guards to be supplied and fitted in luggage compartment and one in driver's compartment at opposite end.
All the necessary switchboards and switches to be provided, and wiring system to be submitted to us for approval.
Four head and tail lights to be incorporated at

*Plate 85:* This fine photograph shows railcar No. 5 after completion at the premises of the Gloucester Railway Carriage & Wagon Co. Ltd., in July 1935 (Order No. 67332, Photo No. 4967).

*Gloucester Railway Carriage & Wagon Co. Ltd.*

each end of body as indicated on drawing No. U.64400.

All lights to be flush fitting, the three lower ones being fitted with bull's eye lenses and the upper one with plain lens.

Tail lamps to be operated by two-way switches from either end of the car, wired up in conjunction with our switchboard indicator lights.

VESTIBULE PARTITIONS
Partitions to be provided at entrance on each side in accordance with drawing No. U.64400 and to be fitted with chromium-plated metal frame windows.

SEATS
Particulars to follow.
Sample seat to be prepared and submitted for approval as soon as possible after placing of order. Two lockers in suitable position under seats to be provided with Autovacs, and to be fitted with airtight lids.

LUGGAGE
No luggage racks are required, but seats to be so arranged as to provide maximum accommodation for luggage underneath.

WINDOWS
Side windows to be fixed and glazed with ¼in. plate glass from inside.
Windows to be made as flush as possible in acdance with drawing No. U.66401, detail 'A'.
Beresord sliding ventilators to be fitted over all passenger compartment windows, except where interfered with by sliding doors. Dummy ventilators to be fitted on all other windows except in driver's compartment, rattling and also ingress of rain.
All windows to be fitted with spring roller blinds with suitable catches; said blinds to be mounted immediately below ventilators.
Windows in partition between passenger and luggage compartments and also in partition at back of driver at other end of car, as well as in doors for same, to be fitted with Peters concertina blinds.
All blinds to match general colour scheme.
Windows opposite seats over raised portion of floor (over engines) to be fitted with dummy window sills to bring height of sill to floor boards to the same as in rear of car; such sills to accommodate destination board, as indicated on drawing

Beresford ventilators to be of double-opening type to provide maximum opening, to be 10in. deep, and every precaution taken to prevent No. U.64401 detail 'B', and special provision to be made to prevent rattling.

If desired, destination boards may be in two pieces to allow stay half-way.

ENTRANCE
All doors to be of sliding type (hand operated) which must be made rigid enough to prevent distortion and to give easy operation.
Arrangement of doors and steps to be as indicated on drawing No. U.64400; special care to be taken to make such doors draught-proof, rain-proof and free from all rattle.
Outer door pillars to be chamfered off as much as possible, as indicated.
All outside doors to be provided with stout bolts on the inside except one which must be provided with a lock so that the car may be securely locked up from the outside.
Doors leading from passenger compartment to driver's compartment or luggage compartment to be fitted with Yale or similar locks.
All doors to be fitted with inside and outside handles, chromium-plated. Entrance steps to be protected by steel treads and nosing.
Emergency step recessed into valance to be provided on each side to allow for entrance or exit from rail level; such recesses to be suitably streamlined.
Single ascending rail to be fitted on left-hand side of each centre entrance, and similar rail on inside of doors to assist in entering car; such handles to be as flush as possible.

BELL
Electric bell to be provided at each end of car near driver; such bells to be operated by push in the centre vestibule or by push in driver's compartment at opposite end of car.

FLOOR
Suitable inspection traps edged with aluminium angle and fitted with flush rings to be provided where indicated on drawing No. U.64402. Floor to be covered with ½in. Insulwood (fireproof quality) and with good quality lino to suit general scheme of decoration.
Raised portion of floor over engines to be provided with ¼in. sheet asbestos betweeen wood and Insulboard.

*VENTILATION*

Trap doors over engine, in addition to asbestos referred to above, to be provided on the underside with sheet metal protected asbestos sheet attached to trap, but separated by suitable air space.

Raised portion of floor over engine, other than trap door, to be suitably protected by metal-covered asbestos, such protection being curved wherever possible.

'Colt' type ventilators to be fitted in roof where desirable; such ventilators to be arranged offset from the centre of roof. In addition, an opening approximately 2ft. 6in. wide x 6in. high to be provided at each end of car in the roof as indicated on drawing No. U.64400, such vent to be fitted with louvres and to communicate with an air duct formed by a false ceiling in the driver's and luggage compartments, such air duct to be connected to the passenger compartment by four or more ventilators fitted in the bulkhead, these ventilators to be adjustable and hinged on their bottom edge in order to deflect air stream on to the ceiling of car and such hinged vents to be fitted with side plates. Means to be provided in the air duct to prevent water passing through into the passengers' compartment and to drain same away.

*LUGGAGE COMPARTMENT*

Double sliding doors, as indicated on drawing No. U. 64400 to be provided fitted with fixed glasses and with dummy ventilators, provided these do not increase the width of the door.

Floor to be covered in hardwood, with metal protecting strips.

Locks on doors, as indicated above, and, as indicated above, also special care to be taken to prevent draught, ingress of rain and noise.

Windows in bulkheads to be fitted as stated above with blinds and also with vertical guard irons, painted to suit interior decoration.

Tip-up seat to be provided for guard, in convenient position.

*TOOL CONTAINER*

A tool container to be provided in a position to be determined later; such container to be large enough to carry loose change speed pre-selecting lever. Fitted with Yale or similar lock.

*VALANCE*

Valance to be generally in accordance with drawing No. U.64402 and to be in aluminium suitably supported, but reduction in price to be quoted if valance be made in steel, and also increase in weight to be stated. As indicated on drawing, valance panels are approximately alternately fixed and detachable.

Detachable panels to be fitted with budget locks or similar means of holding them securely in position and in addition, some form of automatic catch to be provided to prevent panels falling off, if not locked.

Fixed panels to be easily removable from their supporting angles by undoing about four bolts after detachable panels have been removed. A suggested method of doing this is shown on drawing No. U.64401, detail 'C'.

Fixed panels to be turned over and riveted to supporting irons.

As indicated on drawing, louvred panels in front of radiator will be supplied by A.E.C.

Engine panels to be fitted with openings covered on the inside by 16 gauge ¼in. mesh wire netting, as indicated on drawing. Bottom edges of valance to be finished up in line with portion of valance supplied by A.E.C. as indicated above.

Deflector panels to be fitted above and to the rear of auxiliary radiators, as indicated on drawing.

A single line of cut louvres to be arranged along the top edge of the valance, (not shown on drawing).

Valance panels opposite the three driving axleboxes to be arranged so that they may swing outwards on a parallel motion system about 5in. and to be restrained by coil springs which may be attached to the spring hanger bolts of the bogie. A suggested method of doing this is shown on drawing No. U.64402, detail 'D', but suggestions for a better method may be submitted. It may be pointed out that owing to the small clearance between the driving axleboxes and valance, it is necessary to allow for the valance to move outwards at these points when rounding curves.

Inspection covers to be provided in the valance where indicated on the drawing; such covers to be hinged on their upper edges and provided with suitable locks.

Detachable valance plates to be provided with rubber rubbing strips and rubber stops to prevent drumming. A suggested form of valance plate stop is shown on drawing No. U.64402, detail 'E'. Consideration to be given to the spraying of panels with asbestos or to similar means of preventing noise; such to be quoted for as an extra.

All valance panels to be numbered in 1¼in. white numbers on top edge with corresponding numbers on fixed part of body.

*INTERIOR WOODWORK*

Alternative prices to be given for carrying out of interior woodwork, such as window framing, mouldings, etc., in oak, mahogany, walnut or plain whitewood, stained and varnished.

*CARPETS*

Carpets to be provided in centre gangway and vestibule of passengers' saloon; same to match general colour scheme and to be provided with holding down buttons or similar fittings.

*EXTERIOR PAINTING*

Chassis to be well-painted in black before mounting body, and all under parts to be similarly treated.

Rims of wheels to be painted white on outside faces.

Exterior of body to be filled up, rubbed down, painted and varnished in first class style to standard GWR colours.

Transfers, where available, will be supplied by us.

The conditions under which the order was placed with the Gloucester Railway Carriage & Wagon Co. Ltd., also illustrates the terms of the work conditions of the 1930s and was as follows:

**CONDITIONS OF QUOTATION**

Where access is not available to Works by rail, price to include necessary transport of rail car chassis from A.E.C. Works or equally convenient point, to your Works and for return transport of completed coach.

Guaranteed time of delivery from receipt of order and of individual chassis to be quoted.

Penalty Clause for late delivery may be required in contract.

Work to be open for inspection at all times either by this Company's or the GWR Company's representatives.

Guaranteed maximum weight of body to be stated. Alternative weights to be stated if steel panelling used instead of aluminium.

It is to be clearly understood that the drawings forwarded with this enquiry do not, in any way, indicate the exact method on construction, but are merely given to indicate our requirements as regards general construction, and also to assist in the preparation of your quotation.

*Plate 86:* A view taken on 26th August 1935 showing railcar No. 6 in pristine condition. This batch of vehicles had sliding doors on the passenger entrances instead of inward opening doors.

*British Rail*

*Plate 87:* No. W7W in British Railways' service in the 1950s, pictured here running with its engine covers removed.

*R. H. G. Simpson*

*Plate 88:* The interior of No. 6 diesel railcar on 26th August 1935, showing the new sliding doors, the omission of luggage racks and tables, new-style light fittings, roller blinds, clock, etc.
*British Rail*

*Plate 89:* Looking at the other end of railcar No. 6, as compared to the view in *Plate 88*. Note the 3/2 seating arrangement.
*British Rail*

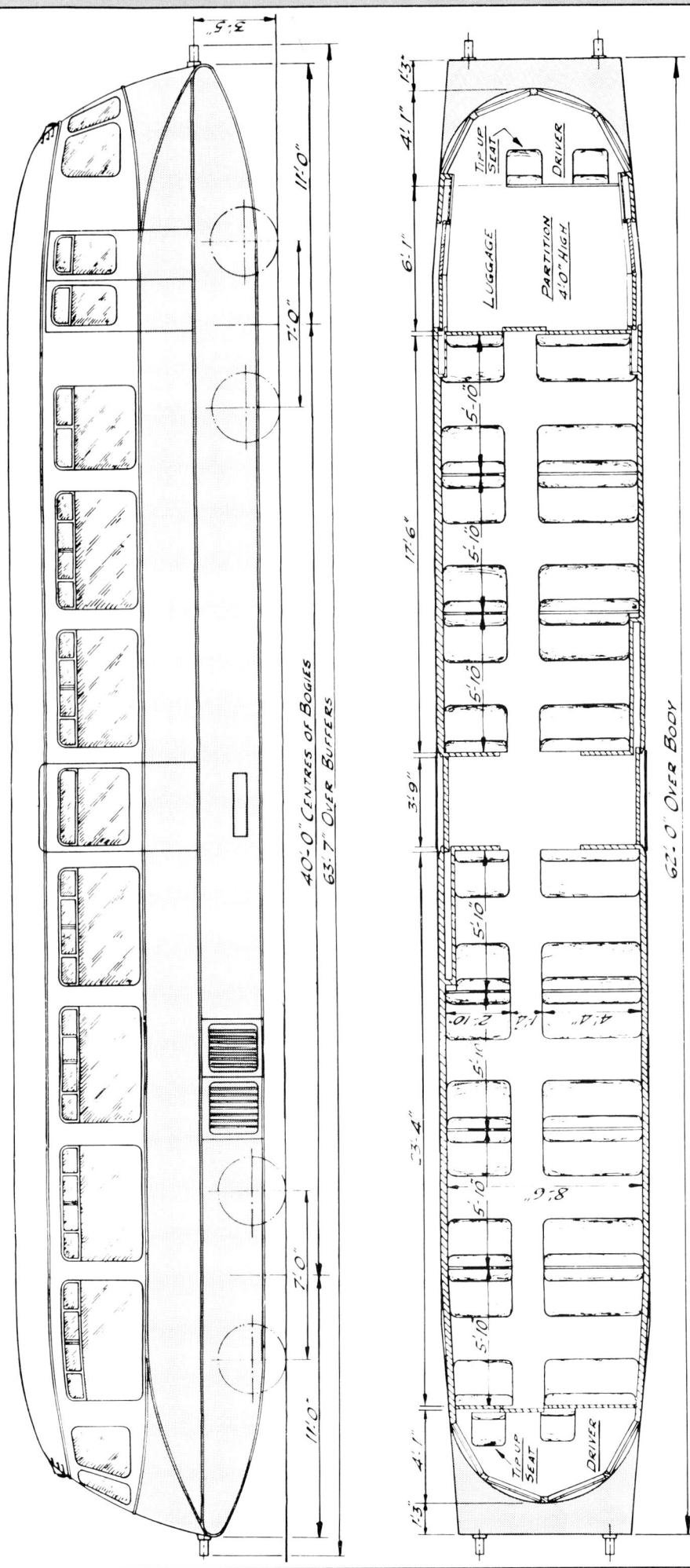

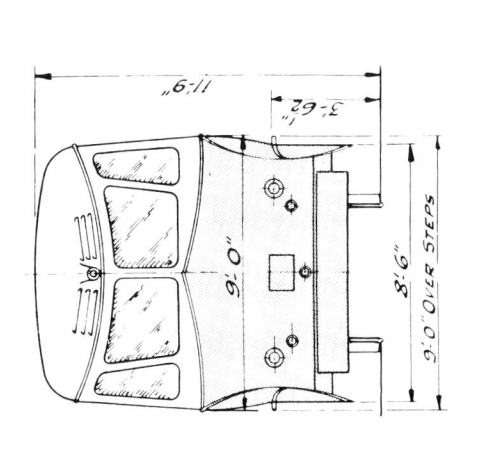

Figure 29

Guarantee to be given with your quotation to cover the making good of any defects in workmanship or materials which may be found during a given period after delivery.

This specification not to be taken as in any way complete. Your complete specification to be forwarded with quotation.

Due to the increase in orders for the railcars, the A.E.C. factory decided to construct a new erecting shop for these vehicles, on a piece of ground adjoining the factory *(Plates 90 & 91).*

One hundred feet long and having a clear span of 60ft., the building was able to contain four tracks, each accommodating one car. Provision was, however, made for a future extension, should this become necessary. One road was provided with a fully lighted inspection pit, 60ft. in length. It was only intended that the building would be used for erecting complete chassis — the various units including bogies, would still be assembled, in the main A.E.C. Works alongside.

Owing to the extremely sharp curve of the then existing spur from the GWR Southall to Brentford branch line, into the Works' grounds, it was necessary to construct a new line with a curve of greater radius. Upon entering the grounds, this immediately divided into five lines; four ran into the erecting shop and the fifth was taken alongside the south wall of the building to act as a siding. Over it, gantries were provided for the handling of chassis frames and heavy components. The junction formation which, with the new spur line, was constructed by the GWR, was believed to be the shortest of its kind ever built by the Company *(Plate 90).*

With all this work being carried out at the A.E.C. factory, the Great Western Railway placed orders for a further ten vehicles after Nos 5, 6 and 7, and these were under the direction of Mr C. F. Cleaver to the requirements and refinements of Mr C. B. Collett, the GWR's Chief Mechanical Engineer.

*The A.E.C. Gazette* of July 1934 gave a good report of the introduction of Nos. 5, 6 and 7, and is reproduced in the quote below.

The heading read:

# G.W.R.'s NINETEEN NEW RAILCAR SERVICES

## Three More A.E.C. "Streamliners" In Operation

### RAILCAR MILEAGE RISES FROM 628 TO 1,193 DAILY

and then continued . . .

When the GWR summer timetable comes into force on the 8th of this month, it will be seen that NINETEEN NEW STREAMLINE RAILCAR SERVICES HAVE BEEN INAUGURATED IN THE WORCESTER AND OXFORD AREAS, and that the GWR RAILCAR MILEAGE HAS INCREASED FROM 628 to 1,193.

These developments are the outcome of the success which has attended the running of the A.E.C. 'streamliners' placed in service by this company in December 1933 and July 1934. Extensions of the first diesel-engined railcar services were foreshadowed by the Chairman of the GWR at its annual meeting last February. Three

*Plates 90 & 91:* These two illustrations show the Railcar Shop and entrance lines in the course of construction.

*A.E.C. Gazette*

additional cars, Nos. 5, 6, and 7, are now ready for work and when running, the GWR will have MORE DIESEL-ENGINED RAILCARS IN OPERATION THAN ANY OTHER BRITISH RAILWAY.

The new cars are basically the same as railcar No. 1 which, with the exception of certain small breaks in service, has run between Southall, Slough, Maidenhead, Reading and Didcot, with trips to Windsor and Henley, for some eighteen months. In its first year, this car covered 60,000 miles and carried over 136,000 people. Propelled by an A.E.C.-Ricardo 130hp oil engine, driving through a fluid flywheel and epicyclic gearbox, railcar No. 1, weighing 21 tons, showed itself in preliminary tests capable of achieving a speed of 61 m.p.h. Although this rate of travel has not been demanded in ordinary running, the numerous station stops on the Thames Valley line has demanded the maintenance of high average speeds.

In the new cars, accommodation is again provided for sixty-nine passengers, but the standard doors have been replaced by those of sliding type to facilitate ingress and egress at busy periods. To give a still better outlook, the windows have been dropped 6in., and this has enabled the depth of the side ventilators to be doubled. Additional ventilation has also been achieved by the fitting of the louvres in the cab roof at each end. As the cars are designed primarily for local services, luggage racks have been dispensed with. The internal decoration, including a walnut finish for the woodwork follows the lines of railcar No. 1, with the exception that brown leather for the seats has now been replaced by the standard GWR moquette covering.

An important function of one of the new railcars will be to provide an earlier morning service from London to Worcester, Malvern, Hereford and the principal stations in that area. This car will connect at Oxford with the 8.40a.m. from Paddington, and reach Worcester at 11.36a.m., Malvern at 11.52a.m. and Hereford at 12.27p.m. A return service from Hereford at 2.05p.m. will connect with the 4.30p.m. from Oxford, reaching Paddington at 5.50p.m.

Another car will be employed to give a new morning business service from Malvern to Birmingham. Leaving Malvern at 8. 54a.m., this car will call at Worcester at 9.10a.m. and then run non-stop to Birmingham at which it is due to arrive at 9.54a.m. The 36¾ miles separating the last two towns will thus be covered in 44 mins., which is equal to a start to stop speed of 50m.p.h.

In the Oxford district, new railcar services will be given between Oxford and Kingham, leaving the former town at 8.15a.m., and the latter at 9.10a.m.; from Oxford to Princes Risborough with departures at 4.50p.m. and 6.37p.m.; and from Oxford to Didcot with a departure at 8p.m.

Apart from the morning business service already mentioned, there will be railcar services from Worcester to Malvern Wells; from Birmingham (10.15a.m.) to Henley-in-Arden (with a return journey from the latter town at 10.45a.m.); from Birmingham (11.40a.m.) to Worcester; from Worcester (2.33p.m.) to Broadway, from Broadway (3.45p.m.) to Stratford-on-Avon, and from Stratford-on-Avon (4.55p.m.) to Oxford. Finally, an evening service will be given from Oxford at 7.42p.m. to Worcester.

Altogether, the new railcars will provide 19 new services *(see*

*Plate 92:* Despite the fact they arrived and departed each day, A.E.C. streamlined railcars still excited the interest of passengers at Birmingham (Snow Hill) Station. Here is one of the buffet-fitted express type railcars awaiting its return trip to Cardiff.
*Railway Gazette*

*Plate 93:* One of the new A.E.C. double-engined 260b.h.p. GWR diesel-mechanical railcars outside the works of the body builder, the Gloucester Railway Carriage & Wagon Co. Ltd., in July 1935.
*Railway Gazette*

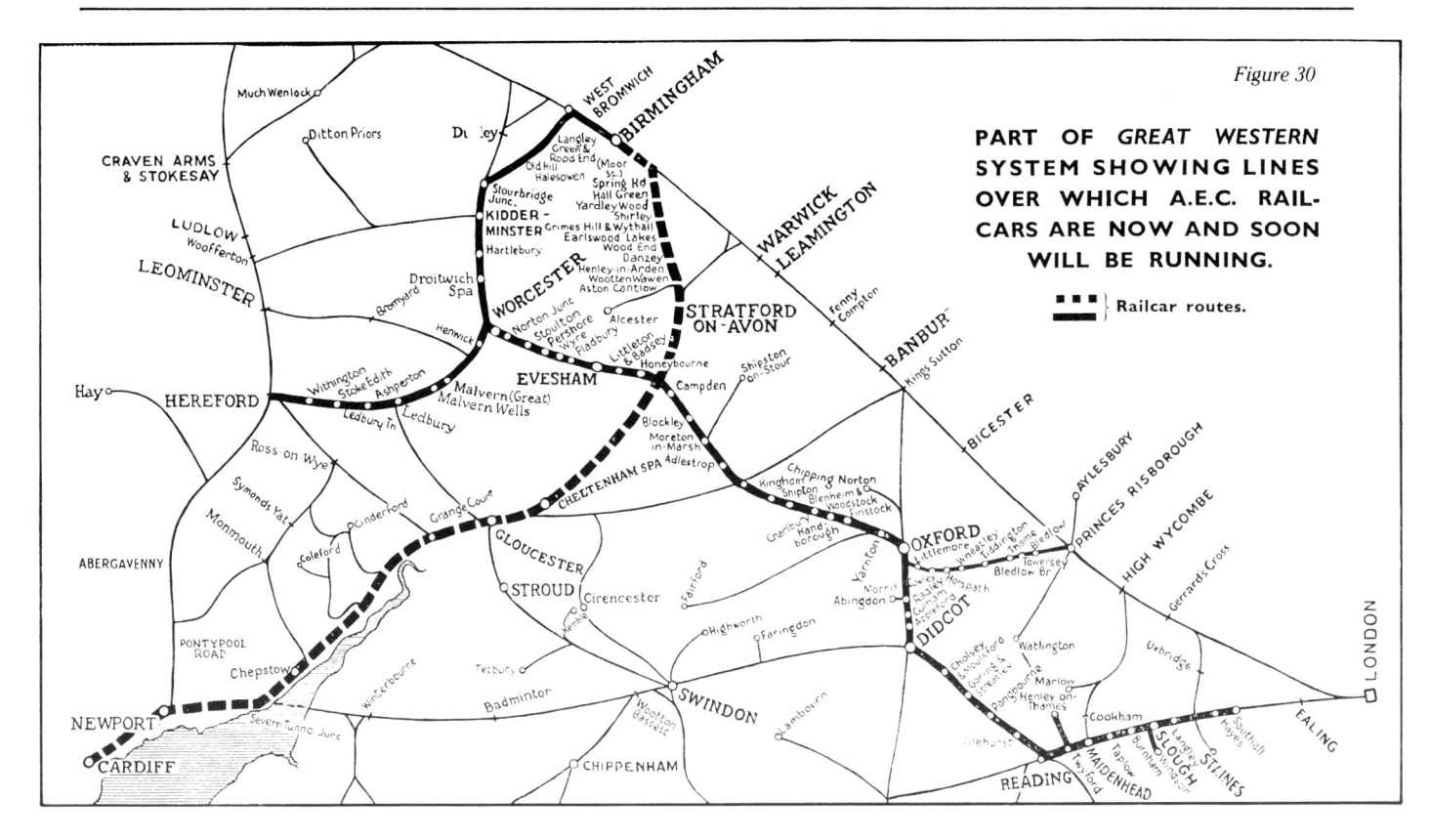

*Figure 30*), and will raise the mileage for this class of vehicle by 89.9 per cent.

No alteration will be made in the running of the A.E.C. twin-engined streamlined vehicles, fitted with buffets, which are maintaining the two daily express services between Birmingham, Gloucester and Cardiff, except that the supplementary charge of 2s. 6d. which has been in force since the service began in July 1934, will be withdrawn.

Also two new railcar services were, last month, inaugurated by the GWR between Birmingham and Stratford-on-Avon. The vehicle used is one of the A.E.C. streamlined, twin-engined, buffet railcars that, since July 1934, have been maintaining the express services between Birmingham, Gloucester and Cardiff. The new trip is being made between two of the long-distance journeys, and the timetable is as follows:
Birmingham (Snow Hill), depart 12.25p.m.; Earlswood Lakes,
12.40p.m.; Henley-in-Arden, 12.49p.m.; Stratford-on-Avon, arrive 1p.m.; Stratford-on-Avon, depart 2.15p.m.; Henley-in-Arden, 2.26p.m.; Hall Green, 2.41p.m.; Birmingham, arrive 2.50p.m.

Contrary to the practice on the long journeys, no supplement is being charged on either of the short runs.

On the first outward trip to Stratford-on-Avon, it was reported in the Press 'that even when the needle of the speedometer mounted almost to the 70m.p.h. mark, the car was so steady that there was hardly any perceptible movement'.

As the extension of the railcar service in the Thames Valley, the Didcot to Oxford service will have now two evening 'streamline' connections at 6.42p.m. and 8p.m.

The remarkable increase in the railcar services affords striking evidence of the value which the GWR places upon this type of unit for the provision of supplementary services over lines where the available traffic would not warrant the running of steam trains.

# Chapter Six: Ten More Ordered

**STILL MORE STREAMLINED RAILCARS**

Although we are still far distant from that Utopia of uniformed prophets in which thousands of railcars will buzz about the country like flies in summer, and the steam engine will be only a museum piece, there is no lack of evidence that British railways in general and the Great Western in particular are devoting considerable thought to the utilisation of this new type of unit for certain forms of traffic. Experimentally, it has already demonstrated its value in the provision of supplementary services over lines where the number of available passengers clearly does not warrant the running of steam-hauled trains; and there seems good ground for the belief that the future will witness a steady increase in the miles run by these lightweight, low-powered, diesel-driven units. The Great Western Railway has shown foresight, enterprise and excellent judgement in its testing of the A.E.C. 'streamliner' on both local and express services. That a certain success has been achieved is shown by the fact that, this month, this same Company is inaugurating no less than 19 new railcar services. And now, as *The A.E.C. Gazette*

*Plate 94:* Railcars Nos. 10, 11 and 12 receive a final clean at the A.E.C. factory before delivery to the Great Western Railway in 1936.
*The BBC Hulton Picture Library*

*Plate 95:* A further look at the 'posed' cleaning of railcars Nos. 10, 11 and 12 at A.E.C., Southall. The bowler-hatted gentleman, one presumes, is the Inspector.
*The BBC Hulton Picture Library*

*Plate 96:* Railcar No. W8 enters Dudley Station on 13th May 1957.
*Michael Hale*

*Plate 97:* Railcar No. 9, photographed on completion in December 1935 at the premises of the Gloucester Railway Carriage & Wagon Company Ltd.
*Gloucester Railway Carriage & Wagon Company Ltd.*

closes for press, comes the announcement that the GWR has ordered a further ten A.E.C. streamlined vehicles for the development of still more services. In effect, this means that at the end of the year, 17 diesel-engined units will be actively working on the Great Western system. When it is remembered that only 17 months have elapsed since the first A.E.C. car — whose potentialities were largely unknown — was put into service, this new order, by far the biggest placed by any British railway for passenger units, provides remarkable testimony as to the essentially sound design of the unit chosen, and its evident worth in specified spheres of railway operation.

The above quote portrays the contemporary enthusiasm for the new diesel railcar, and in order to meet the growing use of these railcars, and with the experience gained from the seven cars in service, a further ten cars were ordered from A.E.C. on 28th January 1935, being built during 1936. The following table summarises the building dates, dates entering service, and the relative cost of each vehicle in this batch of ten.

| Car No. | Built | Into service | Lot No. | Cost | Specification |
|---------|-------|--------------|---------|------|---------------|
| 8 | 1936 | March | 1547 | £5,094 | No buffet, no lavatory |
| 9 | 1936 | February | 1546 | £5,094 | No buffet, no lavatory |
| 10 | 1936 | February | 1547 | £5,164 | No buffet, lavatory |
| 11 | 1936 | February | 1547 | £5,164 | No buffet, lavatory |
| 12 | 1936 | February | 1547 | £5,164 | No buffet, lavatory |
| 13 | 1936 | March | 1546 | £5,093 | No buffet, no lavatory |
| 14 | 1936 | March | 1546 | £5,093 | No buffet, no lavatory |
| 15 | 1936 | April | 1546 | £5,094 | No buffet, no lavatory |
| 16 | 1936 | April | 1546 | £5,094 | No buffet, no lavatory |
| 17 | 1936 | April | 1547 | £4,851 | Parcels Van |

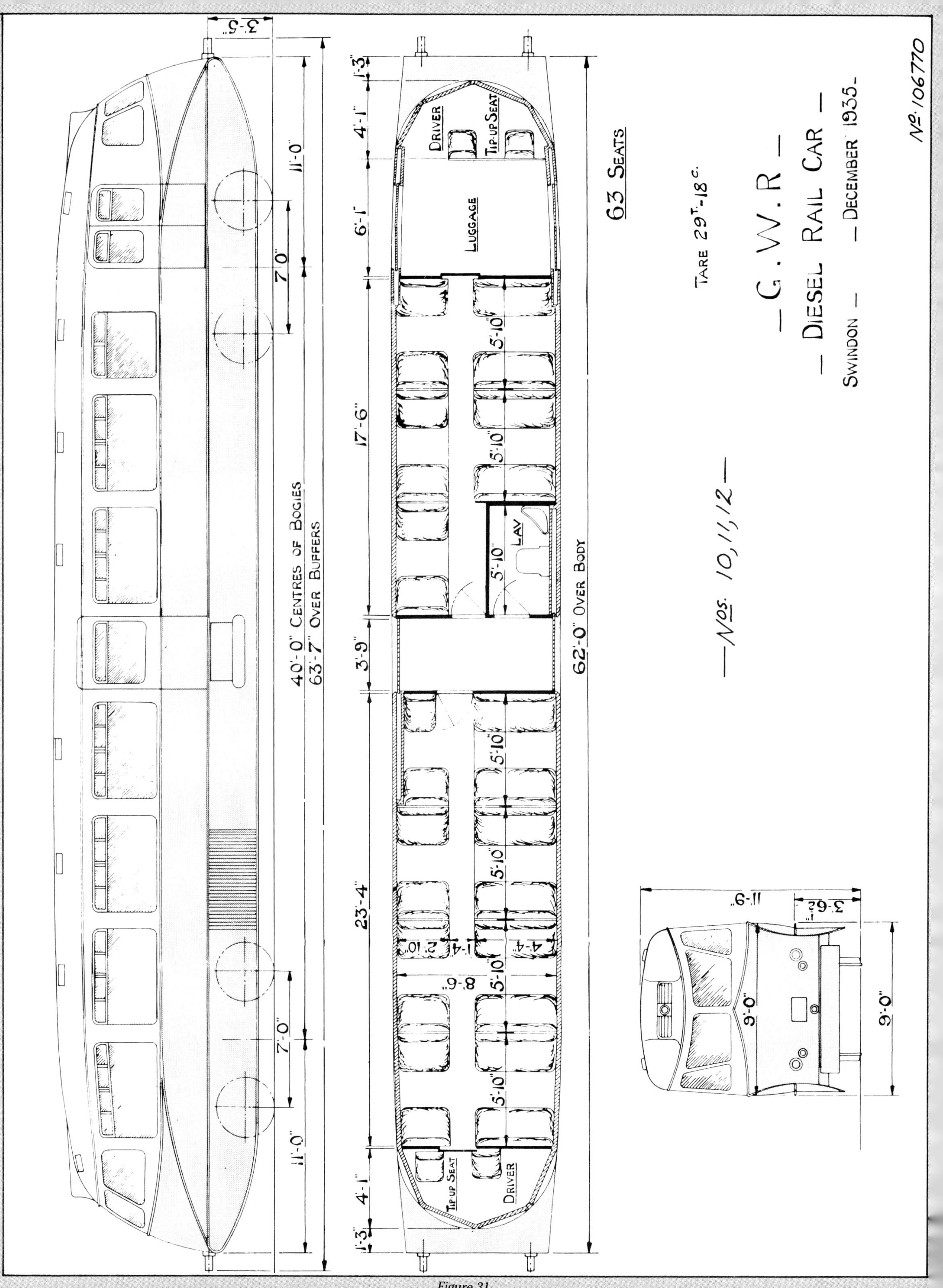

*Figure 31*

## TEN MORE ORDERED

*Plate 98:* Railcar No. W10 on Oxford Shed in the 1950s.

*R. H. G. Simpson*

*Plate 99:* Photographed on 13th January 1936 before delivery to the GWR, railcar No. 11 is seen outside the A.E.C. shops at Southall.

*The BBC Hulton Picture Library*

*Plate 100:* Photographed by the official GWR photographer, railcar No. 12 is seen on the day of delivery to the railway, 11th February 1936.

*British Rail*

*Plate 101:* Many years later, railcar No. W13W stands with paired car No. W17W, both looking in a sorry state of repair.

*R. H. G. Simpson*

*Plate 102:* Picturesque Stourbridge Town Station, on 24th August 1957, with diesel railcar No. W14W waiting to provide the service over the short distance to Stourbridge Junction.

*Michael Hale*

*Plate 103:* The driver of railcar No. W15 has just given up the single line token at Kennington Junction, as it comes off the Oxford-Thame-Princes Risborough branch.

*R. H. G. Simpson*

*Plate 104:* Railcar No. 16, in pristine condition at the A.E.C. factory prior to delivery.

*(A.E.C. Ltd.) Leyland Vehicles Ltd.*

*Plate 105:* Railcars Nos. 16 and 17 (the parcels van) are seen at Southall, prior to delivery to the GWR.

*(A.E.C. Ltd.) Leyland Vehicles Ltd.*

As previously mentioned, these ten cars were designed under the direction of Mr C. B. Collett, the GWR Chief Mechanical Engineer. Two A.E.C. 121b.h.p. engines were used as the propulsion units, and enabled speeds in excess of 75m.p.h. These engines were only slightly modified from the earlier cars, and differed in the design of the sump to increase the oil capacity and oil cooling, as problems had been experienced with engine overheating.

Also, from the experience gained in the running of the first seven cars, the bogies were redesigned with longer side bearing springs, fitted with Spencer-Moulton rubber auxiliaries, and bolster springs and swing links also were considerably improved. The result was that the riding of these later cars was much better than that of the seven earlier ones.

The dimensions of these ten cars are to be seen in the three diagrams in *Figures 29, 31 & 32*. The body designs again were very similar to the earlier cars, but without the buffets, and were contracted to seat 69 passengers. The three cars, Nos. 10, 11, and 12, were fitted with a lavatory compartment *(see Plates 106, 107 & 108)* and No. 17 was fitted out as a 'Special Van' being used purely for the growing suburban parcels traffic, and was an innovation in Great Western and British railways operations *(see Plate 109)*. The final seating arrangements were; Nos. 8 and 9 (70 seats); Nos. 10, 11 and 12 (63 seats); Nos. 13, 14, 15 and 16 (70 seats); No. 17 (no seats, parcel van).

There was no significant difference in the design of the parcel railcar No. 17 *(see Figure 32)*, except that it was designed for the conveyance of parcel traffic on the Great Western, and was put into service 'experimentally' on 4th May 1935. The car was put into service in the London Division, and ran on weekdays between Reading and Oxford, serving also the intermediate stations *(Plates 110 & 111)*.

Included in these duties was an early morning working from Kensington, with Lyons cakes, etc., for Reading and Oxford. It left Olympia (then called Addison Road) at 4.50a.m., arriving at Reading at 5.45a.m., and finally at Oxford at 6.35a.m. The interior as can be seen in *Plate 112*, had stowage racks instead of seating and three glass-panelled sliding doors on each side, one a single middle door, and the two end double doors *(Plate 113)*. Its capacity was 10 tons.

The vehicle, when introduced, did not have the words 'Express Parcels' on the side *(Plate 114)* but only the GWR roundel on the front. The full livery was added by the GWR in April 1935 *(Plate 115)*.

The Great Western also fitted two steps over the buffer bars, as can be seen in *Plates 115 & 116*, as compared with the vehicle outside the Gloucester Carriage Works in *Plate 109*. *Plate 115* also shows the two side valancing covers removed to reveal the easy access to the bogies and drive units.

An amusing 'tale' relates to No. 17 during 1948. It was customary for the 'up' 8.30a.m. Plymouth to Paddington train

*Plate 106:* An interior view of railcar No. 12, taken on 11th February 1936, showing the style of seating and lighting. Note the toilet compartment on the left side.

*British Rail*

*Plate 107:* The vestibule and toilet door of railcar No. 12.
*British Rail*

*Plate 108:* A view looking the other way from that in *Plate 106*, in railcar No. 12. Note the sliding door recess.
*British Rail*

*Plate 109:* An official Gloucester Railway Carriage & Wagon Co. Ltd. photograph, showing railcar No. 17, in March 1936, as completed at Gloucester. The small wording under the number reads 'LOAD NOT TO EXCEED 10 TONS'.
*Gloucester Railway Carriage & Wagon Co. Ltd.*

*Plate 110:* The service it was intended for! Parcels being loaded into railcar No. 17.
*(A.E.C. Ltd.) Leyland Vehicles Ltd.*

*Plate 111:* A further scene at night in Paddington parcel bay. Quite a few staff are on hand to help with the loading.
*(A.E.C. Ltd.) Leyland Vehicles Ltd.*

*Plate 112:* The spacious interior of railcar No. 17, showing the ample floor area available. Note the hinged shelving available.
*British Rail*

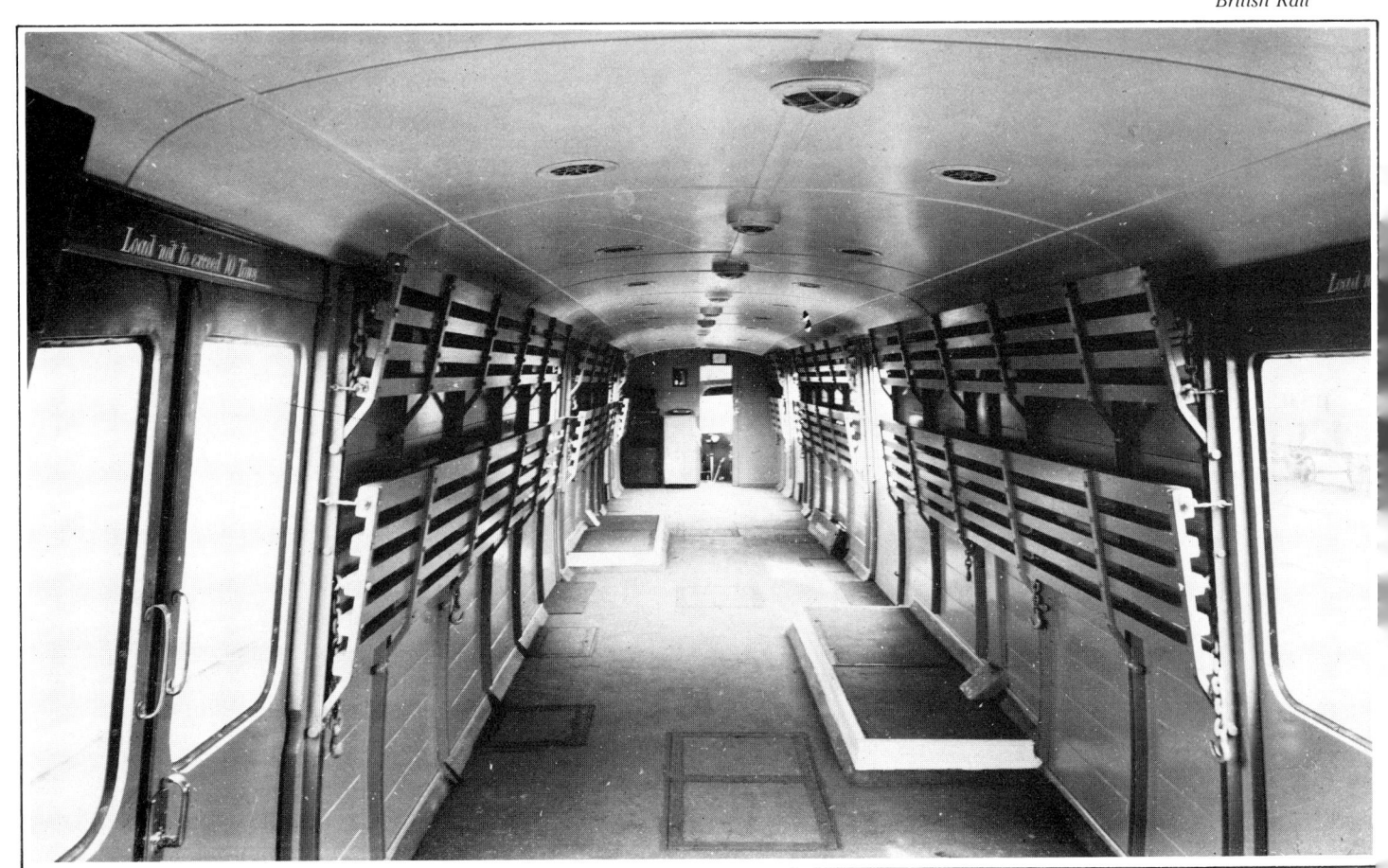

Figure 32

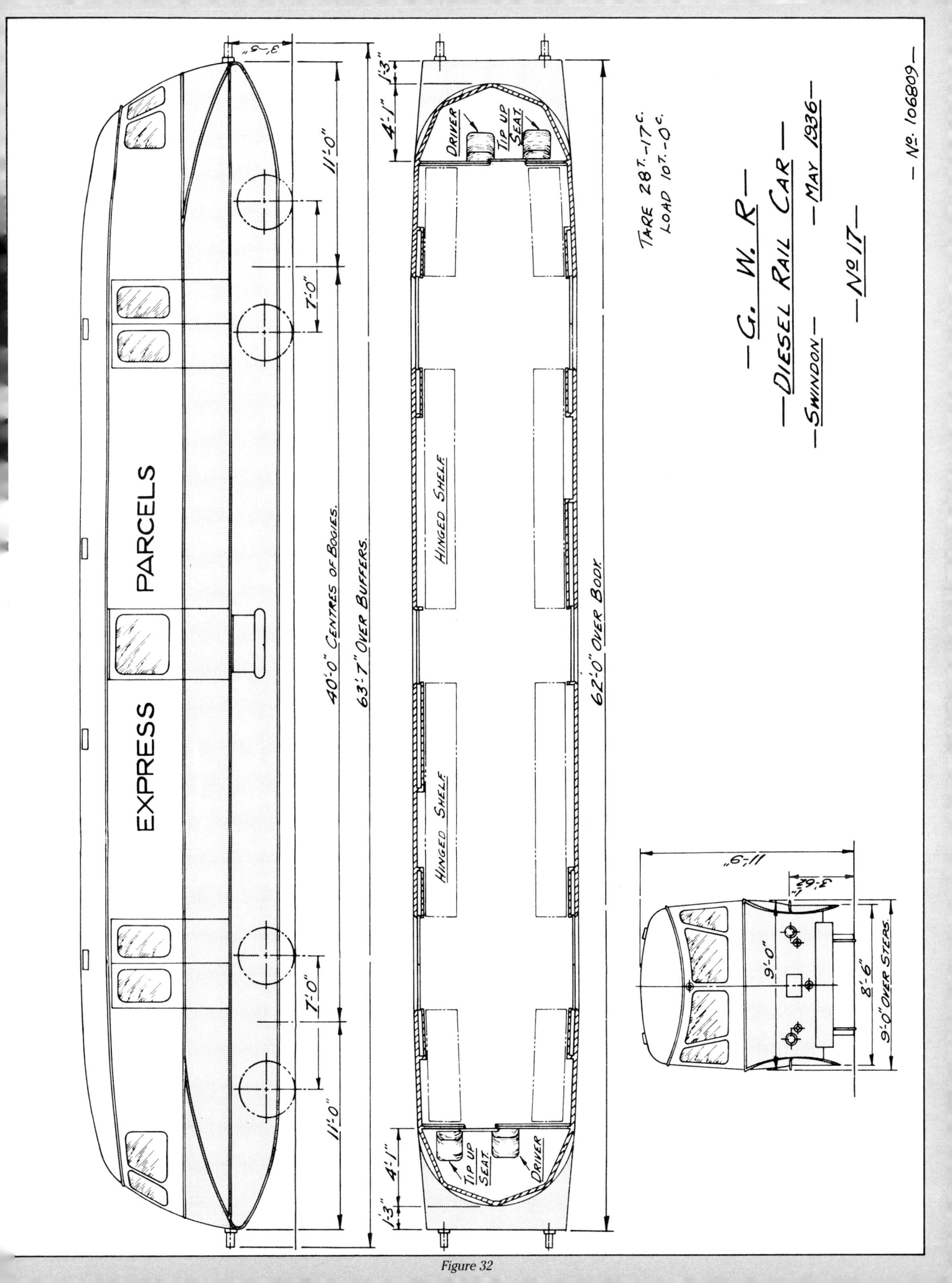

*Plate 113:* Parcels could also be loaded successfully from ground level, as shown in this official A.E.C. publicity photograph.
*(A.E.C. Ltd.) Leyland Vehicles Ltd.*

to 'slip a coach' at Reading, and as this particular day was within the time of the 'locomotive exchanges', in that year, a Southern engine and crew were in charge. Apparently the 'slip' took place at Reading satisfactorily and on arriving at Paddington all the Great Western and Southern enginemen and inspectors (who had been riding in the dynamometer car) were standing talking on the platform, when out of the corner of his eye the Inspector (representing the Southern Railway) saw railcar No. 17 running into Paddington parcels platform. He is reported to have remarked, 'we must have been going some at Reading as our slip coach has just followed us in!'

Various technical details that have emerged from Swindon over the years can now be told, and the first is that cars Nos. 1 to 4 were fitted with 2⅜in. 'Bullseye' head and tail lamps, whereas Nos. 5 to 17 were fitted with 2¹¹/₁₆in. 'Bullseye' lamps. All were electric lamps of 24 volts, 20 watts. Standard tail lamps were also fitted experimentally in car No. 10, to overcome the lamp being dimmed or extinguished by low current from the battery, over periods of slow running. These lamps could also be carried by Nos. 1 to 17 in case of emergency, as a special bracket was fitted by the GWR *(see Plates 116a & 116b)*. The lenses were bought from J. A. Jobling Ltd., Glassworks, Sunderland.

Cars Nos. 1 to 17 were obviously intended for use as single units and had no drawgear, but were fitted with a simple device for the attachment of a towing link to haul the cars dead. Such buffing gear, as was fitted, consisted of two very small spring-loaded plungers, intended only to absorb light impacts and to protect the body ends. Also on these vehicles, internal expanding drum brakes were fitted. On railcars Nos. 1 to 7, these brakes were operated by a vacuum hydraulic system, but the vacuum was 'created' to 'apply' the brakes, whereas on cars Nos. 8 to 17, the vacuum was 'destroyed' to apply the brakes, as is normal practice.

The braking effect produced by these drums was, however, by no means up to normal railway standards and, in particular, retardation fell off rapidly after prolonged braking, due to overheating of the drums. Moreover, two further undesirable results followed from the system of operation adopted. The first affected the operation of track circuits by the cars, which failed to provide satisfactory electrical paths for the current owing to the treads of the wheels not being regularly cleaned, as is the case with the normal rim-type brakes. The other undesirable feature was associated with the ATC apparatus. Owing to the small volume of the vacuum system with both types of gear operating these drum brakes, the quantity of air evacuated through the ATC vacuum valve was sufficient only to produce a note of relatively short duration, indicating a 'caution' signal. Moreover, in the case of cars Nos. 1 to 7 inclusive, the audible signal itself required the provision of a special reed-operated metallic diaphragm horn in place of the normal spinning siren, which meant that ATC cab apparatus for these cars had to be non-standard.

As regards warning devices on the railcars, the first cars were supplied with normal electric klaxon-type horns, one at each end. These were unsatisfactory, due partly to the note produced being liable to confusion with road traffic, and partly to the fact that the sound was insufficiently penetrating. Eventually two-note horns with very strident notes were installed, and provision made for them to be operable whether the car was moving or stationary. These horns were very similar to those used on the former C. F. du Nord in France, and produced almost exactly the same notes. The urgency of this warning device problem was accentuated by the fact that the cars, being lightweight single units with a semi-streamlined profile, gave practically no indication of their approach by way of track noises and/or forward draught, particularly in tunnels. The warning notes produced by the new devices became acceptable to the staff on the track, but were supplemented by special instructions concerning the operation of the cars.

These instructions emphasised that railcars differed from steam locomotives in several respects, and provision was

*Plate 114:* A fine view of railcar No. 17 after completion at the Southall factory of A.E.C.

*(A.E.C. Ltd.) Leyland Vehicles Ltd.*

*Plate 115:* The new livery 'EXPRESS PARCELS' photographed on 23rd August 1939.

*British Rail*

*Plate 116a:* The front end, showing the new bracket for lamps.
*British Rail*

*Plate 116b:* The same view, but with the electric lamp in situ and connected to the socket.
*British Rail*

made, therefore, for the safety of permanent way staff working on the line *(Plate 117)*. The instructions cover reinstatement of the cars after suspension from normal service for a period exceeding seven days and sounding of horns when entering and emerging from tunnels, and also when approaching curves, level crossings, barrow crossings, overbridges and other structures adjacent to the line upon which the car was running.

The 'Look-out' booklet issued to permanent way staff stressed extra vigilance where diesel cars were running. The following is an extract from the booklet:

> Everybody who works on the line or who has to walk on the track must bear in mind that diesel railcars differ from steam locomotives in several important respects:
>
> > Quiet approach at all speeds
> > No smoke or steam
> > Little vibration on the rails
> > Don't trust to hearing — LOOK OUT!
>
> On sighting the car or hearing the horn or whistle, STAND CLEAR IMMEDIATELY.
> Gangers! Remember the necessity for extra vigilance where diesel railcars run, and frequently remind the men in your charge to keep a good LOOK OUT!

Reference was also made in the notices of the special working of these cars for organised parties, society trips, etc.

Permanent way staff were told also (in the interests of their own safety) to acknowledge the warning of the approach of diesel cars as an indication to the driver that his warning had been heard.

As is the case with all non-steam types of railway traction, except for electrification, car heating with these diesel cars had presented a major problem. Various systems had been installed on different batches of cars, *(see Appendix Six)* but complete satisfaction was not claimed for any of them.

Cars Nos. 1 to 16 were all originally fitted with Clayton heaters connected in parallel to the radiator cooling water circuit. Experiments were carried out on car No. 9 to obtain more heat in the driver's compartment by connecting the Clayton heaters in series. This did not prove satisfactory, but it was discovered that prior to the experiments, A.E.C. had removed the thermostats from the cooling water system. Experiments were also carried out on car No. 12, in which the Clayton heaters were removed and copper pipes fitted along each side of the car, and the thermostat replaced in the radiator cooling water system. The results of these experiments showed this arrangement to be the best, and that it could be maintained with the limited amount of heat available from the radiator cooling water, and instructions were issued for all cars of this type to be similarly modified. The A.E.C. Company were requested to restore the thermostats forthwith. The volume of the car to be heated, coupled with the restricted quantity of heat at high temperature in the cooling water, particularly when the engines were running comparatively easily, resulted in very inadequate standards of heating being achieved.

In cars Nos. 1 to 16 and parcel car No. 17, heating in the driver's compartments was supplemented by the installation of Tilley-type paraffin-vapour pressure heaters, which then obviated complaints from the staff concerning inadequate heating of driving cabs. In the guard's compartment of the parcel car, No. 17, Valor paraffin wick stoves were provided.

To summarise the engine, gearbox and transmission systems on the first seventeen railcars, all the cars, except No. 1, had two engines. On cars Nos. 2 to 6 one engine was coupled direct to a reverse box, and thence to the bogie wheels, while the other engine had a change speed gearbox included in the transmission system. The car started on the one engine and, by means of the gearbox, accelerated to about 10m.p.h. at which speed the second engine automatically cut in. All the cars subsequent to No. 6 had two engines, each with its own

## SUMMARY CHART OF FIRST 17 GWR DIESEL RAILCARS

| Car No. | Engine | Gear Boxes | Buffing and Drawgear | Through Driving Gear | Brake Gear | Heating | Accommodation |
|---|---|---|---|---|---|---|---|
| 1 | 1 x 130b.h.p | 1-4 Speed 1-Reverse | | | | | 69 seats Luggage Compt. |
| 2 | | | | | Vacuum Hydraulic (Brake Drums — Internal Expanding Type) | | 44 seats Buffet Compt. Lavatories & Luggage Compt. |
| 3 | | 1-4 Speed | | | | | |
| 4 | | 2-Reverse | | | | | |
| 5 | | | | | | Engine Cooling water with Clayton Dewandre Heat Distributors | 70 seats Luggage Compt. |
| 6 | | | | | | | |
| 7 | | | | Not fitted | | | |
| 8 | 2 x 121b.h.p. | | Emergency Buffing & Drawgear for Towing only | | | | |
| 9 | Total 242b.h.p | | | | | | |
| 10 | | | | | | | 63 seats Luggage Compt. & Lavatory |
| 11 | | 2-4 Speed 2-Reverse | | | Vacuum (Brake Drums — Internal Expanding Type) | | |
| 12 | | | | | | | |
| 13 | | | | | | | |
| 14 | | | | | | | 70 seats Luggage Compt. |
| 15 | | | | | | | |
| 16 | | | | | | | |
| Parcel Car 17 | | | | | | As above but in Driver's Compt. only | Luggage Compt. |

gearbox, and transmission coupled to the wheels of one bogie *(see Figure 33).*

In these first seventeen railcars, reversal was effected by a reverse gearbox in series with the change speed box, the final drive to the bogie wheels from the cardan shaft being by means of worm gearing.

Little change really took place in the engine design over the production of Nos. 1 to 17, except as previously stated, regarding the design of the sump. It is interesting to note that the rating of the engines, prior to World War II, was 130b.h.p., but due to modifications were derated to 121b.h.p. and, also due to wartime difficulties in maintenance, many of the cardan shafts between driving wheels were removed, with the result that the drive was only one axle per bogie.

After the 'honeymoon' period of the diesel railcars, the employees of the Great Western Railway, particularly in Swindon Works, were becoming fairly acclimatised to them after an initial rejection of the 'foreign intruders'. A report in *The Great Western Magazine* is worthy of inclusion to capture the feelings of the men in the Carriage & Wagon Shops of Swindon in the late 1930s.

The diesel railcars receive the same methodical treatment as other vehicles when they come in for their periodical overhaul. The interiors are stripped and reconditioned; the tiny buffets have their equipment thoroughly adjusted by the plumbers; electric lights, patent windows, sliding doors and lavatory fittings, etc., are all attended to by men of various trades.

One of the most surprising things about a diesel car is the way in which the lower part of its outside can be dismantled in a few minutes. This is due to the fact that this lower part is not as solid as it looks. Known as the valance, it consists of detachable panels, locked in position by small hidden catches. With the aid of a special key, a workman can unlock the valance plates and take them down, one after another, all round the vehicle. When these plates are removed, the engines and much of the mechanical gear is revealed, and is

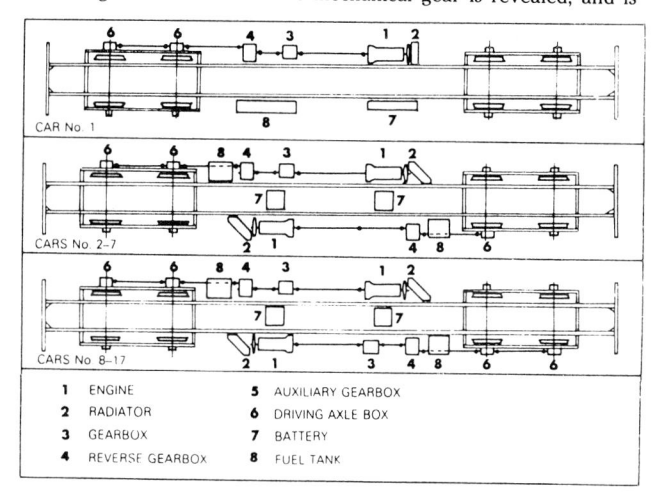

| 1 | ENGINE | 5 | AUXILIARY GEARBOX |
| 2 | RADIATOR | 6 | DRIVING AXLE BOX |
| 3 | GEARBOX | 7 | BATTERY |
| 4 | REVERSE GEARBOX | 8 | FUEL TANK |

*Figure 33:* Schematic comparison of the first 17 railcars.

accessible to the engineers for examination.

A good deal of the machinery is, however, hidden right away under the coach body, and, at first sight, it seems a physical impossibility to reach the undercarriage. Not only is the mechanism closely packed and very unfamiliar to a Great Western man's eye, but the valance reaches down to within a few inches of rail level. A man can get underneath an ordinary coach fairly comfortably, but a cat would not find it easy to pass underneath the side of a diesel car. The only way to get under is via the end. But most of these problems of accessibility are solved by the means of trap doors in the floor of the body. There are anything up to twenty five of these in one vehicle, and each one is situated directly over some vital part of the machinery. Now that these and other conveniences included in the design are being discovered and exploited by the workmen, the 'innards' of a diesel car are losing their former terrors.

Some of the more elaborate appointments which were a feature of the earlier types are gradually being eliminated as the cars come into the shops.

An interesting feature of diesel cars from a locomotive engineer's point of view is the method of carrying the ATC shoe. Owing to exigencies of space, the standard method of securing the shoe to a pair of axleboxes cannot be used. Therefore these cars are provided with a special bearing in the centre of one of the axles. The housing of this bearing is utilised to carry the ATC shoe apparatus, and is prevented from turning about the axle by a torque arm attached to the bogie framework. This torque arm is fitted with 'knuckle' joints designed to accommodate the movement of the bogie framework relatively to the axle.

The 'big noises' of the cars, however, are the horns, and they are real thrillers. If John Peel were still alive he would turn green with envy at the volume of sound which can be produced on these diesel car horns. It is claimed that their notes can be heard over a distance of three miles, and having heard them pierce the quiet air of the paint shop with violent blasts, I can well believe it. The horns provided at each end of the car are operated in pairs, one having a high and the other a low note, and being operated alternatively, by compressed air under the control of the driver, provide an unmistakable warning signal.

A 'stand-by' pair of horns is also fitted at each end, for use when the car is stationary and the main supply of compressed air is not available. These are sounded by small independent compressors, operated electrically, and provide a warning signal similar to that given by the main horns.

Last, but by no means least, in the list of interesting features connected with a diesel car arriving for its overhaul, is the big 'bag' of insects found on the wire mesh of the radiators. These insects are of every conceivable size and species, having come to a violent and sudden end by ignoring the most elementary of railway rules — that of keeping clear of the four foot way.

But there are no flies on a diesel car when it leaves the shops, thoroughly overhauled, clean as a new pin inside, and gleaming with fresh paint and varnish outside.

Recently I watched the departure of one. Two unusual visitors to the paint shop — a driver and a guard — appeared, laden with lamps, flags and tin boxes. These two climbed up into the car, and the big doors of the shop were opened wide.

Suddenly the sound of a self-starter stabbed the silence, followed a second later by the low throbbing rhythm of the diesel engines. Slowly the car began to move forward, proceeding easily through the doorway to the outside world, leaving behind a little knot of work-men of various trades gazing after it, and a painter or two with brushes poised for a moment in order to witness this slight diversion.

The route availability of these early diesel railcars on the GWR lines was governed by the question of clearances, owing to the fact that these vehicles were fitted with valances which came within 10in. of rail level at 8ft. 6in. wide, and also that stepboards were at slightly varying heights from rail level. The chief difficulty experienced in this respect was in the use of crossover roads, particularly between platforms, which had involved the setting back of platform coping and the movement of disc signals to provide sufficient clearance.

As routes were checked, so the railcars could be introduced to more sections, and the routes covered in 1936 are shown in *Figure 34*. The heavy lines on this map showed, in 1936, the portions of the Great Western Railway Company's system over which streamlined railcars were operating. There were sixteen cars on 132 services, covering over 3,000 miles daily. The service from Bristol to Avonmouth operated on Sundays only. The services from Cheltenham and Gloucester to Marlborough, and from Whitland to Tenby, were withdrawn at the end of the summer in 1935.

Four of the sixteen cars were held as spares, a proportion which at first sight may appear high, but which was accounted for by the scattered disposition of services, extending from Tenby in the west to London in the east, and from West Brom-

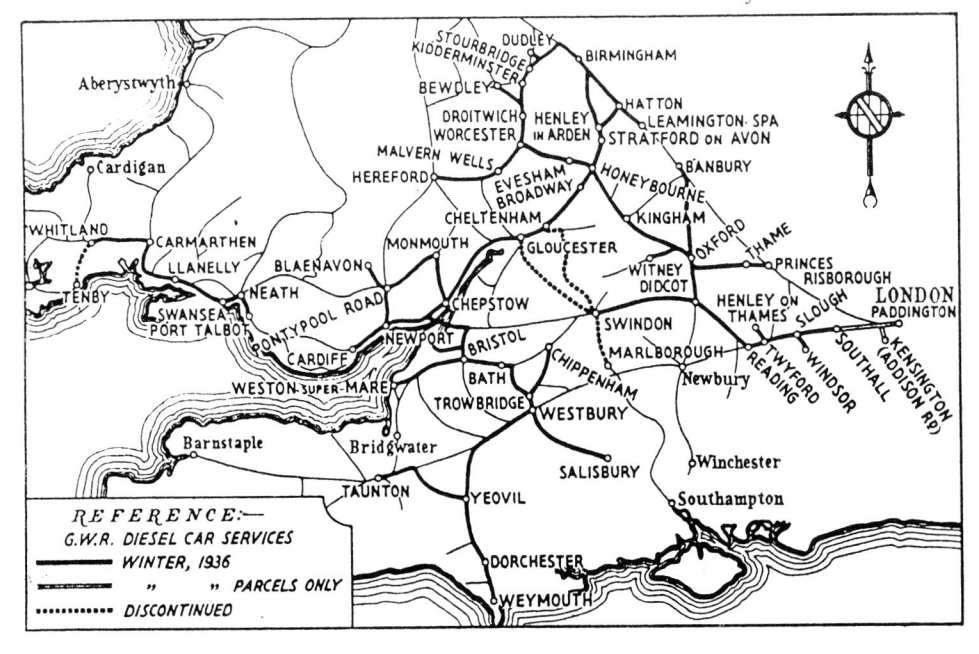

*Figure 34*

*Plate 117:* A publicity photograph taken near Swindon, for use in the *Safety at Work* booklet.

British Rail

wich in the north to Weymouth in the south (as shown in the map).

Nominally, spare cars were held at Birmingham (buffet type), Newport, Bristol and Worcester. As under the regular maintenance scheme, each railcar was withdrawn for examination after 25,000 miles, and as the fleet of cars covered about 20,000 miles a week, it meant that one car was usually out of service for this reason. The average fuel consumption on express services was approximately 8m.p.g., while on stopping services it varied between 6 and 7m.p.g., according to the frequency of stops and the distance between stations.

The busiest railcar centre in 1936 was Oxford (summer timetables). Cars worked from that city in five different directions, namely to Banbury, Hereford, Witney, Princes Risborough and Didcot, and there were 13 railcar departures and 12 arrivals daily, the difference being due to an empty run from Didcot last thing at night. During the 1936 summer timetables, the fleet of cars were running over approximately 767 route miles and serving 217 stations and halts. A table showing an analysis of each car's Monday to Friday working during the summer is reproduced on the right.

It will be seen that the highest mileage run was by the Bristol car, which covered 355½ miles per day; at the bottom of the scale the Swansea car was running only 229 miles. An examination of the figures shows clearly the effect upon average speed of the number of stops made during the day. Thus the Cardiff car, which stopped only 14 times and had an average distance between stops of 20·39 miles, maintained an average start-to-stop speed of 48.1m.p.h. On the other hand, the Pontypool Road and Swansea cars averaged only 29.5m.p.h., the Pontypool car making 135 stops daily with an average

**Summary of Running, G.W.R. Diesel Passenger Railcars**
*Summer Timetables, 1936*

| Car | Miles | Net Time, min. | Start-to-Stop Speed, m.p.h. | No. of Stops | Average Distance Between Stops, miles |
|---|---|---|---|---|---|
| Southall | 238 | 408 | 35.0 | 69 | 3.45 |
| Oxford A | 307½ | 475 | 38.8 | 54 | 5.70 |
| Oxford B | 243¾ | 427½ | 34.2 | 75 | 3.25 |
| Bristol | 355½ | 489½ | 43.5 | 34 | 10.46 |
| Weymouth | 282½ | 378½ | 44.8 | 29 | 9.74 |
| Cheltenham | 272 | 522 | 31.3 | 79 | 3.44 |
| Pontypool | 240½ | 489½ | 29.5 | 135 | 1.78 |
| Worcester No. 1 | 250 | 457 | 32.8 | 102 | 2.45 |
| Worcester No. 2 | 264¾ | 470½ | 33.6 | 101 | 2.61 |
| Birmingham | 305½ | 407½ | 44.9 | 26 | 11.75 |
| Cardiff | 285½ | 356 | 48.1 | 14 | 20.39 |
| Swansea | 229 | 465 | 29.5 | 52 | 4.40 |
| All Cars | 3,273½ | 5,346 | 36.7 | 770 | 4.25 |

distance between stops of only 1.78 miles.

Another schedule of the GWR diesel railcar services included Bristol, Westbury, and Weymouth areas, and was timed at well over 60m.p.h. The 10.10a.m. railcar from Weymouth to Bristol ran from Castle Cary to Westbury, a distance of 19.6 miles (via the Frome cut-off) in 18min., (65.3m.p.h. from start to stop). This was considerably faster than anything else required of this car and, furthermore, included the ascent from Westbury to Brewham Summit, as steep in parts as 1 in 90. Other good

*Plate 118:* A rather perplexed farm horse surveys one of the new Great Western streamlined railcars on 12th February 1936, so unlike the coal-begrimed objects he usually watched.
*The BBC Hulton Picture Library*

timings were those of 16min. from Yeovil to Maiden Newton, a distance of 12.7 miles, which included the steep climb to Evershot for 2¼ miles at 1 in 52. The normal time for steam-hauled trains, start to restart, was 22min. Another smart timing was from Yeovil to Frome (25.9 miles) start to restart, in exactly half an hour.

The longest working day, according to the timetable, was that of the Birmingham car, which was in service for 15hr. 8min., and the shortest time was for the Cardiff car with a 9hr. day, but these figures do not include empty running from shed, etc. The definite relationship between speed and distance station-to-station is shown in *Figure 35*.

In order to prevent delay to passenger trains, an interesting and apparently successful experiment was carried out in the London district. Most services did not convey parcels traffic; this was picked up later by a special parcels railcar, No. 17, as described earlier in the chapter. The mileage of this car was 222 daily, except on Saturdays when it was 150, and on Sundays when it was 132.

Adding the mileage of this car to the table given on *page 101*, and also making allowance for traffic on Saturdays and other special trips, the cars, between them, were running 19,535 miles a week. This was timetable mileage; empty running, shunting and other movements brought the total to over 20,000 miles a week. The mileage being built up by these vehicles was over 1,000,000 a year, which is just about the aggregate mileage that the cars ran in 1936. To this total, the original No. 1 car, working in the Thames Valley, had contributed over 150,000 miles. The average fuel consumption of this car was 8m.p.g.

The figures in *Table II* show that fourteen runs were made daily at a speed of 50m.p.h. or more, the highest booked run being from Castle Cary to Westbury, where the 19¾ miles were booked at 18min., giving a speed of 65.8m.p.h. No. 1 car

TABLE II — RUNS MADE AT OVER 50M.P.H. G.W.R. DIESEL RAILCARS
*SUMMER TIMETABLES, 1936*

| Car | From | To | Time, min. | Distance, miles | Speed m.p.h. |
|---|---|---|---|---|---|
| Weymouth | Castle Cary | Westbury | 18 | 19¾ | 65.8 |
| Worcester No. 2 | Hall Green | Henley-in-Arden | 13 | 12 | 56.5 |
| Birmingham | Newport | Gloucester | 49 | 44½ | 54.5 |
| Birmingham | Birmingham | Cheltenham | 61 | 54 | 53.1 |
| Cardiff | Birmingham | Cheltenham | 61 | 54 | 53.1 |
| Cardiff | Newport | Gloucester | 51 | 44½ | 52.3 |
| Birmingham | Gloucester | Newport | 51 | 44½ | 52.3 |
| Cardiff | Cheltenham | Birmingham | 62 | 54 | 52.2 |
| Bristol | Frome | Yeovil (2 runs) | 30 | 25¾ | 51.5 |
| Birmingham | Cheltenham | Birmingham | 63 | 54 | 51.4 |
| Oxford A | Oxford | Kingham | 25 | 21¼ | 51.0 |
| Weymouth | Castle Cary | Yeovil | 14 | 11¾ | 50.3 |
| Worcester No. 2 | Malvern Link | Worcester | 9 | 7½ | 50.0 |

(with its single engine) did the run from Reading to Appleford daily in 24min., giving a speed of 48.1m.p.h. for the 19¼ miles.

In their spare time, especially at weekends, these cars, as previously mentioned, were often used for football parties, weddings, mystery trips and cheap excursions. On these occasions high speeds were often obtained. For example, on one occasion, the 77¼ miles from Swindon to Paddington was covered in 70 minutes.

Another such private excursion was heralded as probably the first 'Railway Club Special' and was when the Birmingham Model Railway Club chartered a GWR streamlined railcar for a trip to Didcot and Swindon (in 1939) and it was the first time in this country that a club of this kind had engaged a special train.

In America, excursions to railway locomotive works had been tried with considerble success; they were known as 'Fan Trips' and, as the name implied, had as passengers several

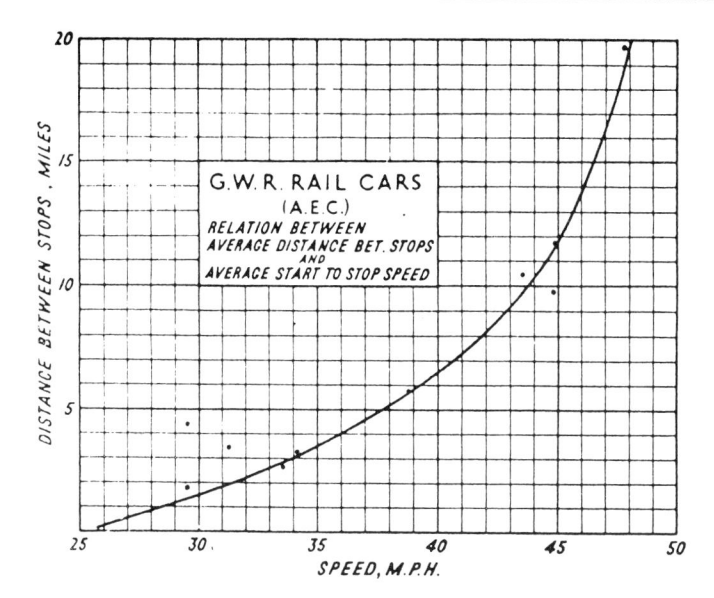

*Figure 35*

*Plate 119:* A photograph taken outside Swindon Works, on the occasion of the Birmingham Junior Chamber of Commerce outing.
*Great Western Railway Magazine*

hundred railway enthusiasts keenly interested in every phase of railway practice.

Over here, the GWR had been pioneers in organising trips of this nature — in their case to the locomotive works at Swindon — and remarkably successful they had been, too *(Plate 119)*.

For an outing such as that arranged by the Birmingham Model Railway Club, the diesel railcar was an ideal mode of travel; it kept members together, it allowed unrivalled views of the railway passed en route to be obtained and, since the railcar itself was easier to work than a lengthy train, it could, in the case of works visits, disregard the orthodox station platform and drop its passengers at the 'front door' of their destination, i.e. Swindon Works.

During the winter services of 1936, alterations were made in the railcar services. The Swansea car service was rearranged and extended to Neath and Port Talbot, and a new one instituted between Bristol, Newport, and Cardiff, via the Severn Tunnel. This was the first railcar to work through that tunnel, and was possibly unique in that a 'daylight' car spent more than 10 per cent of its time in tunnels. Four return runs each way were made, stopping only at Stapleton Road and Newport, except on one trip where a stop was made at Marshfield.

In the afternoon, one trip was continued to Weston-super-Mare and back. The mileage of the Bristol car, which already was the highest, had been increased to 402 miles daily by the addition of a return trip from Trowbridge to Chippenham, and from Bristol to Bath in the evening.

The running time of the 9.10a.m. car from Cardiff to Birmingham was reduced by 5min., bringing the speed from Cheltenham to Birmingham up to 54m.p.h. The 18min. timing from Castle Cary to Westbury was retained. The result of these and other slight changes was that the number of stations served was increased by one, the daily mileage was increased (including the parcels car) by 345 miles to a total of 3,618, the route mileage was decreased by 25 miles to a total of 742, and Newport became the busiest railcar station with fourteen arrivals and fourteen departures daily in 1936.

So with all these diesel railcar services and the new form of 'footplate duty' for the drivers, what was it like 'up front'? To end this chapter and the first phase of the A.E.C./GWR railcars, here is an extract from a series of articles written by a Mr L. M. Crump for *The A.E.C. Gazette* of 1937 and headed:

---

We have the pleasure to announce the receipt of a further *repeat order* from the

**GREAT WESTERN RLY**

**10** for

**AEC SOUTHALL**

★

TWIN OIL ENGINED

**RAILCARS**

The G.W.R. will, from July 8th, operate their fleet of A.E.C. Railcars over 19 important services. The new vehicles will have mounted, 9 passenger bodies and 1 special 'parcels' van body.

This new order will bring the G.W.R. fleet of A.E.C. Railcars up to 17.

Having operated a fleet of A.E.C. Railcars on fast services between important Provincial centres over a long period, the G.W.R. have obtained much knowledge as to their economy and reliability in operation. It, therefore, speaks well for the high performance of A.E.C. Railcars that, after the experience gained, the G.W.R. have favoured A.E.C. with a further repeat order for ten.

**The Associated Equipment Co., Ltd., Southall, Middx.**

## Impressions From The Driver's Cab

### *An Eerie Experience*

#### From Cardiff To Weymouth In Railcar No. 15
#### by
#### L. M. CRUMP

To thousands of passengers comfortably settled in a corridor coach of one of the Great Western Railway's fast South Wales expresses, the Severn Tunnel is no more than a swift transition from light into dark, an awareness that the subdued 'thumpity-thump' of the wheels has changed into a tremendous roar, that reading, or at least concentration upon the text, is no longer effortless and that conversation with fellow travellers is, well, rather difficult. For four minutes or so, an abysmal blackness reigns beyond the windows, and then, suddenly, the train rushes into the daylight and the fields of Monmouth or Gloucestershire again unfold beyond the line.

But what is it like to travel beneath the Severn river, at the very front of the train, on the footplate of the engine, or more pertinently, since the Great Western A.E.C. 'diesels' now traverse the tunnel eight times each day, in the cab of a streamline railcar? How does this four and a half mile tunnel, the longest in Great Britain, appear to the driver as he sweeps through it at nearly a mile a minute — or perhaps at even greater speed?

The writer was privileged to find out for himself when, recently, he travelled from Cardiff to Bristol (and later to Weymouth) occupying a seat beside the driver of railcar No. 15, by kind permission of Mr C. B. Collett, Chief Mechanical Engineer of the GWR. It was a journey of new and vivid impressions, even accompanied by moments of tenseness and, for one so unusually placed, not without thrills.

Yet it might be pointed out that his experience — at least on that part of the trip made in the open — was not entirely unique. A journey in very similar circumstances may frequently be made by railcar passengers who arrive at Cardiff or Bristol stations in good time, and secure a seat immediately behind the glass partition separating the driver's cab from the saloon. For that is one of the intriguing features of railcar travel: in many cases the line ahead — its long levels stretching to the horizon, its sweeping curves, its bridges, cuttings, tunnels — can be seen before they are attained, and thus the journey becomes one of intense interest. In the semi-express railcars, front seat passengers may experience in comfort, and in absolute safety, all the thrills of driving a car at high speed.

'So you're going through the tunnel' (the Severn is always 'The Tunnel' on the Great Western; all others are puny borings compared with this giant beneath the estuary of England's longest river), said Driver Smith, of Bristol, as we took our seat in the cab of railcar No. 15, timed to leave Cardiff on its regular run to Bristol, at 1.15p.m. 'Well you've chosen a poor day for it'.

The weather was not auspicious — at least from the point of view of visibility — grey, menacing clouds hung low in the east; light rain was already falling. While the railcar — its chocolate livery turned a dull green by many trips through the smoke-laden atmosphere of the tunnel — was taking on passengers, we chatted of driving locomotives and railcars. Driver Smith, with over a quarter of a century on the footplate, was still undecided as to which he preferred. There was an ease and comfort in the railcar cab lacking in that of a locomotive; but then when a man has stood up to his job for a good part of a lifetime, sitting down took some getting used to, didn't it? On the other hand, it was cleaner, and one was less exposed to the wind and the weather.

There was the signal from the guard; no whistle blowing or flag waving; a tinkle on the bell; and we began to glide away from the platform. A minute late! Could we pick up those lost sixty seconds in the 11¾ miles run to Newport?

To a man accustomed to driving a car on congested highways, there is something very exhilarating in seeing the starting signal fall, and knowing that for ten, twenty or fifty miles ahead there will be a constant succession of lowered arms or green lights, that there will be no obstruction, no need to slacken speed and, absolute safety all the way. Before such things the spirit soars!

Once clear of the points the gear lever was moved into 'third', into 'top', and we began steadily, but with absolute smoothness, to gain speed. Within a minute from starting, we were travelling at 36m.p.h.; after 5 minutes the speedometer needle recorded 53 m.p.h.; in 6 minutes we were streaming along at more than a mile a minute. This was a straight level 'road'; the sleepers swept beneath the cab window; small bridges and wayside stations rushed at us and were gone in a flash; the lines unrolled like long ribbons of steel from their point on the dark horizon. (Yes! the rain was coming). Marshfield (6½ miles) was no more than a sudden blur of station buildings, for by this time the speedometer needle was flickering between the 63 and 65 marks. So we kept on until the distant derricks and ships' masts foretold the approach to Newport. Speed slackened ... 58m.p.h., 45m.p.h., 36m.p.h., through the dark portal of Hillside Tunnel at 30m.p.h., and then a slow cautious run into Newport Station. The clock showed 1.30p.m. Dead on time! The lost minute had been recovered as Driver Smith remarked, 'with the greatest of ease'.

Two minutes to entrain passengers and we were away on the 26¼ mile non-stop run to Bristol. Once again the needle crept up ... 45m.p.h., 55m.p.h., and after we had been going 7 minutes, 60m.p.h. ... then, as we swept through Llanwern, 63m.p.h. Then came the rain, a torrent that in a second obliterated the line ahead and the fields on either side. Driving a car would be well-nigh impossible in this! Visibility did not exist. Yet there was little slackening of speed; we went through Magor at 60m.p.h., driving into the rain. Here was where that remarkable ATC (Automatic Train Control) showed its worth. Instantly, as we passed over the ramps laid between the rails the bell rang telling Driver Smith (who knows every foot of the line by sound alone) that the signal ahead was 'off'. Fascinated, we gazed at the cab windows where (such is the streamline design of the railcar) the myriad raindrops were streaming up the glass towards the roof. The hiss of the rain rose almost to a scream, making speech impossible. Yet despite these conditions we kept on, and at Severn Tunnel Junction we were before time!

Paramount in rail practice is safety; safety for passengers, safety for men working on the line, and because No. 15 was before time we could not enter the Severn portal. All day in the black bowel of the tunnel men are on duty, maintaining the line, keeping the walls in repair, watching incessantly for any flaw that might spell disaster. Rightfully, they must be protected in conditions where to be taken unawares might easily mean instant death. The quiet running of the railcar is their very danger! And so these men are informed when each 'streamliner' is scheduled to enter the tunnel. None may plunge into that 4½ miles of intense darkness before its allotted time.

Thus we ambled through Severn Tunnel Junction, every 'distant' signal against us, until at last a far-away arm dropped in the cutting, and the 'up' line was ours!

We had hoped to see the tunnel mouth first as a black speck on the horizon, gradually growing larger as we travelled towards it down that 1 in 90 western gradient. But the rain was still falling, the cutting was full of gloom, and from the mouth itself poured great billows of grey smoke. Gathering speed, No. 15 drew nearer . . . the first wraiths swept past the windows . . . now a thick fog suddenly encompassed us . . . the daylight went, a roar smote our ears . . . and we were in . . . plunging down towards the tunnel centre — blindly with ever increasing speed!

A strange eerie — yes, let it be admitted — an alarming sensation! Something like going under an anaesthetic when the world turns dark, a great rushing sound fills the ears and the senses begin to numb. But here we were very wide awake; and although with the reassuring memory of that signal giving us a clear road, not a little fearful of our swift passage through this Cimmerian darkness. And yet all sensation of speed had vanished; only the rising crescendo of the roar of the wheels and the tell-tale needle of the speedometer thrust into our consciousness the fact that we were travelling at 50m.p.h. Blind flying, we thought, must be something like this! We could only sense the close proximity of the driver, the only thing discernible was the faint luminous face of the speedometer . . . and intense blackness engulfed us.

So we speed on, travelling ever deeper into the earth, by now well below the shores of the estuary. And then slowly we realised that the first pall of tunnel smoke had thinned and that the light from the small forward lamps was catching the lines ahead. But the rays were feeble; the lines were revealed for only a few feet beyond the cab window, and since the sleepers were still invisible, there was still no sense of movement.

Suddenly far ahead — though how far, it was impossible to judge — a cluster of lights, like small red stars, pierced the darkness. 'The tunnel gang', shouted Driver Smith. Nearer and nearer they came, growing larger each second — great heavens, some of them were in the middle of the track — coming together, quickly parting, and then assuming two orderly lines, like the street lamps of a town seen from an adjacent hill, until the railcar was upon them. Naked flares they were, and as we flashed past — our speed for a brief second apparent — they revealed the smoke-stained faces of these troglodytic platelayers, huddled in the tunnel refuges. In an instant they were gone, and once more there was only impenetrable blackness.

And then, in the distance, there was discernible a small pinpoint of light — the middle of the tunnel and the mark that indicates the bottom of the western gradient. For a moment the light remained fixed, and then quickly it swelled in size as we drew nearer to that short stretch of level line some 200 feet below the surface of the Severn.

But it should not be thought that even 2¼ miles from each entrance our progress was in the hands of the driver alone. No. 15 was still controlled by the signals! The lights revealed for a second the familiar ramp between the rails and, at that instant, a bell rang in the cabin to tell us that the road was still clear ahead. A friendly sound, that bell! A welcome reminder that so far from daylight, so deep below the waters of that great river, the few of us, isolated in that roaring subterranean darkness, were still in contact with the familiar world of men above and ahead.

For a few hundred feet, the speedometer needle quivered on the 55 mark and then it sank back to 50 — a sign that we had begun the 1 in 100 ascent towards the eastern entrance. But for that tiny indication there was nothing to tell us how fast we were travelling, no reflected light from the tunnel walls, no regular beat of the wheels upon the rail joints (the noise of our passage drowned that), no visibility ahead. Or not for a moment or two after passing the tunnel centre . . . and then a far-off, small, quivering light. Two lights. Three. A blaze of them dancing and pirouetting in the darkness. Gradually drawing nearer, larger, more luminous. No longer lights, but the undulating gleams of fire. Rushing towards us, seemingly in our very path! Now reflecting the tunnel roof. Resolving themselves into what seemed to be streaming flame. And then, great billows of red steam. Here was an express on the 'down' line! With blazing savagery it hurled itself at us. We rocked at the impact. For a moment seemed to be, ourselves, in a core of fire. The screen and roar of its passing smote the cab, enveloped us in a tornado of deafening sound, annihilated every sense. The carriages like the luminous tail of some Stygian dragon, streaked past and were gone. In their wake was a pall of black smoke that rolled up and past the cab windows. Everything in front was obliterated. The windows themselves might well have been wrought of some opaque substance. Our blind progress continued. The speedometer needle showed a steady 50m.p.h.

Another 30 seconds, perhaps, (for the sense of time fades, too, in the tunnel) and we were through the smoke pall . . . again the lines were caught faintly in the rays of the car lamps . . . and then far ahead we discerned a pin point of light. Daylight! The eastern

*Plate 120:* A view on the Bristol-Bath line. An early generation of railway engineers believed that tunnel entrances should look like mediaeval castles. A railcar rushes into Twerton Tunnel at 60m.p.h.

*A.E.C. Gazette*

entrance to the tunnel. For some moments the light quivered. Then it remained steady, unaltered in size or intensity. But as we drew nearer it began, not gradually but suddenly, to grow brighter. The outline of the tunnel mouth could now be discerned. This began to open like the iris of a camera. Faint streaks of light ran down the burnished tops of the rails. There was a hint of green beyond the entrance. A suggestion of blue sky. And then, before we had time to savour our approach to daylight, we were out! The speedometer needle showed 53m.p.h. as we passed the entrance, still climbing that long gradient of 1 to 100. The darkness of the Severn Tunnel was behind us, grass embankments sloped down on either hand, there was a clear sky above and (incredibly strange) we could see the road ahead. It had taken us 5¾ minutes to accomplish the run from the Welsh to the English side.

Onward through Pilning at 1.53½p.m., and then up the 1 in 100 gradient, with the 'down' line below us (the two sets of metals divide and run at different levels at this point) and into Cattybrook Tunnel (very small beer after the mighty Severn!) at 40m.p.h. Driver Smith was taking things easily; we were again getting ahead of time. At 2.01p.m. we had reached Patchway and taken the spur line to Filton Junction. At Horfield the signal was against us; from there we ran easily down the curving 1 in 75 bank to Stapleton Road. Another signal check; but this did not prevent us gliding easily into Temple Meads Station, Bristol, at 2.13p.m. — dead on time.

Those passengers who alighted at Bath, Westbury, Frome, Yeovil and other places were immediately replaced by others; and at the end of the journey it was estimated that for over two hours the car had never, at any point, held less than 70 people. At Yeovil, some six intending passengers were left behind; every seat was filled.

Although on the reverse run, one of the A.E.C. 'streamliners' had the task of covering the 19¾ miles between Castle Cary and Westbury in 18 minutes (which remains still the fastest booked railcar timing in this country), the journey south was not productive of exceptional speeds. It provided, more than anything, an example of the average daily working of a 'streamliner' on a cross-country journey, where the convenience of getting from point to point is of more importance than the speed at which the run is accomplished.

On the gently rising gradients from Bristol to Bath, No. 15 easily maintained 60m.p.h. From Bathampton to Trowbridge — a run abounding in lovely scenery and viewed to the best advantage through the deep, wide windows of the railcar — there are continual curves restricting speed to 40m.p.h. In this instance, the journey from Westbury to Castle Cary, on the main line, including a minute stop at Frome, was accomplished in 24 minutes, and included speeds of 67 to 69m.p.h. down Bruton Bank. Yet the 12¾ miles from Yeovil to Maiden Newton, including a long pull ranging from 1 in 73 to 1 in 51, and traversed against heavy rain and headwinds, were accomplished without difficulty in 17 minutes — an average speed of 45m.p.h. If No. 15 was several minutes late into Weymouth, it was due to extraneous circumstances (including signal checks and the number of passengers at each stopping point) and not to any inherent inability to maintain an easy timing.

# More A.E.C. Railcars for G.W.R.

The G.W.R. recently ordered another 10 A.E.C. Railcars to add to their existing fleet, at present operating on 19 services between important provincial centres.

*We invite your enquiries.*

THE ASSOCIATED EQUIPMENT CO., LTD., SOUTHALL, MIDDX.

*Do not forget to mention the "A.E.C Gazette."*

# Chapter Seven:

# No. 18 — A Radical Departure from the Original Design

At the Commercial Motor Show at Olympia, in late 1935, a new twin oil-engined railcar chassis was exhibited by the Hardy Motor Company Ltd. of Southall. This design again had been influenced by C. B. Collett of the Great Western Railway, and was based on the experience gained in ¼ million miles of service seen by the previous streamlined cars running on the Great Western Railway. Also handed out at this exhibition was a brochure *(Figure 36)* which is included to show how Hardy Motors had incorporated the 'old' streamlined shape of body on to the new No. 18 chassis, whereas, when the GWR eventually purchased this vehicle with a contract on 11th October 1935, a new style body had been designed. This design came from the Swindon drawing office and was supplied to the Gloucester Railway Carriage & Wagon Co. Ltd. for No. 18's body to be built on the A.E.C. chassis. From *Figure 37*, it was clear that Swindon intended to build a trailer coach (rather than use a normal coach) for the 'Lambourn Railcar' (as it was to be known) as the design and layout was extremely similar to that of No. 18. The guard and luggage were to be put in the opposite end to that of the driver (a small compartment indeed), and the vehicle was relatively short compared with the railcar.

The total cost of No. 18 was £5,821, of which the GWR contributed £244, and A.E.C. £5,577. It entered Great Western Railway service in April 1937 under Lot 1564. It is true to say that the Hardy Motor Co. Ltd. had not rested on its laurels, and had made a positive effort to improve these diesel railcars, as can be seen from the chassis drawing in *Figure 36*.

The improved technical specification of this vehicle is somewhat different to the first seventeen, and so the full details are included as a comparison to the earlier vehicles.

It would have been too much to expect that every detail of the first railcars produced by Hardy Motors would have been entirely successful. In fact, it was common knowledge that certain small 'teething' troubles had developed in these cars, and that when they had been rectified, the experience gained was incorporated in the design of the railcars with two 130hp engines.

Further experience had now led the firm to believe that certain refinements in the design of the first railcars were unnecessary in railway operation, while others, absent in the first cars, although not essential, were desirable. Moreover, the first railcar was designed for one engine, and the incorporation of two engines and the resulting duplication of certain controls and mechanisms caused a complication to the connections from the control panel to the units. By redesigning, a reportedly 'better' vehicle was manufactured *(see Plate 121)*.

The most obvious change *(see Figure 36)* was that the main frame had now been designed to accommodate standard buffers and drawgear. In addition, the engines had been re-

*Plate 121:* Railcar No. 18, photographed on 10th December 1936, showing the new shape of the vehicle and its livery. Note the exposed bogies and valancing covering only the engines.

*British Rail*

# FOREWORD

In order to meet the growing demand for Rail Cars, with one built from standard Commercial Motor units, which have been well tried out in arduous service and are produced in large quantities, the first chassis of this type was designed and built in 1933. To a very large degree, with few modifications, such units were incorporated and, where this could not be done, modern commercial motor practice was followed, and advantage taken of up-to-date methods and our many years of experience. In this way reliability was ensured and experimental features reduced to a minimum, while the large production of units resulted in reduced first cost.

The first chassis built was, after exhaustive trials, placed in service by the Great Western Railway, in the Slough-Reading area early in 1934, and so successful was its operating that a further three started work in July of the same year. Three more were placed in service in July, 1935, and now an additional ten are under construction and will be in use before 1936.

Although the first Rail Car was fitted with only one 6-Cylinder Oil Engine, all subsequent vehicles are fitted with two, and while No. 1 Car was used on stopping services, later cars are used on both express and stopping routes with equally satisfactory results.

To meet special demands, these cars are sometimes used for purposes requiring very high speeds and long periods of non-stop operation. To cite only one instance, the $77\frac{1}{4}$ miles run from Swindon to Paddington was covered recently in 70 minutes, giving a start to stop speed of 66 m.p.h., and it is significant to note that the Rail Cars referred to have run to date well over a quarter of a million miles. The experience gained by this extensive service and the many improvements resulting therefrom, have been incorporated in the new design here described.

The many and distinct advantages of this type of vehicle for augmenting existing rail systems is focussing the attention of the leading British and Overseas Railway Companies, and increasing use of this economical and convenient form of rolling stock will undoubtedly be extensively developed in the near future.

Telephone:
SOUTHALL 2424
(17 lines)

**HARDY MOTORS LIMITED**
SOUTHALL, MIDDLESEX, ENGLAND
ALLIED TO THE ASSOCIATED EQUIPMENT CO., LIMITED

Telegrams and Cables
"VANGASTOW"
SOUTHALL

Figure 36a

# SPECIFICATION

**GENERAL CONSTRUCTION** The car is carried on two 4-wheeled bogies, both axles of each being driven. Two independent driving systems are provided, one being connected to each bogie. All driving units are carried on the side of the frame in an accessible position, and all are below floor level. The two engines are mounted at the centre of the chassis, one on each side of the frame, each driving through a 5-speed pre-selective gearbox to the inner axle of the bogie, whence the drive is taken to the outer axle. The reversing gear is incorporated into the inner axle box. The driving systems are so arranged that the left-hand engine drives the rear bogie while the right-hand one drives the front bogie.

**ENGINES** 6-Cylinder A.E.C. Ricardo compression ignition type. Bore 115 m/m. Stroke 142 m/m. Maximum B.H.P. 130. Normal Engine Speed 1,850 R.P.M. Dry Sump Lubrication embodying gilled tube type of oil cooler.

**RADIATOR** Still tube type, with cast-iron tanks and side brackets, and having cooling grid, for oil-cooling water, mounted on front face. Air circulation by 32 in. diameter fan.

**GEARBOX** Wilson pre-selective epicyclic type in conjunction with fluid flywheel.
Gear ratios: 1 : 1, 1·64 : 1, 2·53 : 1, 4·5 : 1, 6·38 : 1.
Reduction gear casing fitted at back of main gearbox, giving easily variable overall ratios.
Alternative reduction gear ratios: 1·03 : 1, 1·15 : 1, 1·37 : 1, 1·73 : 1, 1·96 : 1.

**AXLE DRIVE**—Of spiral bevel type, incorporating reverse gear and mounted in axle-box on outside of wheel. Gear ratio : 2·58 : 1.

**WHEELS**—Cast steel centres with rolled steel tyres, 3 ft. 1 in. dia. on tread.

**CONTROLS**—Pneumatically operated with connection for driving from trailer, if required.

**BOGIES**—Swing link bolster type, built up of solid pressings ½ in. thick. Side bearing springs 4 ft 8 in. long, 3½ in. wide.

**BRAKES**—Internal expanding type, 20 in. dia., 6 in. wide, mounted on axles and automatically vacuum operated.

**FUEL TANK**—Two separate tanks, each of 45 gallons capacity.

**LEADING DIMENSIONS**—
Bogie wheelbase 8 ft. 6 in.
Bogie centres 43 ft. 6 in.
Turning radius 3½ chains.
Length over headstocks 62 ft. 0 in.
Length over buffers (British pattern) 65 ft. 8 in.
Frame width 3 ft. 2 in.
Frame height above rail 3 ft. 11 in.
Overall width (4 ft. 8½ in. gauge) 8 ft. 0 in.

### Alternative Gear Ratios with Corresponding Speeds and Tractive Efforts

| Reduction Gear. | Gear Box Speed. | Top. | 4th. | 3rd. | 2nd. | 1st. |
|---|---|---|---|---|---|---|
|  | Overall Ratio... | 2·66 | 4·41 | 6·74 | 11·98 | 16·97 |
|  | Speed M.P.H. | 75·0 | 45·3 | 29·7 | 16·7 | 11·8 |
|  | Tractive Effort lbs. | 1,000 | 1,600 | 2,450 | 4,360 | 6,180 |
|  | Overall Ratio... | 2·98 | 4·89 | 7·55 | 13·41 | 19·03 |
|  | Speed M.P.H. | 67·1 | 41·0 | 26·5 | 14·9 | 10·5 |
|  | Tractive Effort lbs. | 1,120 | 1,780 | 2,750 | 4,890 | 6,940 |
|  | Overall Ratio... | 3·54 | 5·80 | 8·95 | 15·93 | 22·58 |
|  | Speed M.P.H. | 56·5 | 34·4 | 22·15 | 12·53 | 8·87 |
|  | Tractive Effort lbs. | 1,330 | 2,110 | 3,260 | 5,810 | 8,220 |
|  | Overall Ratio... | 4·48 | 7·35 | 11·35 | 20·2 | 28·6 |
|  | Speed M.P.H. | 44·6 | 27·2 | 17·6 | 9·9 | 7·0 |
|  | Tractive Effort lbs. | 1,690 | 2,670 | 4,140 | 7,370 | 10,400 |
|  | Overall Ratio... | 5·07 | 8·32 | 12·84 | 22·82 | 32·4 |
|  | Speed M.P.H. | 39·5 | 24·0 | 15·6 | 8·75 | 6·18 |
|  | Tractive Effort lbs. | 1,910 | 3,020 | 4,680 | 8,340 | 11,790 |

NOTE:—M.P.H. are given at an engine speed of 1850 R.P.M. and liberal allowance has been made for frictional losses, &c.

*Figure 36b*

69 PASSENGERS & LUGGAGE.
75-80 MILES PER HOUR.

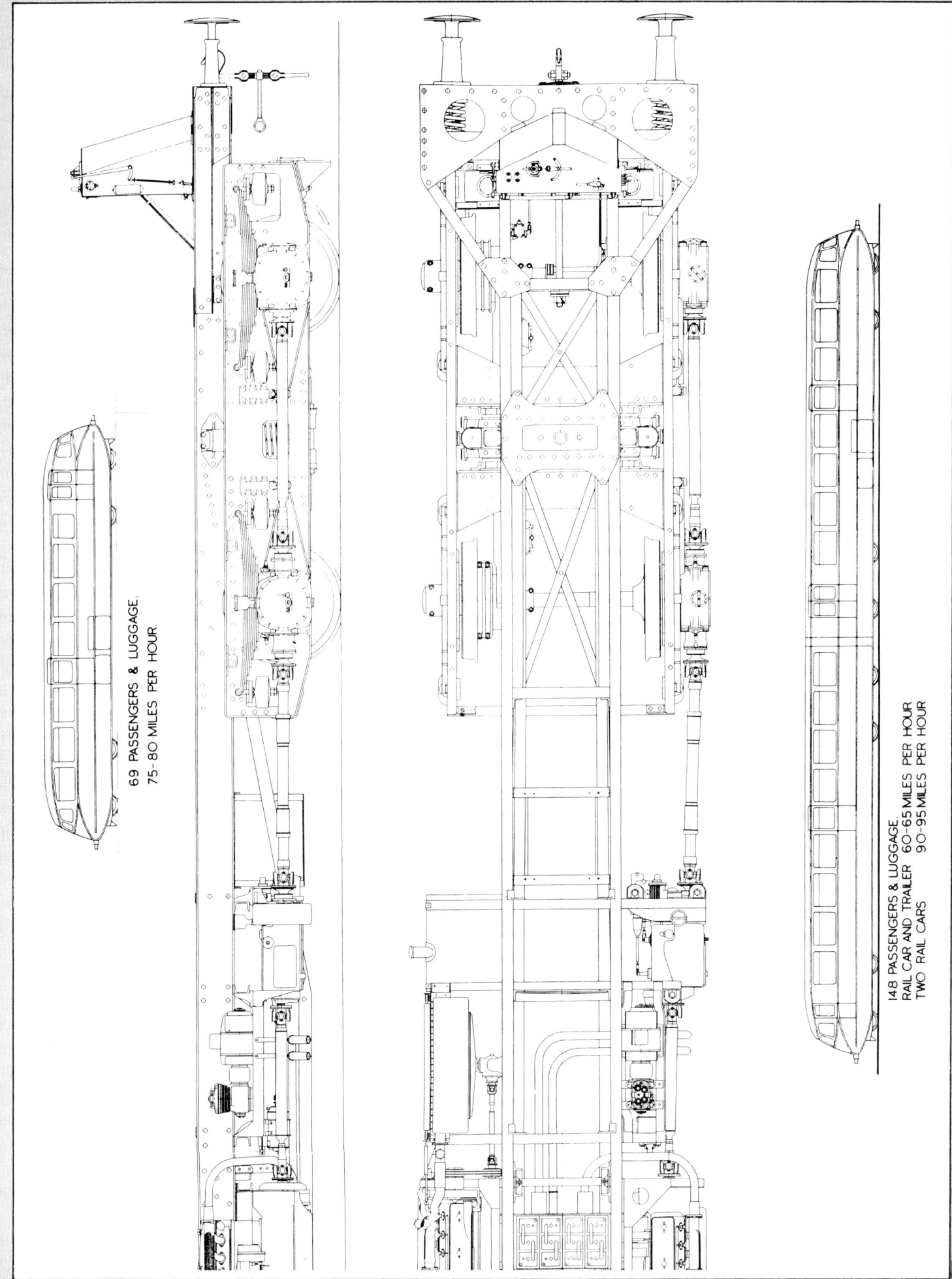

148 PASSENGERS & LUGGAGE.
RAIL CAR AND TRAILER 60-65 MILES PER HOUR.
TWO RAIL CARS 90-95 MILES PER HOUR.

*Figure 36c*

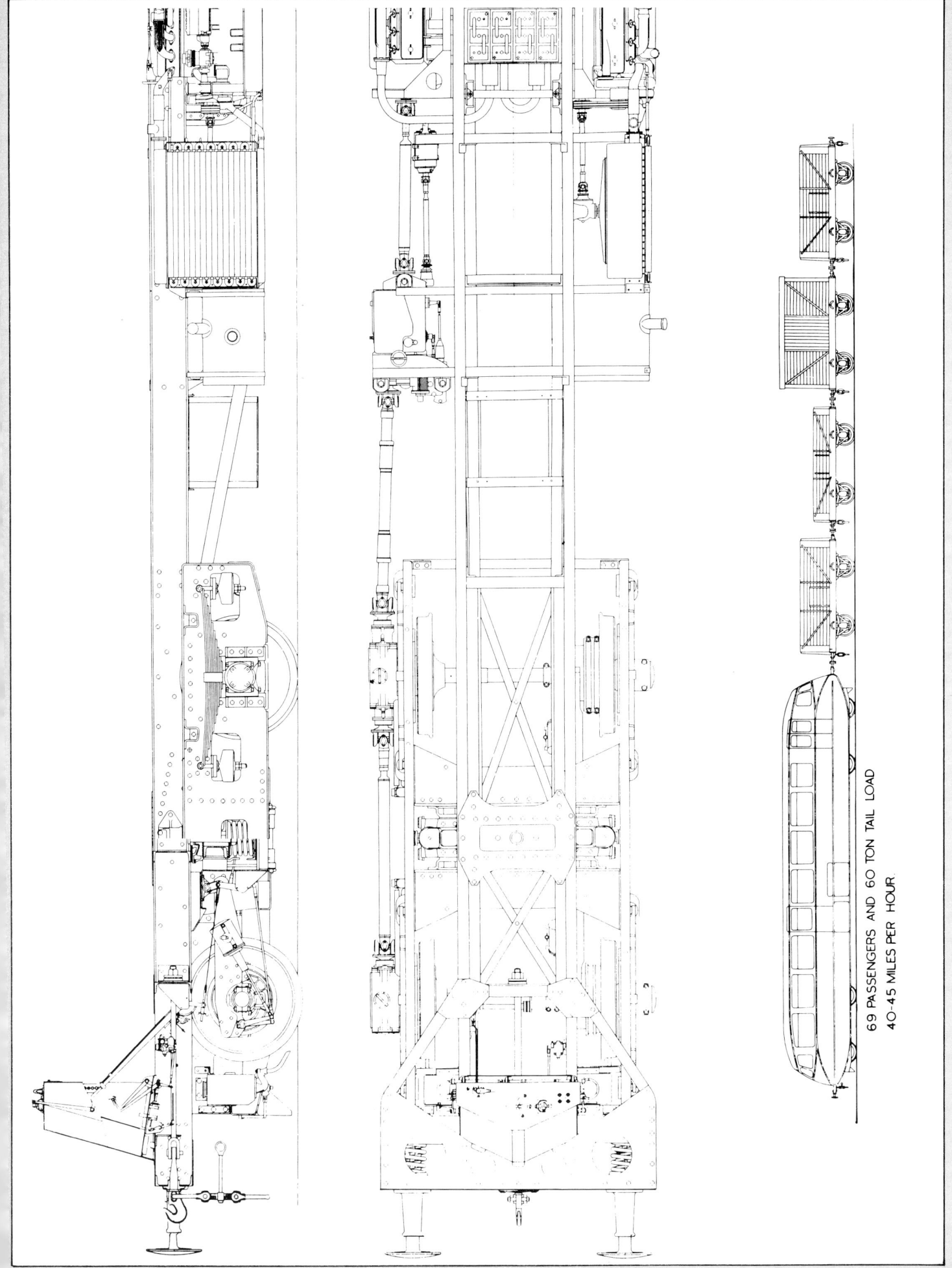

69 PASSENGERS AND 60 TON TAIL LOAD
40-45 MILES PER HOUR.

*Figure 36d*

Above are illustrated Southall built Rail Cars operating at various points on the G.W.R. system. These vehicles are used both on stopping and express services.

Southall built Rail Cars, now an established feature of the G.W.R. system, have successfully operated well over a quarter of a million miles.

**HARDY**
SOUTHALL

Literature No. 189  11/1935

Printed in England by Henry Good & Son, Ltd., London, E.C.2

*Figure 36e*

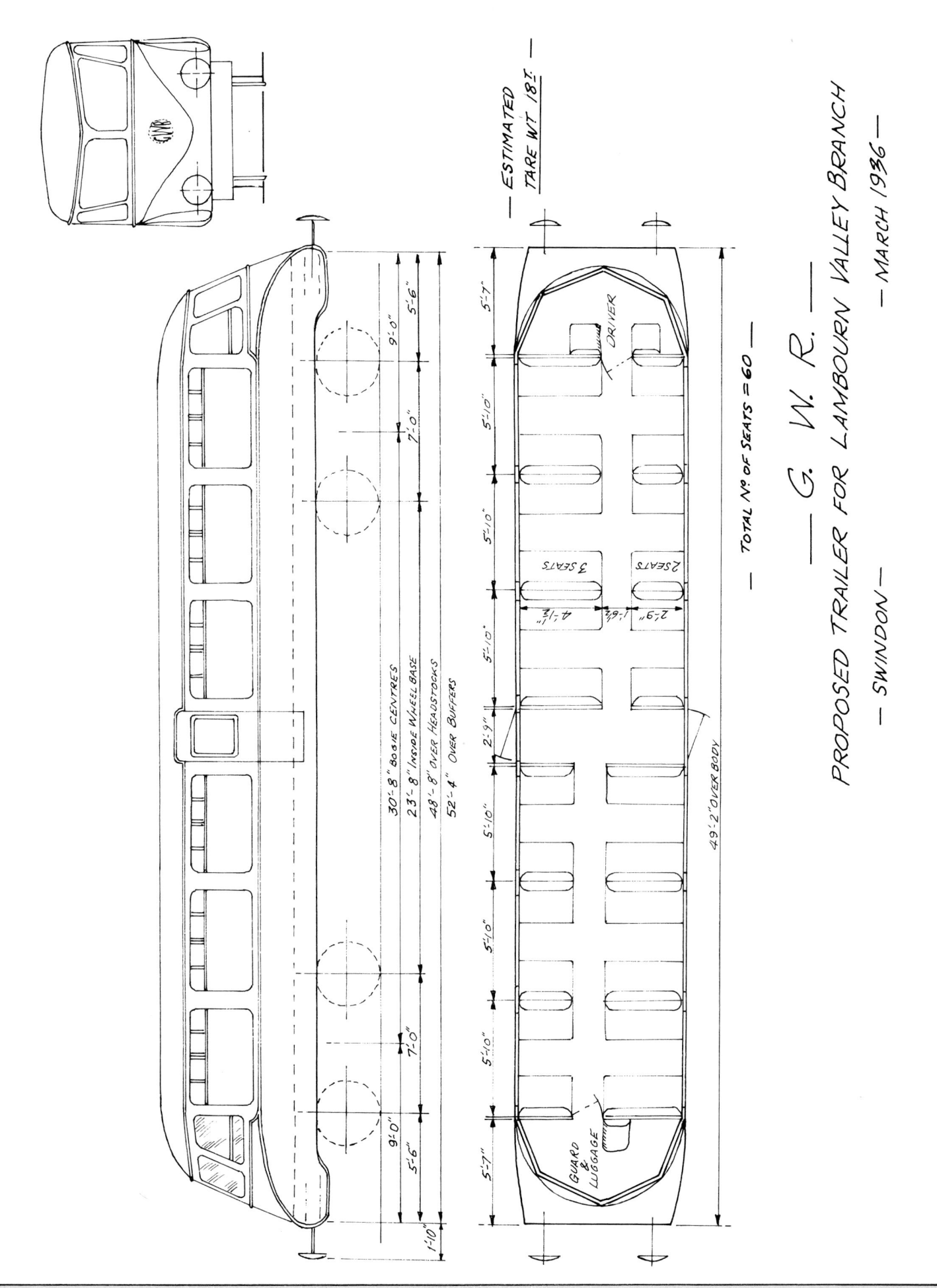

Figure 37

designed to reduce their height, the reverse gearbox had been removed in favour of a different arrangement, five forward speeds were made available instead of four, the engines were placed directly opposite one another on each side of the frame, the position of the radiators had been altered, bogie centres had been increased to give easier riding, and pneumatic controls and vacuum brakes had been adopted. In fact, the chassis had been made 'cleaner' in design. It was also apparent that the firm was laying less stress upon keeping down the weight for, without any increase of power, the chassis had been lengthened and the bogie wheelbase increased. It was, however, pointed out that the only advantage of lightweight design was that high acceleration could be obtained, and that an alternative means of reaching the same result was to lower the gear ratios. Thereby it was true that the top speed was affected, but it must be remembered that high acceleration was only of appreciable value in a local service with frequent stops, in which the attainment of high speeds was rarely possible. An increase of weight had the advantages, to set against this loss of acceleration, of superior strength to withstand shunting shocks and the stresses set up if a trailer was pulled.

### Chassis

The general arrangement drawing of the complete chassis reproduced (see Figure 36 & Plate 122) shows that the railcar was symmetrical about its two centre lines, so that the bogies were also identical. The main dimensions are given in the following table:

| | |
|---|---|
| Length over headstocks | 62ft. 0in. |
| Length over buffers | 65ft. 8in. |
| Bogie centres | 43ft. 6in. |
| Bogie wheelbase | 8ft. 6in. |
| Frame width | 3ft. 2in. |
| Frame height above rail | 3ft. 11in. |
| Overall width | 8ft. 0in. |
| Wheel diameter | 3ft. 1in. |

The main side members and buffer beams were 12in. x 3½in. channel section. Reinforcing members were riveted on the inside of the main side members above the bogies, in order that the car could be lifted from the buffer beams, if required. The comparatively narrow frame width was adopted, in order that the engines could be placed in accessible positions outside the frame. Those interested in the arrangement of structures can observe that all the cantilever members were straight, and that the units carried were so placed that a cantilever on one side of the frame was always 'balanced' by a cantilever on the other side. The bogies were of the swing link bolster type. The main bearing springs were 4ft. 8in. long x 3½in. wide, these being only 4ft. long on previous vehicles, and only 3ft. long on the first seven railcars, while the bolsters were carried on nests of three concentric springs. The bolsters were fitted with centering springs, and the plungers for the latter had large heads which rested against strips of bonded asbestos attached to the solebars thus providing shock absorbers for the vertical movement. Sand boxes with valves of the Westinghouse ejector type, were fitted on the bogies. Remembering that the first seventeen cars had bogies of 7ft. 0in. wheelbase, this had been increased to 8ft. 6in. on this vehicle.

The general arrangement of the units mounted on the frame and of the drive to the axles was similar to that of the earlier twin-engined cars, but, owing partly to the increase of the bogie centres-distance, and partly to the elimination of the reverse gearbox, it had been made possible to place the two engines exactly opposite one another. Actually, with the object of preventing engine vibrations being transmitted to the frame, the two engines were mounted in an independent sub-frame, consisting of two cross members joined up by two longitudinal supports. This sub-frame was suspended from the main frame side members through rubber blocks. Sideways and endwise thrust (adjustable), as well as any upward reaction, was resisted through the same medium.

It is interesting to note that being opposite one another and, as viewed from one end of the car, rotating in opposite directions, the torque reactions of the engines balance out. The weight of the batteries, which were mounted on the sub-frame, further increased its inertia, and thereby reduced vibrations to an even lower degree. The engines were each attached to the sub-frame by a bell housing at the rear and a hanger with a Silentbloc bush at the front end. The situation of other units on the sides of the frame, such as fuel tanks, air reservoirs and other auxiliary equipment, can be seen clearly in Plates 123 & 124.

Like the engines, the gearboxes, too, were suspended through thick rubber pads in order to prevent noise and vibration being transmitted to the main frame.

Standing at either end of the chassis and looking along it, the engine on the left drove the axles of the nearer bogie and the engine on the right the axles of the distant bogie. The two transmission systems were identical in design and arrangement, and as in previous railcar designs, the drive was taken from the engines through fluid flywheels to Wilson preselective gearboxes, and thence (via flexible telescopic propeller shafts) to both axles of each bogie.

Each of the engines were six cylinder A.E.C. Ricardo, with a bore and stroke of 115mm. x 142mm., developing 130b.h.p. and having a speed range from 600 to 2000r.p.m. The normal

*Plate 122:* The complete chassis of railcar No. 18.
*(A.E.C. Ltd.) Leyland Vehicles Ltd.*

*Plate 123:* Another view of the chassis of railcar No. 18, prior to the attachment of the body.

*(A.E.C. Ltd.) Leyland Vehicles Ltd.*

*Plate 124:* A side view of the complete chassis of railcar No. 18.

*(A.E.C. Ltd.) Leyland Vehicles Ltd.*

*Plate 125:* A fine detail side view of No. 18's chassis, showing clearly the engine detail, radiator (with oil cooling system) and gearbox, etc.

*(A.E.C. Ltd.) Leyland Vehicles Ltd.*

design of this engine had been modified for use in the railcar, with the object of reducing the height necessary to accommodate it. Other improvements made on these engines were modifications to the combustion chamber to improve the 'turbulence' in the air before injecting the fuel. The main principle was that a separate combustion chamber, spherical in form, was incorporated in the cylinder head, into which the air was forced through a tangential passage during the compression stroke, thus imparting a high rotational swirl to the air in the chamber. Into this swirling air, the fuel was injected shortly before top dead centre, and a uniform distribution of the fuel throughout the air was achieved, resulting in rapid and smooth combustion and absence of smoke. This modification had made possible the use of a simple type of nozzle which was not liable to choke up. No part of the engine projected above the level of the main frame of the chassis, so that this could be a simplification of the body design. This result had been achieved by adopting a system of dry sump lubrication.

An air compressor, lubricated from the crank case, was mounted on each engine, and supplied air for the operation of the pneumatic controls. Two 45 gallon fuel tanks were provided, one on each side of the frame, each feeding one engine only and thereby maintaining the principle of two self-contained units.

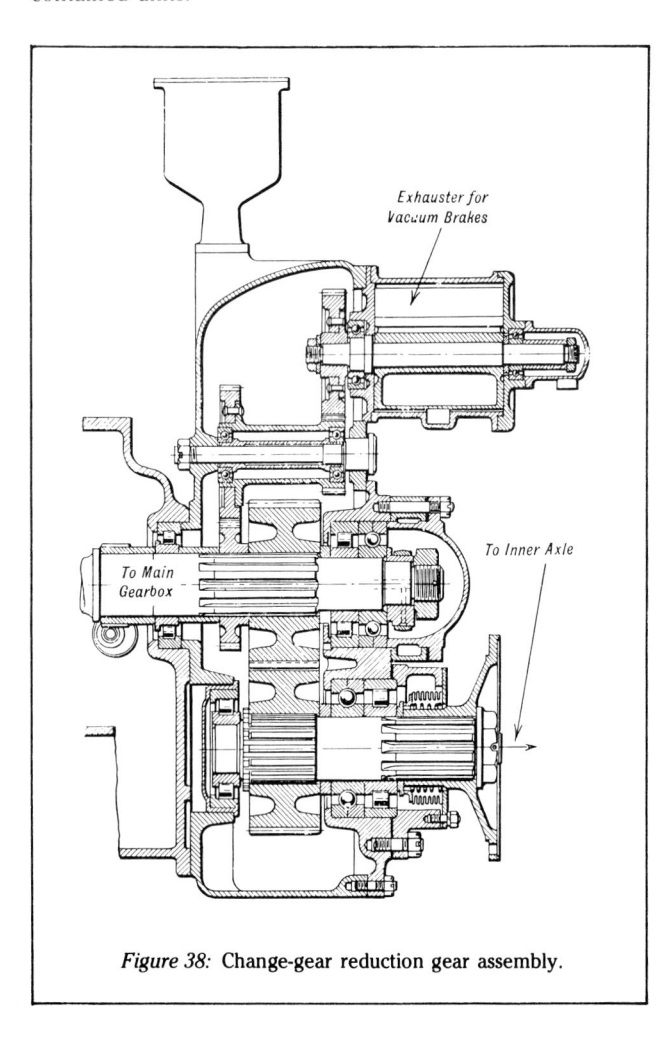

*Figure 38:* Change-gear reduction gear assembly.

In the previous seventeen railcars, it will be remembered that the radiators were set askew to the engines, and that two louvred panels, with blades curved in opposite directions, were situated in the side of the car, and a baffle behind them brought one or the other into operation according to the direction of the vehicle. In the present design, this system had been discarded, as experiment had proved that a simpler arrangement would be equally effective.

As will be seen from *Plate 125*, the radiators were set at right angles to the ordinary position, in front of the engine. A 32in. fan, driven from the engine through a propeller shaft, bevel bearing and a belt, drew the air through the radiator, and delivered it to the space beneath the car. Each radiator was of the vertical 'Still' tube type. On the outer side, a number of similar tubes were arranged 'in series', and acted as the radiator for oil-cooling. Whereas, of course, a relatively small temperature drop of a large volume of water was required by the engine, the oil cooler needed only a small quantity of water, but a larger temperature drop. The connections to the engine sump for oil cooling can be clearly seen in *Plate 125*.

The gearboxes, like those on previous diesel railcars, were of the Wilson preselective epicyclic type. Each gearbox provided five alternative forward speeds, with ratios of 1 : 1, 1.64 : 1, 2.53 : 1, 4.5 : 1, and 6.38 : 1. Each gearbox was lubricated from two eccentric pumps, one driven by the input, and the other by the output shaft. At the front end of the box a chain transmitted a drive to a lay shaft, which, in turn, drove a dynamo through a universally-jointed shaft. At the rear end of the box there was a reduction gear assembly, so designed that alternative reductions could be fitted to make the railcar suitable for various classes of service. The output shaft of the main gearbox *(see Figure 38)* carried a single helical ground gear meshing, with a similar gear on the driven shaft, which was offset to one side and below, and transmitted the drive to the axles. It will be seen that it was a comparatively simple job to remove the covers and slide the gears off the splined shafts, replacing them by others with a different ratio. The following table indicated the ratios that were available, the resulting top speeds, tractive efforts in bottom gear, and the class of work for which they made the railcar suitable.

| Ratio | Top Speed m.p.h. | Maximum tractive effort lb. | Service |
|---|---|---|---|
| 1.03 : 1 | 75.0 | 4,360 | Express |
| 1.15 : 1 | 67.1 | 4,890 | Express |
| 1.37 : 1 | 56.5 | 5,810 | Local with trailer |
| 1.73 : 1 | 44.6 | 7,370 | More than one trailer; |
| 1.96 : 1 | 39.5 | 8,340 | or heavy gradients |

The drawing *(Figure 38)* also shows the arrangement of the drive to one of the exhausters for the vacuum brakes. A pneumatic system of operating the controls had been adopted on this new vehicle, and for preselecting the gears in the Wilson gearbox, an ingenious device had been designed and is illustrated in *(Figure 39)*. A handle on the driver's control table operated a self-lapping valve, which altered air pressure in an air line, in five steps. The other end of the line at the gearbox end was connected to the space 'A' of the operating device seen in *Figure 39*. This device consisted of a cylinder having a piston upon which four springs 'B', 'C', 'D', and 'E', were

*Figure 39:* Pneumatic gear selector.

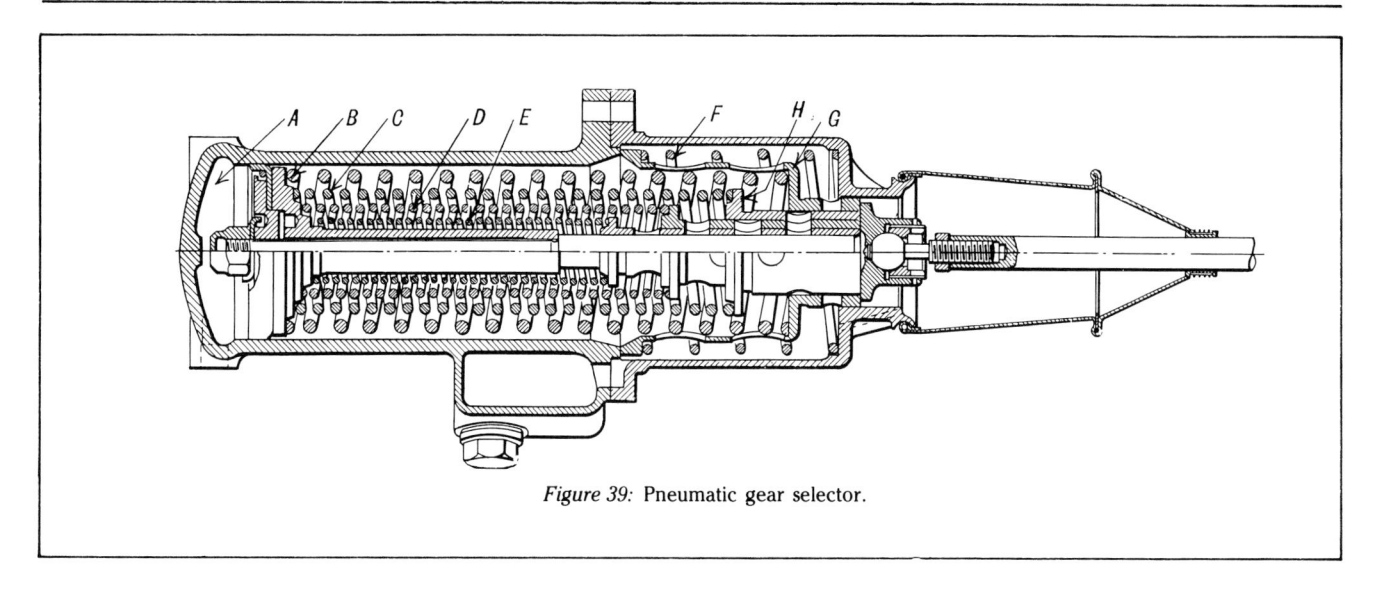

arranged to act in opposition to the air pressure. In addition, there was a return spring 'F'. The drawing shows the device in the 'neutral' selected position. On moving the control handle on the driver's table to first gear position, air at a pressure of about 10p.s.i. was admitted to space 'A'. This pressure was sufficient to compress the spring 'F', and consequently the piston travelled until the cage 'G' of spring 'B' abutted against the casing. As the pressure was not sufficient to compress both springs 'F' and 'B', the motion of the piston ceased. By this action the first gear was selected. On further motion of the control handle, the pressure in space 'A' was increased to about 21p.s.i. Spring 'B' was then compressed until the cage 'H' of spring 'C' hit against the stop, when the piston could travel no further; thereby second gear was selected. Third, fourth, and top gears were selected in a similar manner, the final air pressure being 80p.s.i.

**Calibration Curve of Gear Changing Cylinder**

The camshaft with five equal rotational movements was required to correspond with the five gear steps, and these movements were provided by an air cylinder which was controlled through a series of five coiled springs, as described above. Each of these had a definite initial compression, and as is shown in the accompanying graph *(Figure 40)*, the springs were held by a series of sleeves on which shoulders were formed at spacings, which made the sleeves abut against the outer casing at five equidistant points of the piston travel.

From the gearbox *(Plate 126)*, the drive was transmitted to the axles through a telescopic propeller shaft mounted between universal joints. The final drive to the axles had been completely redesigned. The arrangement, formerly adopted, consisted of a worm drive to each axle with an inter-axle differential, and had proved very satisfactory and efficient in service, but it was now considered that the inter-axle differential was an unnecessary refinement. Its elimination had not only allowed a very simple bevel drive to be adopted, but had also made it possible to incorporate the reverse gear very neatly in the same arrangement. The design of the drive to the inner axle of the bogie is shown in *Figure 41*. Two pinions, carried freely in 'ball and roller' bearings, were constantly in mesh with a crown wheel bolted to the wheel hub. The driving shaft passed through the bore of the first pinion, and was guided at its end in the bore of the second by a small roller bearing. Sliding dog-clutches allowed either of the two bevels to be engaged with the driving shaft. Since the bevels were situated at opposite sides of the crown wheel, forward or reverse gear was engaged according to which bevel was transmitting the drive. The arrangement of the drive to the outer axle of the bogie *(Plate 127 & Figure 41)* was similar, except that there was only one bevel pinion situated at the edge of the crown wheel furthest from the engine. It was driven from the corresponding bevel pinion on the inner axle, to which it was connected by a propeller shaft. The arrangement of these two bevels constituted a definite linkage between the two axles, so that the outer axle would always rotate in the same direction as the inner one.

The pneumatic reversing device is also shown in *Figure 41* (marked 'A'). The forks which operate the dog clutches were carried by an overhead rod. The latter had, at each end, a piston working in a pneumatic cylinder, and either clutch could be engaged by admitting air to one or other of the cylinders. It will be seen that no provision was made for engaging a 'neutral' position, but in the case of an emergency arising such that it became desirable that the whole of the transmission system on one side of the coach should be put out of action, arrangements had been made for holding the clutch rod in the neutral position.

At the head of each pneumatic cylinder there was a stop in the form of a double-ended set screw. These screws were placed in a position easily accessible from rail level and, if withdrawn and replaced with the long end inwards, prevented the movement of the clutch rod from the central 'neutral' position.

In order that the driver should be unable to attempt to engage reverse when the train was in motion, an interlock was provided and operated by the vacuum in the brake train pipe. As long as any vacuum existed in this pipe, the reversing handle on the control desk could not be put in the reverse position. Thus the handle could only be moved when the car was at rest with the brakes fully applied.

The torque reaction from the axle boxes was taken on to the bogie soleplate by means of pressed arms bolted to the axle box casing, and held at their outer ends by shackles and pins fitted with 'Silentbloc' bushes. Owing to torsional movement, it followed that the axle casing could not remain exactly verti-

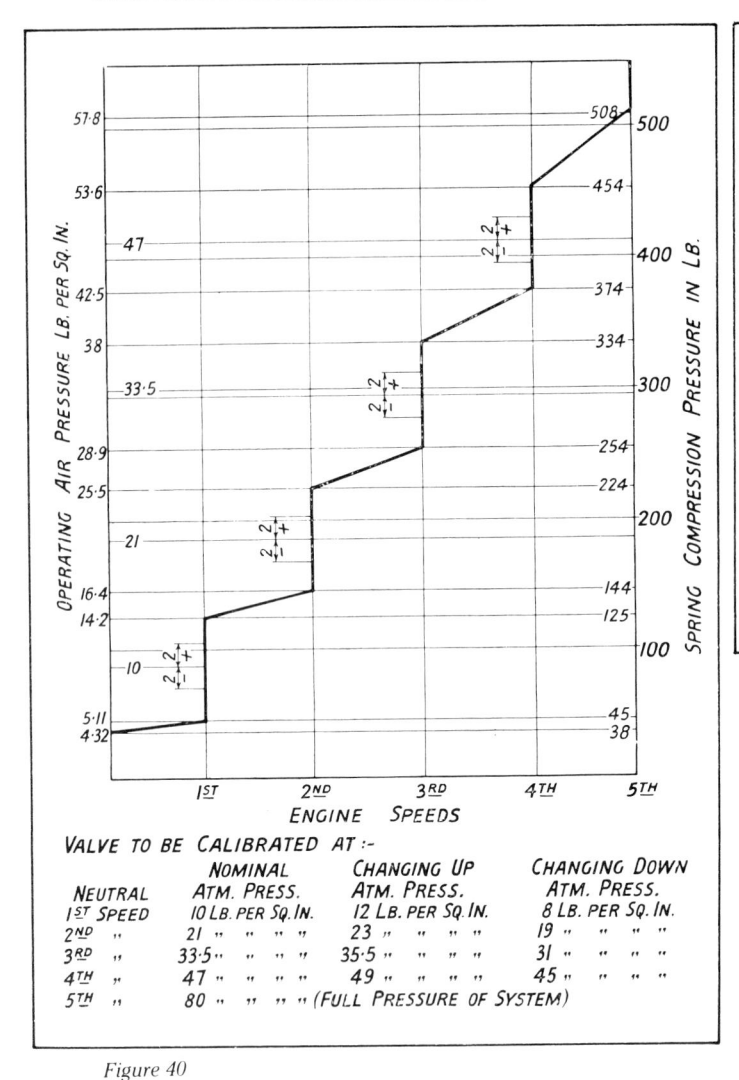

Figure 40

VALVE TO BE CALIBRATED AT:-

| NEUTRAL | NOMINAL ATM. PRESS. | CHANGING UP ATM. PRESS. | CHANGING DOWN ATM. PRESS. |
|---|---|---|---|
| 1ST SPEED | 10 LB. PER SQ. IN. | 12 LB. PER SQ. IN. | 8 LB. PER SQ. IN. |
| 2ND " | 21 " " " " | 23 " " " " | 19 " " " " |
| 3RD " | 33.5 " " " " | 35.5 " " " " | 31 " " " " |
| 4TH " | 47 " " " " | 49 " " " " | 45 " " " " |
| 5TH " | 80 " " " " (FULL PRESSURE OF SYSTEM) | | |

*Plate 126:* The Wilson gearbox as fitted to No. 18 diesel railcar.

(A.E.C. Ltd). Leyland Vehicles Ltd.

*Plate 127:* Details of bogie and drive to axles on No. 18 diesel railcar.

(A.E.C. Ltd.) Leyland Vehicles Ltd.

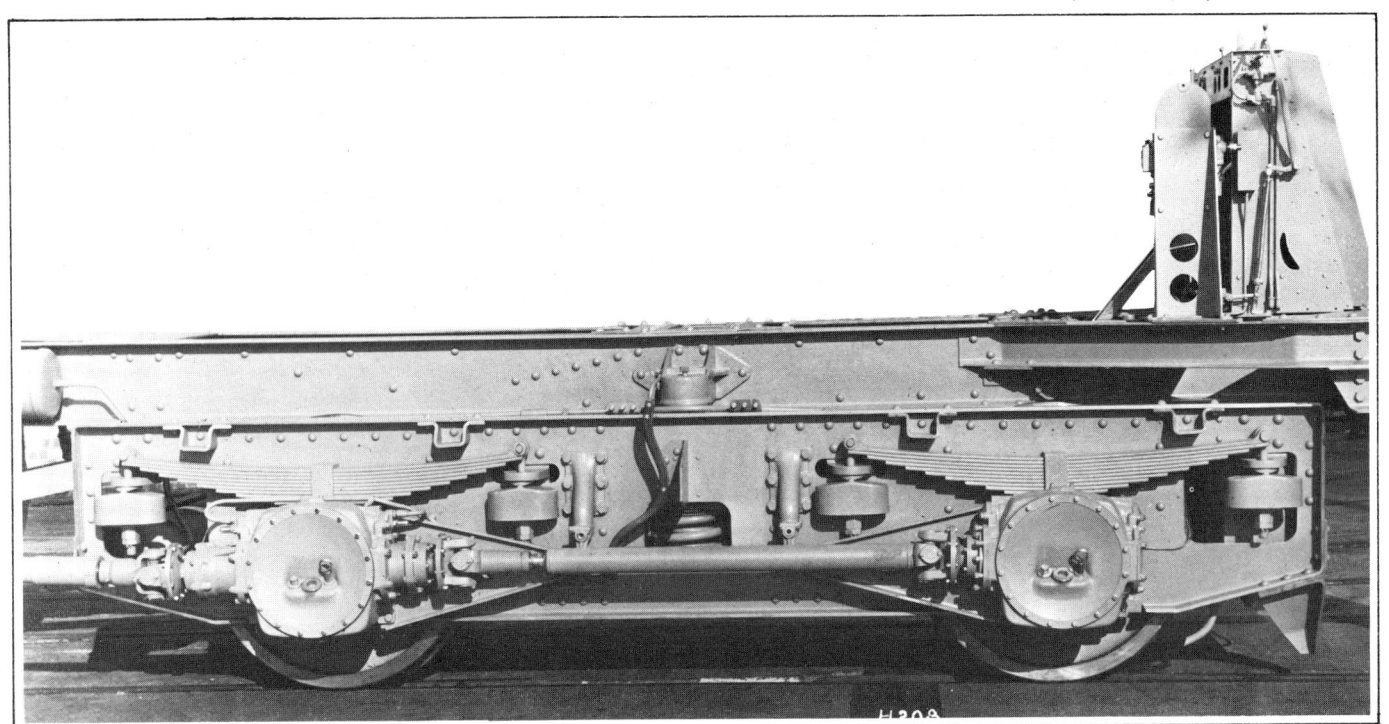

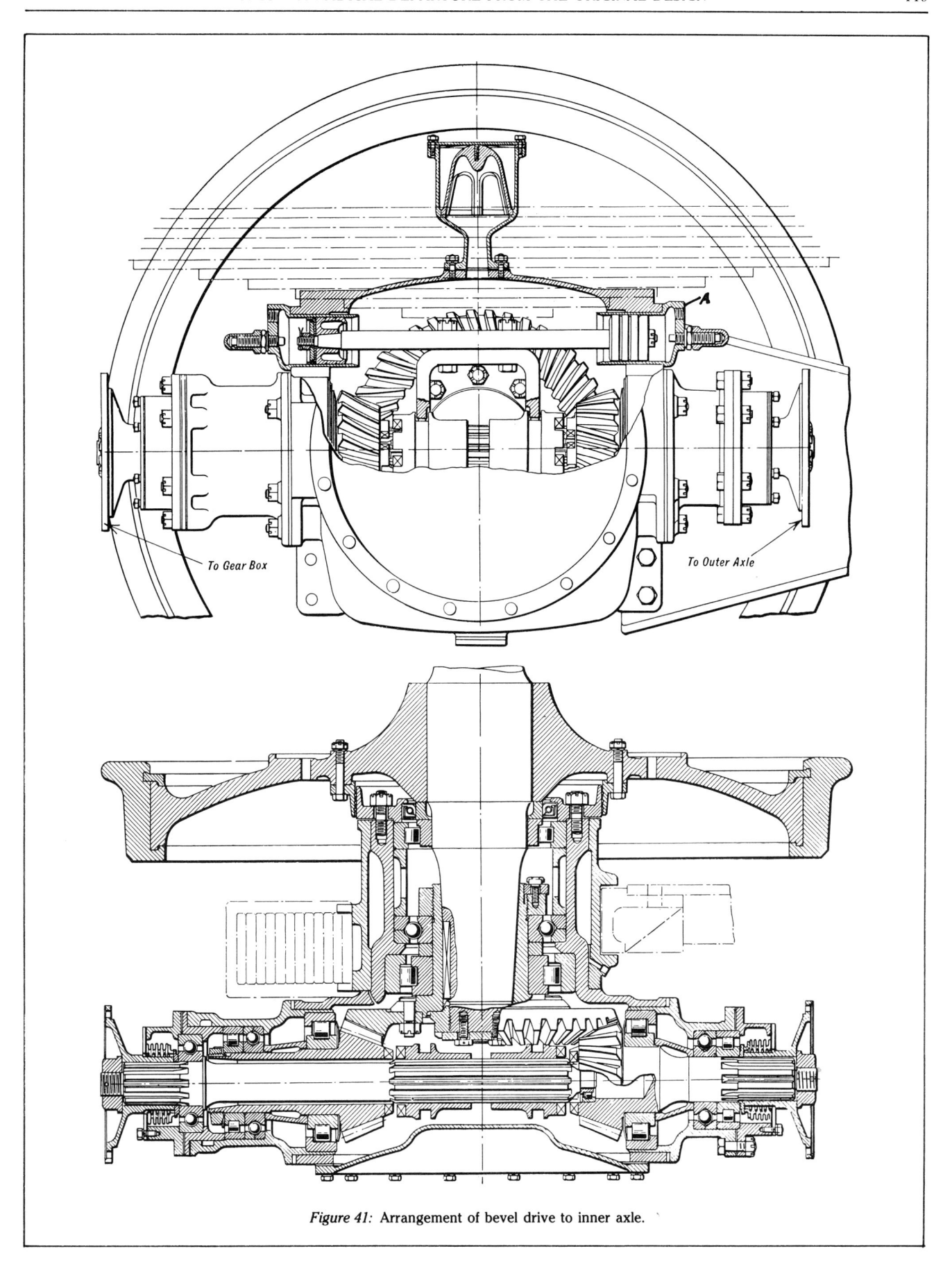

*Figure 41:* Arrangement of bevel drive to inner axle.

*Figure 42:* Full bogie details of railcar No. 18.
*(A.E.C.) Ltd. Leyland Vehicles Ltd.*

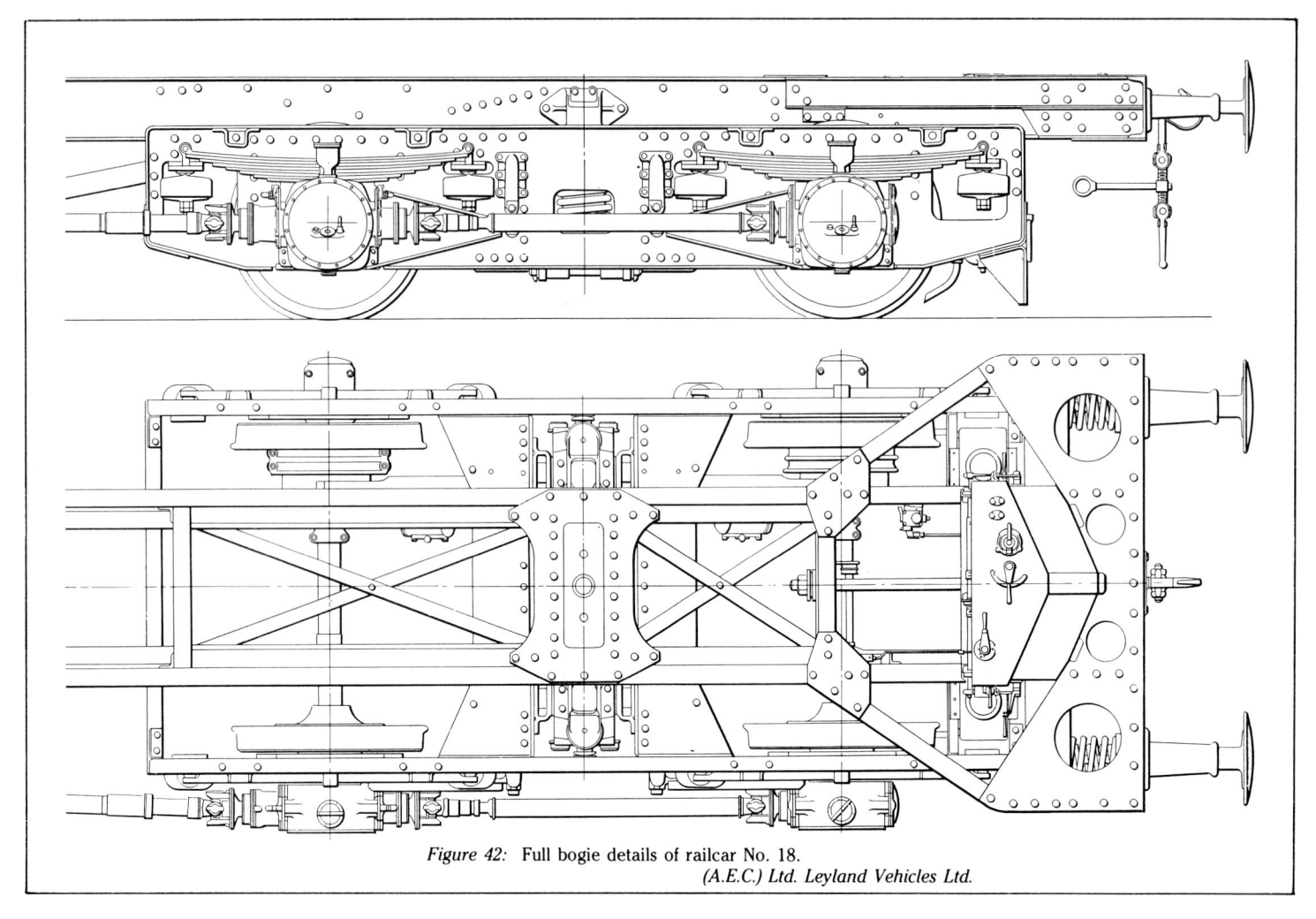

cal under all conditions of loading, and in order that the thrust from the axle box to the horn guides could be square, the thrust faces of the axle box were carried on a sleeve, which was free to rotate around the main axle casing, and remained square with the horn guides. The large axle box inspection covers were fitted with oil filler plugs, oil dipsticks, and a magnetic filter. The bevel wheel ratio was 2.588 : 1.

The general design of the braking system remained unchanged, with internal expanding brakes. The drums were machined from steel stampings, and were 20in. in diameter and 6in. wide. The brake shoes were cam-operated, and the cams and pivot pins were mounted on a casting which was carried on the axle by roller bearings. Brake reaction was taken by a torque arm bolted to this casting, and attached to the bogie frame through shackles and 'Silentbloc' bushes. The brakes were operated by an automatic vacuum system, the cylinders for which were mounted on the torque arm, so that there was no relative movement or lost motion. Vacuum for the operation of the brakes was provided by two rotary exhausters, one mounted on the rear of each main gearbox. A third exhauster (motor-driven) was carried on the side of the main frame, and utilised for creating vacuum, initially before the engines were started. Large capacity vacuum reservoirs were carried between the main frame members.

As No. 18 car was intended for working with standard vacuum-fitted stock, provision had to be made for creating far more vacuum than had previously been required. At first, an electrically-driven exhauster was tried, but this was totally inadequate and the Daimler-Benz system was used. In this, the air intake of three cylinders of each engine was connected through a non-return valve to the brake reservoir, and when the driver's throttle was brought back to idling position, fuel, as well as air, was shut off from these cylinders. The result was a three cylinder exhauster, of large capacity (115mm. x 142mm.) driven by the other three cylinders. This gave very good results, but idling on three cylinders caused a certain amount of vibration, when the car was standing with the engines running, and a torque reaction.

It was found that, often, the car would be standing at a station idling in this way for some minutes, when the necessary vacuum could be obtained in a matter of seconds, especially when the car was working alone. Therefore an automatic valve had been designed and fitted, which closed the air valve when the vacuum dropped to a certain point, and opened it again when the necessary amount was obtained. The valve was held closed by a coil spring, which was overcome when the desired degree of vacuum was reached in the train pipe to which the cylinder containing the spring was connected. To make the action more positive, and to allow for the delayed action between open and closed positions, the air

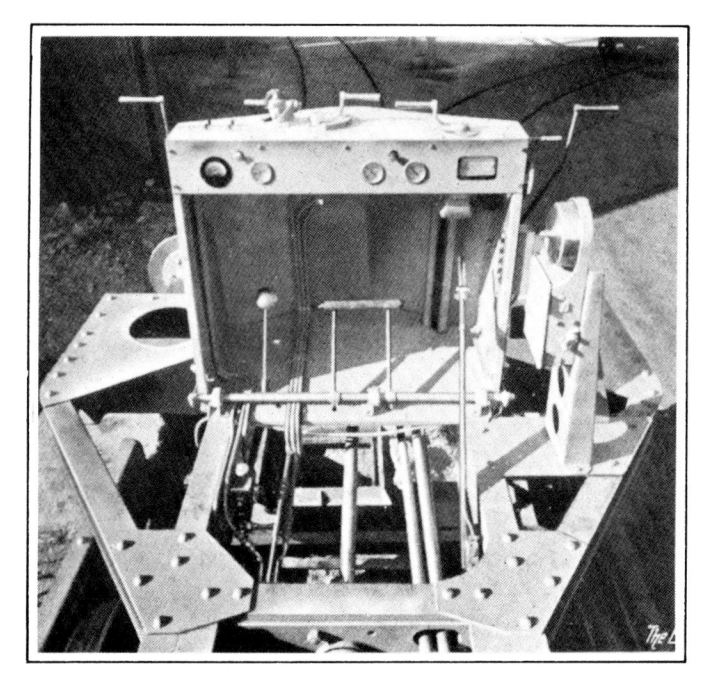

# NO. 18 — A RADICAL DEPARTURE FROM THE ORIGINAL DESIGN

*Plate 128:* The control table of railcar No. 18, before the body was attached.

*The Engineer*

*Plate 129:* An engine revolution meter replaces the former speedometer on the driver's control table which has, on the left, starter buttons and reverse switch; in the centre, finger-tip pre-selective gear switch; and, on the right, a vacuum brake handle.

*(A.E.C. Ltd.) Leyland Vehicles Ltd.*

valve was made up of a 'pilot working' in the main valve.

Another advantage of this system was that vacuum could be created more quickly by increasing the engine speed, where previously it could only be done at idling speed. This was not desirable at stations, owing to the smoke caused by fuel being admitted when the throttle was opened up, but not burnt owing to the lack of air compression. It was, however, useful away from platforms, for example after a signal check.

Before this valve was fitted, an unexpected weakness of the system came to light during the tests of No. 18 when running with two trailers. One of these trailers was defective and the brake connections were leaking rather badly, with the result that, in the interval between the driver opening the throttle, and so cutting the engine out as an exhauster, and the time that the car had attained sufficient speed for the gearbox exhauster to become effective, the brakes had leaked on. To overcome this and fill up this gap, a further exhauster was fitted to each engine, giving the requisite vacuum, while the engine was speeded up in accelerating.

In this new design of railcar, pneumatic connection of the controls had been adopted rather than the previous mechanical connections, allowing a much neater arrangement. The throttle was still mechanically connected, and the reason for this exception was that this control must necessarily be used while starting the engine, and before any pressure could be developed. Air for the operation of the controls was obtained from small compressors mounted on the engines. The control panels at each end of the car were identical in arrangement and can be seen in *Plates 128 & 129*.

On the top of the panel to the left were four buttons, a starter and heater button for each engine. Next came a valve for controlling the reverse switch which had an interlocking cylinder connected to the brake train pipe, and could not be moved until the brakes were applied and the vacuum in this pipe was destroyed.

The reverse switch handle was loose, and was taken by the driver to whichever end he was driving from. It could not be withdrawn, except in the neutral position, and when it was withdrawn, it automatically engaged neutral in the gearbox and isolated the pre-selecting and clutch switches.

A new feature of the driver's control table was the fitting of an engine revolution meter which, when the car was running in top gear, also acted as a speedometer.

The reverse switch was followed by a valve, operating the pre-selector mechanism for the gearbox. The handle to the right, on top of the panel, was the brake. Two pedals operated the gear change and throttle respectively. In addition to the foot throttle, there was, on each side of the control table, a hand throttle so placed as to be within easy reach of the driver, for use when leaning out of the window during fog, or when shunting. The face of the control panel carried push valves for the whistle and engine stop, vacuum gauge, reservoir air pressure gauge, and gear selector gauge, which indicated at night what (during the day) was shown by the position of the gear selector handle. The remaining handle, that on the right side of the desk panel, operated the sanding gear. The handbrake acted only upon the bogie at one end of the car (as before), and was chiefly used for holding the vehicle when the engines were stopped. Indicator lights were arranged on a panel to be easily seen and not to confuse the driver when looking out at the signals. Two green lights indicated that the engines were running, and gave warning that the temperature of the water or oil in one or both of the engines was too high. The remaining lights (a red and white) indicated at which end of the car the tail lamp had been switched on.

Underneath the buffer beam a control coupling was fitted, to

*Plate 130:* Warmth for trailer vehicles was supplied by exhaust-heated boilers in the luggage compartment, as seen in this photograph taken of railcar No. 18, when new.

*British Rail*

*Plate 131:* The new design of ventilation is apparent in this official photograph, taken on 10th December 1936. Apparently, at speeds in excess of 30m.p.h., a good flow of air conditioning was achieved.

*British Rail*

which all control pipes were connected. It was arranged to connect up with a similar coupling on a trailer or a second car.

To allow for heating in any trailer car a boiler was installed in the luggage compartment, and consisted of a Clarkson thimble tube-type boiler and an economiser, both heated by the engine exhaust *(see Plate 130)*.

An improvement had been made in the ventilation of the passenger compartment by the fixing of an air scoop across the full width of the roof *(see Plate 131)*. The scoop was connected to a series of adjustable hinged ventilators fitted to the top of the panel, dividing the driver's and passengers' compartments giving a continuous current of fresh air just beneath the ceiling.

With the extra weight, caused by the fitting of standard drawgear and buffers, the use of a stiffer frame and the carrying of steam heating boilers, etc., railcar No. 18 was heavier than its predecessors at 33 tons 12cwt.

The interior decorations *(Plates 132 & 133)* of No. 18 car, which accommodated 49 passengers, followed the same lines that characterised the others in service. New style rectangular light fittings were mounted down the centre of the ceiling and between the windows.

So this new development of the diesel railcar was born, to the revised specification, for trailer haulage *(see Plate 134, Figure 43)*. Apparently there was a delay in delivery as, in contra-distinction to the preceding ten cars of the order, and indeed to all 17 GWR railcars, trailer haulage had been stipulated, and some investigation was desirable to produce the necessary combination of speed, seating, luggage capacity and tractive effort, which would satisfy all concerned. In fact, extensive trials were carried out with this design and the results of an interesting test showing its haulage capacity are given in the graph below.

These tests were carried out between Brentford and Southall on a generally rising gradient, and a trailing load of no less than 124 tons was hauled in addition to the weight of the car (with its test load), although this represented twice the load for which the car was intended.

And so with the chassis tested, the body was completed by the Gloucester Railway Carriage & Wagon Co. Ltd. to order No. 110075. This body differed greatly from the first 17 cars and *Plate 135* shows the buffing gear allowing it to pull tail loads of either passenger or goods vehicles up to 60 tons. Notice how the valancing does not now cover the whole vehicle but leaves the bogies free for inspection.

For coupling up to other cars, the standard jumper couplings used on electric trains had been adopted as shown in *Plate 136*. The other connections used consisted of a Bowden control for the throttle, two brake pipes, one the train pipe and the other release, and an air connection for pressure gauge and whistle if required. A standard steam connection was also provided, delivering steam from the exhaust-heated boiler.

When the vehicle was completed by the Gloucester Railway Carriage & Wagon Co. Ltd., it was returned to A.E.C. at the end of November 1936 for further exhaustive tests, which were carried out in December 1936 on the Reading-Oxford-

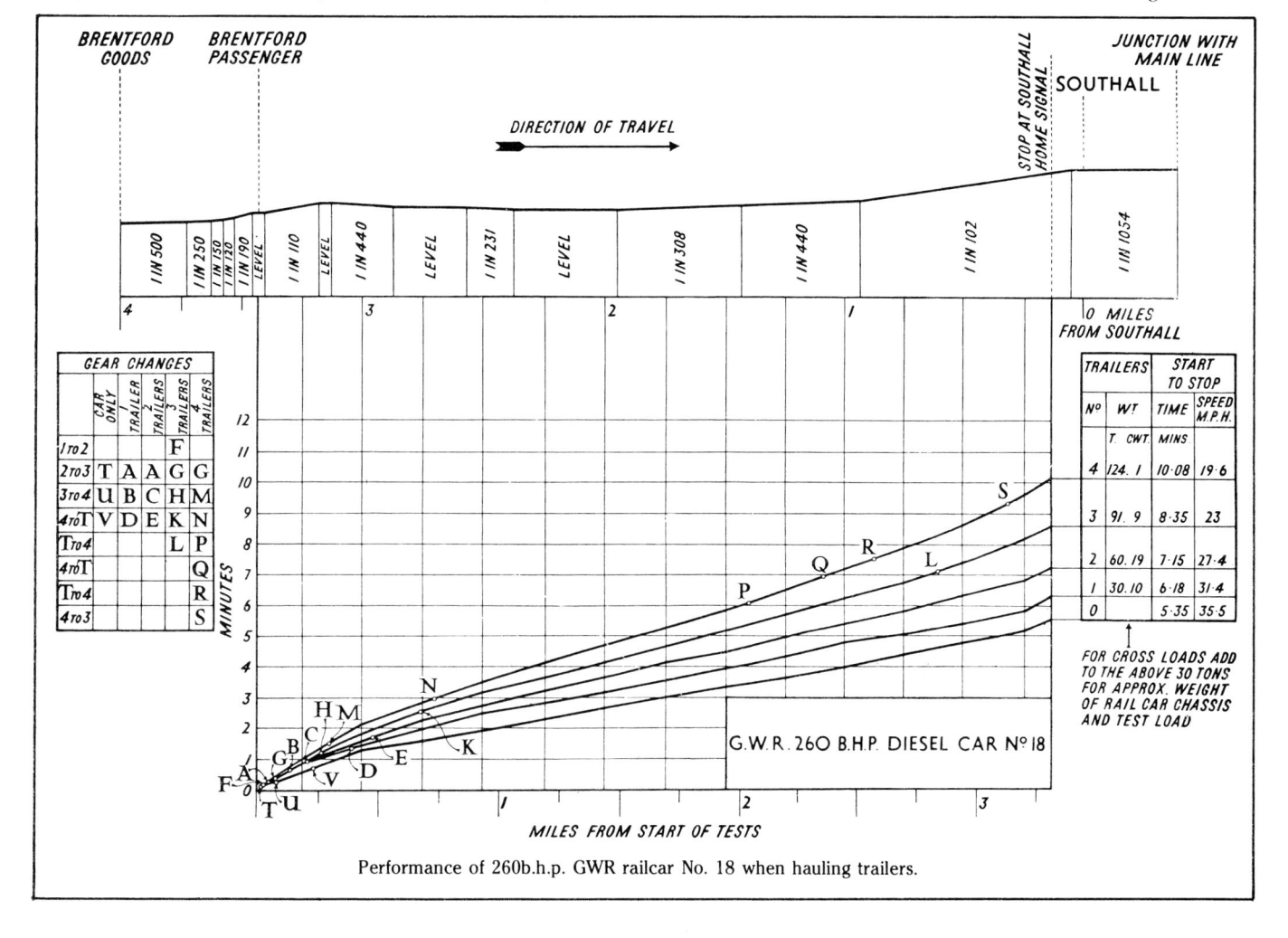

Performance of 260b.h.p. GWR railcar No. 18 when hauling trailers.

Figure 43

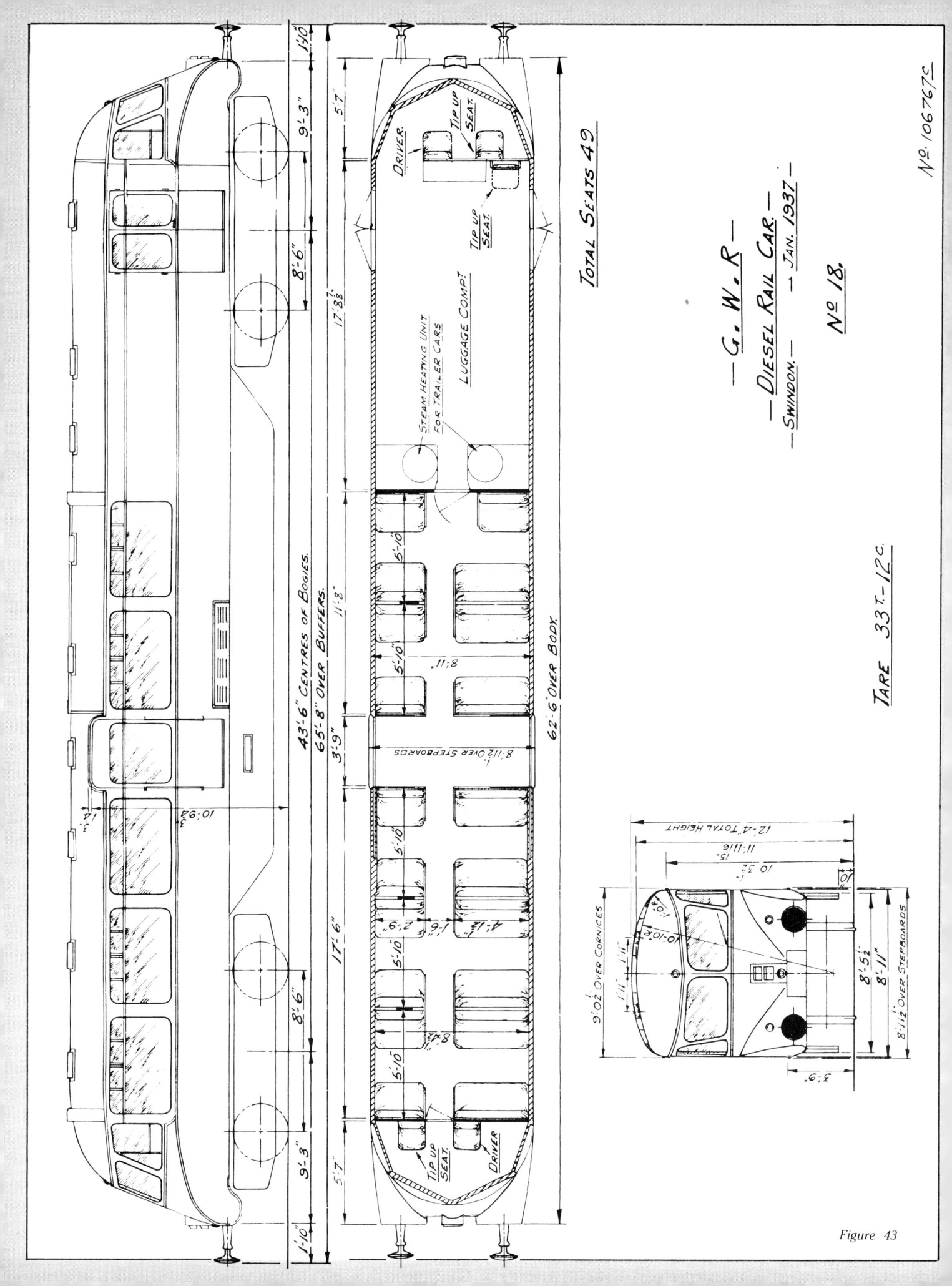

*Plate 132:* Looking towards the passenger end of railcar No. 18, the spaciousness of these railcars can be appreciated.
*British Rail*

*Plate 133:* Looking in the opposite direction to that in *Plate 132* (towards the luggage end), this photograph (taken on 10th December 1936) shows the sliding door recesses and new light fittings. Note the lack of luggage racks in this vehicle.
*British Rail*

*Plate 134:* Railcar No. 18 with a standard coach attached. This was photographed during trials with various loads.
*British Rail*

*Plate 135:* Diesel railcar No. 18, having arrived from the Gloucester Railway Carriage & Wagon Co. Ltd. before being passed over to the GWR.
*(A.E.C. Ltd.) Leyland Vehicles Ltd.*

*Plate 136:* For coupling up to other cars, the standard couplings had been adopted as shown here. The connections consisted of a Bowden control for the throttle, two brake pipes, one the train pipe and the other release, and an air connection for pressure gauge and whistle if required. A standard steam connection was also provided, delivering steam from an exhaust-heated boiler.

*Gloucester Railway Carriage & Wagon Co. Ltd.*

Banbury, then the Banbury-South Ruislip, the Banbury-Oxford-Reading, and finally the Southall lines. All these tests were recorded on the four accompanying graphs *(Figures 44, 45, 46 & 47)*, and show the performance of this vehicle. The Great Western Railway also managed to record the event on film and *Plate 134* shows one photograph of No. 18 with a coach attached.

Unfortunately (it was documented), the fog interfered badly with these trials but the Great Western Railway and A.E.C. pressed on, even in these conditions.

In the tests, times were taken with an ordinary watch and were between stations, while distances were as given in the public timetable. It was thought that this was of greater commercial value than anything more exact, and the milepost method would have been impracticable owing to failing light, and weather conditions, the last part of the runs being made in the dark. Some points of interest from the Banbury-South Ruislip trials *(Figure 46)* follow.

With the car only, the gear ratio gave a top speed of 71 m.p.h. A check at the bottom of the bank, just after passing King's Sutton, put the car behind schedule, but this was caught up at Brill, and more than maintained to the stop at Gerrards Cross. From passing Ardley to the stop at Gerrards Cross, 39¾ miles were run at 61m.p.h., while the 22½ miles from passing Ardley to passing Princes Risborough were covered at 67½m.p.h.

On the second run with one trailer weighing 33 tons 6 cwt., the ratio had been altered to give a 60m.p.h. maximum. Again, the car was checked at King's Sutton, but the time had been regained at West Wycombe. Passing times at Ardley and Seer Green showed 37 miles run at 48½m.p.h.

On the last run, two trailers, totalling 63 tons 18 cwt., were hauled, and the gear ratio allowed for a top speed of 47½m.p.h.

The car was slightly behind time at Bicester, possibly due to brake drag caused by a leaky brake pipe coupling but, from there to Gerrards Cross, time was easily maintained and from passing Ilmer was run at 45m.p.h. for the 19¾ miles, while the 39¾ miles from passing Ardley to stopping at Gerrards Cross were covered at 39½m.p.h.

During these trials, temperature readings were taken at regular intervals, at different points on the car. The outer axle box was hottest when the car was running alone, indicating possibly that gear tooth speed, and the churning of oil,

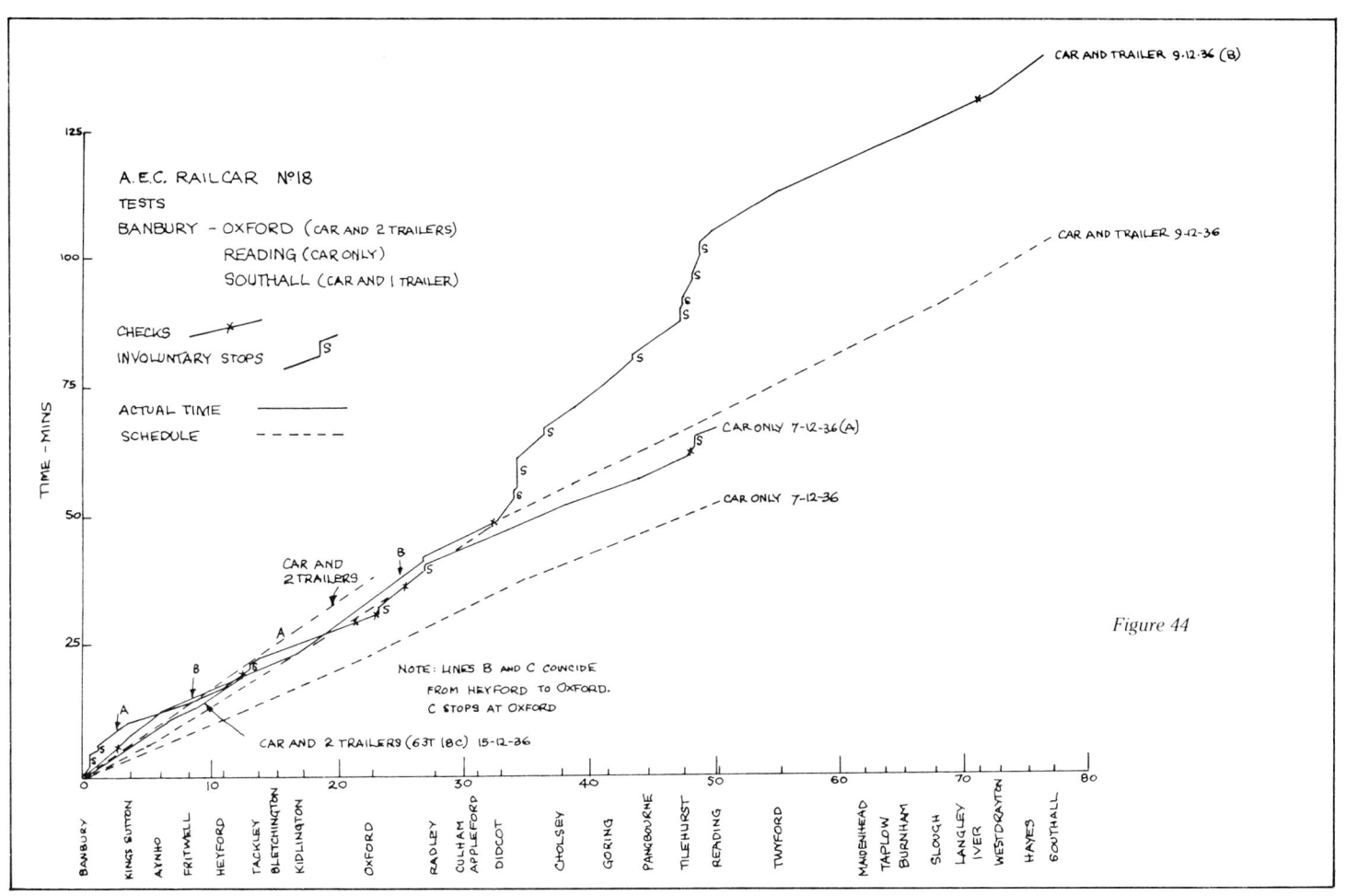

# NO. 18 — A RADICAL DEPARTURE FROM THE ORIGINAL DESIGN

*Figure 44*

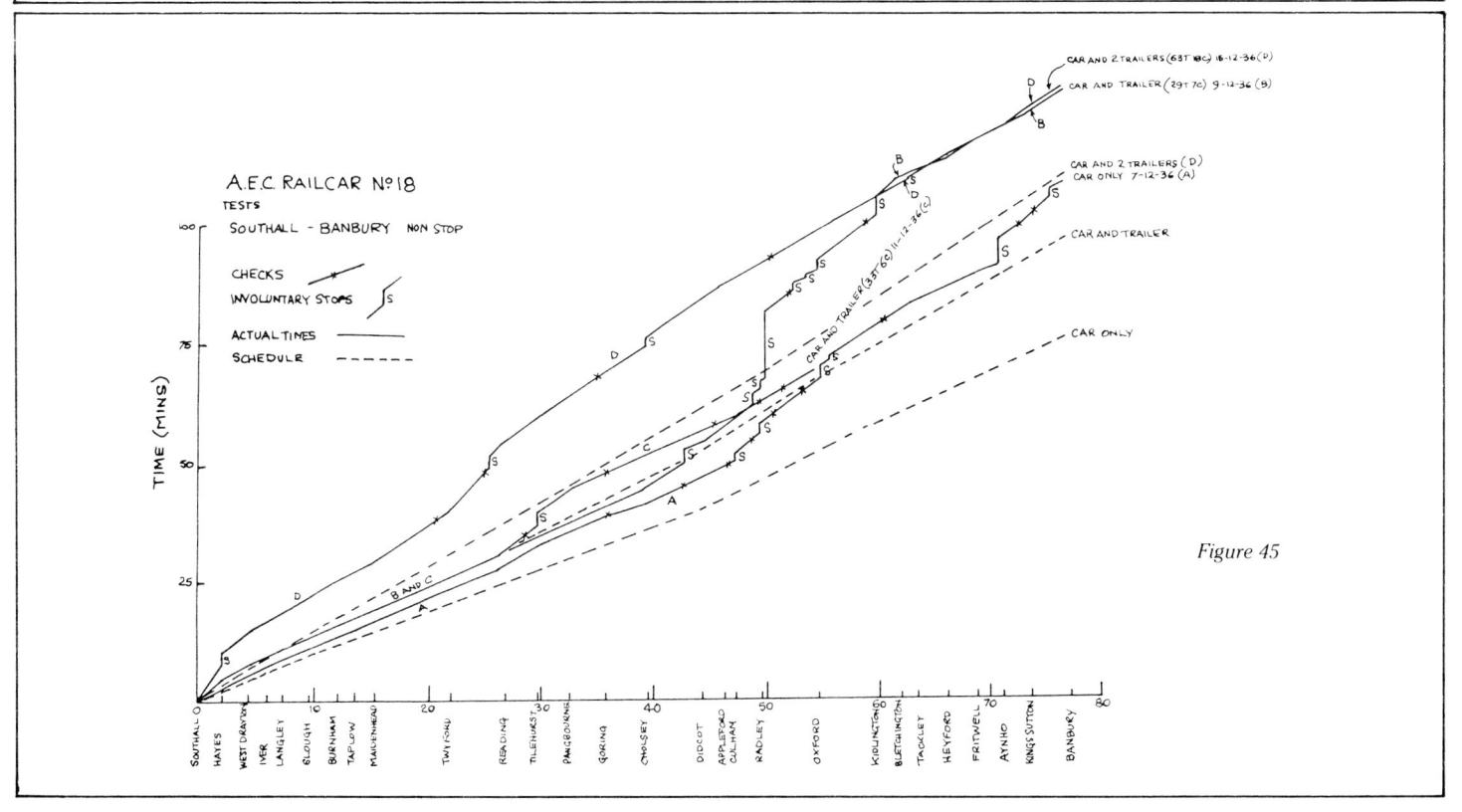

*Figure 45*

*Figure 46*

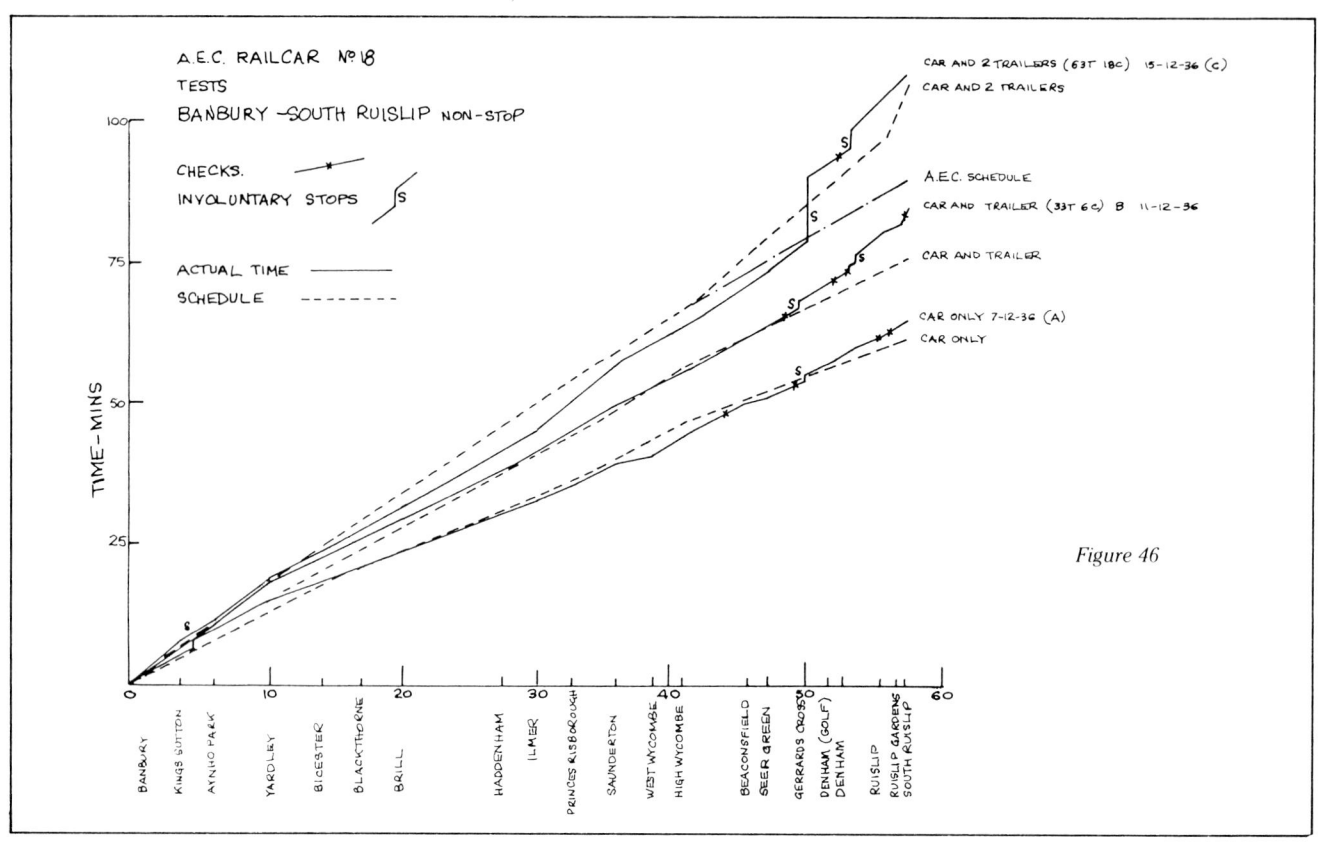

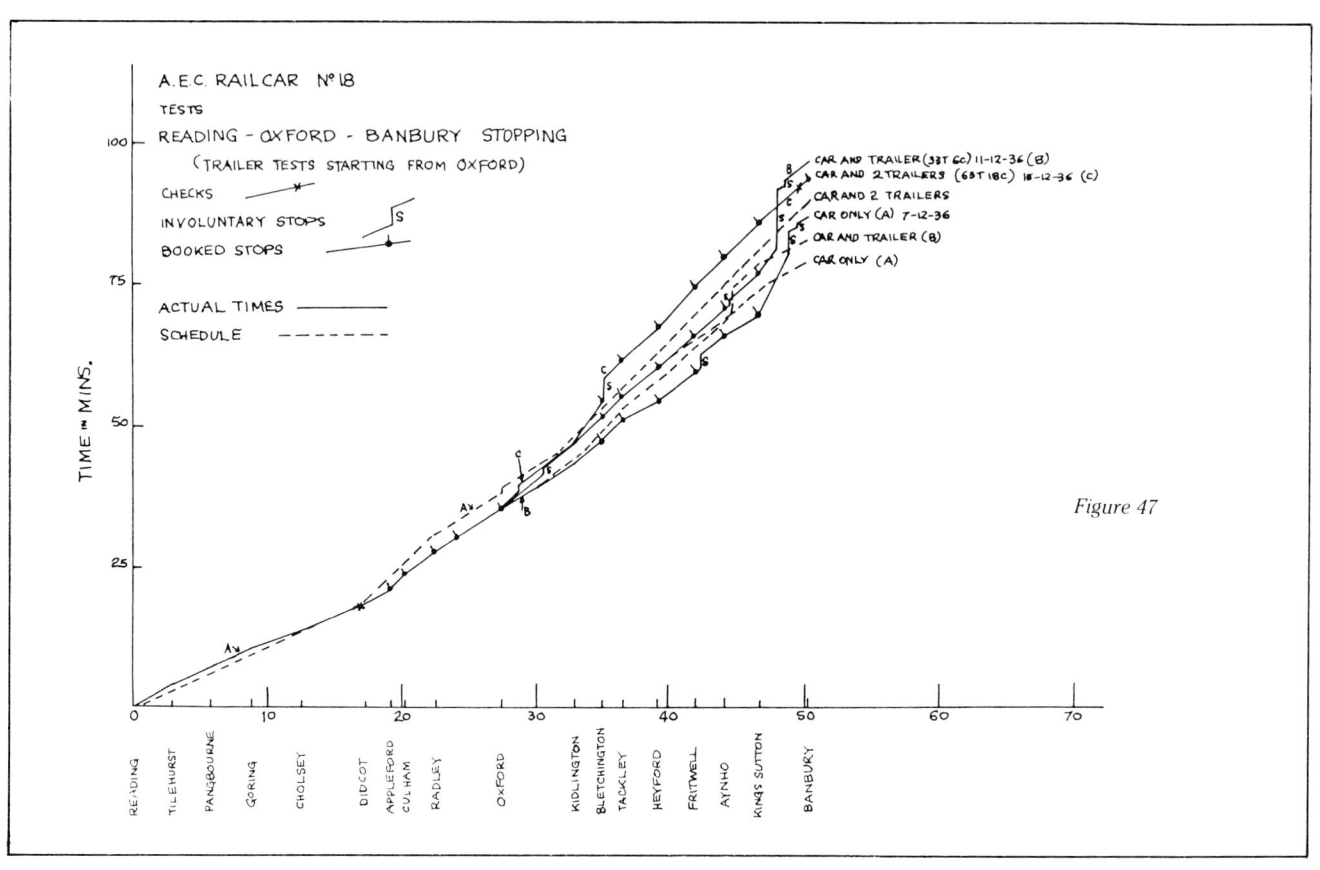

*Figure 47*

governed the temperature. The figures for the other two runs did not bear this out, however, as the box was hotter at the lower speed when hauling two trailers than when hauling one. However, with one trailer, this box was leading and may have been cooled by the air stream, while on the other two runs it was trailing.

Temperatures for the inner axle box bore the same relation to one another as for the outer one, and probably the explanation was that, due to the reversing gear, when running in one direction, the drive was reversed, while in the other it was direct. In other words, in one direction 150 per cent of power was transmitted, while in the other, the figure was only 50 per cent. With the car only, and with two trailers, the drive was reversed, but was direct when hauling one trailer.

The temperature figures for the gearbox were influenced by the temperatures at the start and, as stopping tests had just been carried out, the car with the heaviest load had had most gear work and therefore was the hottest.

It is interesting to note that when running with two trailers *(see Plate 239)*, it was necessary to drop out of top gear for about a minute, at the top of the long bank at Princes Risborough. Following this, the two axle boxes showed a drop in temperature, while the gearbox showed a rise, which was to be expected.

Radiator temperatures followed the temperature gradient profile fairly closely, and engine oil temperatures remained reasonably constant.

After these tests, the A.E.C. Company released, in March 1937, (just before No. 18 went into GWR service) a review of the vehicle in their internal staff Gazette, and this article is reproduced in full. The heading read:

## A.E.C.'s 18th "STREAMLINER" HAS IMPORTANT NEW FEATURES

### Principal Is Electro-Pneumatic Control For Trailer Work

### G.W.R. NOW OPERATES 72 PER CENT. OF BRITAIN'S DIESEL RAILCARS

Briefly referred to in last month's issue of this journal, the eighteenth A.E.C. oil-engined railcar to be ordered by the Great Western Railway, whose seventeen 'streamline' units have between them covered over one and a quarter million miles since the first single-engined car was placed in service in February, 1934 — and which, incidentally, has itself travelled over 170,000 miles — is now ready for duty.

Designed to haul a tail load comprising a trailer coach, horse-boxes or other vehicles amounting to about 60 tons, the new railcar differs in several respects from its forerunners, embodies a number of improvements, and incorporates certain features rendered necessary by the class of work in which it will be engaged. It has, for instance, standard drawgear, buffers, steam heating and vacuum brake pipes, and carries, in a specially large luggage compartment, an exhaust-heated boiler for heating the trailer coach.

In general principles of construction, the chassis remains the same as those used for previous cars and has two A.E.C. 130b.h.p. oil engines mounted on either side of the main frame, each driving through a fluid flywheel, a pre-selective epicyclic gearbox, and suitable variable reduction gear to a separate bogie; that on the right drives the leading bogie, that on the left, the trailing bogie.

But whereas in former cars the engines stood slightly above the frame, in the new design, the power units have been altered and the height reduced so that the floor is quite level. Also, the engines are now mounted opposite to one another at the centre of the chassis. The radiators remain as before, ahead of the engines, but they are now parallel with their centre lines and are cooled by large, slow speed fans, driven by belt and bevels.

The drive is similar in principle to that previously used, but the epicyclic gearbox now has five speeds instead of four, and the reverse gear is incorporated in the final drive.

The final drive itself, formerly by a centre worm and wheel mounted in both axleboxes, is now by double reduction gear. One reduction is by constant mesh helical gears carried in a casing at the rear of the main gearbox, and the second reduction is by spiral bevels in the inner driving axlebox of the bogie. Two pinions are used, either of which may be engaged to give opposite directions of motion. The outer axlebox is also bevel-driven, but needs no reverse gear.

To improve riding qualities, both the bogie wheelbases and centres have been increased, the former from 7ft. to 8ft. 6in., and the latter from 40ft. to 43ft. 6in., also longer side bearing springs have been fitted.

The probability that in the future the railcar may be coupled up to and driven from another similar railcar or trailer, has necessitated a change in the type of control gear. Formerly mechanical, this is now electro-pneumatic, except for the engine throttle which has to be brought into use before the engine can work up the required air pressure.

The reverse engine stop and clutch are operated by air cylinders, but the admission is controlled by electric pneumatic valves, wired up to switches or press buttons on the driver's control table; air is also admitted to the sanding valves by the same system.

The struts in the gearbox for pre-selecting the gears are pushed forward by a series of solenoids bearing directly on them, and carried as a unit in the side-cover of the box.

To save current, the return circuit from these solenoids passes through a pneumatic switch connected to the clutch-operating cylinder air inlet pipe and thus, although a gear may be pre-selected, no current passes to the solenoid until the clutch switch pedal is depressed; when the pedal is released the current is cut off.

The reverse switch has an interlocking cylinder connected to the brake train pipe and cannot be moved until the brakes are applied and the vacuum in this pipe is destroyed. This prevents the driver trying to reverse the car when running.

The reverse switch handle is loose and is taken by the driver to whichever end he is driving from. It cannot be withdrawn except in the neutral position, and when it is, it automatically engages neutral in the gearbox and isolates the pre-selecting and clutch switches.

Yet another safeguard is found in the mounting of a switch on each reversing axlebox. These are connected to the striking gear and are wired up in such a way that unless both axles are set for the same direction, the clutch in the gearbox cannot be engaged. This prevents the car being driven with the dogs not fully home.

A new feature of the driver's control table is the fitting of an engine revolution meter which, when the car is running in top gear, also acts as a speedometer. There are two pointers, each recording the speed of a separate engine. The advantage of this type of instrument — apart from its instant record of lag on the part of either engine — is that with a clearly marked scale, the engine driver can see exactly when to change gear. The pointers by dropping to zero also give warning of any excessive heating.

For trailer heating, the boiler installation in the luggage compartment consists of a Clarkson thimble tube-type boiler and an economiser, both heated by the engine exhaust. The feed is automatically controlled by a switch gear connected with an electrically driven feed pump. Water tanks are carried beneath the floor.

*Plate 137:* A good view of railcar No.18 pulling an auto-trailer to increase seating capacity. The photograph nicely emphasises the vehicle's livery.
*(A.E.C. Ltd.) Leyland Vehicles Ltd.*

An improvement has been made in the ventilation of the passenger compartment by the fixing of an air scoop across the full width of the roof. Inside it are a number of pipes, passing through the roof, but projecting out of it in order to prevent the ingress of rain. If any should enter the tube, it is caught in a galvanised tank from which it drains into the gutter.

The scoop is connected to a series of adjustable hinged ventilators, fitted to the top of the panel dividing the driver's and passengers' compartments. By means of the two sets of ventilators — one at the front and the other at the rear of the passenger compartment — air is drawn in at the front, and extracted at the rear, giving a continuous current just beneath the ceiling.

With the extra weight caused by the fitting of standard drawgear and buffers, the use of a stiffer frame, and carrying of steam heating boilers, auxiliary water tank and other equipment, railcar No. 18 is heavier than its predecessors. In running order it has a total weight of 33 tons 12 cwt. Apart from the alterations connected with the bogie centres and wheelbases, the other principal chassis dimensions remain the same, i.e.:

| | |
|---|---|
| Length over headstocks | 62ft. 0in. |
| Length over buffers | 65ft. 8in. |
| Frame width | 3ft. 2in. |
| Frame height above rail | 3ft. 11in. |
| Overall width | 8ft. 0in. |
| Wheel diameter | 3ft. 1in. |

The interior decorations and fittings of the new car which, as mentioned previously, seats 49 passengers, follow the same luxury lines that characterise the others in service. Woodwork is of polished light oak, walls and ceiling are covered in cream shaded rexine, and the seats are upholstered in an attractive green and brown ribbed moquette. Rectangular light fittings are mounted down the centre of the ceiling and between the windows. The windows themselves are wide and deep, and with a glass fitted partition between the driver's cab and the passenger compartment, an unusual degree of visibility is obtained.

The exterior of No. 18 differs a little from that of earlier types by the dropping of the valances, except over the immediate area of the engines, and by the necessary adoption of standard drawgear, buffers, etc.

Tests have shown that the new car rides smoothly, both at low and high speeds, and with its high standard seating comfort, its attractive interior and excellent outlook, it should have a particular appeal for passengers. From the viewpoint of hauling trailer coaches *(Plate 137)* and other vehicles — which, of course, widens considerably its sphere of operation — its performance will be watched with keen interest in railway circles.

Whilst in actual service it will not be called upon to make fast runs, its ability to do so has been demonstrated by the fact that it has covered, at different periods by itself, 22½ miles at 67½ m.p.h., 39¾ miles at 61 m.p.h., 19¾ miles at 62½ m.p.h., and with one trailer coach, 35¼ miles at 55½ m.p.h., and 16 miles at 56½ m.p.h. to quote just a few of many examples.

# NO. 18 — A RADICAL DEPARTURE FROM THE ORIGINAL DESIGN

*Plate 138:* Loading up racehorses at Lambourn Station. The horse-box is attached to streamlined railcar No. 18.
*Great Western Railway Magazine*

*Plate 139:* Interested staff and passengers watch the loading of seven horse-vans at the horse landing on a trial run from Lambourn Station in 1937. If all seven vans were hauled, then this would have exceeded the maximum allowance.

*(A.E.C. Ltd.) Leyland Vehicles Ltd.*

Once in GWR service, No. 18 became known as the 'Lambourn Valley Car' as it was set to work on that branch, near Newbury, in May 1937, almost immediately after officially joining the GWR fleet. This branch was 12½ miles in length with a ruling gradient of 1 in 60. As this railcar was specially designed for this line, it is seen in *Plates 138 & 139* loading the horse-boxes with racehorses from stables adjacent to the branch, its maximum permitted load being six vehicles. On market days, when there was an increase in passenger traffic, the horse-boxes were replaced by a trailer coach and even goods vans, and this railcar was reportedly the first vehicle to be employed on mixed traffic work. Also included in its rostered duties was the first run of the day from Reading to Basingstoke with the 'Royal Mail', after which it returned to Reading to carry the newspapers to Newbury and then on to Lambourn. Two days a week it hauled trailers, and on other days an occasional horse-box or two. Because of this haulage work, it was geared for a top speed of 47½m.p.h. to which ratio it was limited when running alone. It is obvious that with a dual-ratio gearbox, the majority of its working would be speeded up to a higher figure.

Two other runs made may also be taken as examples. On one, the 63½ miles from Oxford to Paddington were covered in 65 minutes, including two stops, and over forty consecutive miles were run at 68½m.p.h. On another occasion, with a different gear ratio, the 44 miles from Southall to Newbury were run, start to stop, with two trailers weighing about 60 tons in 63 minutes.

With the new dual-ratio gearbox, it was possible to make these two runs consecutively without the driver leaving his seat (this must not be taken too literally, as the car could not very well stop at Paddington and immediately start for Southall). In other words, this arrangement was equivalent to fitting driving wheels of two different diameters to a locomotive, and having either set immediately available to suit traffic requirements.

The 'Royal Mail' duty was heralded in *The A.E.C. Gazette* with the following photographs and article:

# THE 'MAILCAR'
## Streamliner 18 Becomes A 'Down Postal'

The Royal Mail is now being carried, for the first time in Britain, by a streamlined railcar.

'No. 18', the latest addition to the GWR's fleet of A.E.C. diesel-engined cars, makes a special journey early each morning from Reading to Basingstoke with letters and parcels.

In 1938 a newspaper reported the following interesting story:

### FALSE ALARM!
*Or Two Horns With a Single Note*

There's a bit of an argument on at Lambourn, where A.E.C. diesel railcar No. 18 is working the branch line traffic. And it's all because one evening, recently, the railcar driver's sleeve accidentally touched the electric horn button.

The amazing result of this was that the Lambourn Fire Brigade — or at least most of it — turned out with its engine and full fire fighting paraphernalia.

'Where's the fire?' demanded the men of the Brigade, on arrival at the Police Station.

'Fire?' queried the sergeant, 'I've never sounded the alarm for no fire'.

So in due course the Captain went along to the Station Master of Lambourn (GWR). Then the argument started.

'You can't do that kind of thing', said the Captain. 'Why the next time your driver presses his horn button accidentally the Brigade will turn out again'.

'It's a bit difficult, I admit', replied the Station Master, 'because one day there might be a real fire, and your men might think the alarm was only that . . . . . . railcar again, and take no notice at all'.

'I had my horn first', said the Captain.

'Well, I don't see how the railcar horn can be altered', said the Station Master. 'There's been a lot of experimenting before that particular note was decided upon'.

'Something's got to be done about it', added the Captain, very heatedly.

'Well, what can I do?' asked the Station Master.

And so the argument continues.

Meanwhile, Lambourn laughs and laughs and laughs.

The driver of the Lambourn railcar reported that on 22nd June 1939, 'the sand injectors had failed to operate in the wet conditions'. Almost immediately Mr Cleaver, design engineer for A.E.C. ordered the A.E.C. maintenance staff at Reading Shed to alter the outlet pipes to allow better sand flow. A test trip was carried out on the branch on 4th July 1939 with A.E.C. and Westinghouse Brake personnel on board. All the sanders operated well at Newbury with an air pressure of 50p.s.i. On arrival at Lambourn, the left-hand leading sander did not function, although all air pressures were satisfactory, necessitating prolonged braking, and the railcar sliding towards the buffer stops. It was found that the sand was 'too fine' and causing the injector to 'pack', and samples were taken for analysis at Swindon and at A.E.C. On 10th July, new pattern nozzles were fitted to No. 18, two each off different patterns; one short straight pipe and the others long and bent. The sand boxes were also thoroughly cleaned out and were found to contain

*Plate 140:* Diesel railcar No. 18 seen at Cowbridge, on arrival from Llantrisant. Railcar No. 18 (although originally withdrawn with all the other railcars) soon resumed its duties within months of the commencement of World War II.
*R. C. Riley*

paper and other wastes, plus a dead mouse! On 12th July the operation with the new nozzles was quite satisfactory but the short straight type was definitely better than the bent type. This shows clearly how even small problems were dealt with on these early railcars, and the report ends that the railcar would run with the two different types, with the driver being required to comment on the operation of both.

Also in the year 1939, a reporter recorded his impressions of one of the first 18 railcars again in *The A.E.C. Gazette* and it is here reproduced to summarise the achievement in those few short years of diesel railcar development.

For several years past, travellers who make use of the Great Western Railway have noticed the smartly streamlined railcars operating on cross-country services, without realising the enormous importance of modern railcars in supplementing the work of main line rolling stock, and helping to maintain our national railway facilities at maximum efficiency.

All the railcars operating on the Great Western Railway system have been designed and constructed as the result of close co-operation between The Associated Equipment Co. Ltd., the Gloucester Wagon & Carriage Co. Ltd., and the GWR Chief Mechanical Engineer, Mr C. B. Collett, OBE, and his assistants. Eighteen A.E.C. railcars are at present in service. In view of the above facts, therefore, I obtained permission recently to glean first-hand information for publication in *The A.E.C. Gazette*.

On my arrival at the works I was met by a member of the railcar design and development staff who conducted me, first of all, to that part of the factory where the railcar chassis are erected. Four railway tracks, having direct access to the GWR Brentford-Southall branch line, run into the railcar shop, which is also provided with pits and the usual equipment in the way of overhead gear for handling heavy units during chassis assembly operations. It will be realised, therefore that when the A.E.C. railcars are completed they can proceed direct from the factory to Southall Station, and thence by main line to any part of the GWR system for duty as required.

I suppose most people familiar with the technicalities of heavy automobiles would feel somewhat bewildered by the apparent complications of the modern railcar chassis. It must be confessed that I was until the purpose of each part of the mechanism was demonstrated to me in the most practical manner possible.

Having heard that a railcar was available at Southall Station, I tramped along the permanent way to board it, the idea of the proposed demonstration being to show how it worked and to convey a clear conception of the general design and construction.

Taking the seat normally occupied by the pilot or guard, I sat alongside the driver to watch events as we started on the run to Brentford which, although only a distance of 4¼ miles, was a most interesting journey, becoming even more interesting on the return trip.

From the streamlined cab, one has a perfectly uninterrupted view of the permanent way ahead, and it is therefore quite easy to pick out the signals in plenty of time to take the appropriate action.

In accordance with standard railway practice, the A.E.C. railcars are equipped with automatic signalling apparatus which, operated by means of ramps between the rails, brings the brakes into action when signals are against the vehicle. One thing that impressed me very forcibly in connection with the A.E.C. railcar cab layout was the relatively few controls needed, and the clever way those controls are grouped for easy manipulation.

From his comfortable bucket seat, the driver can handle the car with much less physical effort than that needed to control a road vehicle, mainly because the engine, transmission and brake mechanism respond to electro-pneumatic control, thus practically eliminating all physical effort on the part of the man in charge. He is also relieved, of course of any need for steering.

By the time we reached Brentford on the outward journey, the purpose of the various controls had been explained quite clearly and, to prove how easily the railcar could be operated, I was invited to take charge of the controls for the return journey to Southall.

'Shut off everything' came the initial order from the official in charge of the demonstration and, thereupon, sitting in front of the control panel with a clear line ahead, I was expected to carry on.

Actually, the task was far less complicated than I had anticipated for, in effect, the railcar chassis bears a strong family resemblance to A.E.C. road vehicles, being equipped with standard units such as oil-engines, fluid flywheels and Wilson gearboxes, all of which, adapted for railcar work, have simplified the constructors' problems and raised this form of railway rolling stock to a level of efficiency that exceeded most people's expectations.

When about to set the railcar in motion, the first thing one does is to press the two small buttons on the panel, which action causes the two engines to start and continue running at the governed idling speed.

As all railcars must be capable of being driven from either end, one has to be sure of putting the 'forward' and 'reverse' control lever in the proper position to set the direction of travel. Omission of this golden rule would produce serious complications at a terminus.

Selection of the required gear in the Wilson gearbox is also effected by means of electro-pneumatic control, operated from a miniature gate on the panel.

Having selected first gear, one simply depresses the bar-type accelerator and the railcar glides smoothly along the track, gathering speed as the accelerator is depressed more fully. The engine cannot be heard at all from within the cab, so a revolution counter, mounted on the control panel, is used to show the driver when to change from one speed to another. I found that with little practice, changes up and down could be effected without causing the slightest jerk on the transmission. As in the case of road vehicles embodying the fluid flywheel and the Wilson epicyclic gearbox, the act of changing consists merely of preselecting the required gear ratio, releasing the accelerator and allowing the bands to operate in the normal manner. Transmission of the A.E.C. railcars is exactly the same as on a bus fitted with fluid tranmission, i.e. the gear is preselected and then engaged by depressing and raising the bus-bar. On A.E.C. railcars this is done electro-pneumatically (button-operated). At the driver's right hand is a lever which controls the automatically-operated vacuum brakes, while a multiple stroke handbrake lever actuates the brakes used to hold the railcar stationary at stopping places.

Other items of the control system calling for the driver's attention are the electro-pneumatic sander and the gauges indicating the amount of vacuum, and pressure existing in the brake system and pneumatic control arrangements respectively.

My first experience of railcar driving passed off without any untoward incident, my earlier attempt on the trolley bus test track having made me very respectful of vehicles strange to my experience and handling. Anyone accustomed to handling a bus or coach with similar transmission can become an efficient railcar driver after very little tuition. At present, the job of driving a car might perhaps seem a little strange to a steam locomotive man, for I think with regard to controls, the railcar favours the bus cab more than the locomotive footplate. On putting this view forward on the occasion of my visit to Southall, I was shown certain modifications in control arrangements which are to conform as far as possible with established methods of locomotive control as applied to railcar development.

So the first phase of the diesel railcar development on the Great Western Railway was now complete, but one of the difficulties that had arisen was the staffing of these 'different' vehicles.

With 18 railcars in service, it was interesting to see how the Company tackled the problem of training drivers in handling the new 'streamlined stock' especially with new orders about to be placed for more vehicles, and thus more drivers needed.

The first problem was that of recruitment. The trainees were men who were already main line drivers and knew the various

**RAILCARS**
maintain
branch
services
profitably
by reason
of their
sheer
**ECONOMY**

WRITE FOR DETAILS

THE
ASSOCIATED EQUIPMENT
CO. LTD.
SOUTHALL   MIDDLESEX

roads upon which they would be operating, or if they knew only a proportion of the appropriate roads, could soon acquire familiarity with the remaining sections. Among the attractions of streamline train driving was the cleanliness and comfort of the work.

The training was not a lengthy business, because it amounted to instruction in the handling of the vehicles themselves, and acquiring a knowledge of safety regulations applicable only to diesel-engined vehicles.

As regards handling the cars, the first step was for the trainee to accompany one of the existing drivers on his daily runs for two or three weeks, to become familiar with the routine methods, principally on account of the differences between steam and internal-combustion engine working. He had to learn the essential variations in braking practice (without a large tail load) and, if necessary, to become acquainted with any portion of a route not previously covered by him in regular working.

During this period, the first two or three days were spent merely as an observer; the learner then taking over the controls under the guidance of the more experienced man. In addition to learning the actual driving system, it was necessary for him to understand what had to be done when he started the normal shift, in the way of checking car conditions and reporting at the end of his shift. A mechanical inspector or foreman gave instructions on those items of trouble diagnosis and cure which came within the province of a driver, as distinct from the running shed staff. For example, if one engine of the two should fail, the driver had to know whether the matter could be put right by means of a spare water connection or spare fuel injection pump carried on the car, or whether the engine should be regarded as 'dead'. In the last-named case, he would have to disconnect it from the transmission sysstem so that the car could continue its journey on the remaining engine.

The driving training generally occupied a period of two or three weeks. When the learner driver was satisfied with his own progress, he applied for a test.

The test covered all aspects of driving, such as engine starting, gear changing, braking, and the careful observance of safety regulations, both general and particular. The examination also dealt with diagnosis and mechanical emergency work. It was important that the driver should not regard an engine as 'dead' because it had stopped for a minor cause, which could easily be rectified by the exercise of a little knowledge. He must also know how to get the car home with the least possible dislocation of normal service, because there was not only his train to think about, but many others, the schedules of which were interdependent.

Special attention was given to familiarity with the Company's safety regulations for the operation of diesel rolling stock on single line sections. The guard had to signal to his driver when the latter was manoeuvring an empty car, for example, in stations. When there were any passengers aboard, the driver had to change ends before reversing the direction of travel, so that the guard's signalling assistance was not then necessary.

Railcar guards had to satisfy the inspector that they knew what steps must be taken in the event of signal checks, and the respective emergency responsibility for action on the part of both driver and guard.

In July 1939, there were nearly 100 trained men for handling railcars on the GWR. These vehicles were based at Southall, Reading, Oxford, Tyseley (Birmingham), Bristol, Weymouth, Cardiff, Pontypool Road and Landore (Swansea).

The provision of some four men per car was necessary, owing to the number of shifts worked (several of the cars operated for the major portion of each 24 hours), and to allow for sickness, holidays and other causes of absence from duty, there was always available a spare man at any base who could take over at very short notice.

All the foregoing remarks related to the practice of the GWR which at that time was the largest British operator of railcars. In other countries, working conditions and training routine were often quite different. In cases where whole sections of line were worked exclusively by diesel cars, and schedule speeds were practically the same (as opposed to sandwiching local cars between expresses), the signalling procedure was so simplified as to call for little special education.

In such circumstances, young men with internal combustion engine experience could learn to handle their vehicles in a short space of time, and they had no steam experience to 'unlearn'. Such drivers usually handled only diesel stock, whereas the men to whom reference has been made previously had to drive steam or diesel-engined vehicles.

# Chapter Eight:	Swindon-Built — Nos. 19 to 34
## — The New Design

With the headline reading *A Million miles a year. Three Year's Experience of widely differing Services Performed by the Eighteen GWR Railcars*, a leading technical journal reviewed the progres of the Great Western vehicles. It went on to say that no British company had a greater experience of railcar operation than the Great Western Railway. Excluding the most recent unit (No. 18), the mileage covered from February 1934 to 29th May 1937 was 1,671,045, whilst the fleet in service exceeded 21,000 miles per week. In fact, during 1938, the total reached 1,076,000 miles, which was an increase of 97,000 miles on 1937.

A table was also included to show how the 18 cars were utilised in their daily routine in 1937, and is an update of the table shown in *Chapter Six*.

| Car Located at: | Daily miles | Net time mins. | Start-to-stop speed m.p.h. | No. of stops | Av. distance between stops, miles |
|---|---|---|---|---|---|
| Southall | 238 | 408 | 35.0 | 69 | 3.45 |
| Oxford | 307½ | 475 | 38.8 | 54 | 5.70 |
| Oxford | 243½ | 427½ | 34.2 | 75 | 3.25 |
| Bristol | 355½ | 489½ | 43.5 | 34 | 10.46 |
| Weymouth | 282½ | 378½ | 44.8 | 29 | 9.74 |
| Bristol | 342 | 488 | 42.0 | 28 | 12.20 |
| Pontypool | 240½ | 489½ | 29.5 | 135 | 1.78 |
| Worcester | 250 | 457 | 32.8 | 102 | 2.45 |
| Worcester | 264¾ | 470½ | 33.6 | 101 | 2.61 |
| Birmingham | 305½ | 407½ | 44.9 | 26 | 11.75 |
| Cardiff | 285½ | 356 | 48.1 | 14 | 20.39 |
| Swansea | 229 | 465 | 29.5 | 52 | 4.40 |
| Reading (trailer) | 214 | 545 | 23.3 | 96 | 2.22 |
| Parcels car | 222 | 433½ | 30.7 | 59 | 3.76 |

With A.E.C. maintaining these railcars at Southall, the vehicles were called in every 25,000 miles to give them an inspection and top overhaul. At 100,000 miles or more they were then recalled and given a thorough overhaul including possibly a body lift, if needed.

The article continued by saying that with any new vehicles, like these, breaking new ground, all concerned had to learn by experience. A feature of the working of the fleet in question was the way in which improvements had been, and were being, embodied in existing machines as they came in for overhaul. For instance, cast-iron crankcases had been found better than those of aluminium, whilst later-type bogies had given better results than the first pattern, so that these features were being standardised throughout the railcar fleet.

The article concluded with the following paragraph:

Throughout the three years' working, a truly refreshing candour had been apparent with regard to inevitable difficulties; the result was that everybody concerned could honestly say that useful lessons had been learned.

The chairman of the Great Western Railway, at the annual meeting in February 1938, stated that:

The new diesel car (No. 18) with a trailer for passenger traffic, which we introduced, experimentally, had proved a success and had enabled appreciable working economies to be effected. We now have altogether 18 of these cars which run nearly 1,000,000 miles per annum, and while the original intention was to use them to provide additional services where the traffic was insufficient to justify the working of a train, our experience shows that owing to the increasing cost of operating steam locomotives, considerable economies can be effected by replacing them with diesel cars on certain sections of the lines. We are, therefore, now negotiating for the purchase of 20 cars somewhat similar to those already in use.

So the question was then, 'Should not this success warrant the GWR proceeding to further experiments'? This experiment had shown that diesel traction could effect 'appreciable economies' and, in view of the rising cost of coal, which seemed likely to continue, it would certainly be worth while to experiment further, with three or four-car trains, to ascertain whether similar economies could not be made.

There were certain main line services on the Great Western Railway route which would lend themselves well to the employment of high speed diesel-engined cars, as well as uneconomic branch lines.

Based on their considerable experience, the GWR, in 1938, decided to increase its fleet of 18 diesel railcars by a further 20, but with the proviso that they constructed the underframes, bogies, brake-gear and also the bodywork. The design, although closely monitored by the GWR at Swindon, was to the A.E.C. specification, as was the power unit. Several points regarding the general specification presented by the GWR are worthy of mention. The design was requested to be similar to that of No. 18, in that the new cars should be capable of hauling additional vehicles, or carrying out light shunting. Controls were to be electro-pneumatic, so that two or more cars could be coupled together, as required, and run as a single train unit, being controlled by one driver only. The length of the new vehicles was to be 63ft. over headstocks. Four of the new cars would be built in pairs (with vestibule connections) to form twin-car sets capable of 70m.p.h. (dealt with in *Chapter Nine*) and would be used to replace the single unit railcars serving the Cardiff to Birmingham business services which were now too small to carry the traffic which the diesel service had developed.

The main batch of fifteen cars, Nos. 19-33, *(Plate 141)* was intended for branch line and local services, and were geared to give a maximum speed of about 40m.p.h., but also capable of hauling a load of 60 tons (equivalent to two standard coaches). The following routes were scheduled for the new cars: Banbury-Kingham; Kidderminster-Bridgnorth; Leamington, Stratford-upon-Avon and Honeybourne; Newport, Pontypool Road, Chepstow and Monmouth; Weymouth, Abbotsbury and Yeovil; Trowbridge, Devizes, Westbury and Chippenham; Frome, Castle Cary and Taunton; the Teign Valley line; Banbury; and Princes Risborough.

Two of the 15 branch line cars were, however, fitted with a dual-range gear, giving a maximum speed of about 40m.p.h. or 60m.p.h. when the cars were running alone or hauling light loads. All the cars had a seating capacity for 48 passengers, and larger luggage accommodation than was available on previous cars.

One car was intended solely for parcels traffic (No. 34) to supplement the existing parcels railcar, which had been running for two years in the London area.

All the new railcars were also to be fitted with the GWR Company's system of Automatic Train Control (ATC).

A.E.C. introduced the new order with the following article in their company journal of October 1938:

# G.W.R. TO DOUBLE ITS RAILCAR FLEET

## A.E.C. Receives Order For Further Twenty

### NEW TWIN UNITS FOR EXPRESS SERVICES

#### Railcar Fleet That Now Runs 1,000,000 Miles A Year

News that the Great Western Railway was going to increase its fleet of diesel engined railcars was confirmed, last month, when A.E.C. received a contract for the supply of 20 twin engined units to supplement the 18 cars already in service. This is the largest order ever placed by a British railway with any manufacturing company for the supply of railcars of this type.

It was in February of this year that Viscount Horne, chairman of

*Plate 141:* The new design; Swindon designed, Swindon built!

British Rail

## OCTOBER "A.E.C. GAZETTE"

**1934** Running 238 miles a day, veteran, single-engined A.E.C. "Railcar No. 1" began service in 1934. Here it is with a G.W.R. crack express on Maidenhead bridge.

the G.W.R., revealed to shareholders that, whilst the company's original intention had been to use diesel railcars for additional services where traffic was insufficient to justify the working of trains, experience had shown that, owing to the increasing cost of operating steam locomotives, considerable economies could be effected by replacing them with diesel cars on certain sections of the line.

Viscount Horne announced, on that occasion, that negotiations were then proceeding with the object of augmenting the existing fleet.

The signing of this new order, which has the effect of doubling the Great Western diesel railcar fleet, sets the seal of satisfactory service upon the first 18 A.E.C. "stream liners," which have now run some 3,000,000 miles.

An innovation is, that this time, the bogies, under-frames, brake gear and bodies, previously supplied by sub-contractors, will be constructed at the

**1934** Waiting to leave Birmingham for Cardiff, A.E.C. "Railcar No. 2" was, in 1934, Britain's first express diesel car with buffet and toilet facilities.

Great Western Railway's own works, at Swindon.

Not all the new cars will be alike. For the highly successful business men's service between Birmingham and Cardiff the G.W.R. intend to use two twin car sets provided with buffets and lavatories and having accommodation for 104 passengers.

Started experimentally in 1934,

this service—the first diesel car buffet express service in the country—has attracted such a steadily increasing volume of traffic that single cars are no longer adequate for requirements.

The new units will be geared for speed of 70 m.p.h. and will replace the original cars which have now run over half a million miles on this route.

Another experiment, the parcels car, introduced by the G.W.R. in 1936, has justified the introduction of a second similar car. The first car by handling traffic which would otherwise be carried by passenger trains has, in eliminating the delays caused by "smalls," materially assisted in maintaining punctuality.

**1935** The first diesel-railcar to be privately booked in this country was used, in 1935, by football supporters travelling between Birmingham and Cardiff. It is here seen leaving Chepstow bridge.

**1934** On board No. 2. In 1934, for the first time in this country, passengers could obtain refreshments while travelling in diesel-engined railcars.

As the new car, geared to run at 40 m.p.h., is designed for trailer haulage, its load capacity will be more than doubled.

The remaining 15 cars will be built on lines generally similar to car No.

OCTOBER "A.E.C. GAZETTE"

will thus be able to employ whichever gear is the more suitable for the loads hauled and the gradients traversed.

Certain modifications, to give 3 ft. of additional length, will be made to the bodies of the new fleet; but they will not be greatly dissimilar from the body of car No. 18, the last to be placed in service.

A number of technical improvements will, however, be embodied in the chassis, of which the principal is the latest design of A.E.C. oil engine which has among its features approximately 50 per cent. increase in the area of its main bearings and a new type of oil cooler which can be easily extracted for cleaning without the removal of the sump.

Gearboxes will have five speeds instead of four as hitherto and will embody a new form of electro-pneumatic pre-selection equipment. All controls will be of the electro pneumatic type and so arranged that two or more cars may be coupled together and driven by one man.

The fact that it will be made impossible for the master control handle to be removed until all other controls, including the pre-selector equipment itself, are locked in "neutral," will provide an added safeguard.

A feature of particular interest is the braking system which will be the employment of two exhausters which, by the use of automatic change-over valves, will act as either compressors or exhausters, thereby making one piece of equipment perform two distinct functions.

The brake gear itself will now conform to standard railway practice and include clasp brakes with two shoes to each wheel. This has been made possible by the necessity for providing an increased vacuum capacity to cover tail load working.

Excluding the twin car sets, allocated to the Birmingham—Gloucester—Cardiff route, the new cars will work between the following points, in several cases over stretches of line which already have regular railcar services.

Banbury—Kingham.
Kidderminster—Bridgnorth.
Leamington—Stratford-on-Avon—Honeybourne.
Newport—Pontypool Road—Chepstow—Monmouth.
Weymouth—Abbotsbury—Yeovil.
Trowbridge—Devizes—Westbury—Chippenham.
Frome—Castle Cary—Taunton.
Teign Valley line.
Banbury—Princes Risborough.

Now owning 70 per cent. of the diesel passenger railcars in this country, the G.W.R. has rightly earned a considerable reputation for its enterprise in inaugurating a new type of service which, as experience has proved can, in certain circumstances, be operated

**1936** An enormous expansion of railcar services had taken place by 1936, and this car—seen at Moreton-in-the-Marsh—opened new links in the Oxford, Worcester, Hereford districts.

18 which, since April, 1937, has been working in the Reading, Newbury and Lambourn Valley areas.

Intended for branch line and local services, these cars will, with two exceptions, be geared to give a maximum speed of about 40 m.p.h., and will be capable of hauling a tail load of 60 tons, equivalent to two standard 60 ft. coaches or five or six horseboxes. All will have larger luggage compartments than existing cars and a seating capacity for 48 passengers.

**The two cars referred to will be fitted with a special dual range gearbox giving an alternative speed of 60 m.p.h. when they are running alone or hauling light loads. On these cars the drivers**

**1936** An interesting experiment in railway working, this A.E.C., twin-engined unit, Britain's first diesel-parcels car—here seen loading at Paddington—was put into service in 1936 to reduce passenger train delays.

**1937** Following the parcels car there came, also in 1937, No. 18, the first car to draw a tail load, to be fitted with electro-pneumatic controls—and to carry Post Office mails.

more economically than one employing steam locomotives.

Indeed, the development of railcar travel on the G.W.R. during the four years which have elapsed since the first A.E.C. "streamliner" was placed in service on February 5th, 1934, between Southall and Reading, is one of the most interesting developments in recent railway history.

It is worth recalling that the first A.E.C. single-engined diesel car — at that time a unit of revolutionary design—reached, on its inaugural run, a maximum speed of 63 m.p.h. and carried in its first month of regular working no less than 12,000 passengers.

**Now the veteran of the fleet, A.E.C. Railcar No. 1, with its single 130 h.p. engine, is still in service, having travelled well over a quarter of a million miles.**

The inauguration of the semi-express service between Birmingham and Cardiff, in July, 1934, with double engined buffet cars, was an entirely new development of railway travel in this country; and its success is reflected by the new order for twin car sets to cope with the traffic which has been created entirely by this type of unit.

In July, 1934, three more cars were acquired for work in the Worcester, Hereford and Oxford areas. 19 new services were provided and the daily mileage of all units rose from 628 to 1,193.

A year later, A.E.C. railcars appeared for the first time in the Carmarthen, Llanelly, Bristol, Yeovil, Weymouth, Monmouth and Swindon districts. By that time the fleet had grown from one car running 1,500 miles per week, to 17 cars travelling over 20,000 miles per week. Streamlined railcars were operating in regular daily services over 770 of the G.W.R. 3,801 route miles, equivalent to 20 per cent. of the system.

In September, 1936, the railcars attained their first 1,000,000 miles of running.

Three months previously the G.W.R. had placed in service between London, Reading and Oxford, the first diesel parcels car in this country, a unit powered, as in the case of previous cars, by twin A.E.C. 130 h.p. engines.

Then, in February, 1937, came "Railcar 18," the first of the G.W.R. fleet designed to haul a tail load and to embody among a number of new and improved technical features, electropneumatic controls. This car, as previously related, is now working with conspicuous success over the 1 in 60 gradients of the Lambourn Valley branch and has been used as the basis of design for the new fleet of 20 units to be placed in service during 1939.

In February 1939, the GWR announced that the first of the 'new design' of the 20 railcars was nearing completion at Swindon Works. The chassis had been tested during December 1938 and January 1939 on the GWR's Southall-Brentford branch, and all the 'manufacturing difficulties' had been overcome. Since then, A.E.C. had been making steady deliveries of the chassis to Swindon, for the fitting of bodies, etc.

The general improvement in design over the preceding 18 cars was as follows:

Body shell angular rather than smooth streamlined.
Engines staggered and moved outwards towards the bogies instead of being mounted opposite to one another at the mid-length of the chassis.
Detail modifications to the side mounting and engine suspension.
New type of engine with improved oil-cooling arrangement.
Radiators carried behind engines, at mid-length of chassis, and fitted with intermediate header tanks for de-aeration.
Cooling by two fans per radiator.
Axleboxes redesigned with SKF roller bearings.
Two tread brake shoes to each wheel, in place of internal-expanding brakes.
Hydraulic shock absorbers of the piston type, instead of the previous disc pattern.
Electro-pneumatic controls with new design of preselector.
Self-contained control table.
Single-lever shunting controls at each side of the driving cabin.
Improved layout of control wiring.

The technical specification for these 20 vehicles was as follows, with a further detailed specification for the dual ratio vehicles, Nos. 19 and 20, drawn up by Swindon drawing office in January 1944.

**TECHNICAL DATA**

| | |
|---|---|
| Type (Wheel arrangement) | Two bogies each with two axles |
| Weight in Running Order | Nos. 19-33, 35 tons 13cwt. |
| | No. 34, 34 tons 18cwt. |
| | Nos. 35 & 37, 36 tons 14cwt. |
| | Nos. 36 & 38, 37 tons 12cwt. |
| Wheelbase (Overall) | 52ft. 0in. |
| Bogie | 8ft. 6in. |
| Wheel Diameter | 3ft. 2in. |
| Width Overall | 9ft. 3in. |
| Length Overall | 65ft. 8in. |
| Height Overall | 12ft. 2⅜in. |
| Minimum Curve Negotiable | 3½ chains |
| Fuel Tanks | 100 gallons |
| Lubricating Oil Sumps | 8 gallons per engine |
| Cooling Water Radiator & Engine | 36 gallons |
| Carriage Warming Boiler | Vapor Clarkson Steam Generator |
| Carriage Warming Boiler Fuel Tank | 50 gallons |
| Carriage Warming Boiler Water Tank | 100 galllons |
| Brakes, Vacuum | Standard GWR type brake blocks |
| Sanding | Compressed Air Operated |

**POWER EQUIPMENT**

| | |
|---|---|
| 6 cylinder Diesel Engines | A.E.C. Type 105h.p. at 1,650r.p.m. |
| | Single and double ratio cars |
| | 2 engines = 210h.p. |
| | Twin Cars, 4 engines = 420h.p. |
| Cylinder Bore and Stroke | 120mm. x 142mm. |
| Firing Order | 1.5.3.6.2.4. |
| Fuel Injector Nozzle Type | CAV multi-hole long stem 1500 |
| Fuel Injector Holder Type | B.K.B. L. 67.S 567 |
| Pressure at which fuel Injector nozzles should be set | 2,500lb. per sq. inch |
| Fuel Pumps | C.A.V. 38. P.E. 86B8C |
| | Q.320S626 |
| | 38 B.P.E. 6 B80 N.320S626 |

## AUXILIARIES

| | |
|---|---|
| Battery | Oldham Lead Acid 24 cells 224 Amp/hrs. |
| Lighting Circuit | 24 volts |
| Dynamo | Split Field Shunt Wound 8in. C.A.V. D8C40 |
| Starter Motors | C.A.V. Clockwise axial BS 624C2 |
| Compressors | Rotary Type Clayton Dewandre G. A. 6AC |
| Exhausters | Rotary Type Clayton Dewandre REGA 131 5½in. bore, 7¼in. long |

| | Gear | Twin Ratio Cars | Single Ratio Cars |
|---|---|---|---|
| | 1st | 15.2 | 26.9 |
| | 2nd | 10.7 | 19.0 |
| Overall | 3rd | 6.02 | 10.66 |
| Ratio | 4th | 3.9 | 6.92 |
| (To Unity) | 5th | 2.38 | 4.22 |
| Maximum | 1st | 11380 | 10060 |
| Tractive | 5th | 1840 | 1630 |
| Effort (lb.) | | | |
| Maximum | 1st | 11.8 | 6.7 |
| Speed | 2nd | 16.8 | 9.4 |
| m.p.h. | 3rd | 29.9 | 16.8 |
| | 4th | 46.1 | 26.0 |
| | 5th | 75.5 | 42.5 |

Drawing Office,
SWINDON.
3rd January, 1944.

### Diesel Cars Nos. 19 & 20 (Dual Ratio Cars).

*Specification*

| | |
|---|---|
| Engine Size | 6-cylinder 120mm. bore x 142mm stroke |
| Output/Max. r.p.m. | 105b.h.p. at 1,650r.p.m. |
| Number per unit | 2 |
| Total power of Car unit | 210h.p. |
| Gearbox: Type | 5 Speed Epicyclic |
| Ratios : 1st | 6.3.8 : 1 |
| Ratios : 2nd | 4.5 : 1 |
| Ratios : 3rd | 2.53 : 1 |
| Ratios : 4th | 1.64 : 1 |
| Ratios : 5th | Direct |
| Auxiliary Reduction | High 1.09 : 1    Low 1.63 : 1 |
| Reverse Gear | In axlebox |
| Final Drive : Type | Bevel Gear |
| Ratio | 2.59 : 1 |
| Wheel Diameter | 3ft. 2in. |

| *Overall Gear Ratios* | *High* | *Low Ratios* |
|---|---|---|
| 1st | 18.0 : 1 | 26.9 : 1 |
| 2nd | 12.69 : 1 | 19.0 : 1 |
| 3rd | 7.12 : 1 | 10.66 : 1 |
| 4th | 4.62 : 1 | 6.92 : 1 |
| 5th | 2.82 : 1 | 4.22 : 1 |

| *Maximum Speeds m.p.h.* | *High* | *Low* |
|---|---|---|
| 1st | 10.0 | 6.7 |
| 2nd | 14.1 | 9.4 |
| 3rd | 25.2 | 16.8 |
| 4th | 38.8 | 26.0 |
| 5th | 63.7 | 42.5 |

| *Maximum Tractive Effort (lbs.)* | *High* | *Low* |
|---|---|---|
| 1st gear | 6720 | 10060 |
| Top | 1090 | 1630 |

*Leading Dimensions:*

| | |
|---|---|
| Bogie Wheelbase | 8ft. 6in. |
| Bogie Centres | 43ft. 6in. |
| Length over Headstocks | 62ft. 0in. |
| Length over Buffers | 65ft. 8in. |
| Height of Frame above Rail | 3ft. 11in. |
| Width of Frame | 3ft. 2in. |
| Overall width of Frame | 8ft. 0in. |
| Width over Body | 8ft. 11in. |
| Width over Handles | 9ft. 3in. |
| Height over Roof | 12ft. 1in. |
| Total Height | 12ft. 2⅜in. |
| Minimum Turning Radius | 3½ chains |
| Fuel Capacity — gallons | 100 |
| Weight of Complete Car | 35tons 13cwt. |

### Diesel Cars Nos. 19 & 20 (Dual Ratio Cars)
**Acceleration**

| *Acceleration, Time & Distance* | *High Ratio* Min. Sec. Miles | *Low Ratio* Min. Sec. Miles |
|---|---|---|
| Car only 0 to 20 m.p.h. | – 26 .08 | – 28 .09 |
| 0 to 30 m.p.h. | – 54 .28 | – 55 .28 |
| 0 to 40 m.p.h. | 1 38 .7 | 1 32 .62 |
| 0 to 50 m.p.h. | 2 56 1.7 | – – – |
| 0 to 60 m.p.h. | 5 0 3.6 | – – – |
| Car and One Trailer (30 tons) | | |
| 0 to 20 m.p.h. | – – – | – 45 .16 |
| 0 to 30 m.p.h. | – – – | 1 42 .46 |
| 0 to 40 m.p.h. | – – – | 3 8 1.38 |
| Car and Two Trailers (60 tons) | | |
| 0 to 20 m.p.h. | – – – | 1 8 .24 |
| 0 to 30 m.p.h. | – – – | 2 50 .98 |
| 0 to 40 m.p.h. | – – – | 5 36 2.55 |

Drawing Office, SWINDON.    3rd January, 1944.

Dealing with the chassis first, this was of a similar design to No. 18, and can be seen in some detail in *Plates 142 to 147*.

The frames were made up of standard rolled-steel sections, riveted together, the main trussed members being of 12in. x 3.5in. x 4in. channelling, and were situated at the centre of the frame and took the buffing and drawgear, which were of the standard GWR pattern. The body sides were carried on cantilever brackets from the main members, as also were the engines, transmissions and ancillary equipment.

The two engines were of the A.E.C. 6-cylinder type, fitted with Ricardo heads, direct injection type, having a bore and stroke of 120mm. x 142mm., and giving an output of 105b.h.p. at 1,650r.p.m. This engine included the newly introduced oil cooling system.

In order to cool the oil, a gilled tube grille was fitted into the engine sump in such a position that all the oil that was splashed around the crankcase had to pass over and through this grille on its way to the oil pump. Water from the rear cylinder head was passed through an auxiliary radiator carried on the outer face of the main radiator, and was then drawn through the crankcase grid by a connection with the suction side of the main water pump. This auxiliary radiator was virtually one long continuous pipe, which insured a much greater reduction in temperature than was obtained from the 'parallel' tubes of the main radiator.

*Plate 142:* A view of the complete chassis for railcar No. 19, before delivery to Swindon Works. The new more complex control panel and boxes can be seen.

*(A.E.C. Ltd.) Leyland Vehicles Ltd.*

*Plate 143:* After delivery to Swindon, the official GWR photographer took this picture on 14th December 1939. The new painted chassis is standing in front of two 'Hall' class locomotives, Nos. 5933 and 4921, which are in for maintenance.

*British Rail*

The engine oil grid *(Figure 48)* was attached to one of the bottom inspection covers of the sump, and was easily withdrawn for cleaning if necessary.

The engines were mounted on the outside of the narrow chassis frames by cantilever arms and fixed below floor level to avoid taking up the valuable floor space. These were also staggered and placed ahead of the centre line of the railcar in relation to the bogie which they drove, to avoid a shaking movement that had occurred in previous designs when the engines were at the centre.

The transmission was on the same general principles as adopted for previous A.E.C. railcars, and comprised (down each side) a fluid flywheel, cardan shaft, Wilson epicyclic gearbox, cardan shaft, and bevel axle-and-reversing gears on the end of the inner axle, and a cardan shaft and bevel drive to the outer axle of the bogie.

The drive through the fluid flywheel (a Daimler type No. A.E.C. D150) to the gearbox, was taken by a propeller shaft. The relatively long distance between engine and gearbox was therefore occupied by the radiator, and by a fixed coutershaft which formed part of the transmission line between these two units. The radiator, although of conventional design, (i.e. cast top and bottom tanks with vertical tubes between) was mounted on the outside face of the car, parallel with, instead of at right angles to, its centre line.

As the engine cylinder head was almost in line with the radiator top tank, a header tank was employed to maintain the water level when on gradients. Water from the engine was pumped into this tank, and after passing through baffles (which released any suspended air) it flowed by gravity to the radiator. This tank could be placed in any convenient position, so that it was under a seat and did not encroach on floor space.

The countershaft was carried in self-aligning ball bearings mounted in brackets attached to the radiator support members, and was behind and parallel with the radiator. At each end were two fans of opposite helices which drew air through the radiator and expelled it endwise via a suitable air duct which shrouded the fans.

One end of this duct (which extended right across the rear face of the radiator, as well as one of the fans), can be seen in *Plate 145*, showing the chassis.

'Vee' pulleys for driving exhausters and air compressors were carried on the countershaft, which could be 'broken' for removing the inner belts by means of a splined flange joint.

One of the most important improvements made on A.E.C. railcars had been the introduction of free wheels, and by careful design it had been possible to incorporate the free wheel into a cardan shaft, interchangeable with that taking the drive from the fluid flywheel to the countershaft (and thence to the gearbox) — *see Figure 49*.

With the increasing demand for multi-unit trains, which included from two to four twin-engined power cars, it was

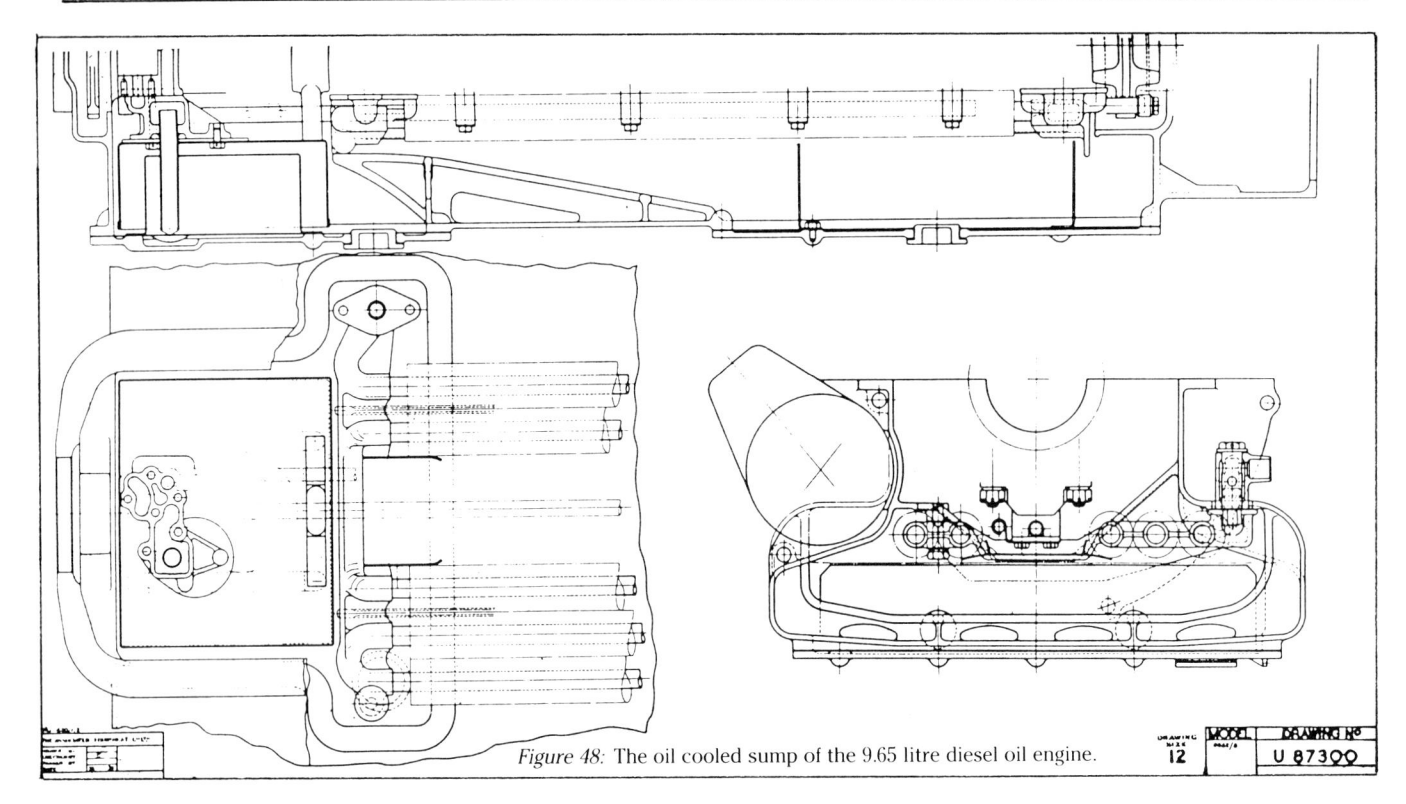

# THE HISTORY OF THE GREAT WESTERN A.E.C. DIESEL RAILCARS

*Figure 48:* The oil cooled sump of the 9.65 litre diesel oil engine.

Plate 144: The non-driving axle, together with the accompanying official Swindon drawing *(Figures 48A & 48B)*.
(A.E.C. Ltd.) Leyland Vehicles Ltd.

**Figure 48A**

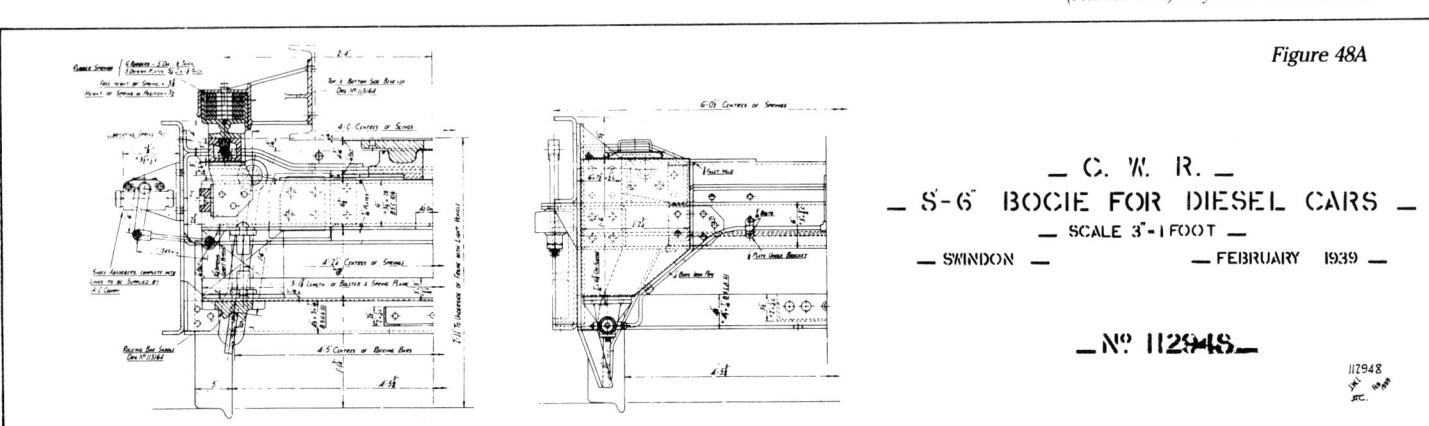

G. W. R.
8'-6" BOGIE FOR DIESEL CARS
SCALE 3"= 1 FOOT
SWINDON — FEBRUARY 1939
N° 112948

*Plate 145:* Fuel tanks, air reservoirs, engine, radiators, etc.

*(A.E.C. Ltd.) Leyland Vehicles Ltd.*

*Plate 146:* Gearbox, final drive and control boxes.

*(A.E.C. Ltd.) Leyland Vehicles Ltd.*

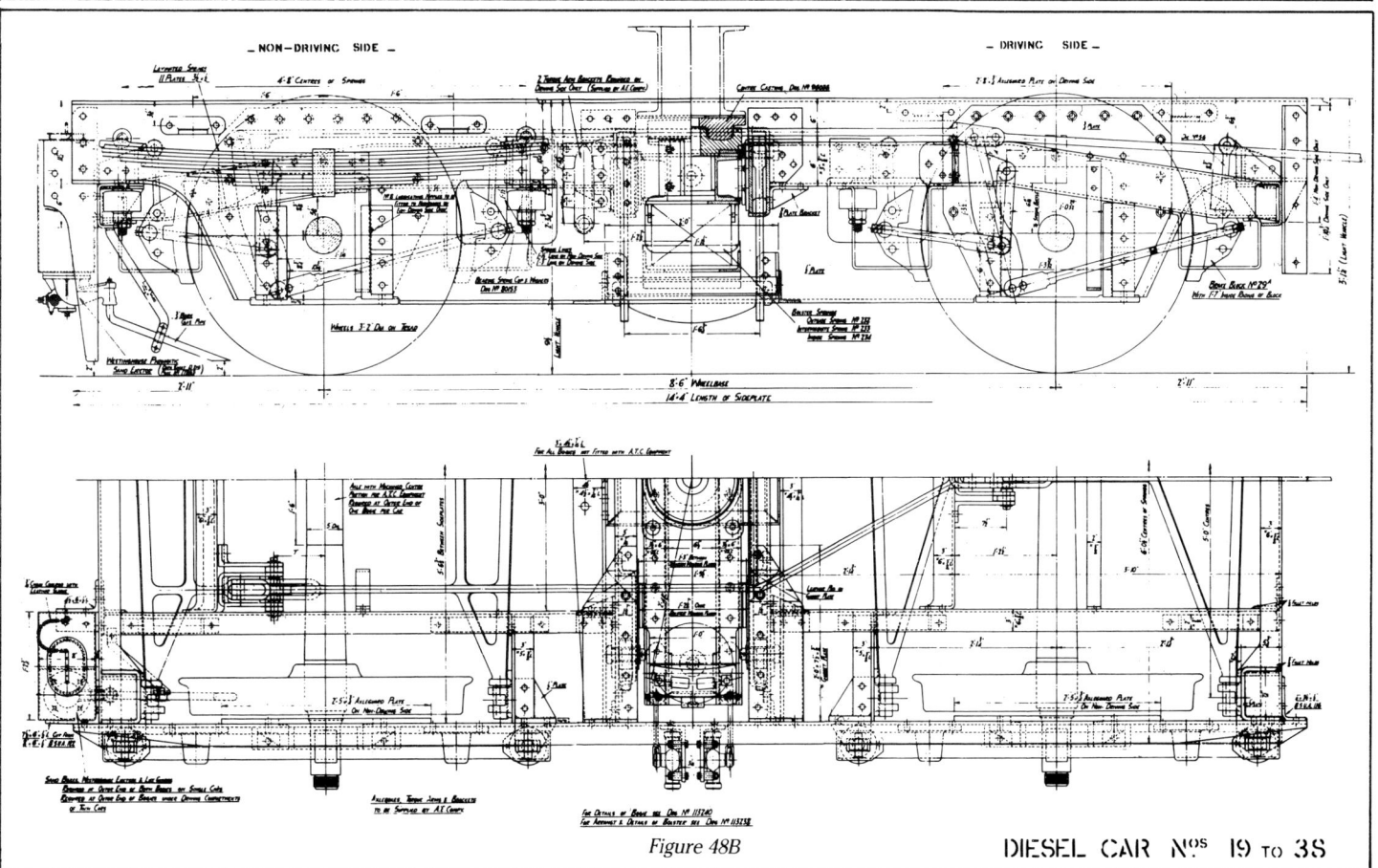

*Figure 48B*

DIESEL CAR Nos 19 TO 38

*Plate 147:* Powered bogie and control console.

(A.E.C. Ltd.) Leyland Vehicles Ltd.

*Figure 49*

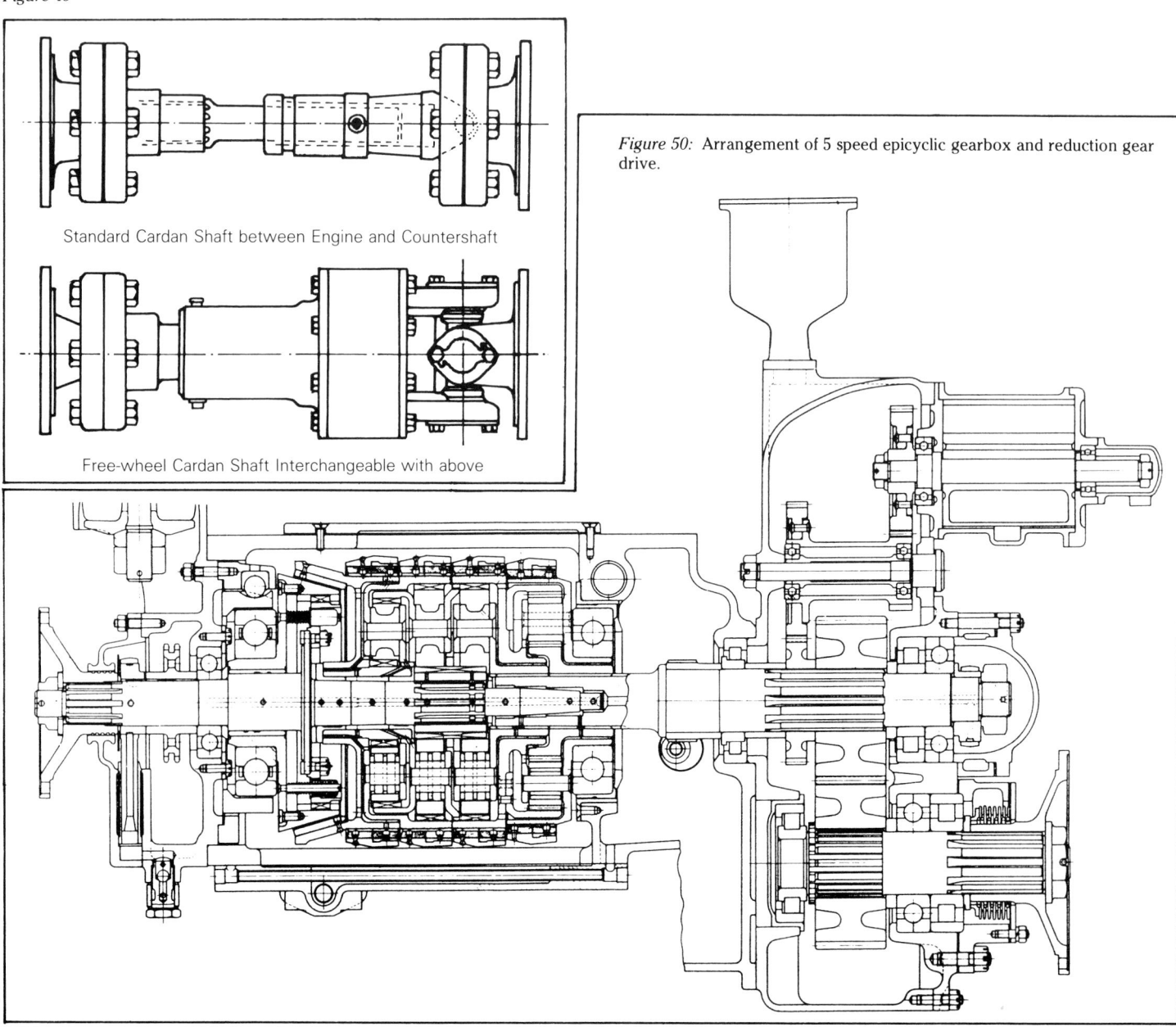

Standard Cardan Shaft between Engine and Countershaft

Free-wheel Cardan Shaft Interchangeable with above

*Figure 50:* Arrangement of 5 speed epicyclic gearbox and reduction gear drive.

realised that some safety device such as a free wheel was essential. In case of a partial piston seizure (and unfortunately such things did sometimes happen), the loss of power on a single engine car was easily noticeable by the driver, but with multi-engines it was difficult. In one case, the loss of power would be 50 per cent, but in the other only 25 per cent, and before the train could be stopped, the engines would 'motor' the faulty one to destruction.

On the test bed, it had been found that even on full throttle and at full power, a partially-seized engine would stall before serious damage was done. In practice, one particular engine lost all its water because of an obstruction on the line, but was saved by the free wheel, before anything serious happened.

Another very valuable feature was that the free wheel prevented an engine from being overdriven when the car was running downhill at excessive speed with gears engaged.

The gearbox on this series of railcars was basically of the same design as the previous units, being a five-speed, preselective, epicyclic No. A.E.C. U87067 gearbox *(see Figure 50)*, having ratios of 6.38, 4.5, 2.53, 1.64 and 1.0 to 1, and the axle-bevel ratios of 2.59 to 1. The auxiliary gear reductions were 0.919 to 1 for the twin-car express sets, and 1.63 to 1 for the single-unit cars; the dual-geared cars had auxiliary gear ratios of 1.09 to 1 (high) and 1.63 to 1 (low).

One of the basic problems in the control of the two gearbox selections was that both had to be simultaneous and also controllable from either driving end, plus the possibility of them being operated from a further coupled car. Therefore, a further improvement over No. 18's pneumatic device, was the introduction of the electro-pneumatic system.

This system had been adopted where the moving of gears or shafts used in the control sequence was needed. This was effected by cylinders and pistons using compressed air, and the admission or release of this air was by valves (electro-magnetically operated) and was designed to give definite movements for all the motive power equipments under the control of the driver for up to, say, eight engines and gearboxes.

Compressed air was supplied by two rotary compressors, one mounted on each engine, so that if it was necessary to cut out one engine, the supply of air was not lost completely. The air was stored at 80p.s.i. in two reservoirs, one of which contained a diverter consisting of a small inner reservoir which had to be filled to full pressure before it, in turn, fed the main ones. In this way a limited amount of air at full pressure was quickly available for initial movements of the car soon after the engines were started.

The chief control operations of the car were as follows:
1. Engine throttle regulation.
2. Gear pre-selection.
3. Gear engagement (bus-bar).
4. Forward and reverse engagement.
5. Gear-range control where dual-range gearboxes were fitted.

Generally speaking, air was supplied from the reservoir to a bank of magnetic valves, *(see Plate 148)* each of which controlled a separate operation, and from each valve, air was delivered to the necessary pair of cylinders. These were at varying distances apart, (i.e. the reverse cylinders were each approximately 22ft. from the valve) but although the driver's control tables were at the extreme ends of the car — about 60ft. from each other — no air connections were required, as the valves (placed about amidships) were electrically-

*Plate 148:* Electro-magnetic air valves in their control box alongside the radiator.

*(A.E.C. Ltd.) Leyland Vehicles Ltd.*

controlled and grouped in a very accessible place near the radiator, and enclosed in a casing, with a hinged drop-cover. The dual-ratio cars, Nos. 19 and 20, had eleven magnetic valves, and the other single cars had nine magnetic valves. Nothing more was needed, in fact, than a single delivery pipe to the pressure gauge and horns. For throttle operation and pre-selection, a patented air motor was used which is illustrated in *Figure 51*.

The motor, which consisted of three concentric cylinders, was bolted to the side of the gearbox, and air was admitted independently to the cylinders or in combination. The pistons butted against one another, and the outer one was held up against the cylinder cover by a return spring. An extension of the inner piston had grooves of tooth form, and these engaged with teeth on a quadrant fixed to the gearbox pre-selector shaft, so that when the piston moved inwards or outwards, it caused this shaft to turn. This construction had been adopted

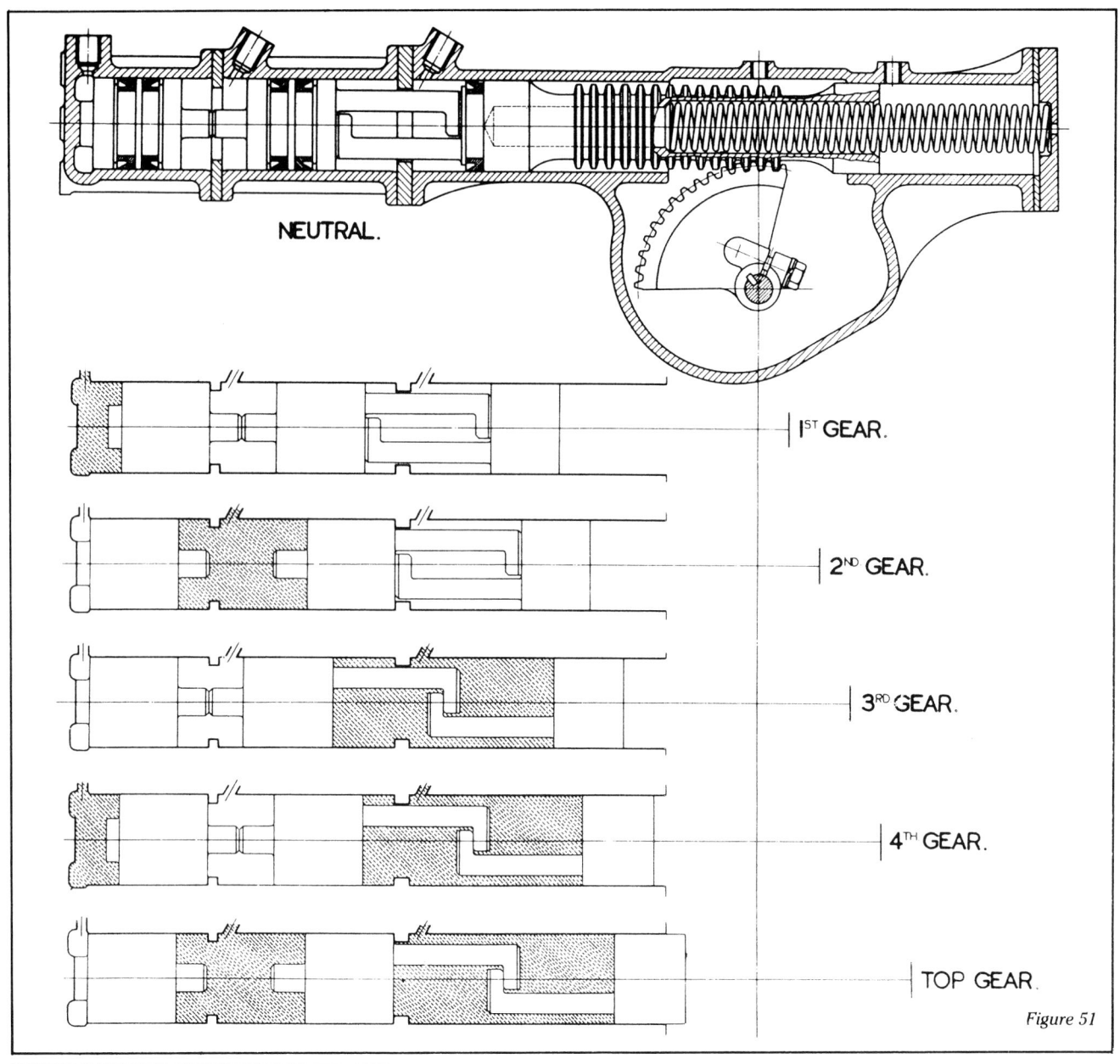

NEUTRAL.

1ST GEAR.

2ND GEAR.

3RD GEAR.

4TH GEAR.

TOP GEAR.

Figure 51

Figure 52

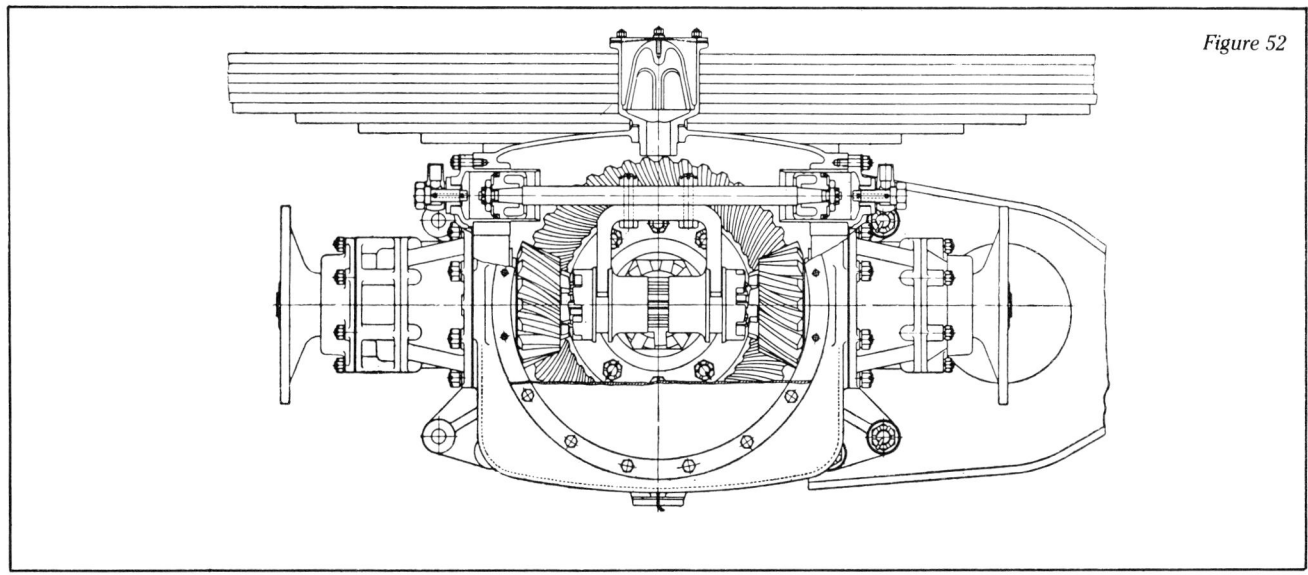

# SWINDON-BUILT — NOS. 19 TO 34 — THE NEW DESIGN

to give accurate angular movement. The travel of the two outer pistons was limited by annular stops, while that of the inner one was controlled by jaws formed integrally on it and on the middle piston.

If then, air was admitted to, say, the outer cylinder, that piston would move forward a distance equal to its travel, at the same time forcing the other pistons forward, and so causing rotation of the pre-selector shaft.

The piston travels were in the proportion of one, two and three, and gave three equal increments according to which cylinder was used. Two further increments were obtained by admitting air to either of the outer cylinders at the same time as air was retained between the centre and inner pistons. These five positions are best understood by studying the diagram in *Figure 51*, where the shaded sections indicated compressed air in the various cylinders.

The throttle motor was similar to that used for pre-selection, except that the throttle cross-shaft lever was connected to the inner piston by a link, and the grooved portion and the quadrant were eliminated.

The advantage of such a system was that it did not depend upon exact air pressure or upon calibrated springs, and so each movement was always exactly the same, irrespective of the value of the air pressure available, as long as it was up to the necessary minimum.

For the electrical bus-bar operation, a simple single-acting air cylinder was used, and was bolted to a facing, on the auxiliary casing.

*Figure 52* is a drawing of the driving axle box on the inner axle of each bogie, and shows how forward and reverse gears were obtained. A crown wheel *(see Plate 149)* was bolted to a flange on the axle itself and meshed with two pinions, carried freely in the casing on opposite sides of the crown wheel. The inner pinion, (i.e. that nearer the gearbox) was hollow, and the driving shaft passed through it and was spigotted into the outer pinion. It was splined at its centre *(see Figure 53)* and carried two 'dogs' which, by sliding, engaged with one or other of the pinions. In this way, either pinion could transmit the drive to the crown wheel, and as they rotated in the same direction, but were on opposite sides of the wheel, forward or reverse rotation could be given to the axle.

Movement of these 'dogs' was obtained pneumatically by means of two cylinders and pistons at opposite ends of the box. A common rod joined the two pistons and had on it a fork engaging with the 'dogs'. By admitting air to one cylinder, and releasing it from the other, the 'dogs' were moved endwise along the driving shaft, and so connected it to the pinion by which the drive was to be transmitted to the crown wheel and axle, thus giving forward or reverse travel.

It can be seen that the banjo pins of the air connections form stops to limit the movement of the pistons. An interesting feature was that when it was necessary (in emergencies) to disconnect one transmission line and run with that side of the car 'dead', these pins were taken out and replaced by longer dummy ones which, when screwed in, brought the 'dog' into mid-position, and locked it there.

Two cars, Nos. 19 and 20, were fitted with dual-range auxiliary boxes which provided alternative ratios, (i.e. single or dual). The former was generally adopted for high speed work-

*Plate 149:* The inner axle box with its cover removed, showing the crown wheel and pinions. Note the two dogs connected to the actuating push rod. The air pipe connections to each end of the reverse operating pistons can also be seen.

*(A.E.C. Ltd.) Leyland Vehicles Ltd.*

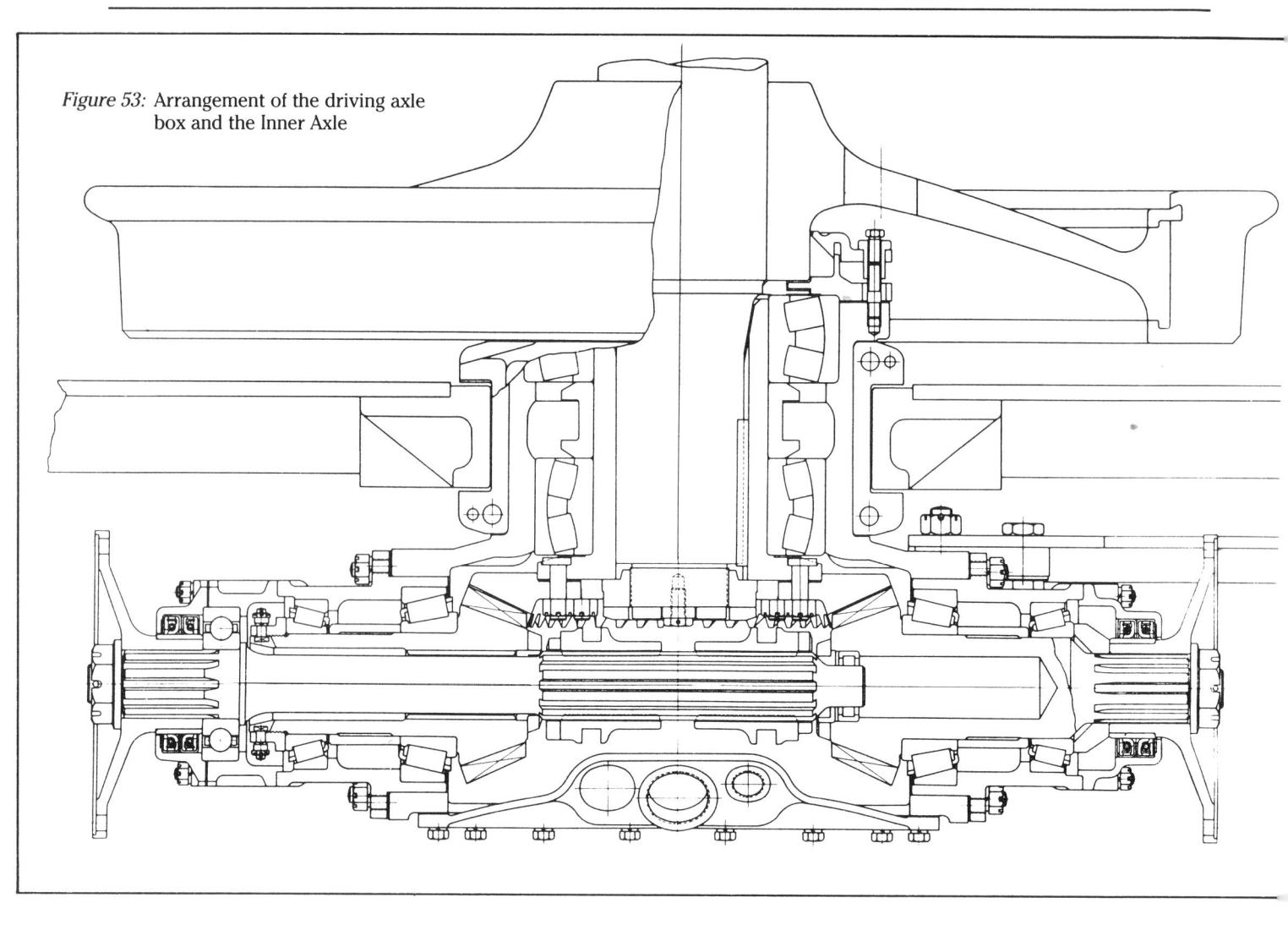

*Figure 53:* Arrangement of the driving axle box and the Inner Axle

ing with a light load, and the latter for mixed traffic purposes. In the latter case, the top speed and tractive effort could be varied to suit gradients and tail loads. In fact, it may be said that it is like having two alternative diameter driving wheels available on a locomotive. Both single and dual-ratio boxes comprised a driving shaft, which was an extension of the output shaft of the main gearbox, and a second shaft, geared to and parallel with it, from which the drive was taken to the axle. *Figure 54* is of the dual-range auxiliary box, in section.

The driven shaft was actually slightly below, and about 6½in. offset to the outside of the chassis, allowing it to line up with the final drive without encroaching on the loading gauge. Two gears, fixed on the driving shaft, meshed with the two mounted on roller bearings, on the driven one. This latter shaft was splined at its centre and carried a sliding 'dog', which engaged one or other of the gears and so transmitted the required drive. As can be seen, the movement of the 'dog' was controlled by two opposing air pistons mounted on a striking shaft to which a fork was attached.

On the rear of the driving shaft was an oscillating-type oil pump, similar to one at the front of the main box, which ensured adequate lubrication if the car coasted down a long gradient, in neutral, when the front pump would not be operating.

Finally the propeller shaft, coupling the dual or single box to the axle box, had a special double-ended shaft, which allowed for the full movement of the bogie.

The brakework for these railcars was now of the standard railway pattern, with the brake blocks of the two-tread type acting on the wheel tyres instead of on the internal brake drums used on the first 18 cars, and can be seen in the photographs depicting the complete bogie *(Plate 144).*

Compressed air was used for sanding, and *Plate 150* shows the arrangement of the sand box and feed pipe on railcar No. 19.

Although the riding of the first railcars was entirely satisfactory on the branch lines, it was found that side-sway was a very serious problem when running the cars at high speeds on the Birmingham-Cardiff services. A single railcar lacked the 'snubbing' effect of buffers rubbing against those of another car, and some equivalent had to be found. The early cars were withdrawn, and experiments were carried out with hydraulic shock absorbers exactly as used on buses. The results were so good that all the early railcars were fitted with two shock absorbers, mounted back to back on a bracket riveted to the solebars on both sides of both bogies, and were connected by links to the spring bolsters. In this way, the movement of the bolster was controlled but not limited *(see Plates 151 & 152).*

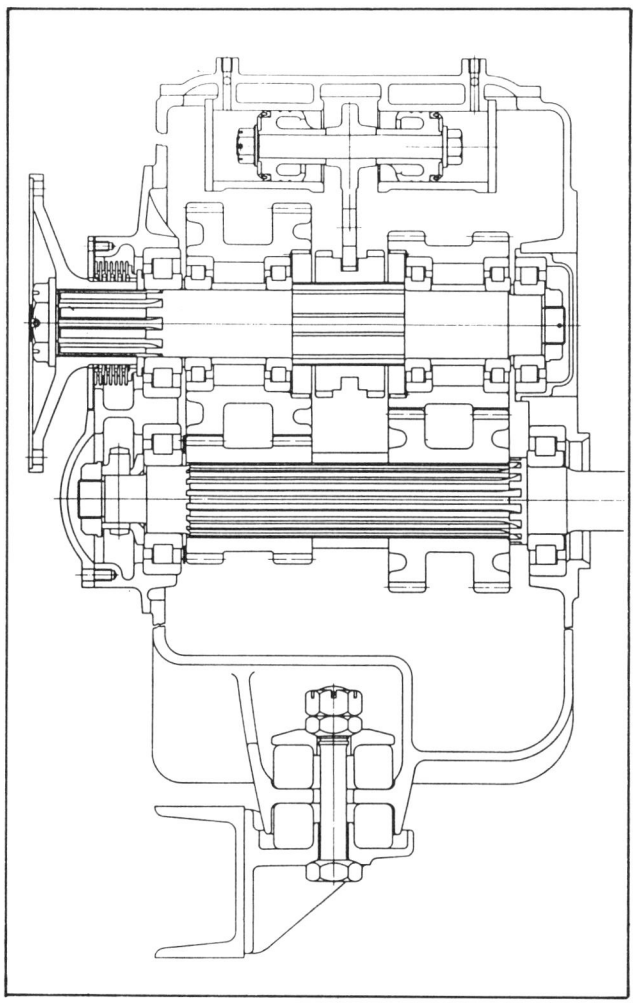

*Figure 54:* The dual-range gearbox.

*Plate 150:* The arrangement of the sand box and air pipe for railcar No. 19.

(A.E.C. Ltd.) *Leyland Vehicles Ltd.*

*Plate 151:* The rotary shock absorbers fitted to models before railcar No. 19.

(A.E.C. Ltd.) *Leyland Vehicles Ltd.*

*Plate 152:* The newer plunger-type shock absorbers fitted to vehicles from No. 19 onwards.

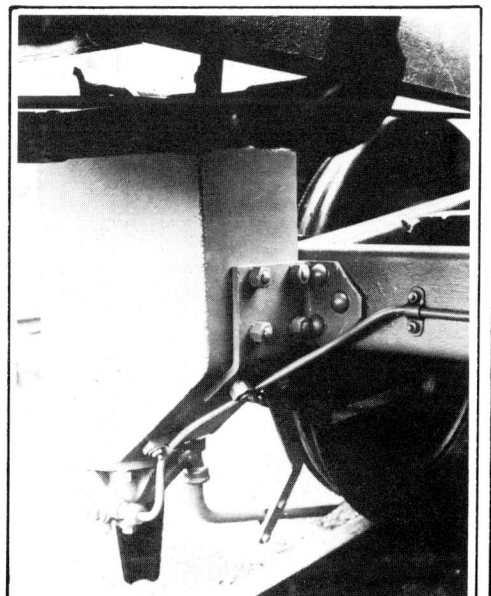

(A.E.C. Ltd.) *Leyland Vehicles Ltd.*

From railcar No. 19 onwards, the shock absorbers were changed to plunger-type rather than the valve-type previously fitted *(see Plate 152)*.

Automatic Train Control (ATC) apparatus, similar in action to that on Great Western steam locomotives, was also fitted, the ATC shoe being carried on the outer axle of one bogie of the single cars, and two outside axles of the later twin-sets.

Simplification of driver controls, easier operation, and increased protection against misuse of the controls were, in general terms, the main improvements in the new cars. All had been made possible by the adoption, (for twin-car working) of the electro-pneumatic operating system, first tried experimentally on railcar No. 18 and described in detail earlier in the chapter.

Whereas in former cars the pre-selector, reverse levers, and the clutch pedal occupied widely separated positions in the driving cab, these controls were now grouped together in one box, as shown in *Plates 153, 154 & 155*. As each lever was connected only to a series of electrical contacts *(see Figures 55 & 56)*, physical effort required for its movement was almost negligible. 'Finger tip control' had, in fact, become almost a reality. This was a big improvement upon the former method of driving, which called for a certain amount of manual effort.

The new safeguards not only ensured that the railcar could not be moved without first unlocking the controls, but also made certain that all the driving operations were performed in the correct sequence.

An additional locking device made it impossible for the driver to engage reverse gear before the clutch had been disengaged. This ensured that the reverse lever was not inadvertently used in mistake for the clutch lever, nor could the driver, when relinquishing the car or changing from the front to the rear driving cab, withdraw the master key until the pre-selector handle and the reverse lever had been placed in neutral, and the clutch lever operated to engage neutral (already pre-selected).

The method of driving was that the driver, having inserted the key which unlocked the controls, placed the reverse lever in the required position, pre-selected the gear for starting, de-clutched, and then operated the foot accelerator pedal. As momentum was gained, so each gear was pre-selected and, by de-clutching, brought into action.

In the earlier cars, the time for changing gear was, to some extent, left to the driver's judgement, although guidance was provided by a small speedometer and a list of speeds at which it was recommended that changes should be made. The new system was much more positive and had as an integral feature, a large centrally-placed speed indicator similar to that adopted for the first time in railcar No. 18 *(see Plate 154)*. In all gears up to top, when it became a speedometer (in the true sense of the term), this indicator acted as an engine revolution counter and was provided with clear and easily read instructions as to when gear changes should be made, both in and upward and downward directions. Two of its main advantages were that it prevented over-revving of the engines, and enabled maximum power to be obtained at all speeds and under all conditions. It provided, also, (by means of its two pointers) a constant indication of the behaviour of the twin engines and, when the car was at rest, showed if they were running or stopped.

With the introduction of 'free wheeling', it was realised that a driver could release the throttle and have no idea at all of the car speed. Consequently, as both engines must run at the same speed when driving the car, only one pointer was necessary to indicate the gear changing speed, and so the second

*Figure 55:* A section of the control box.

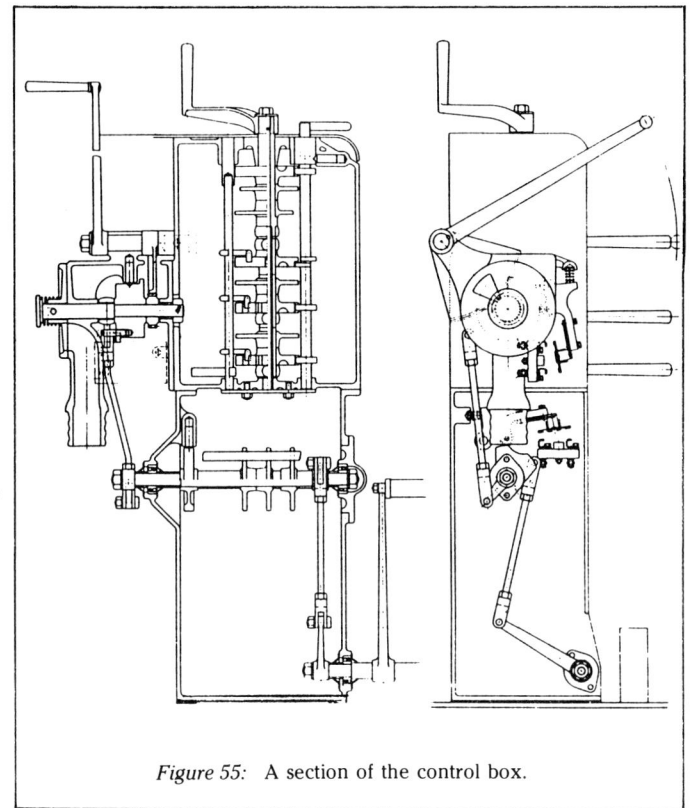

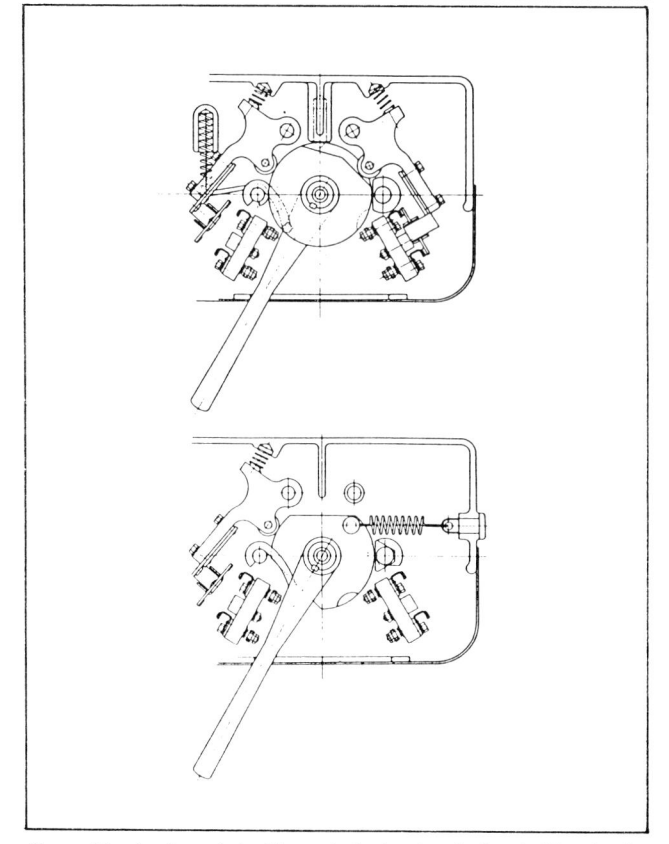

*Figure 56:* A plan of double and single electrical switching in the control box.

# SWINDON-BUILT — NOS. 19 TO 34 — THE NEW DESIGN

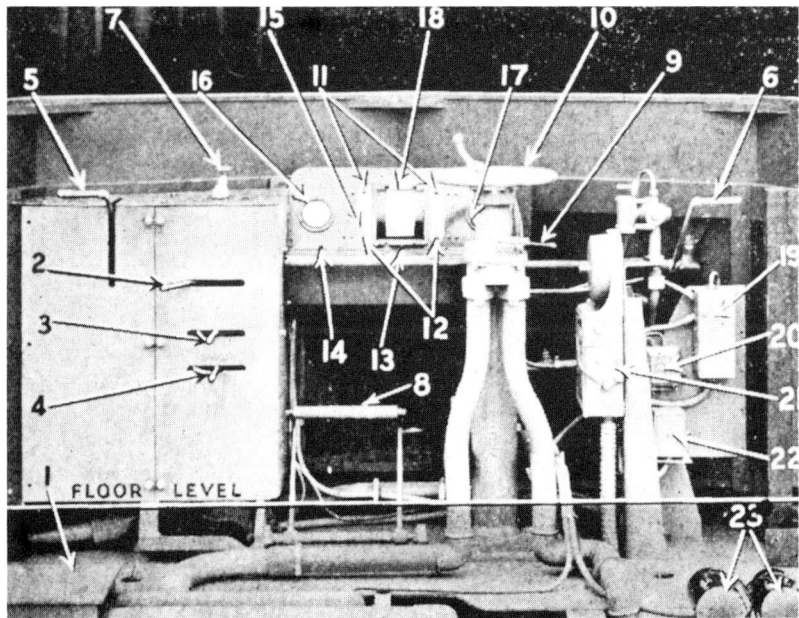

1. Junction box. 2. Clutch lever. 3. Forward and reverse lever. 4. High and low gear ratio lever (dual-range only). 5. Shunting lever, left hand. 6. Shunting lever, right hand. 7. Pre-selector lever. 8. Accelerator pedal. 9. Driver's vacuum brake valve. 10. Hand brake wheel. 11. Engine starter buttons for car. 12. Engine starter buttons for trailer. 13. Engine stop button. 14. Sanding button. 15. Horn switch lever. 16. Vacuum gauge. 17. Air pressure gauge. 18. Speedometer. 19. Sanding magnet valve (in case). 20. Switch and fuses (controls only). 21. A. T. C. Apparatus. 22. Air pressure switch—indicates on trailer by lamp. 23. Motor compressors for standby horns. Not shown—oil pressure indicator lamps for both engines of car and trailer—air pressure indicator lamp showing pressure on trailer is at predetermined minimum.

*Plate 153:* The full control table, with an explanation of all the controls.
*(A.E.C. Ltd.) Leyland Vehicles Ltd.*

*Plate 154:* The control box, with covers removed to show the electrical switchgear. Note the main speedometer/engine rev. counter.
*(A.E.C. Ltd.) Leyland Vehicles Ltd.*

*Plate 155:* A general view of the back of the control console of railcar No. 19.
*(A.E.C. Ltd.) Leyland Vehicles Ltd.*

pointer was connected to an axle-driven generator.

In order, however, that the driver was able to check the 'balance' of his two engines when starting up in the morning, a two-way switch was provided so that either engine generator could be connected to the instrument head.

One of the greatest advances made in the driving controls, of the new cars, several of which would include shunting among their normal duties, was the provision on either side of the cab, of hand throttle levers, which could be conveniently operated by the driver while leaning out of the cab windows *(see Figure 57 & Plates 156 & 157)*. Hand levers coupled to the accelerator pedal had been employed on all the cars since No. 1, but they were not made so easily accessible for a driver leaning from the cab until railcar No. 18 had been built, and this was the first time in which (in a single upwards and downwards movement) they had been capable of completely controlling the car.

Now a progressive upward movement of either handle performed the operations of engaging the gear already preselected and of opening the throttle, similarly, a downward movement closed the throttle, selecting neutral, disengaging the clutch, and applied the automatic vacuum brake.

The compact arrangement of the controls and indicators can be seen in the accompanying photographs *(Plates 156, 157 & 158)*.

Mention has been made of the control box; it might here be added that this contained (on dual-range cars) an additional lever for selecting high or low gear, according to the duties upon which the cars were engaged.

The instrument panel contained, on the left and right sides respectively, vacuum and air pressure gauges. There was also an indicator light that showed (when two cars were coupled together) that the pressure in the trailing unit was sufficiently high for the proper operation of all the electro-pneumatic controls.

Flanking the central speed indicator were the engine starter buttons for both leading and trailing cars, and on the left was the two-position handle for the dual (main and standby) horns *(see details later in this chapter)*; these were operated by compressed air. Also included on the panel were an engine stop button, oil pressure indicator lights for both leading and trailing car engines, and the sanding control button.

On the right-hand side of the driving cab were the automatic vacuum and handbrake controls, the GWR standard ATC apparatus, the duplicated hand throttle control, the sanding magnetic valve, and a main switch for the electro-pneumatic control system.

The abandonment of manual controls operating through rods and ribbons had (as shown by the working of railcar No. 18) appreciably reduced maintenance work. It had also, by eliminating the apertures in the floor through which the former control levers passed to the link mechanism, made the driver's cab less draughty than was formerly the case. Another gain was that of 'increased accessibility', for cleaning and adjustment. The control box cover panels could, for instance, be removed within a matter of seconds when it was required to reach the electrical contact mechanism.

From car No. 19 onwards, the railcar bodies were also built at Swindon, and the most apparent difference between these new cars and the earlier cars was that although the general outlines had been retained, all curves and rounded surfaces had been replaced by corresponding straight lines and flat panels. This procedure had even been extended to the roof, where the former elliptical shape was now made up of a series of flats. The value of scientific streamlining had only been proved at relatively high speeds, and as nearly all these new

*Plate 156:* The left side of the driving cab. Note the hand throttle for shunting, at the extreme left.

*(A.E.C. Ltd.) Leyland Vehicles Ltd.*

*Plate 157:* A view of the right-hand side of the cab of railcar No. 19.
*(A.E.C. Ltd.) Leyland Vehicles Ltd.*

*Plate 158:* A final view of the left-hand side of the driving cab.
*(A.E.C. Ltd.) Leyland Vehicles Ltd.*

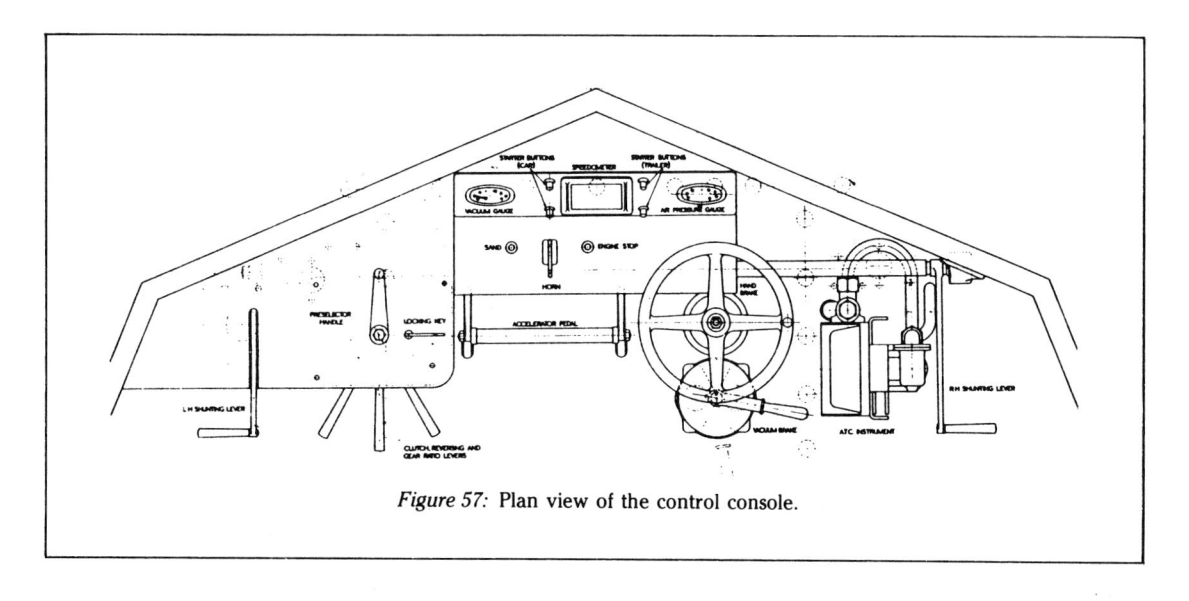

*Figure 57:* Plan view of the control console.

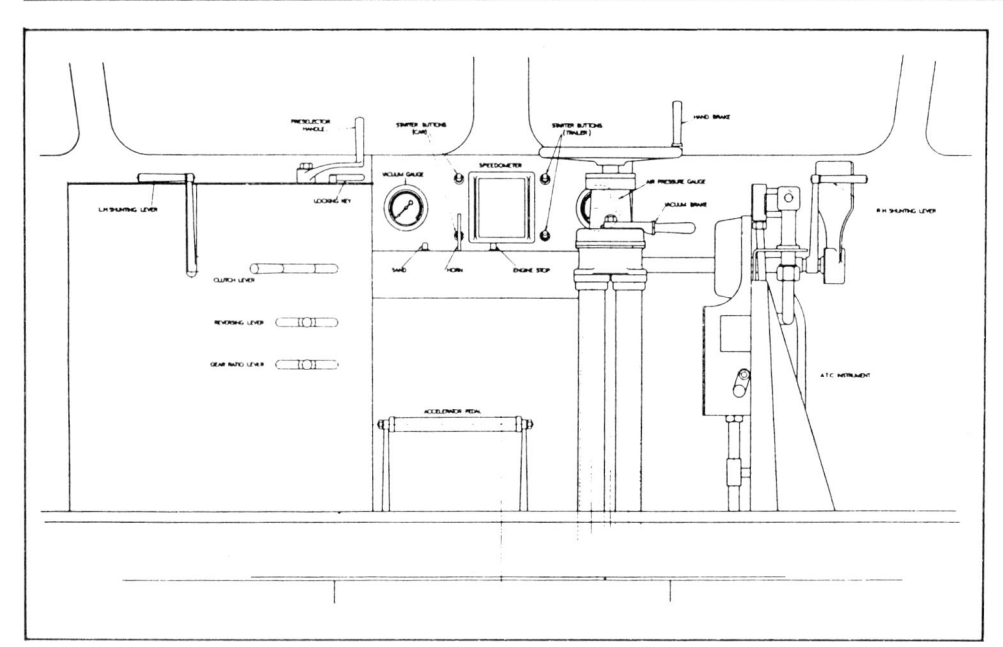

*Figure 58*

cars were intended for relatively slow speed (branch line) working it had now been considered justifiable to abandon the original shape for something more utilitarian. Replacing the downswept rounded front, for instance, by framing, which in its lower part was nearly vertical, had resulted in an aggregate gain of 2ft. in the body length of the car, to which could be added a further 1ft. obtained by continuing the body for 6in. over the headstocks at each end. The extra 3ft. thus achieved had provided additional and useful floor space for passengers and luggage, also the driver's compartment in these cars, and the controls were arranged for easy manipulation. The compartment was heated by steam pipes and had a drop window on either side. The front windows, of Triplex glass were both fitted with wipers. Following the practice instituted with car No. 18, headstocks were now of standard railway pattern, and screw couplings and vacuum brake pipe connections were fitted for use when hauling trailer coaches and other standard rolling stock.

Two saloons were provided in each car, one carrying 32 and the other 16 passengers *(see Figure 59)*. The seating layout in these vehicles became two each side of the gangway instead of the three and two as in earlier cars. They were divided by a vestibule, and between the large saloon and the driver's cab was a luggage compartment approximately 15ft. long. Steel panelling had been used throughout, the panels being secured to light teak framing, stiffened with steel inserts. Floor members were in the form of flitched beams with steel diaphragms connecting them to the body sides, and the flooring itself was made up of fire-proofed boarding covered with insulwood ½in. thick for sound-proofing and insulation. Specially shaped members had been employed to maintain the straight line appearance of the roof, and to provide curved ceilings in the interior *(see Plates 159 to 171 inclusive)*.

In both saloons, green was the prevailing decorative colour *(Plates 172 & 173)*. Mottled, olive green rexine covered the side panels, from the green enamelled steam grille at floor level to the top of the seat backs, after which cream rexine was employed to the cantrail level. The ceiling was finished in the same material, but in a paler shade of cream. Patterned green moquette of the same shade was used for the upholstery of the seats, now fitted in pairs on either side of a central gangway;

an arrangement that provided greater comfort than when the gangway was offset. Like the mouldings, the seat ends were of polished mahogany and had mottled green rexine insets. Mahogany was also used for all the window framing, which was designed with square corners. The effect was perhaps more severe than in the former cars, but nevertheless pleasing.

Mottled green linoleum was used for the floor — the gangways and vestibule being laid with hair carpet, incorporating the GWR monogram — and the windows were provided with pale green, silk-finished curtains. These were clipped in position with green silk cords and when fully drawn covered the windows so effectively that full lighting could be maintained during black-out hours, in World War II. The actual lighting was obtained from three lamp clusters arranged along the centre of the ceiling, one cluster being provided for each group of eight seats. Luggage racks ran the whole length of the saloons. To avoid distracting reflections, dark blinds were fitted to the windows of the driving cab partitions. Wartime restrictions had compelled the adoption of additional measures to prevent the infiltration of light into the vestibule and luggage compartment.

An oil-fired automatic steam generator provided heating sufficient for the car itself and any trailer coaches that might be attached. Steam, it must be mentioned, was available within a few seconds of starting up. The oil was supplied from a tank mounted on the underframe, and the water from a tank carried near the generator. These two were housed in the luggage compartment (about 15ft. long) which had double swing doors on each side for easy loading, and which contained the usual standard items of railway equipment — emergency tool cabinet, first-aid box and fire extinguishers, as well as a guard's seat, letter rack and cupboard.

*The A.E.C. Gazette* reported the following in their pages following a visit to Swindon Works in late 1939:

*The A.E.C. Gazette* recently had the opportunity of seeing bodies of the new cars being constructed at the GWR Works at Swindon, which covers an area of some 326 acres. The Carriage & Wagon section (some 138 acres) comprises sawmill, body repair, finishing, painting, trimming, wheel fitting and smith's shops.

*Figure 59*

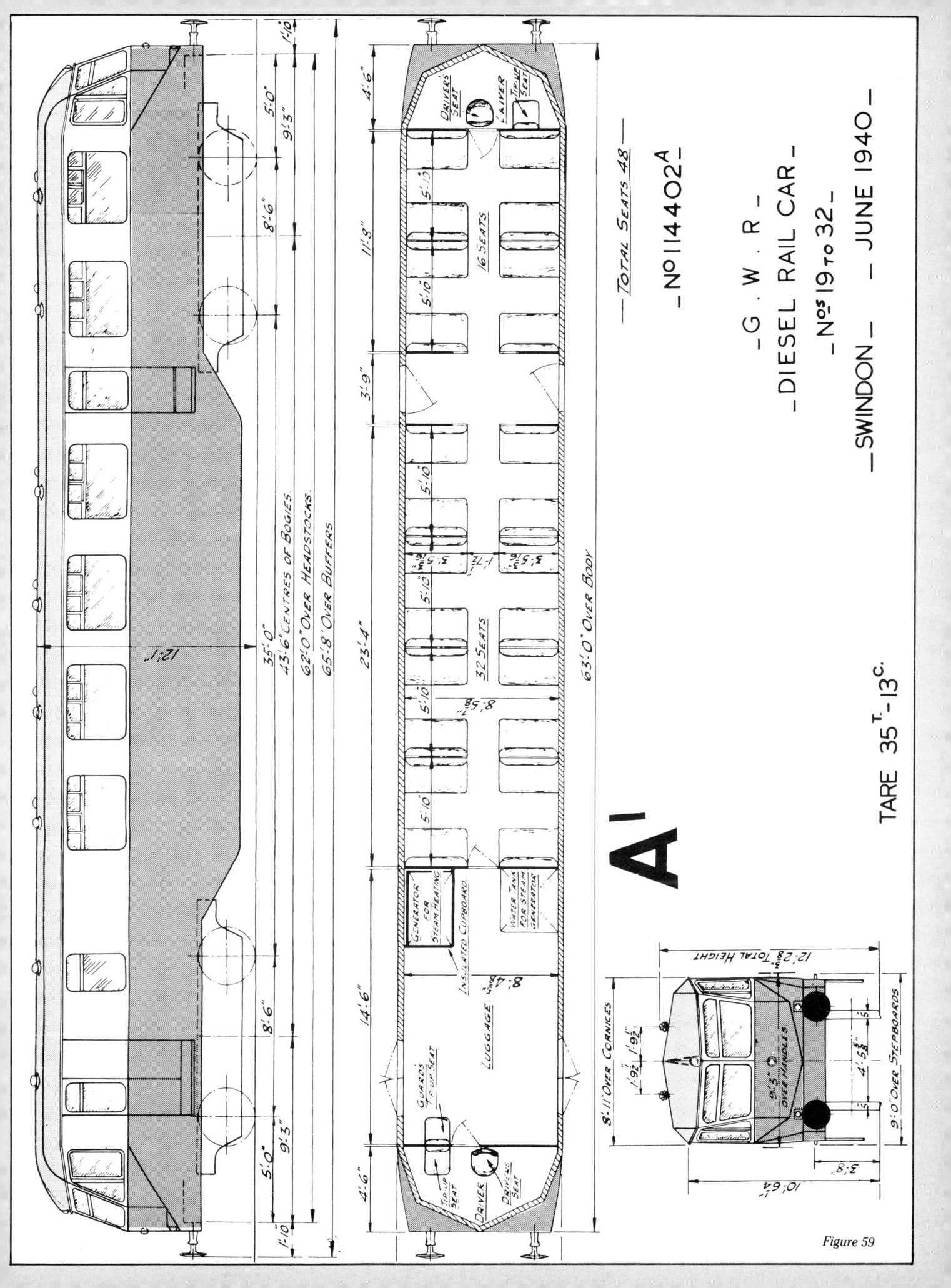

Figure 59A

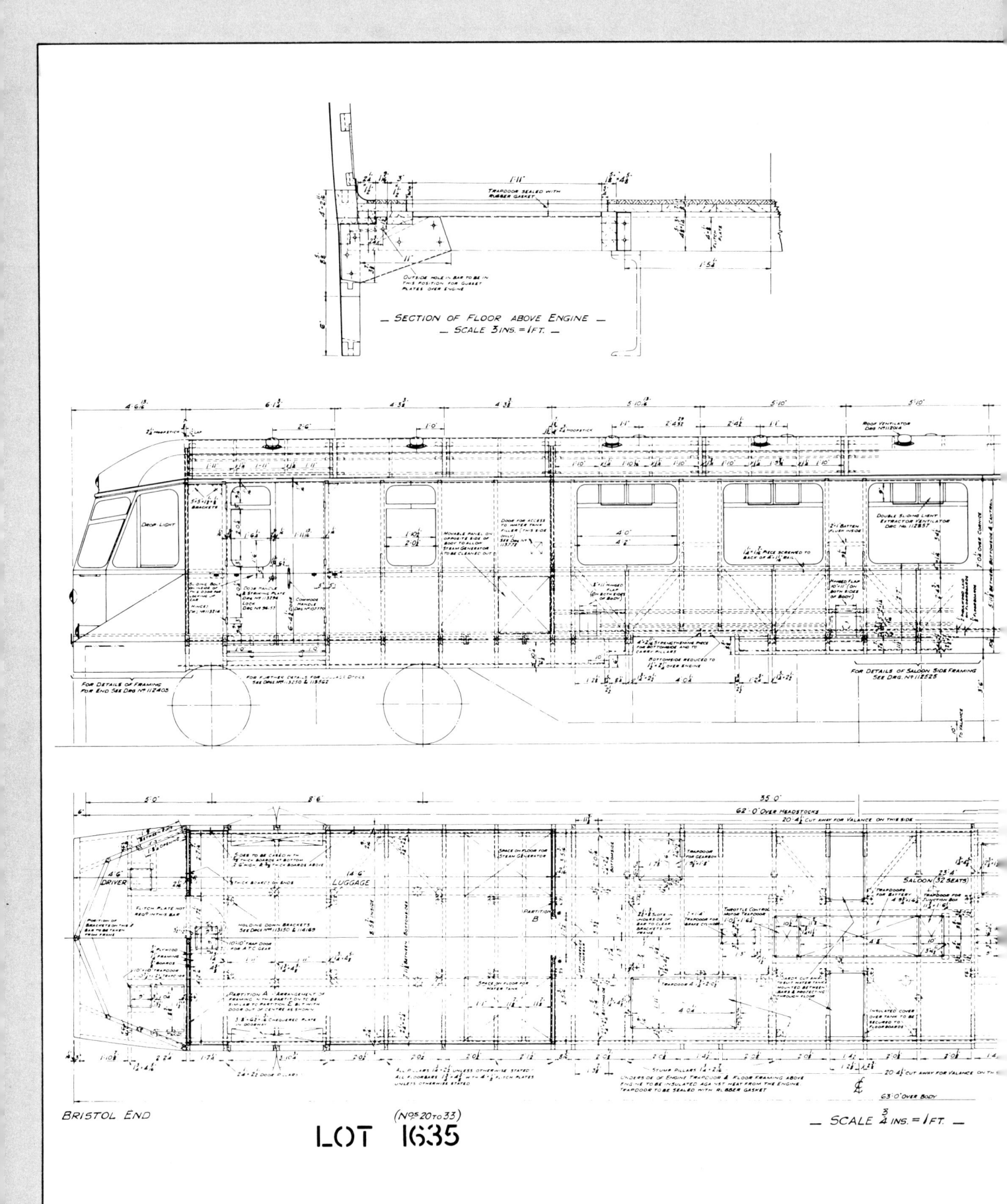

# G. W. R.
## DIESEL CAR
SWINDON — NOV. 1939

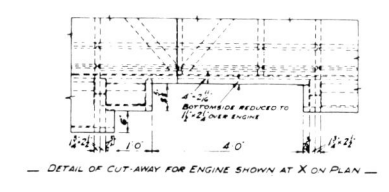

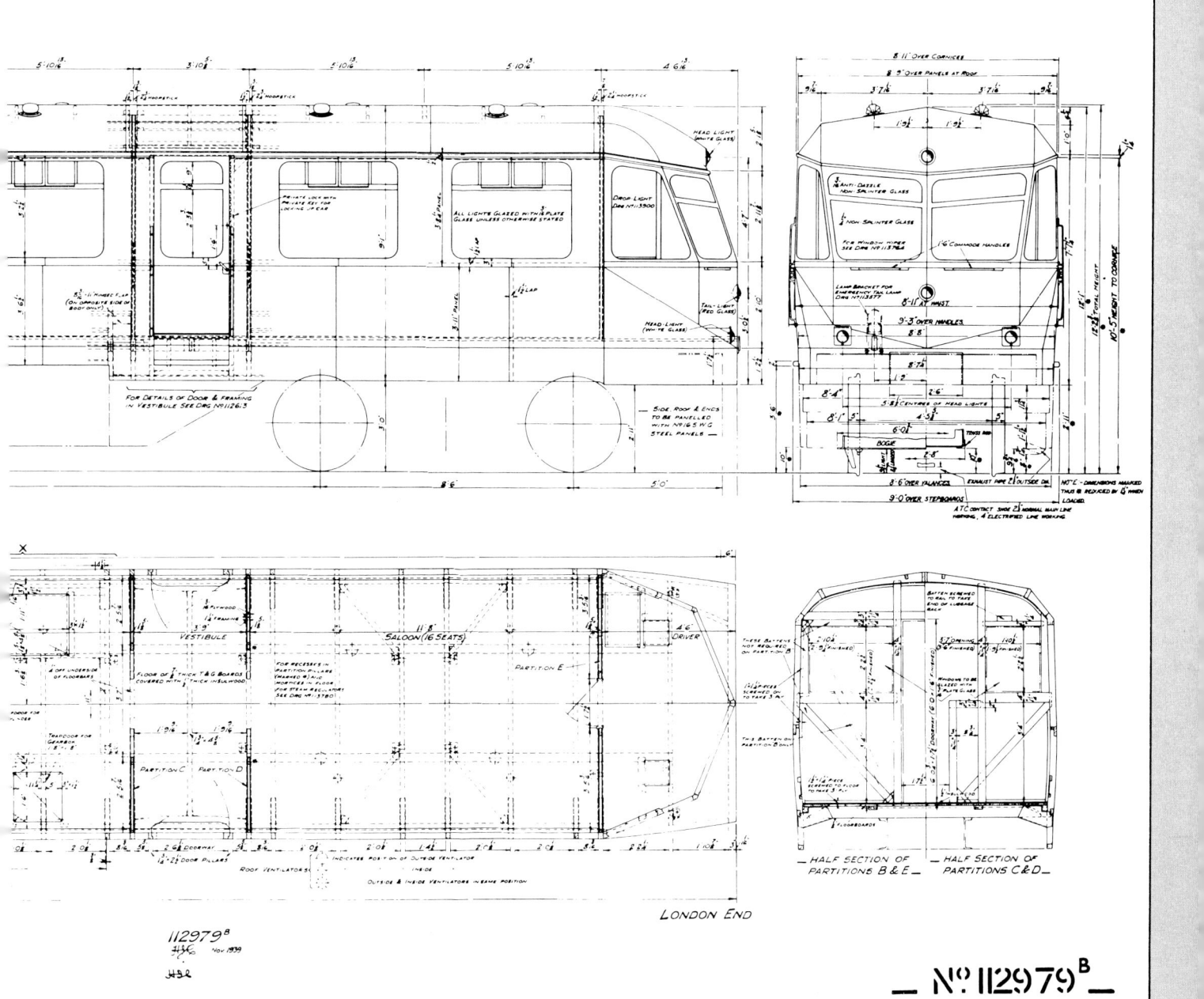

No. 112979 B

*Plate 159:* The new chassis for railcar No. 19, just after arrival from A.E.C., Southall on 14th November 1939, at Swindon Works.
*British Rail*

*Plate 160:* The start of the timber framing. Note the jig standing down by the front.
*British Rail*

*Plate 161:* The wooden structure now complete, ready for panelling.
*British Rail*

*Plate 162:* A view of the inside, showing the wooden construction very clearly.
*British Rail*

*Plate 163:* With most of the panelling attached, railcar No. 19 is nearing completion.
*British Rail*

*Plate 164:* White roofed and fully primed, railcar No. 19 awaits final undercoating and painting. Note one of the earlier series railcars alongside, just having been repainted.

*Plate 165:* The finished body, awaiting glazing at the cab ends.
*British Rail*

*Plate 166:* A side view of railcar No. 19, fully glazed and awaiting final painting and lining out. Note that the side valance panels are not yet fitted.
*British Rail*

*Plate 167:* A final 'angled' view of the primed body of the 'new style' diesel railcars, built at Swindon, and photographed on 29th December 1939.
*British Rail*

*Plate 168:* Finished; but why the rubbing out around the 'No. 19'? Perhaps various liveries were tried out, when painting the numbers. It was photographed in this form on 15th March 1940.
*British Rail*

*Plate 169:* A good front three-quarter view of railcar No. 19 at completion.
*(A.E.C. Ltd.) Leyland Vehicles Ltd.*

*Plate 170:* A fine series of three sequence photographs showing the engine, gearbox and axle/bogie details of railcar No. 19 after completion. The grill and livery detail is clearly visible.

*(A.E.C. Ltd.) Leyland Vehicles Ltd.*

SWINDON-BUILT — NOS. 19 TO 34 — THE NEW DESIGN

*Plate 171:* A view giving all the front detail of railcar No. 19.
*British Rail*

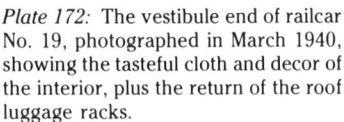

*Plate 172:* The vestibule end of railcar No. 19, photographed in March 1940, showing the tasteful cloth and decor of the interior, plus the return of the roof luggage racks.

*British Rail*

*Plate 173:* A view looking towards the luggage compartment of railcar No. 19.

*British Rail*

Any timber used in the latest A.E.C. railcars for framing, cross-members, etc., has passed through the drying shed and sawmill in the normal way before being sent to the body shop. The Sturtevant compartment system is used for artificial seasoning.

In the sawmill are many examples of modern woodworking machinery for sawing, planing, mortising, multiple boring, shaping and joinery work. It is here that the timber is cut to size by circular saws, planed, squared and milled, as well as being further treated ready for the coachbuilders. Every scrap of waste, it might be emphasised, is collected and burnt in the generation of steam for shop heating, etc.

In the body shop, the procedure, so far as railcars are concerned, is to build the bodies direct on the underframe by first laying the floor cross-members on the chassis, following this by the erection of the side-members, fronts and roof, and then completing with the panelling. Before the last operation, the doors already made as complete units, have been fixed and the seat frames have been fitted. When making standard coach stock, both framing and doors are built up in jigs, the former in the form of quarters.

The exterior completed, the body is ready for finishing and painting. Finishing includes, in most cases, the laying of fireproof flooring. This is put down in the form of paste, and allowed to set solid before subsequent operations are undertaken. In the finishing shop, also equipped with up-to-date machinery, most of the interior woodwork, comprising gangway and driver's cab doors, frames for seat backs, mouldings, etc., are prepared. Adjoining are the french polishing shop, where the staining, filling and polishing of interior doors and decorative woodwork is undertaken, and the carriage trimming shops, where seats are upholstered and a variety of incidental items are made, such as blinds, curtains, signalling flags, towels, etc.

So to the paint shop, where railcars and coach stock are run on to rails, with steam piping laid between them to assist in maintaining the necessary drying temperature. No spray painting is undertaken, all work being carried out by hand from the first stopping to the final coat of varnish. Altogether, eight coats of paint and varnish, consisting of filling coats, body colours, body coat varnishes and final varnishes, are brushed on before painting is pronounced complete. The coats are applied at the rate of roughly one per day, and before the two final varnishes, the GWR monogram, car numbers, etc., are affixed in appropriate positions by means of transfers. All railcars are finished in the Company's standard colours of cream and Windsor-brown. It might be mentioned that before the bodies are fitted, the chassis are scaled and given two coats of red oxide. During the normal painting of the complete unit they receive one coat of black paint and one of black japan.

In the Wagon Works, operations follow in similar sequence, although the work is, of course, considerably simplified. Here, every form of goods vehicle is built from the simple 12 ton truck to a monster all-steel 'crocodile' with a tare weight of anything up to 85 tons, capable of transporting complete boilers, transformers and similar outsize loads. Bodies are also built and repaired at Swindon for the GWR fleet of road vehicles, and at the time of *The A.E.C. Gazette* visit, one or two Southall-built lorries were seen in the shops having their bodies put into good condition after several years' service.

The impression left by a visit to Swindon is that modern machinery and good solid craftsmanship combine effectively to produce passenger vehicles that, whilst attractive both in appearance and comfort, are also properly utilitarian and of quite outstanding durability.

With production going well and the cover of *The A.E.C. Gazette* of July 1940 showing five of the 20 new vehicles complete outside Southall Works, it was time for the GWR to put some of the vehicles through a series of trial runs. One of the cars fitted with dual-range gearboxes (No. 19) was used, with the object of proving the haulage capacity and speed under different conditions, and with various loads. The first trial was a week's running during the period 20th May to 25th May 1940 on the GWR main line between Southall and Westbury; a distance of 86½ miles. High and low ratios were used on alternate days, and tests were made (a) with a single car, (b) with a car and one trailer, and (c) with a car and two trailers. The trailers were standard rolling stock, each weighing 33 tons 6 cwt.

The characteristics of the line chosen are as follows (see also the gradient profile in *Figure 59*). From Southall to Newbury the line was practically level. It then rose gently to Bedwyn,

A line-up of five 'new' design GWR railcars outside the A.E.C. works at Southall, as shown on the cover of their 1940 *Gazette*.

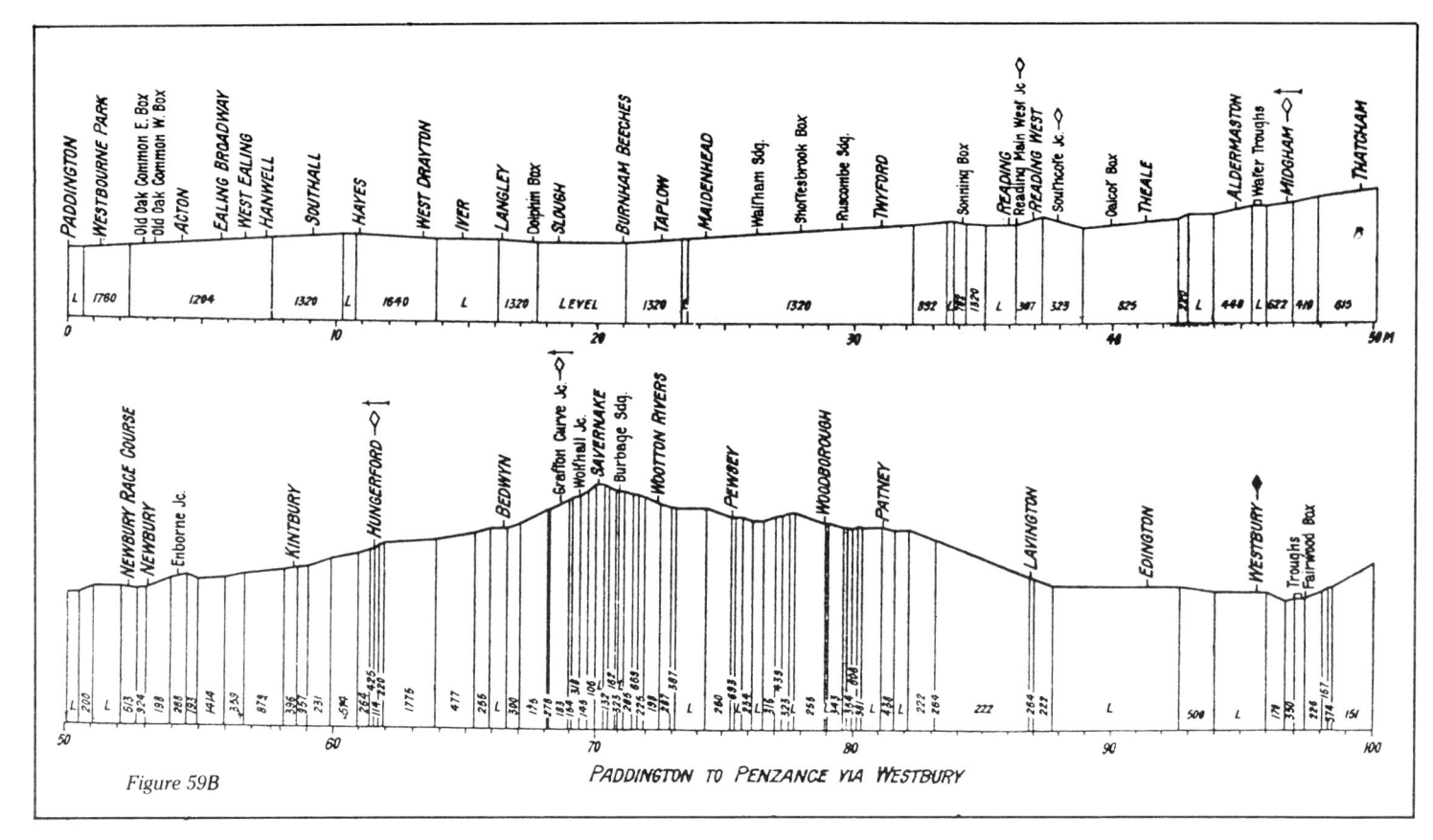

Figure 59B    PADDINGTON TO PENZANCE VIA WESTBURY

where the gradients became steeper to Savernake Summit. Thence it fell to Pewsey and followed an undulating course to Patney before falling steeply to Lavington. The final stretch to Westbury was fairly level.

Near Lavington, on the return trip, the car had to climb for about four miles at 1 in 222. This may appear a negligible gradient, but it is interesting to note that when the car was hauling two trailers, making a total moving weight of over 102 tons, the average speed attained of approximately 38m.p.h. represented an expenditure of 104hp for 'lift' alone.

On each outward journey, stops were made at Slough, Reading, Newbury, Bedwyn and Patney, to obtain results from comparatively short runs. The last two stops were chosen in order to test the acceleration of the car against and with the gradient respectively. The return journey was made non-stop.

The following tests runs were carried out over the route:

1. Car only — low ratio (Car Low)
2. Car only — high ratio (Car High)
3. Car hauling one trailer — low ratio (Car and 1 T.L.)
4. Car hauling one trailer — high ratio (Car and 1 T.H.)
5. Car hauling two trailers — low ratio (Car and 2 T.L.)
6. Car hauling two trailers — high ratio (Car and 2 T.H.)

In the following table a summary of the start to stop speeds for all trials are given, and it will be noted that even with two trailers, the car was able to average as high a figure as 38.3m.p.h. for the day.

The difference in running time between high and low ratio is not very marked, except in the case of the car alone; but here signal checks interfered with the true result. On the whole, there appears to be some advantage in the high ratio

## SUMMARY OF TESTS
### Average Start to Stop Speeds

| Between | Ratio Dist. | Car only Low | Car only High | Car +1T Low | Car +1T High | Car +2T Low | Car +2T High |
|---|---|---|---|---|---|---|---|
| | miles | m.p.h. | m.p.h. | m.p.h. | m.p.h. | m.p.h. | m.p.h. |
| **Outward Trip.** | | | | | | | |
| Southall—Slough | 9½ | 35.8 | 49.5 | 34.5 | 38.0 | 33.5 | 36.2 |
| Slough—Reading | 17½ | 43.8 | 56.1 | 39.0 | 42.8 | 35.0 | 36.8 |
| Reading—Newbury | 17 | 35.2 | 49.8 | 38.8 | 38.4 | 32.4 | 35.2 |
| Newbury—Bedwyn | 13½ | 42.0 | 50.5 | 39.6 | 39.6 | 33.7 | 34.4 |
| Bedwyn—Patney | 14½ | 41.5 | 48.3 | 38.7 | 43.5 | 32.8 | 37.4 |
| Patney—Westbury | 14½ | 42.9 | 52.7 | 41.5 | 45.8 | 38.6 | 42.5 |
| Total | 86½ | 40.0a | 51.3 | 39.2 | 41.2 | 34.2b | 36.9 |
| **Return Trip.** | | | | | | | |
| Westbury—Southall | 86½ | 38.6c | 54.9 | 42.6 | 45.1d | 38.9 | 39.6e |
| **Both Trips** | 173 | 38.4 | 53.0 | 41.0 | 43.0 | 36.4 | 38.3 |

a = Three signal checks totalling 5 mins.
b = One signal check totalling 1½ mins.
All outward trips had P.W. check to 15m.p.h. on the Reading–Newbury section lasting about 1½ mins.
c = Three signal checks totalling 13¼ mins.
d = Three signal check totalling 3¾ mins.
e = Three signal checks totalling 2 mins.

on comparatively level runs, and the average of 53m.p.h. for the car alone (in high ratio) could not possibly have been maintained in low ratio, where the governed speed gave a nominal 42½m.p.h.

The times in the table were taken with an ordinary watch between stations, but occasional checks were made over half-mile stretches with a stop watch. On the level, maximum speeds of 65m.p.h. with the car alone, 61m.p.h. with one trailer, and 55½m.p.h. with two trailers, were recorded when running in high ratio, while higher speeds were obtained on slightly falling gradients.

In assessing operating expenses, the question of fuel consumption was naturally of great interest, and the relevant figures have been set out in the following table. These show a consumption of between 7m.p.g. for the car alone, in low ratio, and 4.86m.p.g. for the car and two trailers, when running in high ratio.

**FUEL CONSUMPTION**

|  | Ratio | Car only Low | Car only High | Car & 1 Trailer Low | Car & 1 Trailer High | Car & 2 Trailers Low | Car & 2 Trailers High |
|---|---|---|---|---|---|---|---|
| Consumption | m.p.g. | 7.0 | 6.6 | 5.23 | 5.85 | 4.95 | 4.86 |
| Total weight, unladen tons |  | 35.6 | 35.6 | 68.9 | 68.9 | 102.2 | 102.2 |
| Ton miles per gallon |  | 249 | 235 | 360 | 403 | 505 | 497 |
| Average speed per day |  | 38.4 | 53.0 | 41.0 | 43.0 | 36.4 | 38.3 |
| Comparison of ton miles per gall x speed |  | 1 | 1.36 | 1.55 | 1.81 | 1.93 | 1.98 |

These figures, taken in conjunction with the load hauled, and the average speed obtained, are remarkable in comparison with road haulage figures, since, with two trailers, the ton/m.p.g. was almost 500, and the average speed 38.3m.p.g.

While these trials were being undertaken, temperatures were checked at various points for oil and water, and the results obtained were in every way satisfactory.

## MAXIMUM SPEEDS

Taken at intervals over half-mile stretches.

*Car only*: Low ratio not taken. High ratio, outward; 65m.p.h. at Twyford, 68m.p.h. at Woodborough. Return; 66½m.p.h. at Bedwyn, 65m.p.h. at Twyford.

*Car and 1 Trailer*: Low ratio, outward; 48m.p.h. at Savernake. Return; 47m.p.h. at Aldermaston.

*Car and 1 Trailer*: High ratio, outward; 61m.p.h. at Pewsey. Return; 65m.p.h. at Bedwyn.

*Car and 2 Trailers*: Low ratio, outward; 44m.p.h. at Edington. Return; 47m.p.h. at Maidenhead.

*Car and 2 Trailers*: High ratio, outward; 55½m.p.h. at Woodborough. Return; 60m.p.h. at Bedwyn.

A further trial was carried out using car No. 19 on the Bristol to Weymouth route on 23rd July 1941. The test was made to ascertain whether the wheel flanges would foul the underframe, under service conditions. The following official Swindon drawing shows the buffer heights with the railcar fully loaded, but with no 'overload' margin.

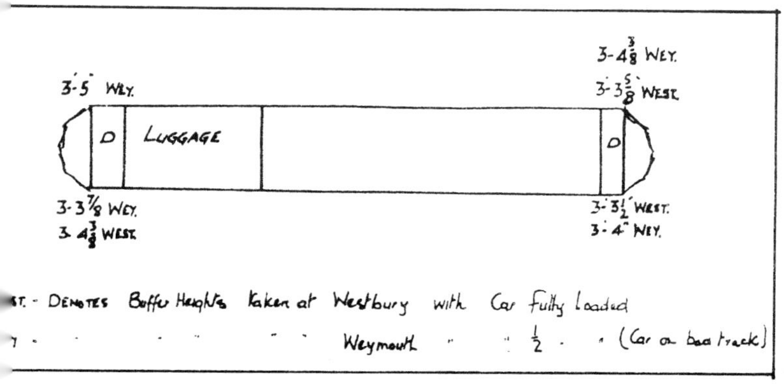

The following points were listed in the report:

1. Laminted springs had approximately 1in. camber which is correct to the drawing.
2. Deflection of side springs and bolster springs 1¼in. for 5 tons load.
3. Clearance between wheel flange and brace on frame = 1⅞in. (Car Light).
4. Wheel fouled frame twice when passing over crossings near Bath, but at no other time.
5. Buffers were generally about ¼in. to ⅜in. low.
6. Suggested that cars should be sent out from shops at 3ft.—5½ft. in future.
7. Divisional Superintendents asked to raise those railcars already out in service.
8. Sand pipes and lifeguards did not foul rail and had correct clearance from rail.

*Swindon 1941*

Railcar No. 19 was lent to the LNER and used on regular traffic in April and May of 1942 for experimental purposes.

It is of interest to observe that in connection with the Bristol-Cardiff service, which entailed a car passing through the Severn and other tunnels four times each way daily, a satisfactory horn to warn gangers of the approach of a diesel railcar had been introduced. It had been somewhat difficult for men on the line to distinguish between the horns of railcars and those on road vehicles, and in the Severn Tunnel, it was difficult to hear the horn at all. All sorts of warning devices were tried out before the final equipment was adopted, which comprised eight Desilux horns per car, four at each end. They were arranged in pairs, with two pairs at each end of the car, one pair operated by the main supply of compressed air, while the other pair, for use as a 'stand-by', was operated by independent air compressors. The pairs of horns *(see Figure 60)* sounded alternately to make them absolutely distinct from road vehicles. They could be heard upwards of three miles away.

It is interesting to read the actual order for the warning horns sent by the GWR. First the requirement:

**WARNING HORNS**
To be supplied by C. V. Desiderio,   March 1939
143 Whitfield Street,
London, W1

*Requirements per car*
*Main Horns* operated from main compressed air supply.

| Quantity | Description | Drawing |
|---|---|---|
| 2 | E Flat Horn and Sound Assembly | A.E.C. — U87149 DESILUX — No. SK6 |
| 2 | G Flat Horn and Sound Assembly | A.E.C. — U87150 DESILUX — No. SK6 |
| 2 | Double Air Valves | A.E.C. — U87153 |

(E flat and G flat)

*Figure 60*

```
                    C.V.Desiderio
                143 Whitfield St., London.W.1.
        ==========================================


    Great Western Railway,
        Stores Dept.,
            Swindon, Wilts.           May 30th.1939.

            For the attention of the Stores Superintendent.

        Your Order FK1198/N2314 (part).   Our Advice  A/C3716
                                          Note No.   A/3717.


    To supplying:

    8 sets  Compressed Air Horns type SK6 as below:

            8 "Sound Assembles" E Flat, (bronze housings,
                black trumpets).

            8 "Sound Assembles" G Flat, (bronze housings,
                black trumpets).

            8 "Double Valves" hand operation.

                        Each set £6.12.0 Net.    £52.16.0.
                                                  =========
                                                    Nett.

    Despatched per G.W.Rly., carriage prepaid, in
    2 cases Nos.31 and 32; each case 4 sets, addressed
    to:-
            Mr E.T.J.Evans,
                G.W.R.Chief Mechanical Engineer's Dept.,
                    Swindon.
```

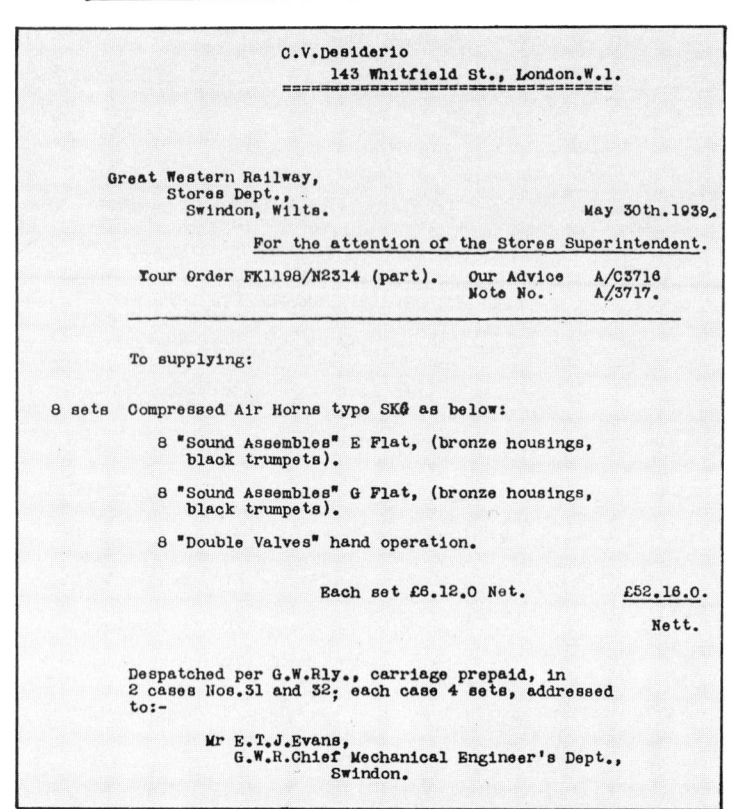

```
                    C.V.Desiderio
                143 Whitfield St. London.W.1.


    Great Western Railway,                      15th.June 1939.
        Stores Department,
            Swindon, Wilts.

            For the attention of the Stores Superintendent.

        Your order FK1198/N2314(Part).   Our Advice A/C3719/20.
        No.                              Note No.

    To supplying:-

            Three Sets "Desilux" Electric Horns,
            24 Volts, each set consisting of:-

            2 Groups (2 IR24V/2 SK2) of 4
            motors, 4 aluminium sound assembles
            and 4 black trumpets per car.

                        Each set £35.16.0. net.    £107.8.0.
                                                   =========
                                                     Nett.

    Despatched per G.W.Rly., carriage prepaid, in
    2 cases Nos.33/34, addressed to:-
            Mr E.T.J.Evans,
                Chief Mechanical Engineer's Dept.,
                    G.W.Rly., Swindon.

    Case No.33 - 12 Sound Assembles SK2
                             6 E flat, 6 G flat.

    Case No.34 - 12 Electric Compressors,
                         Standard, 24 Volts.
```

Copies of the invoices for the railcar 'horns'.

*Plate 174:* The second parcels railcar, No. 34, with dark grey roof paint and hinged doors.

British Rail

*Figure 61*

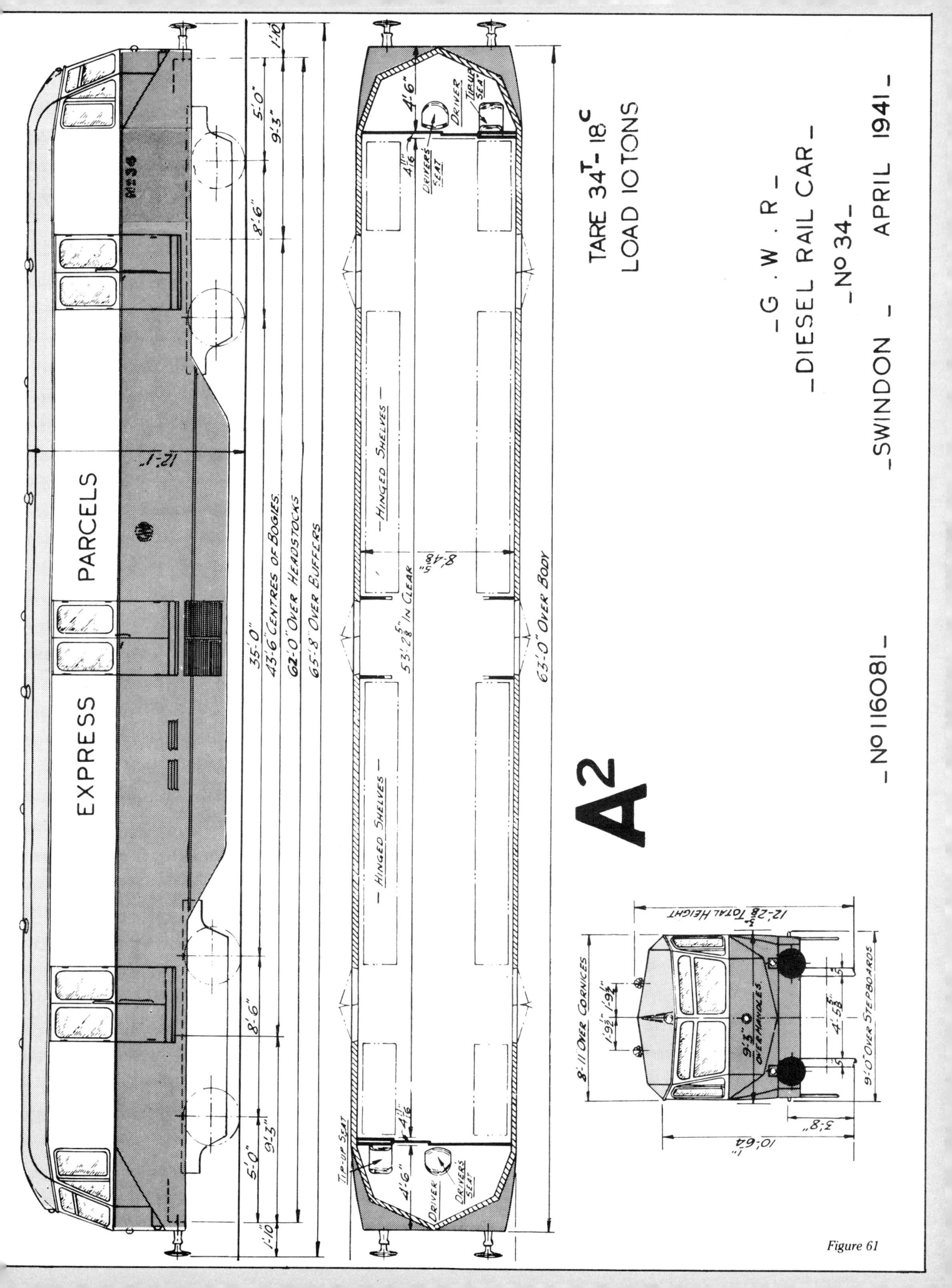

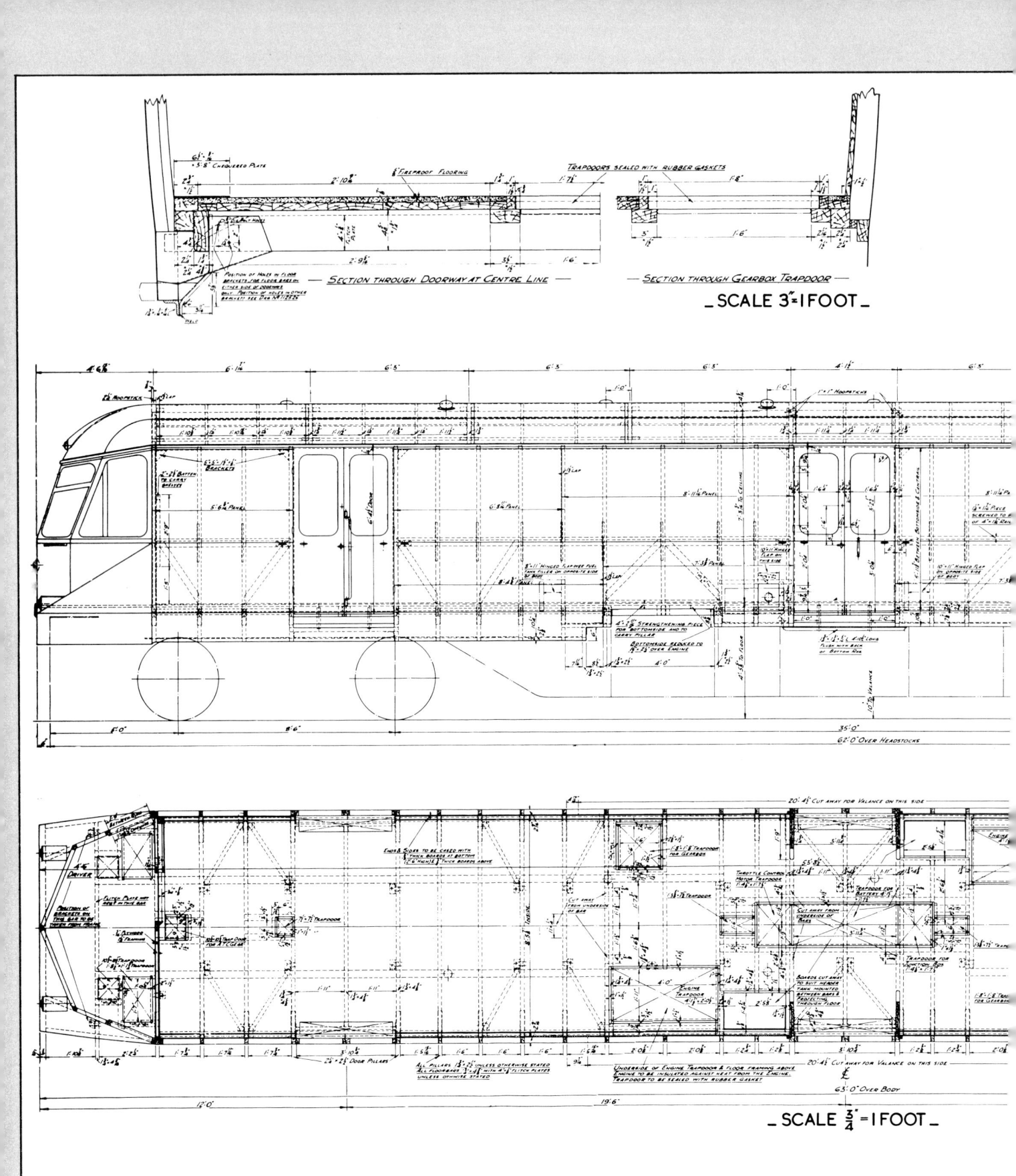

LOT 1636

*Figure 61A*

# G.W.R
## DIESEL PARCEL CAR
### SWINDON  APRIL 1940

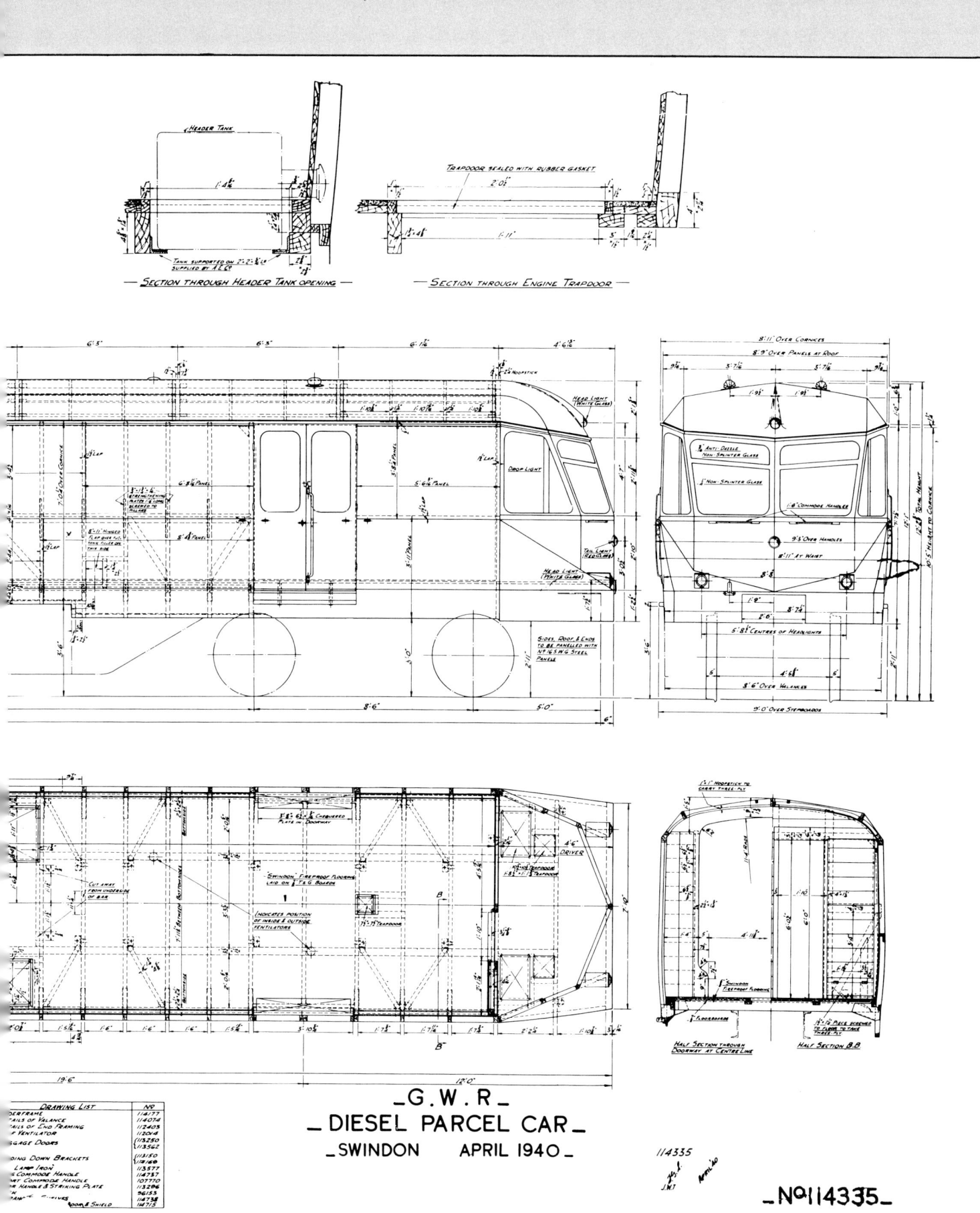

No 114335

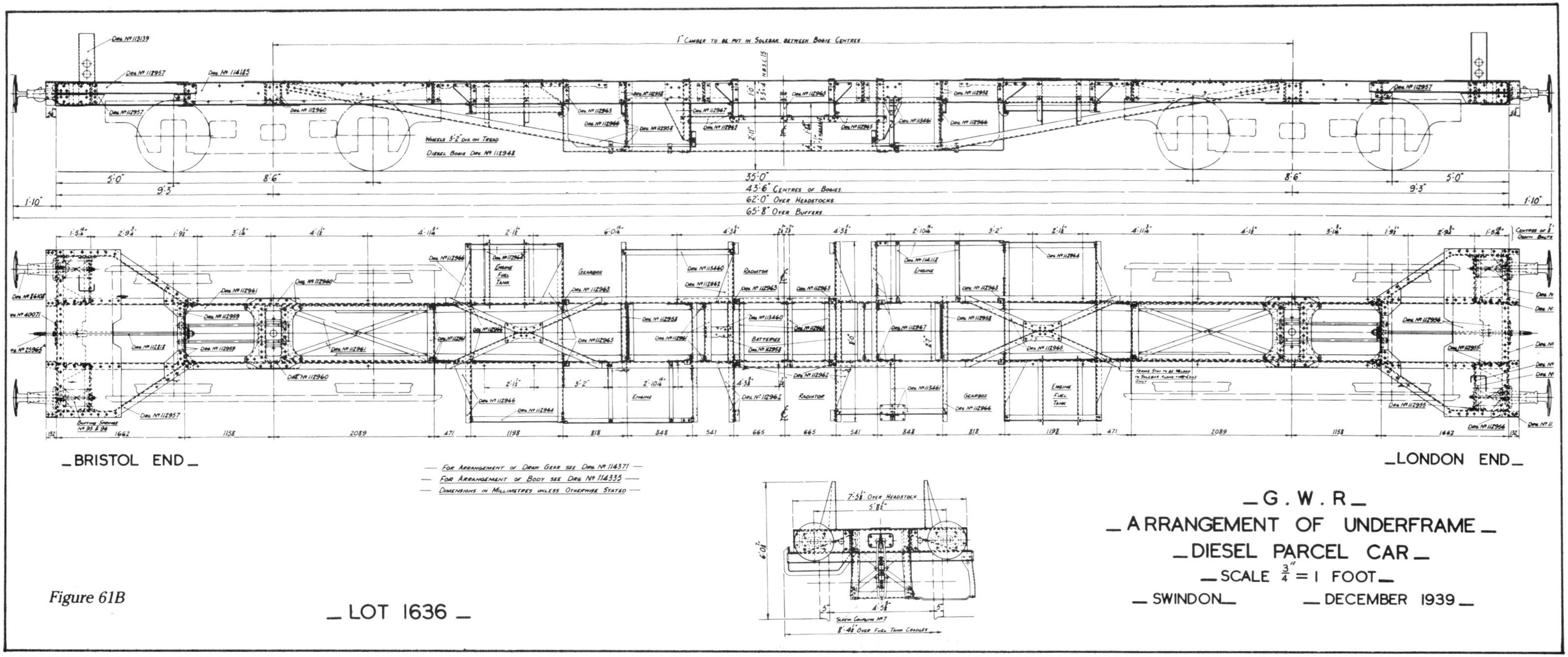

— G.W.R. —
— ARRANGEMENT OF UNDERFRAME —
— DIESEL PARCEL CAR —
— SCALE $\frac{3}{4}" = 1$ FOOT —
— SWINDON —   — DECEMBER 1939 —

— LONDON END —

— BRISTOL END —

— LOT 1636 —

Figure 61B

*Standby Horns* operated from electric compressors

| Quantity | Description | Drawing |
|---|---|---|
| 2 | E Flat Horn and Sound Assembly | A.E.C. — U87151 DESILUX — IONC — 1938—SK2 |
| 2 | G Flat Horn and Sound Assembly | A.E.C. — U87152 DESILUX — IONC — 1938—SK2 |
| 4 | Electric Compressors | A.E.C. — U87154 DESILUX — 15NC — 1938—SK2 |

Secondly, two invoices showing the air horns (8 sets) and electric horns (3 sets) with their relative cost and delivery instructions are included; these are reproduced on *page 166*.

With the completion of the fifteen new single railcars, came the second Express Parcels Railcar, No. 34 *(Figures 61, 61A, and 61B)* built to supplement the overworked car, No. 17.

This new parcels car had the exterior design of body standardised for the new fleet, and is seen in *Plates 174 & 175*.

Six double doors, which this time were hinged rather than sliding, gave access to the interior, which had a floor space of approximately 450sq. ft. Eight folding slatted shelves were fitted at each side, and there were seven roof lights for night work. The car could carry 10 tons of parcels, and the spacious interior can be seen in *Plate 176*. The driver's compartment was the same as on the passenger cars, as was the technical specification and equipment. No. 34 was seen extensively in the London area and was based at the Southall Shed.

Before the last phase in GWR diesel railcar production is reached (the twin-car units to be discussed in the next chapter) a picture gallery of the new design has been included, and shows a view of each of the railcars, Nos. 19 to 34.

*Plate 176:* A view of the interior of railcar No. 34, showing the hinged shelving and spacious floor area.
*British Rail*

*Plate 177:* Railcar No. 19 at Reading Shed in 1950, with a tunnel gauging van in tow. This is a good view for studying the front detail of these vehicles. The small letters and figures 'S.P.5.52' to the right of the right-hand buffer indicate that the vehicle will be proposed for shopping in May 1952.
*National Railway Museum, Maurice Earley Collection*

*Plate 178:* Diesel railcar No. W20W on a local service, seen at the GWR's Birmingham (Snow Hill) Station in the late 1950s.

*R. H. G. Simpson*

*Plate 179:* Railcar No. W21W on shed with a BR diesel multiple unit behind.
*R. H. G. Simpson*

*Plate 180 (below):* Railcar No. W22W hauls a trailer coach on the local Stratford-upon-Avon to Leamington Spa service, and is seen approaching Hatton West Junction on 15th May 1956.

*R. J. Blenkinsop*

*Plate 181:* A further view of railcar No. W22W showing the British Railways overall green livery with yellow flash and stripe.

*British Rail*

*Plate 182:* Railcar No. W23 in crimson and cream livery with a grey roof. Note the boiler chimney and only inner axle drive. The negative of this photograph is damaged, causing the black line across the print.

*British Rail*

*Plate 183:* Railcar No. 24 in immaculate GWR livery.

*(A.E.C. Ltd.) Leyland Vehicles Ltd.*

*Plate 184:* Railcar No. W25W seen at a typical location for these vehicles; waiting in a bay for a branch line service.

*Lens of Sutton*

*Plate 185:* Seen leaving Burlish Halt on 4th July 1959, railcar No. W26W is in the overall green livery.

*Michael Hale*

*Plate 186:* Railcar No. W27W stands at a station in the hot weather (note all ventilator windows open). The drive to the outer axle has been removed.

*Lens of Sutton*

*Plate 187:* Two 'razor edged' railcars coupled together, Nos. W24W and W28W, enter Bristol (Temple Meads) on 12th May 1958.

*N. E. Preedy*

*Plate 188:* Railcar No. 29 is seen with a GWR auto trailer in tow, to increase the seating capacity. Looking at the railcar, it appears to be well-loaded.
*R. G. Simpson*

*Plate 189:* Railcar No. W30W, showing the new-style windscreen wipers coming downwards instead of the original fitment at the bottom of the centre strut of the windscreen.
*Lens of Sutton*

*Plate 190:* Colnbrook Station, with railcars Nos. W27 and W31 running as a coupled unit on 23rd June 1957.
*C. Gammell*

*Plate 191:* Railcar No. W32W, in the overall green livery and grey roof, showing up the position of the BR crest.

*Author's Collection*

*Plate 192:* A fine photograph of railcar No. W32 in the crimson and cream livery, and showing clearly the livery and lining details.

*British Rail*

*Plate 193:* Railcar No. W33, after alteration from a single car unit to a dual-car unit, to replace No. 37 which was destroyed in a fire, seen on Reading Shed on 24th February 1952.

*National Railway Museum, Maurice Earley Collection*

*Plate 194:* Railcar (parcels van) No. W34W at Paddington parcels platform on 1st June 1951, with a Class 61XX 2-6-2T hauling a local service away from the terminus, in the right background.

*Brian Morrison*

*Plate 195:* Parcels car No. W34W, seen here passing Iver on the Paddington-West Ealing-Slough parcel service of 25th June 1955 is in overall maroon livery. Note the small GILL SANS lettering of 'EXPRESS PARCELS'.

*Philip J. Kelley*

# Chapter Nine: The Twin-Coupled Units — Nos. 35 to 38

From July 1934, until the commencement of World War II, the Great Western diesel express railcars ran twice daily (in each direction), between Cardiff and Birmingham. With the provision of a buffet facility and toilets and more luxurious seating (replacing the 70 seats in the first railcars), capacity was reduced to 44 available seats. As these railcars were rated at a maximum speed of 70m.p.h., they were able to reduce the overall time of 3½ hours (average) to 2hr. 20min. (depending on the path available). But because of this, their seating capacity became heavily taxed, so the replacement units, namely Nos. 35, 36, 37 and 38, were to be built as twin-car units, with toilets and buffet facilities *(see Plate 196)*. The war delayed their delivery but this did not really matter as the Cardiff-Birmingham service was withdrawn during this time. Later, however, it was reinstated with a morning train from Birmingham at 9.10a.m., and a return from Cardiff at 4.45p.m. As these, in effect, combined both a diesel and a steam service in each direction, a steam train had been necessary to cope with the demand, but with additional stops at Stratford-upon-Avon in both directions (and at Chepstow and Hall Green also, northbound), the Birmingham to Cardiff time of 2hr. 44min. was still 16min. less than the best pre-war steam time, and 2hr. 51min. from Cardiff to Birmingham was 4min. less than in 1939. The problem now was how the first of the new twin diesel units, which had just been completed, could cope with the greatly increased traffic. Taking advantage of the easier timing, therefore, it was decided to use a standard GWR 70ft. ten compartment corridor coach as a trailer between the two railcars, bringing the total seating of the unit up to 184. Thus the train made its appearance in this form *(see Plates 197 & 198)*.

The new twin-coupled set had a tare weight of 74 tons 6cwt., which increased to 108 tons when the ten compartment corridor coach was inserted. Loaded with passengers and luggage, the gross weight was approximately 120 tons. The full specification is given below:

## TRANSMISSION

| | |
|---|---|
| Fluid Coupling | Daimler-type Fluid Flywheel under license A.E.C. J.150 |
| Gearboxes Pre-selective Wilson | No. A.E.C. U.87067 5 Speed |

Epicyclic (Electro-pneumatic operated)

| | 1st | 2nd | 3rd | 4th | 5th |
|---|---|---|---|---|---|
| Gear Ratio | 6.38 : 1 | 4.5 : 1 | 2.53 : 1 | 1.64 : 1 | Direct |

| | |
|---|---|
| Reverse Gear | Bevel Gear and Pinions in Driving Axle Box |
| Final Drive | Bevel Gear; Ratio 2.59 : 1 |

| | Gear | Twin Cars |
|---|---|---|
| Overall Gear Ratio (To Unity) | 1st | 15.2 |
| | 2nd | 10.7 |
| | 3rd | 6.02 |
| | 4th | 3.9 |
| | 5th | 2.38 |
| Maximum Tractive Efforts (lb.) | 1st | 11,380 |
| | 5th | 1,840 |
| Maximum Speed M.P.H. | 1st | 11.8 |
| | 2nd | 16.8 |
| | 3rd | 29.9 |
| | 4th | 46.1 |
| | 5th | 75.5 |

## AUXILIARIES

| | |
|---|---|
| Battery | Oldham Lead Acid 24 cells 224 amp/hrs. |
| Lighting Circuit | 24 volts |
| Dynamo | Split Field Shunt Wound 8in. C.A.V. D8C40 |
| Starter Motors | C.A.V. Clockwise axial BS 624C2 |
| Compressors | Rotary-Type Clayton Dewandre G.A. 6AC |
| Exhausters | Rotary-Type Clayton Dewandre REGA 131 5½in. bore 7¼in. long |
| Type (Wheel Arrangement) Weight in Running Order | Two bogies each with two axles |
| | Nos. 35 and 37 (36 tons 14cwt.) |
| | Nos. 36 and 38 (37 tons 12cwt.) |
| Wheelbase Overall | 52ft. 0in. |
| Wheel Diameter | 3ft. 2in. |
| Width Overall | 9ft. 3in. |
| Length Overall | 65ft. 8in. |
| Height Overall | 12ft. 2⅜in. |
| Minimum Curve Negotiable | 3½ chains |
| Total length over twin-sets | 131ft. 4in. |
| Fuel Tanks | 100 gallons |
| Lubricating Oil Sumps | 8 gallons per engine |
| Cooling Water, Radiator and Engine | 36 gallons |
| Carriage Warming Boiler | Vapor Clarkson Steam Generator |
| Carriage Warming Boiler Fuel Tank | 50 gallons |
| Carriage Warming Boiler Water Tank | 100 gallons |
| Brakes, Vacuum | Standard GWR type brake blocks |
| Sanding | Compressed Air Operated |

## POWER EQUIPMENT

| | |
|---|---|
| 6 cylinder Diesel Engines | A.E.C. Type 105hp at 1,650r.p.m. Single and double ratio cars 2 engines = 210hp Twin Cars 4 engines = 420hp |
| Cylinder Bore and Stroke | 120mm. x 142mm. |
| Firing Order | 1.5.3.6.2.4. |
| Fuel Injection Nozzle-Type | C.A.V. multi-hole long stem 1,500 |
| Fuel Injector Holder-Type | B.K.B.L. 67.S 567 |
| Pressure at which Fuel Injector Nozzle should be set | 2,500p.s.i. |
| Fuel Pumps | C.A.V. 38. P.E. 86B8C Q.320S626 38 B.P.E. 6 B80 N.320S626 |

As previously stated, these two twin sets were built to operate on fast services, with a top speed of 75.5m.p.h. and seating capacity for 104 passengers. They were equipped with standard buffing and drawgear, and access from one car to the other was afforded by means of a flexible gangway between the vehicles *(see Plate 199)*. The train set could be driven from either of the two driver's compartment situated at the extreme ends of the set.

The new sets were fitted with the usual comforts for the passengers and, in addition, were equipped to supply light refreshments en route. The car which carried the buffet portion comprised two saloon compartments *(see Figures 62 & 63)*, one of which could seat 32 passengers whilst the other, (besides seating 12 passengers) was fitted with the serving counter *(see Plates 200, 201 & 202)*. Between saloon

*Plate 196:* Railcars No. 35 and 36, as new, and coupled as a twin-car unit, photographed in November 1941.

*British Rail*

*Plate 197:* Railcars No. 35 and 36 with the 70ft. coach sandwiched between the power units to increase the seating capacity to 184.

*British Rail*

*Plate 198:* A side view of the 3-car train.

*British Rail*

*Plate 199:* The railcar to corridor coach connections showing the special fitments to couple one to the other.

*British Rail*

Figure 62

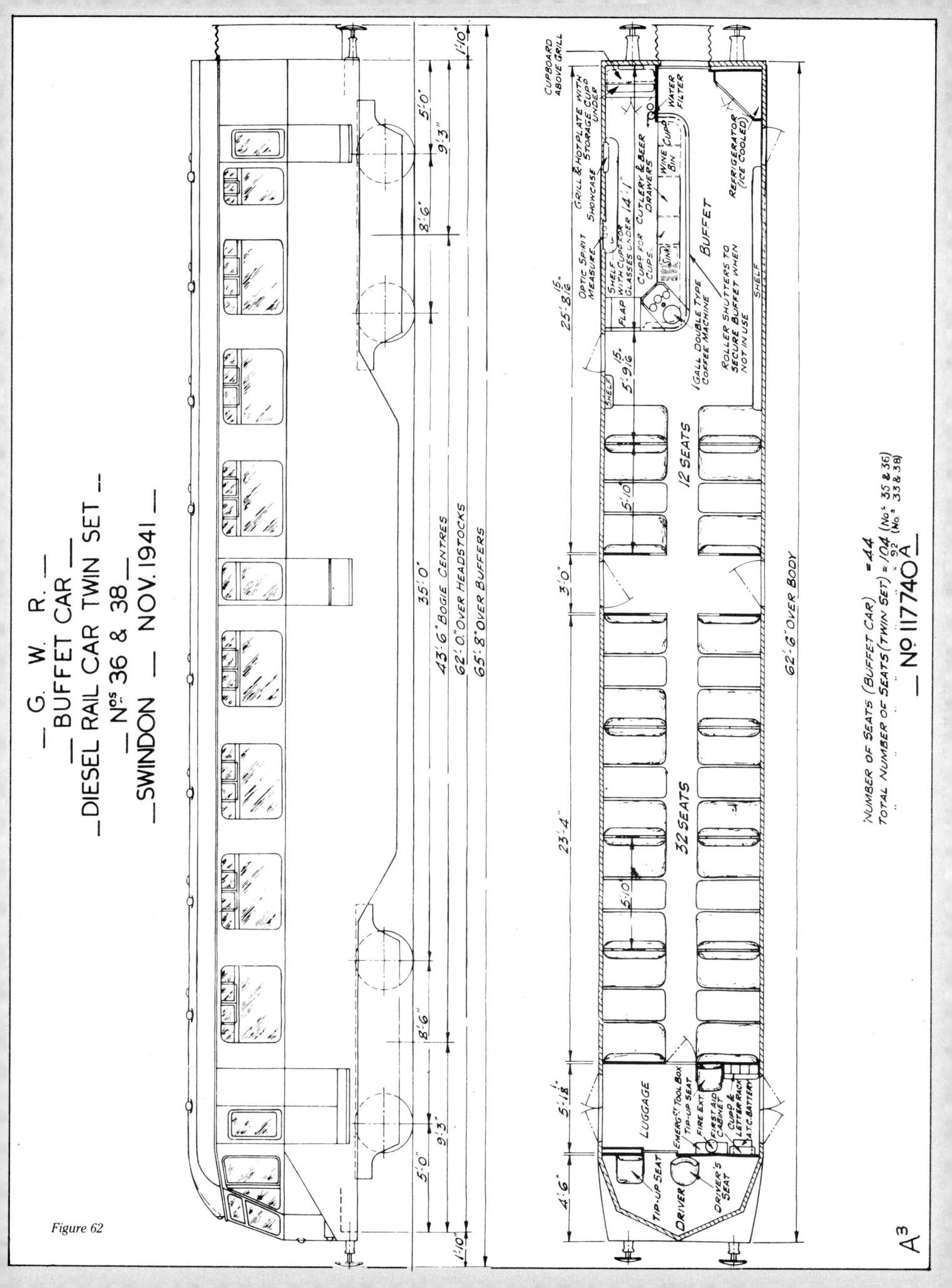

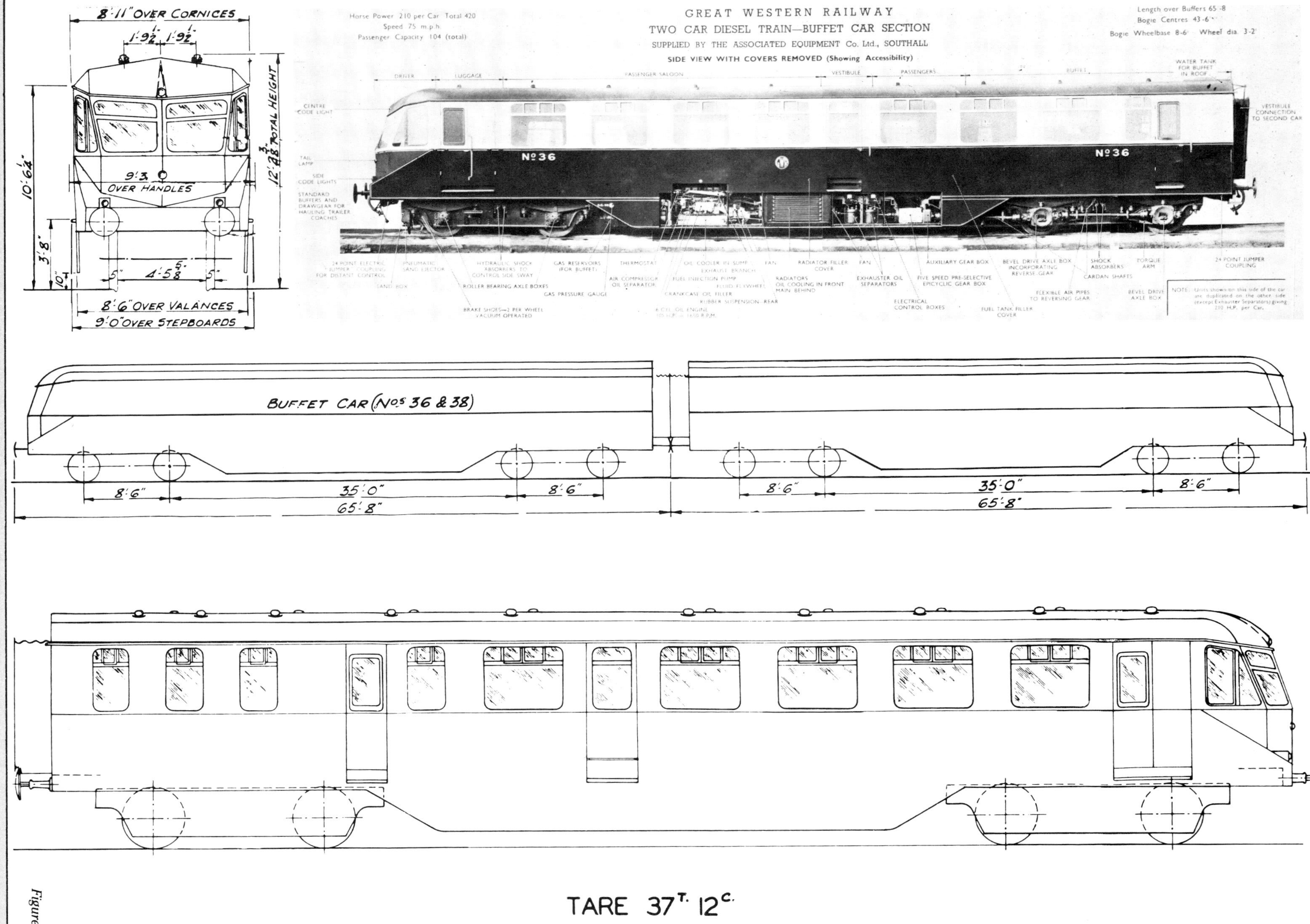

*Figure 62A*

*Figure 63*

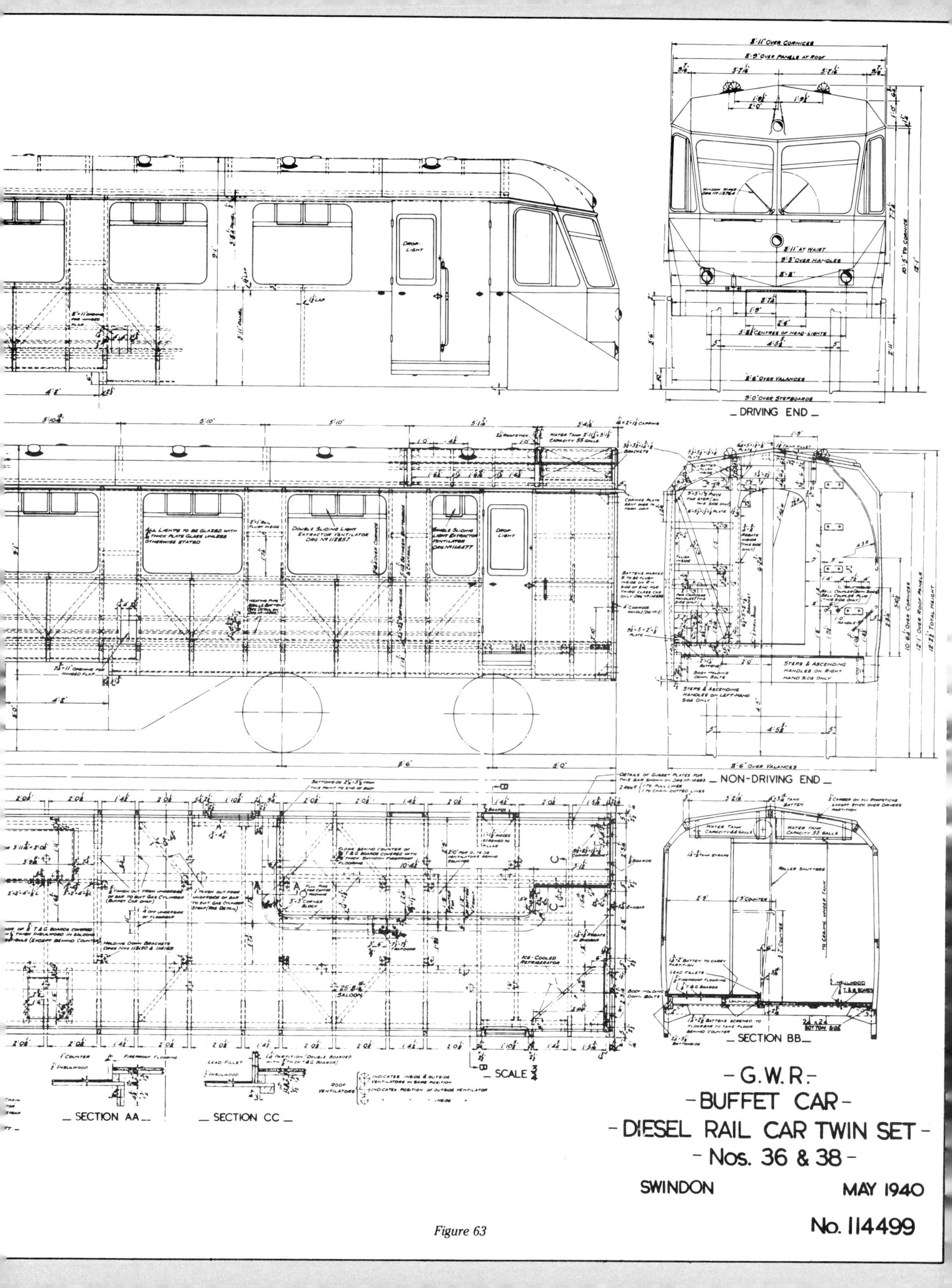

Figure 63A

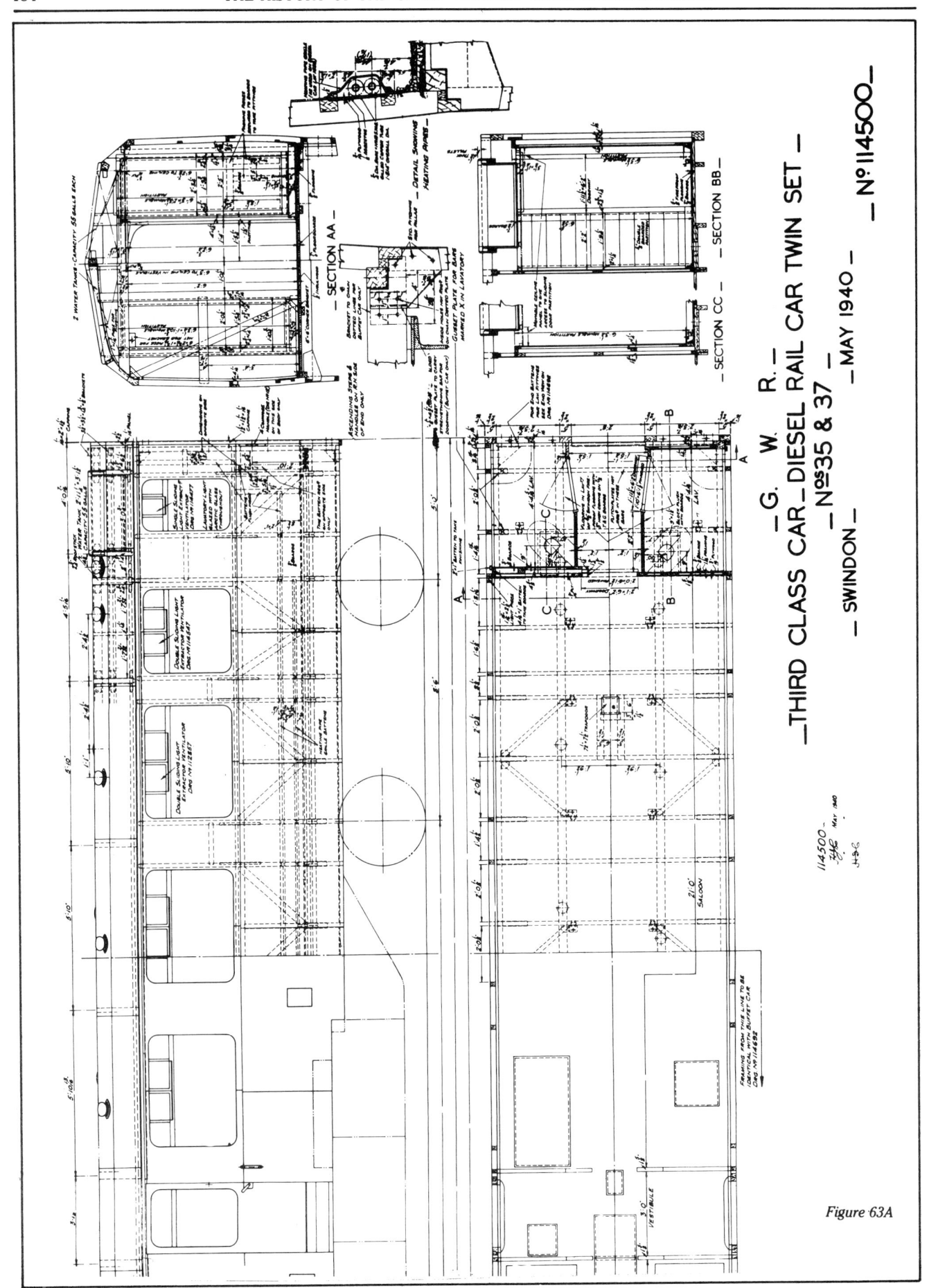

*Plate 200:* An interior view of the buffet car No. 36, photographed on 20th September 1941.

*British Rail*

*Plate 201:* The highly-polished buffet counter of railcar No. 36.

*British Rail*

*Plate 202:* A further view looking in the other direction from that in *Plate 201* of the buffet section of railcar No. 36.

*British Rail*

*Plate 203:* A view of railcar No. 35; the unit with toilet and steam generator compartments.

*British Rail*

*Plate 204:* Details of the coffee, water boiling and cooking facilities of railcars Nos. 36 and 38.

*British Rail*

compartments was the entrance vestibule with a wide doorway in each side, while at the opposite end to the buffet compartment was a small luggage compartment and the driver's compartment.

The other car had two saloon compartments, one of which seated 28 passengers and the other 32 passengers *(see Plate 203)*, between which was the entrance vestibule. Toilet accommodation was provided adjacent to the smaller saloon while the luggage compartment and the driver's compartment were at the opposite end of the vehicle *(Figure 64)*.

The bodies were mounted on steel underframes, and the side framing secured to the floor members with steel brackets like the other cars, and were panelled throughout on the outside, with steel panels fastened to the teak framing. The outside straight-lined appearance of the roof, and at the same time the curved inside ceiling, was achieved by using shaped members. The floor was insulated from noise by using ⅞in. boards covered with ½in. insulating material, as on the other cars of similar design.

The twin units were decorated in a similar manner to the existing single diesel units with coloured rexine, offset with polished mahogany mouldings, the lower portion of the walls being covered in olive green and the top portion in cream, with the ceiling in a paler shade of cream. The seats were comfortably upholstered in patterned olive green moquette, the seat ends being inlaid with green rexine. The floor was covered with mottled green linoleum (to tone with the walls) whilst in the central passageway, and in the entrance vestibules, hair carpet was laid.

The cars were illuminated with three lamp clusters arranged along the centre of the ceiling, while the windows were all fitted with curtains. Passenger luggage racks ran the whole length of the passenger section. The cars were heated by hot water taken from the engine cooling system, and the pipes ran the entire length of the saloons on either side, a vast improvement on earlier designs.

The buffet saloon was equipped with a coffee machine *(see Plate 204)*, a grill, boiling rings, etc., and was easily capable of supplying light refreshments to all the passengers. The

Figure 64

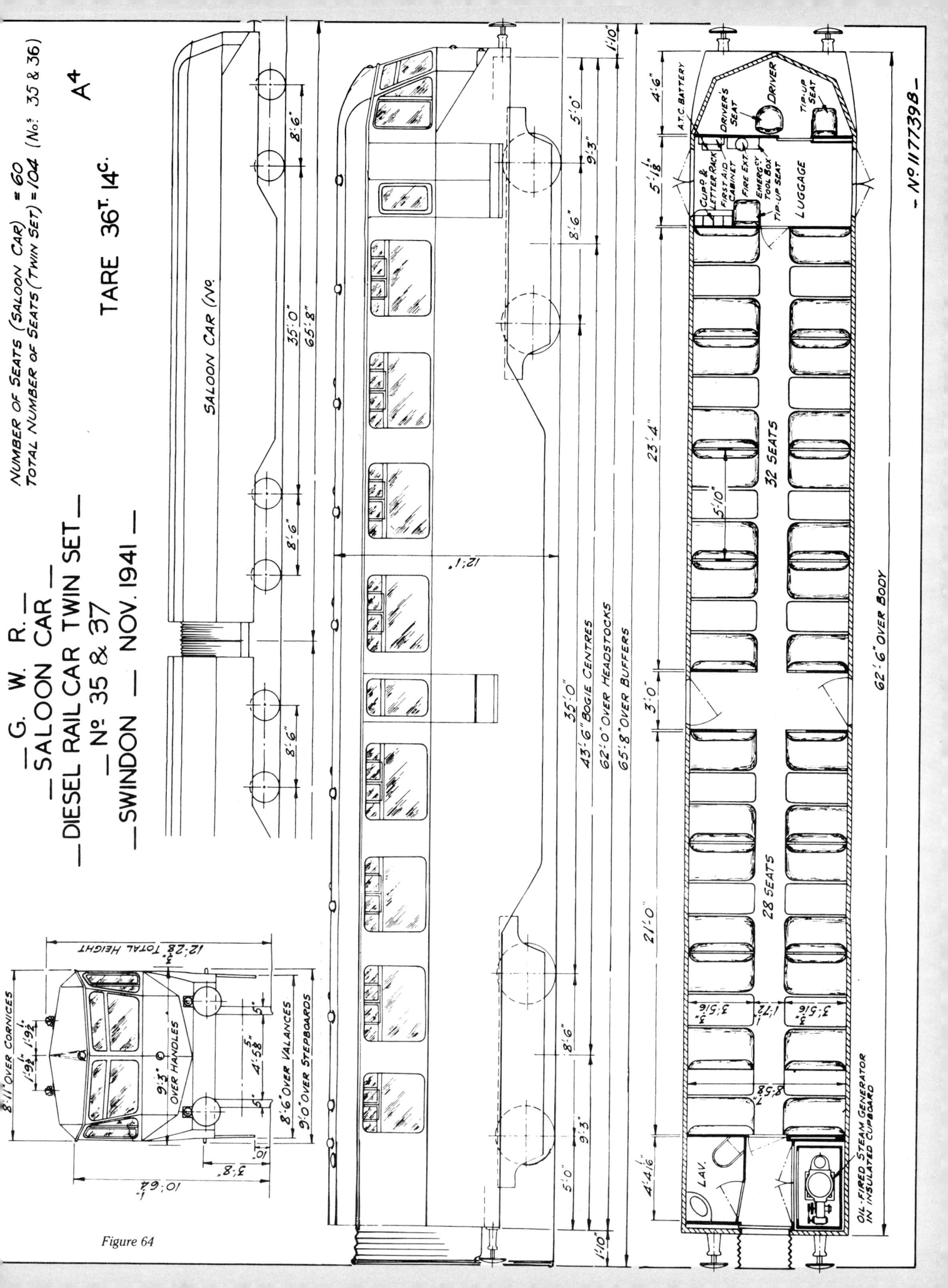

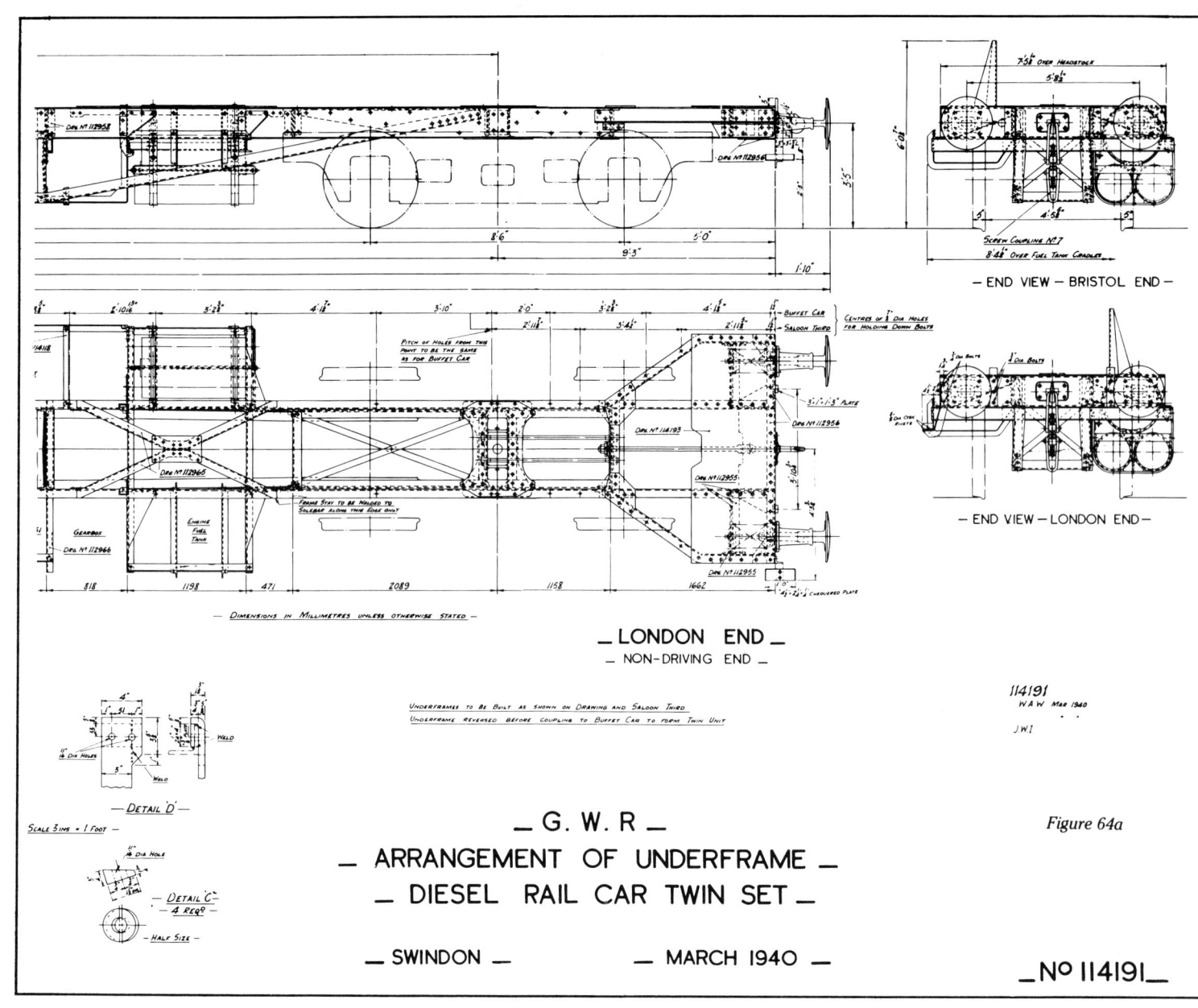

**G.W.R**
**ARRANGEMENT OF UNDERFRAME**
**DIESEL RAIL CAR TWIN SET**

_ SWINDON _ — MARCH 1940 —

*Figure 64a*

N° 114191

counter was not equipped with seats, but tables were provided between all the passengers' seats, enabling them to be served in their seats.

In the luggage compartment were the emergency tool cabinet, first-aid outfit and fire extinguishers, as well as the guard's seat, letter rack and cupboard. The driver's compartment was arranged to enable the driver to manipulate all the various controls in comfort, and was a vast improvement over the earlier cars. Droplights were provided on both sides of the compartment, which was heated with hot water pipes. Window wipers were also fitted to the front Triplex glass windows.

The twin sets were adapted to take an extra vehicle, inserted between the two driving cars, and the necessary cables, etc. (for operating the sets from either end) were carried underneath this middle coach *(Plate 199)*. Steam heating was supplied to this middle coach by a special steam generator fitted in one of the driving cars. This generator was fired from a fuel tank mounted on the underframe, the necessary water being carried in the roof tank. It was automatic and, once started, maintained a constant steam supply to the extra coach.

A test run of the twin-unit railcars (with a standard corridor coach coupled between them), was made on 15th October 1941 from Southall to Westbury and back; a total distance of 172½ miles. The tare weight of the complete unit was 108 tons, and with passengers was approximately 110 tons. The addition of the trailing coach reduced the horsepower per ton by approximately 30 per cent, and obviously had some effect on the speeds obtained, especially when accelerating or on gradients. Nevertheless, on the return journey, speeds of 70½ m.p.h. were officially observed at Bedwyn and Newbury. A feature common to both runs was the remarkably smooth riding, even at 70 m.p.h., of both leading and trailing cars.

On the outward trip, stops were made at Reading, Newbury,

Figure 65

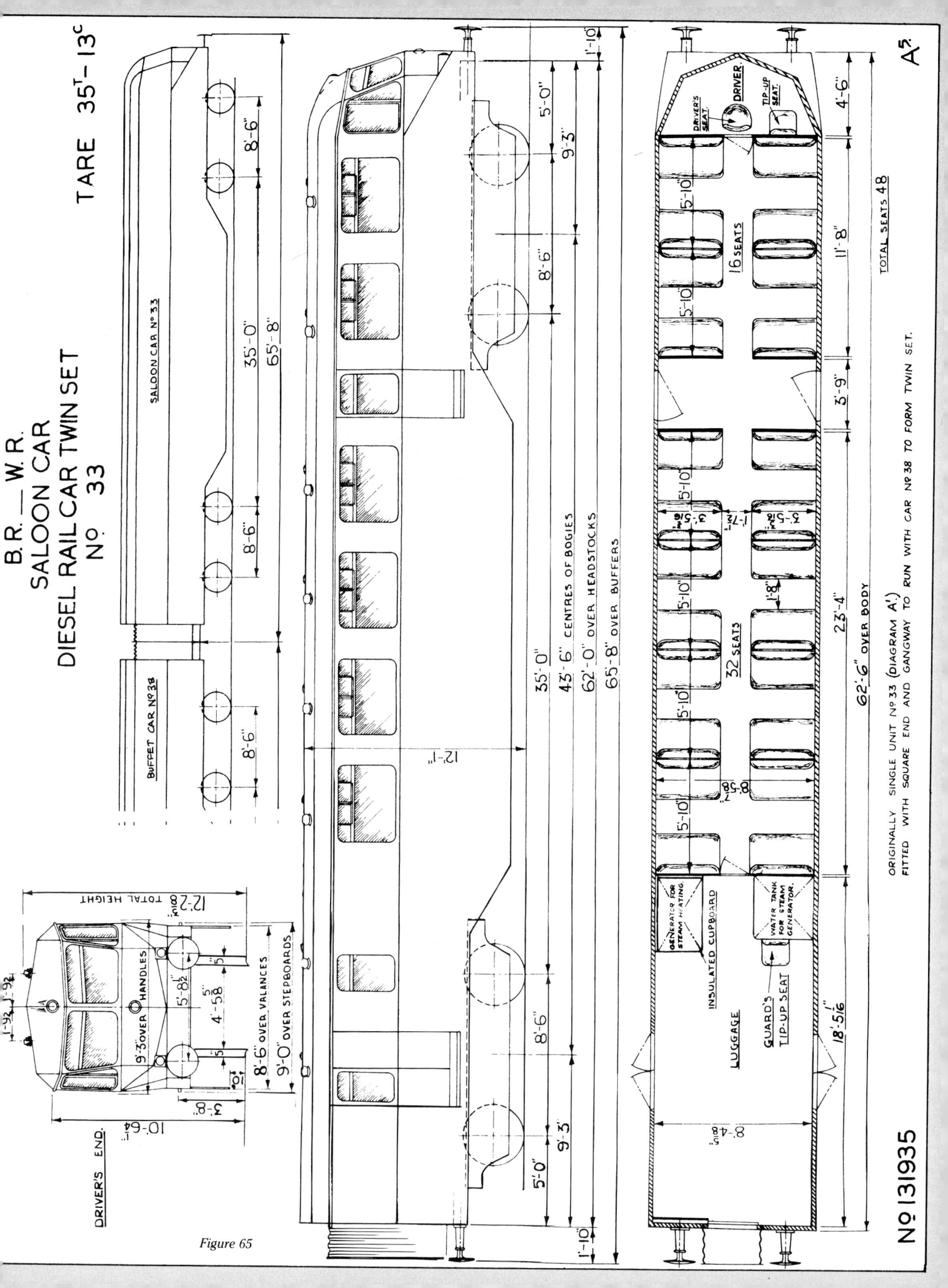

*Plate 205:* Railcar twin set Nos. 35 and 36 on acceptance trials in October 1941 before entering service in November.

*British Rail*

Bedwyn and Patney; but on the return run, planned as non-stop, adverse signals brought the unit to a standstill for 3min. at Reading. Thereafter, speed was affected by the presence of an express ahead, although the 27 miles to Southall were accomplished without a stop. From Southall to Newbury, the line was practically level. It then rose gently to Bedwyn where the gradients followed to Pewsey after which the line undulated to Patney.

The following speeds were obtained; thence it dropped steeply to Lavington.

*Outward:* Southall-Reading, 27 miles at 43½m.p.h. (2 checks); Reading-Newbury, 17 miles at 45m.p.h. (1 check) Newbury-Bedwyn, 13¼ miles at 42½m.p.h.; Bedwyn-Patney, 14¾ miles at 44½m.p.h.; Patney-Westbury, 14½ miles at 27m.p.h. (stopped outside Westbury for 12½min.).

*Return:* Westbury-Reading, 59½ miles at 54m.p.h. (2 checks); Reading-Southall, 27 miles at 46½m.p.h. (4 checks).

Average speed for both trips; 173 miles at 45m.p.h. On the return trip passing times were: Westbury start to Patney pass, 14½ miles at 45m.p.h.; Patney pass to Bedwyn pass, 14¾ miles at 56m.p.h.; Bedwyn pass to Newbury pass, 13¼ miles at 65m.p.h.; Patney pass to Newbury pass, 28 miles at 60m.p.h.; Newbury pass to Reading stop, 17 miles at 32m.p.h. (checked).

Fuel consumption for the day was 49 gallons, which equalled 3.6m.p.g. or 396 ton miles per gallon.

So came the end to the building of this revolutionary fleet of vehicles, and with many of them lasting into the early 1960s, they served the Great Western Railway and British Railways (Western Region) with a high degree of efficiency and operational reliability, in fact covering a total of 14,643,357 miles. This includes No. 33's mileage before it was converted to be coupled to No. 38, to take the place of No. 37 (damaged and destroyed by fire in 1947). The diagram for the rebuild is seen in *Figure 65*.

**AEC**

**SOUTHALL**

**RAIL CARS**

**SOUTHALL, MIDDLESEX**

# Chapter Ten: The Power Plant and its Construction

**The 130hp High Speed Diesel Oil Engine**
Over three years' whole-time intensive research work was carried out by A.E.C. engineers, and many long-duration service tests by independent operators, before the 1932 model of the A.E.C. high speed oil engine was introduced. The degree of success attained in bringing the new unit up to the standard of the current petrol engine can be judged from the fact that road speeds of over 3,000r.p.m. were obtained, and that cruising speeds of 2,000r.p.m. could be maintained. Light weight, made doubly important by the restrictions of the Road Traffic Act that had been recently introduced, the weight of the latest model had been brought down, complete with flywheel and all accessories, to 1,414lb.

To improve the engine, from a thermo-dynamic standpoint, the experiments carried out in the early stages had been continued and, as a result of investigations made simultaneously with Mr Ricardo, material improvements — including reduced fuel consumption — and the elimination of the so-called diesel knock, had been achieved.

Other improvements made included modification of the combustion chamber, producing a greater and more definite state of turbulence to the air before injecting the fuel. This had resulted in much better and cleaner conbustion, and the production of a higher mean-pressure at a lower fuel consumption.

The new cylinder head contained a spherical combustion chamber, which was connected to the cylinder barrel by means of a conical passage arranged tangentially to the surface of the chamber. As much as possible of the compression volume was contained in this sphere, only the necessary mechanical clearance being left between the top of the piston and the underface of the cylinder head when the piston was at the upper end of its stroke. The injector was so placed that the fuel was sprayed into the chamber, the injector itself being placed at a slight angle to the vertical. The idea of the design was to produce an orderly swirl of the air in the combustion chamber. The air was then forced from the cylinder through a tangential passage into the combustion chamber, taking up a rotary action within the sphere, and the body of air was thus flowing at a rapid rate past the injector nozzle during the period of injection. This brought a continual supply of fresh air to each particle of fuel as it entered the combustion chamber. As a result of this action, a high percentage of the air was utilised, and the combustion was virtually complete. A perfectly clear exhaust was repeatedly obtained, while developing mean effective pressure of over 100p.s.i.

The crankcase was ribbed to provide the maximum support for the crankshaft and cast in Elektron alloy. The main bearing caps were of drop-forged steel, with white metal bearing surfaces running directly into them. The cylinder was in the form of a monobloc casting which, when bolted to the crankcase, formed an exceedingly stiff construction for supporting the crankshaft.

The crankshaft, partially balanced by counterweights to relieve the main bearings of some of the dynamic loading, was of very generous proportions, and of sufficient rigidity to avoid any problems from torsional vibration. The seven main bearings were 85mm. in diameter, and the crank pins 75mm. in diameter, with webs of corresponding proportions. The pistons were heat-treated aluminium alloy, and the connecting rods were of drop-forged alloy steel.

Adjustment of the big end bearings was achieved by the use of shims. Lubrication was effected by means of a gear type pump, having a patented device for providing a supply of low pressure oil to the valve gear. The valves operated through push rods and rockers from the camshaft, and the ends of the valve stems had specially hardened caps to obviate any wear. The fuel pump and injectors were standard Bosch equipment, and worked at an injection pressure of 1,000p.s.i. A special exhaust pump — driven at half engine speed in tandem with the fuel pump — was fitted for brake operation. The exhauster maintained a vacuum of 22-24in. mercury on a tank carried inside the frame, and thus did away with the necessity for throttling the engine air-intake, and making elaborate arrangements for fuel cut-off when the brakes were applied.

The electrical equipment consisted of twin 24 volt generators, driven in tandem, and a C.A.V.-Bosch electric starting motor. All the auxiliaries were mounted on the nearside of the engine, leaving the offside free for forward drive chassis. Accessibility was thus provided to those parts which occasionally required attention. The engine was of particularly clean design, and its appearance was greatly enhanced by the elimination of the inlet manifold. This had been incorporated in the cylinder head valve-gear cover, which was provided with a passage inside the top, with extensions downwards to meet ports cast in the upper face of the cylinder head. A gasket provided the necessary oil-tight seal at the junction with the cylinder head. The air was admitted to an air cleaner attached to the forward end of the cover. The outstanding feature of the A.E.C. engine at this period in development was the fuel economy achieved. Consumptions obtained in actual service showed from 75 per cent to 95 per cent improvement over those for similar vehicles in the same service, running on petrol. This saving illustrated the possibilities which the oil engine provided for a reduction in operating costs, as compared with a petrol engine. In ton-miles-per-gallon, figures of over 170 were registered, while instances of over 150 ton-miles-per-gallon were achieved over a distance of 10,000 miles. A great forward development of the diesel engine.

The engines fitted in the Great Western railcars were relatively of the same design throughout the series of railcars Nos. 1-38, and were based upon the successful A.E.C. 6-cylinder oil engine described in the previous paragraphs. This engine had been designed basically for buses, and the company had produced many units before the first railcar was fitted out. This meant that considerable experience had been already gained, both in manufacturing and the running of this power plant. By March 1935, over 2,300 units were recorded as having been constructed.

During its use in the railcars, several modifications were necessary, one being the cooling of oil and, as a temporary measure, external coolers were fitted. These consisted of a large diameter pipe through which the oil was passed, while water, cooled by an auxiliary radiator, circulated through gilled tubes contained in the cooler. It may be noted that the auxiliary radiator consisted of a continuous tube, whereas the main one was made up of a number of tubes in parallel, as the oil cooler called for a relatively small flow of water and a large temperature drop. To get the most efficient working temperature for the engine, the main radiator gave a large flow, and a small drop. A drop of about five degrees was all that was required in the main radiator, whereas a drop of about 85-90 degrees was necessary for the cooling of the oil.

Owing to the risk of fracture in external oil pipes, (although none was experienced), it was decided to make the cooler self-contained in the crankcase *(Figure 66)*. In this, a grid, through

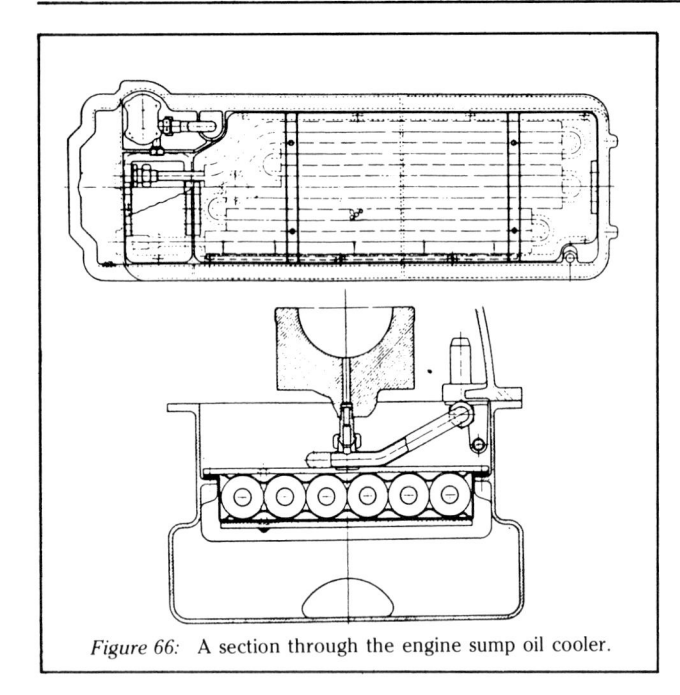

*Figure 66:* A section through the engine sump oil cooler.

*Figure 68*

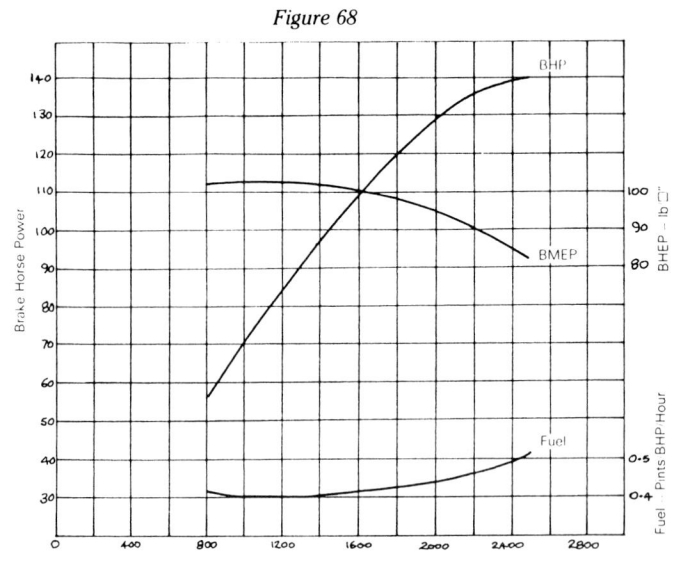

Performance Curves of AEC 6 cyl High Speed Oil Engine (Ricardo Head) 115mm x 142mm

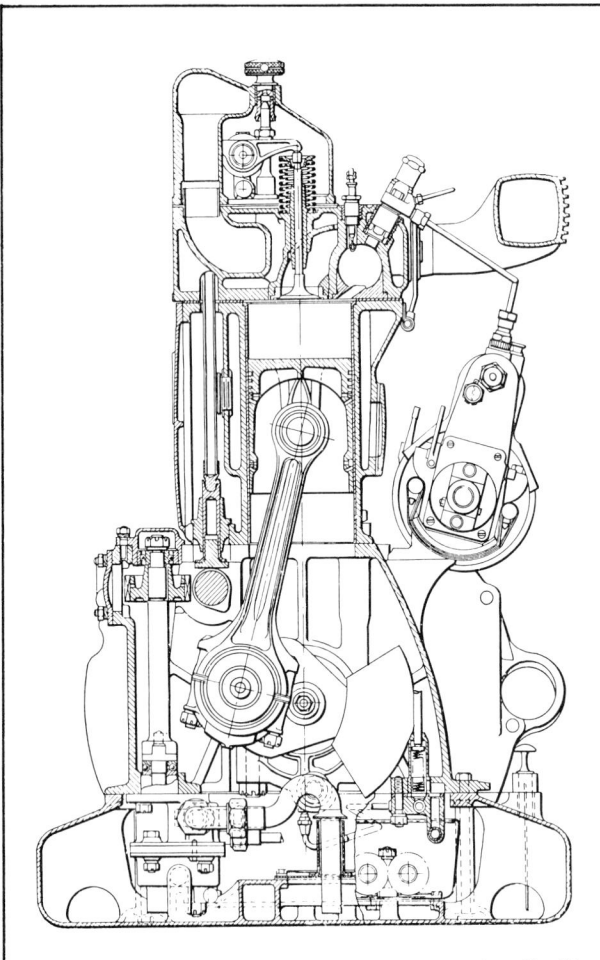

*Figure 67:* A section through the engine on railcar No. 18.

which water was passed, was laid in the crankcase sump, and all the oil thrown off from the bearings and relief valve had to pass through this grid before it reached the oil pump.

*Figure 66* also shows the larger oil pipes that were fitted to all engines, owing to the tendency of the smaller type to close-in at the unions, when they were liable to get clogged by particles of carbon, etc.

On railcar No. 18, a different system was employed *(Figure 67)*, this being of the dry sump type. The cooling element was contained in a tray or bath, and the oil, after passing over the cooling grid, was pumped out by the scavenge half of the pump into the space outside the tray, and then by the other half of the pump to the bearings. In this way, the height of the engine was considerably reduced, and the raised portions of the floor over the engines could be dispensed with. In this cooling system, the object was to keep the cooling tubes clear of the oil stored in the sump, so that when the engine was standing, the oil would not remain in the tubes and 'sludge-up' as it cooled off. As previously pointed out, rigidity and lack of 'give' necessitated more robust units, and for this reason it had been found necessary to change over from aluminium to cast-iron crankcases, to avoid bearing trouble caused by distortion. Also on the early cars, considerable trouble had been experienced with broken timing chains. Timing gears were substituted, but even these gave trouble, owing to crankshaft torsional vibration and, although these gears should theoretically have been capable of transmitting about 15hp continuously, they had to be replaced by gears almost equal to those used in a gearbox, and capable of transmitting the full power of this engine.

After the modifications and new design features on No. 18's engine, the final engines on railcars No. 19-38 were the A.E.C. 6-cylinder direct injection type, having an increased bore of 120mm. and the same stroke of 142mm., but giving a reduced brake horsepower of 105 at 1,650r.p.m. The next few pages contain some extracts from the service manual for one of these railcar engines.

THE POWER PLANT AND ITS CONSTRUCTION 193

*Plate 206:* This photograph shows how access to the engine and various other items was made easy by the panels and trap doors.
(A.E.C. Ltd.) Leyland Vehicles Ltd.

The power plant.

### GENERAL DATA.

| | |
|---|---|
| Bore | 115 mm. |
| Stroke | 142 mm. |
| Cubic Capacity | 8·85 litres |
| R.A.C. Rating (Types A165 and A180) | 49·2 H.P. |
| Governed Speed | 1,800 R.P.M. |
| Oil Capacity (without oil filter) | 3¼ Gallons |
| Valve Clearance | 0·010" to 0·012" |
| Max. Brake Horse Power { Type A165 | 130 B.H.P. |
| Type A180 | 114 B.H.P. |

---

## 8·8 Litre 6-Cylinder
### O.H.V.
## HIGH SPEED
## OIL ENGINE

A.E.C. LIMITED,
AN A.C.V. COMPANY.
SOUTHALL, MIDDLESEX, ENGLAND.
Telephone : SOUthall 2424 (19 lines). Telegrams and Cables : "Vangestow, Telex, Southall."
A.E.C. SOUTHALL SERVICE DEPOT : 20, Windmill Lane, Southall, Middlesex.
Telephone: SOUthall 2300 (5 lines) Telegrams : "Repaircar, 'Phone, Southall."

# THE 6-CYLINDER OIL ENGINE.

The original "8·8 litre" oil engine (type A165) was of the indirect injection type; many of these have been converted into direct injection engines (type A180).

This Instruction Book fully describes the original indirect injection engine, and where information is not applicable to the direct injection version, an asterisk refers to the Appendix at the back of the Section, where amended instructions are given for the converted engine.

## DESCRIPTION.

The engine is fitted with overhead valves which are operated by means of push rods and rockers from a camshaft carried in the crankcase.

The camshaft is driven from the crankshaft by a chain which also forms the drive to the fan, the water pump, the dynamo, the exhauster and the fuel-injection pump. The latter two are mounted in tandem on the nearside of the engine, whilst the water pump, which is mounted on the forward side of the crankcase, is driven by an extension of the dynamo drive shaft. The water pump is fitted with a special graphite packing which requires no attention, and this eliminates constant repacking of the gland.

Full pressure lubrication is fitted for the main and big-end bearings, and a patented metering device feeds a small quantity of oil, at low pressure, to the overhead valve gear.

A large capacity oil filter, which also acts in some degree as a cooler, is sometimes fitted in series with the main oil supply to the bearings. The oil is thus maintained in good condition, and the dirt and carbon in it is reduced to a minimum. The filter element can be removed very quickly for cleaning or renewal without the loss of any oil other than that which is contained in the filter chamber itself.

Three point suspension is provided for the engine unit, the front of the engine being carried by a removable crossmember bolted to the dumb irons and fixing to a bracket on the front of the crankcase which carries the cranking handle.

## THE CYLINDER HEADS.

The cylinder heads are formed in two units, each covering three cylinders, and they are, as regards their essential details, interchangeable.

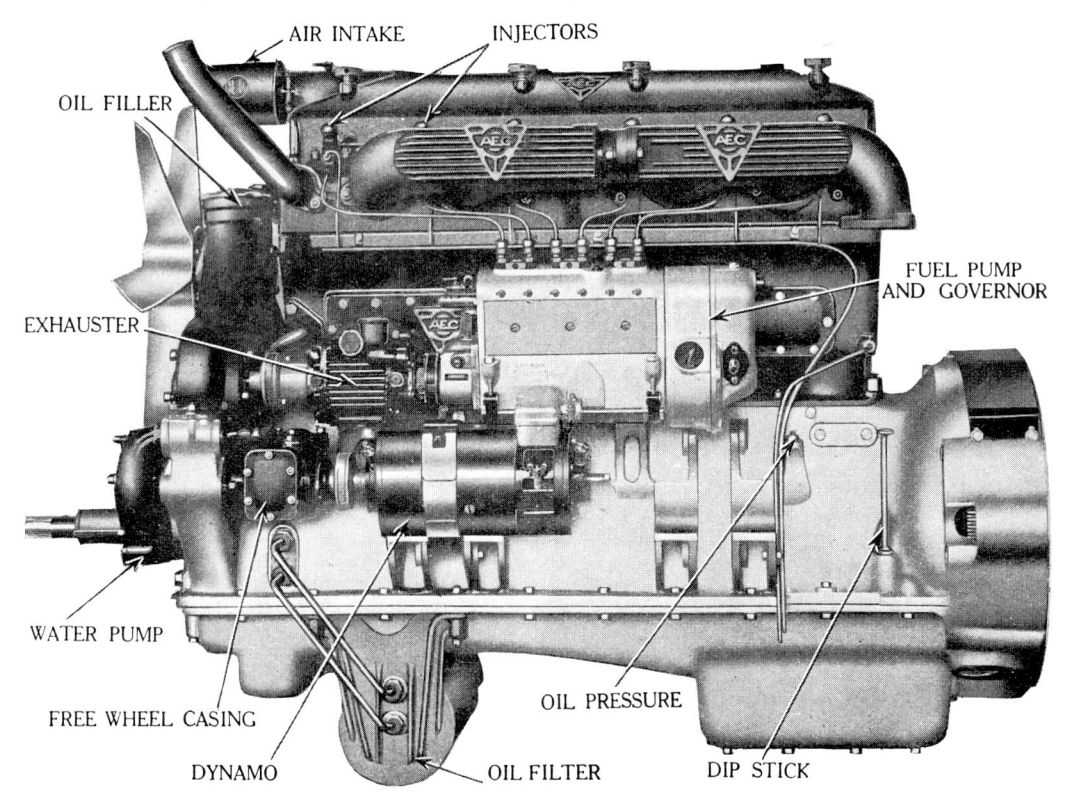

# THE POWER PLANT AND ITS CONSTRUCTION

The valve gear mechanism is carried in the head and the valve seatings of a special alloy cast iron are screwed in. This ensures long and efficient valve operation without constant regrinding.

## REMOVAL OF VALVE SPRINGS.

Valve springs can be easily replaced without removing the valves. Remove the rocker shaft complete with brackets and rockers, after first disconnecting the oil pipes feeding the rocker bearings.

Bring the piston under the valve, the spring of which is to be removed, on to its top dead centre, depress the valve spring with a suitable valve lifter and remove the split collar from the valve stem.

## REMOVAL OF CYLINDER HEADS.

The cylinder heads are removed separately and the process is practically identical for both the front and the rear.

Remove the cylinder head cover. Disconnect the top water pipe; it is generally easier to break the flanged joint on the cylinder head than to disturb the rubber connection. Remove the buss bar from the heater plugs (type A165 engines only), and disconnect injector pipes.

Disconnect the exhaust pipe flange and uncouple the two halves of the exhaust manifold where it is joined in the centre. Remove the water pipe coupling the two heads together at the nearside of the engine, remove the rockers and brackets, and, for convenience, lift out the push rods operating the valves.

Remove the thimbles from the tips of the valve stems.

Two special jack nuts are fitted to each head to facilitate removal, and are so arranged that as they are unscrewed they will lift the head clear of the cylinder block. *These two nuts must, therefore, not be unscrewed until all the other nuts have been removed.* When this has been done, unscrew the two jack nuts evenly until the nuts are disengaged from their studs.

## REGRINDING VALVES.*

The seating angle for the valves is 30°, and as this differs from our usual petrol engine practice, we would call particular note to this point to obviate any chance of the valve seats being incorrectly cut when re-cutting becomes necessary.

It should never be necessary to remove the venturi from the cylinder head, and in the few cases where this is found necessary from one cause or another, the complete head should be returned to the factory for inspection and replacement.

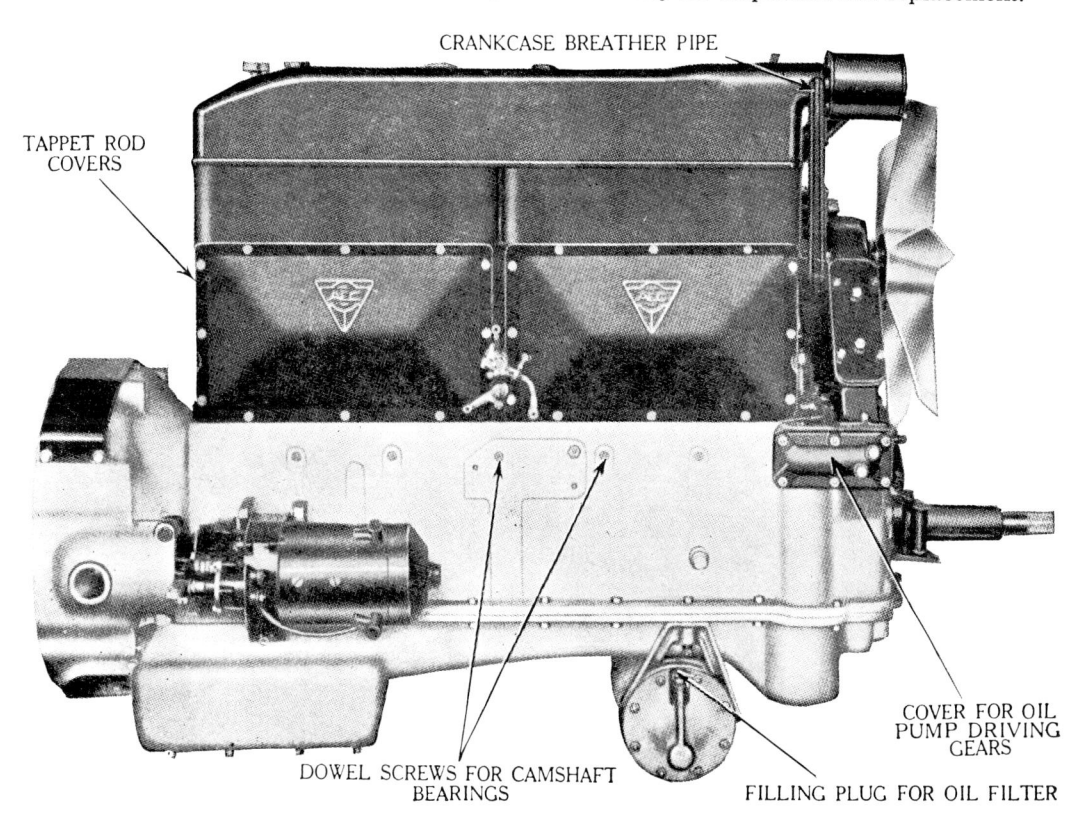

TAPPET ROD COVERS

CRANKCASE BREATHER PIPE

DOWEL SCREWS FOR CAMSHAFT BEARINGS

FILLING PLUG FOR OIL FILTER

COVER FOR OIL PUMP DRIVING GEARS

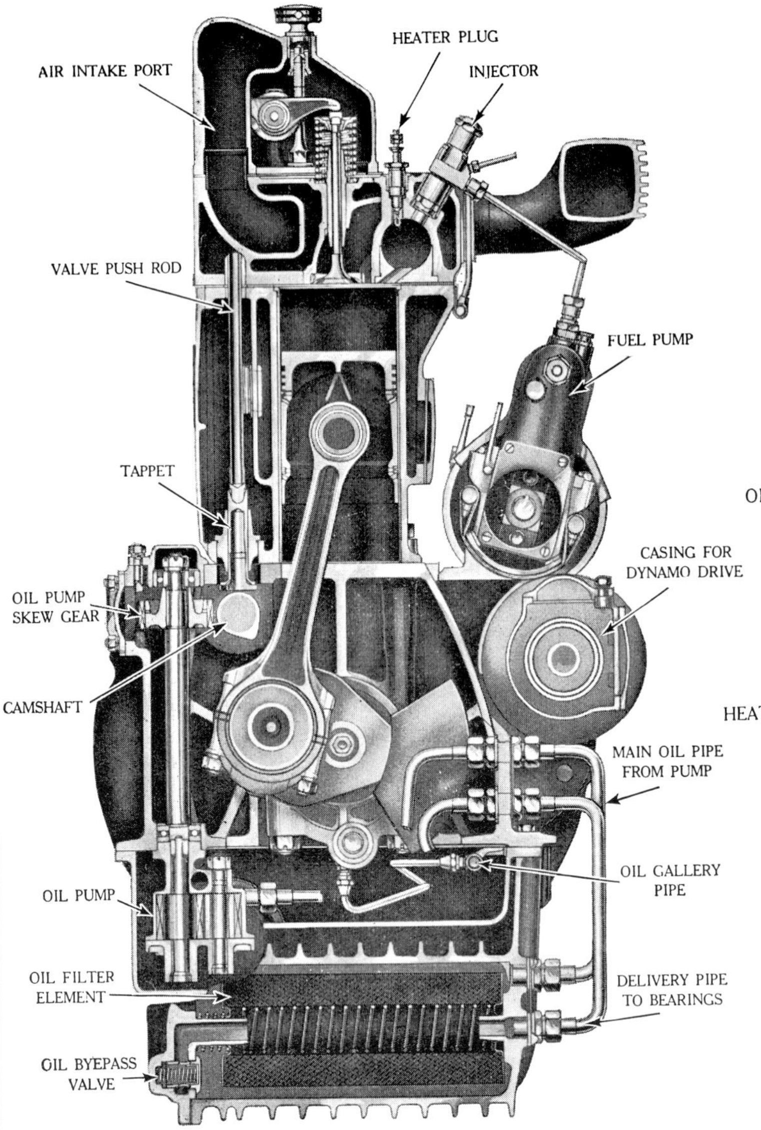
HEATER PLUG
AIR INTAKE PORT
INJECTOR
VALVE PUSH ROD
FUEL PUMP
TAPPET
CASING FOR DYNAMO DRIVE
OIL PUMP SKEW GEAR
CAMSHAFT
MAIN OIL PIPE FROM PUMP
OIL GALLERY PIPE
OIL PUMP
OIL FILTER ELEMENT
DELIVERY PIPE TO BEARINGS
OIL BYEPASS VALVE

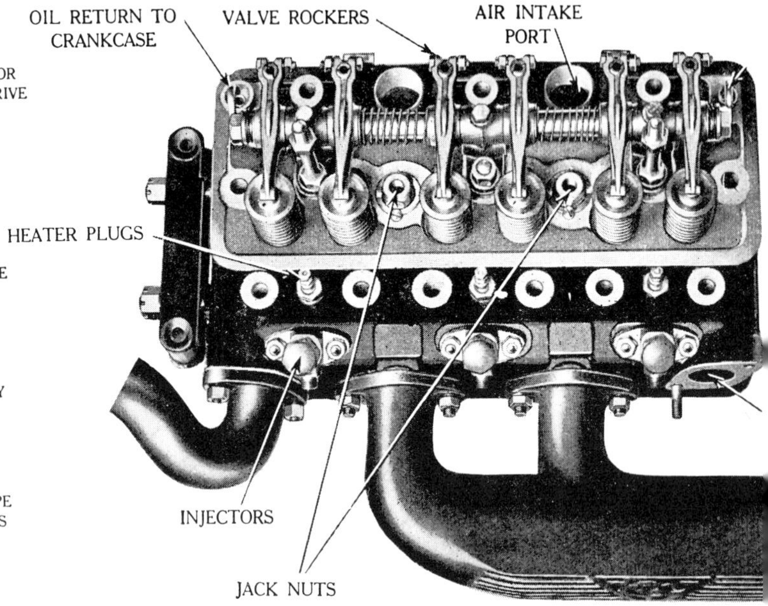
OIL RETURN TO CRANKCASE
VALVE ROCKERS
AIR INTAKE PORT
HEATER PLUGS
INJECTORS
JACK NUTS

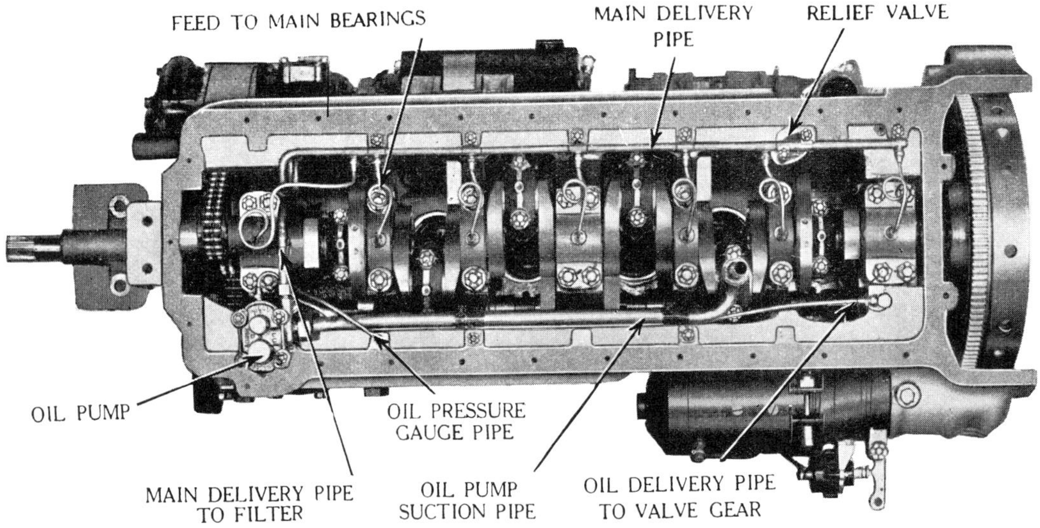
FEED TO MAIN BEARINGS
MAIN DELIVERY PIPE
RELIEF VALVE
OIL PUMP
OIL PRESSURE GAUGE PIPE
MAIN DELIVERY PIPE TO FILTER
OIL PUMP SUCTION PIPE
OIL DELIVERY PIPE TO VALVE GEAR

# Chapter Eleven: Three are still Preserved

The Great Western railcars are as much a part of railway history as the steam locomotives, and therefore it is fortuitous that three examples have been preserved, namely No. 4, the original streamlined 'flying banana', and Nos. 20 and 22 of the squarer, 'razor edge' GWR-built type.

Railcar No. 4 was acquired by Swindon Corporation (later the Borough of Thamesdown) and, due to lack of space in the museum, was placed on loan to the Great Western Society at Didcot, Oxfordshire. No. 4, however, later left Didcot for the National Railway Museum at York, and arrived there on 6th February 1979, where it went into store, pending a decision as to its future. The National Railway Museum decided to rebuild this vehicle to its original splendour and sent it (by rail) to a company named RESCO Ltd., Erith, Kent, who specialise in restoration works, on 5th January 1981. The subsequent rebuilding is shown in *Plates 222 to 225*. The vehicle then left in July 1984 and finally, was put into the GWR Museum at Swindon on 12th July 1984, replacing *City of Truro*, the steam locomotive, which was removed to be reconditioned for the GWR's 150th Celebration Year.

Railcar No. 20, however, was purchased in 1966 by the Kent & East Sussex Railway from a Worcester company (where it had been in store), in a derelict state. After its arrival, it was fully restored to operational condition and, happily, its new Kent & East Sussex livery of chocolate and cream coincided with its former Great Western colours. It is known to have operated, in its 22 years of Great Western and British Rail service, in the Bristol, Newport and Weymouth areas. It was operational by Christmas 1972, and formed the first fare-paying public train in February 1974. For the next five years it ran regular Saturday morning and November services. Regrettably, although mechanically sound, it was withdrawn in 1980 suffering badly from corrosion and its fate now hangs in the balance. The delivery of this railcar was by rail, arriving at Robertsbridge on 3rd April 1966 (see Special Traffic Notice). Because of width restrictions on the Hastings line, it was hauled as an 'out-of-gauge' load by an electro-diesel locomotive from Tonbridge, with nothing permitted on the lines either side of it, during its 80 minute journey.

*Plate 207:* No. 4 railcar in Swindon Works.

CCE's Department representative and Freight Trains Inspector will travel with this train.

---

**SPECIAL TRAFFIC NOTICE NO. 295 SED (contd.) 1.4.66**

**SUNDAY 3rd APRIL 1966**

**DEPARTMENTAL TRAIN ARRANGEMENTS**

Tonbridge, Robertsbridge, Tonbridge (CM & EE A/c.)

| | arr. | dep. | |
|---|---|---|---|
| Tonbridge W.Yd. | LD | 14.43 | LD — ex-GWR Diesel Railcar W20W and brake van, hauled by EDL |
| Tonbridge Station | 14.49 | | |
| Grove Junction | 15.09 | | |
| Wadhurst | 15.28 | | |
| Etchingham | 15.56 | | |
| Robertsbridge | 16.04SD | 17.15 (EBV) | |
| Wadhurst | 17.34 | | SD — Shunt and Detach Railcar |
| Grove Junction | 17.44 | | |
| Tonbridge Station | 17.55 | | Class: 8. Headcode KE. |
| Tonbridge W.Yd. | 18.00 | ST | |

---

*This train will run as an OUT-OF-GAUGE load, and the following instructions will apply between Tonbridge and Robertsbridge.*

1. Train conveying this load must travel on Through Line at Tonbridge.
2. Must NOT exceed speed of 20m.p.h. throughout, and NOT more than 10m.p.h. from TONBRIDGE EAST JN., to country end of SOMERHILL TUNNEL, through WELLS TUNNEL, GROVE HILL TUNNEL, STRAWBERRY HILL TUNNEL, WADHURST TUNNEL, and through BRIDGE NO. 87 (at 40M.P.). Also NOT to exceed 5m.p.h. through all platforms.
3. Running lines and/or sidings on right-hand side of load, looking in direction of travel, must be clear, and nothing OUT-OF-GAUGE must be allowed on the running lines and/or sidings on the left-hand side of the load. To be signalled by the special 'Is Line Clear', or 'Description of Train' signal 2-6-3 (Two-Six-Three) from TONBRIDGE EAST JN. to ROBERTSBRIDGE.

A report in *The Farmers Line* (the old house magazine of the Kent & East Sussex Railway) records how this vehicle was purchased.

*Photomatic*

*Plate 208:* Railcar No. 4, seen outside the Peter Allen Building at the National Railway Museum, York, in 1980, awaiting restoration.
*National Railway Museum*

Plate 209: Standing at Swindon Works on 18th March 1960, the livery details of railcar No. 4 are well displayed.
*National Railway Museum*

*Plate 210:* A further view of railcar No. 4 at Swindon Works on 18th March 1960.

*National Railway Museum*

*Plate 211:* A detail photograph of the buffet counter in railcar No. 4, before restoration.

*National Railway Museum*

*Plate 212:* No. 4 in splendid 'new' condition, seen at Cardiff posing for official photographer prior to the new express service between Cardiff and Birmingham. Note the single horn. A fine photograph for details.

*British Rail*

*Plate 213:* Ex-GWR railcar No. W4W inside the stock shed at Swindon Works on 20th September 1959.

*N. E. Preedy*

*Plate 214:* Railcar No. 22, preserved on the Severn Valley Railway, hauling a trailer carriage.

*R. H. G. Simpson*

Back in the early days of the K&ESR Preservation Society, equiries to the Western Region about these cars had elicited the fact that they were charging £600 apiece for them and, not having this amount of capital to spend, the matter was temporarily dropped.

However, in due course, the sale of rolling stock became centralised at a department of BR near Euston in the old Railway Clearing House offices at Eversholt House. This department became responsible for the sale of all scrapped materials on the whole of BR valued at more than £25, and soon earned themselves an unenviable reputation of driving hard bargains to the extent that most preservation organisations came to regard those in charge as being, to coin a phrase, 'a right lot of Scrooges'. Much emnity was aroused when Eversholt House began asking sums for engines and coaches wanted for preservation which were far in excess of their value as scrap, even though such vehicles — often irreplaceable historical relics — would simply be burnt and cut-up for a fraction of the price being asked from preservation groups.

This, then, was the scene when, unexpectedly, the Preservation Society's secretary received a form inviting Tenders for the purchase and delivery of the last of the GWR railcars then remaining. This was a rather unusual step since, normally, Eversholt House sold items at fixed prices, and opportunities to make offers rarely occurred. However, after inspecting the cars listed on the Tender form at both Worcester and Swindon, an offer was made of £415 for No. W20W delivered to Robertsbridge, or £365 as standing at Worcester.

Being fully aware of the fact that the car was officially much too wide for delivery through the tunnels on the Hastings line, we never really expected the Tender to be accepted to include delivery, even if it were successful at all, but some weeks later we were all confounded and delighted when a letter arrived stating that our Tender had been successful, and would we please forward £415 immediately so that arrangements could be made for delivery. Due to the generosity of one of the Society members, Mr Brockman, who allowed funds which he had already paid into the Society's Appeal Trust to be used in payment, we were able to send off the sum required, and we sat back to speculate wildly on how the railcar would be got through the Hastings line tunnels with their very restricted clearances.

Several months later, no word having been heard since payment was made, we discovered, to the intense amusement of all who heard about it, that Eversholt House had suddenly realised that they had made a rather large and expensive blunder, and that the car would not be accepted by the Southern Region due to the tunnel clearances. This information came in a letter from Eversholt House which asked us to give them alternative consignment instructions to some other point not on the Hastings line. Naturally, we replied that no other delivery point would be acceptable, as Robertsbridge was our only junction point with the main line. This letter was followed by another space of several weeks, during which time our 'spies' in the appropriate SR department kept us informed that Eversholt House were pleading with the SR to allow them to deliver the car, somehow. The reply was evidently in the negative, for we received a rather curt note from Eversholt House stating that unless alternative consignment instructions were received by them within a few days, they would cancel the sale, and refund the money paid. They were promptly and equally curtly informed that acceptance of our Tender placed them under Contract to deliver the car to us as provided for in the Contract, and that any attempt to wriggle out of this obligation would be followed by legal action by the Society.

A further long pause occurred, at the end of which we received a letter from Eversholt House couched in tones which were positively honeyed, in comparison with the rather threatening tones of previous correspondence, and inviting us to meet the appropriate officer at Eversholt House to discuss the possibility of our accepting some mutually acceptable alternative vehicle to No. W20W. We accordingly did so, and Messrs Cann, Doust, Dunlavey and Sinclair proceeded to beard the ogres in their den. In contrast to the previous occasion when we had met the gentleman concerned, when we had a thoroughly unpleasant time arguing furiously to try to get the price of the 4 Maunsell coaches reduced from £1,260 to the eventual price of £1,000 — their actual value being about £750 for scrap — all was conciliation, on this occasion. Unfortunately, the only vehicles which we could suggest as alternatives were some of the 4-wheeled railbuses running on various regions and built in about 1958 at a cost of some £18,000 each. They seemed quite discomfitted when we turned down the offer of some ancient locomotive-hauled coaches, and eventually undertook to look into the possibility of letting us have one of the 4-wheeled railbuses instead.

However, from the fact that we understood that frantic overtures were again being made to the SR authorities for permission to move No. W20W to Robertsbridge as an out-of-gauge load, we realised that our hopes of a nice new railbus for £415 were not to be realised. The whole business having by now taken over two years, we began pressing for an early delivery of the vehicle, as open store at Worcester was not improving its condition. This pressure resulted in repeated assurances that early delivery could be expected and, at long last, we learned that the SR had decided that the car could be accepted as an out-of-gauge load providing that it could be tilted inwards some 3 inches to clear tunnel sides.

Progress from then onwards was rapid — the car was moved first to Reading, and then to Tonbridge, where it stood for a week in the West Yard there until it could be tilted, after which it was hauled cautiously down to Robertsbridge on a quiet Sunday afternoon, where it got a little of its own back at being kept hanging about at Worcester so long by delaying a 'down' Hastings train for nearly 20 minutes, as it could not be moved from a siding adjacent from the main line in time.

And so it came about that the Association came into possession of the excellent 48 seat A.E.C. railcar and, at the same time, managed to deliver a few pokes at one of British Rail's less popular departments. And they all lived happily ever after . . .

The future, at the time of writing this book, seems a little uncertain for No. 20, but one hopes that the vehicle can find a new lease of life and again be restored to running order.

The last preserved vehicle, No. 22, is owned by the Great Western Society at Didcot, and was purchased in 1967. It was on loan to the Severn Valley Railway until 1978, when it returned to the Great Western Society's premises at Didcot. Whilst at the Severn Valley Railway, it operated a Saturday morning shoppers' service between Bridgnorth and Hampton Loade. The Severn Valley Stock Book records the following about this vehicle:

Our railcar, No. 22, is amongst the batch of 15 which were built at Swindon Carriage Works to a new angular design, often known as 'razor edged', as opposed to the totally streamlined appearance of the first 18 cars. No. 22 was typical of the batch in possessing twin A.E.C. engines, developing a total of 210b.h.p. They carried 48 passengers, included a large luggage compartment, and were suitable for attaching a 60 ton tail-load. For some time in the 1940s, railcar No. 22 inhabited the Bristol district.

From 1956 to 1958, No. 22 became familiar in the Midlands. Stationed at Leamington, it was seen on the service to Stratford and Worcester. In 1958, transfer to Worcester was effected, and for the next three years it became a common sight on the SVR, often working to Shrewsbury, also on the Wyre Forest branch to Tenbury. In August 1958, it was the first of several cars to be repainted in the new BR livery of mid-green (previously it was maroon and cream),

*Plate 215:* A scene at Rolvenden Shed, on 18th September 1977, with ex-GWR railcar No. W20 being worked on by two Kent & East Sussex volunteers.

*Brian Morrison*

*Plate 216:* Railcar No. 20 in service on the Kent & East Sussex Railway in Kent, and already looking in need of repair.

*Lens of Sutton*

and remained at Worcester, the last stronghold of GWR railcars. After the introduction of BR single-unit diesels in 1961, it was retained as standby, and finally withdrawn with all the last GWR cars in October 1962.

It was moved to Swindon Works stock shed, and bought early in 1967. Great Western Preservations are owners of the vehicle, with the GWS Midland Group as custodians. It was moved dead from Swindon to Bridgnorth from 3rd to 13th May 1967 (Kidderminster to Highley pulled by No. D5008 and Highley to Bridgnorth pulled by No. D3205).

Restored at both Bewdley and Bridgnorth, No. 22 made its debut as the first item of restored SVR stock in 1968, and its chocolate and cream livery restoration has been the source of much favourable comment. From June 1970, it continuously worked the Saturday shoppers' service to Hampton Loade until August 1971, and after a further repair, resumed the duty, which is now extended to Bewdley.

And so in 1985 the three are preserved; two in running condition, with at least one of each design change available for closer inspection and comparison. Perhaps if this book has roused in the reader an interest in these vehicles, a visit to the Great Western Society's premises at Didcot, and the GWR Museum at Swindon, will allow the reader to see, at first hand, the ingenuity of these vehicles.

*Plate 217:* Diesel railcar No. W22 at Hampton Loade on the preserved Severn Valley Railway on 29th September 1973, forming the 10.35 service to Bridgnorth. A useful vehicle for this railway.

*Brian Morrison*

*Plate 218:* The same day at Hampton Loade, but showing more details of the railcar.
*Brian Morrison*

*Plate 219:* The end of the journey at Bridgnorth, with railcar No. W22 standing framed by the footbridge.
*Brian Morrison*

*Plate 220:* Shortly after its arrival on the Severn Valley Railway, still in the British Rail green livery, railcar No. W22W stands awaiting its fate. A useful view to show how the panelling for servicing was arranged.

*C. L. Caddy*

*Plate 221:* The last view of railcar No. W22W, seen here in service just before withdrawal, in the BR green livery with crest.

*Lens of Sutton*

*Plate 222:* The next four photographs show railcar No. 4 in the restoration works of RESCO Ltd. at Erith during 1981. The details of the construction of the cars is well covered, and this vehicle is now at Swindon Railway Museum for all to see.

*Brian Morrison*

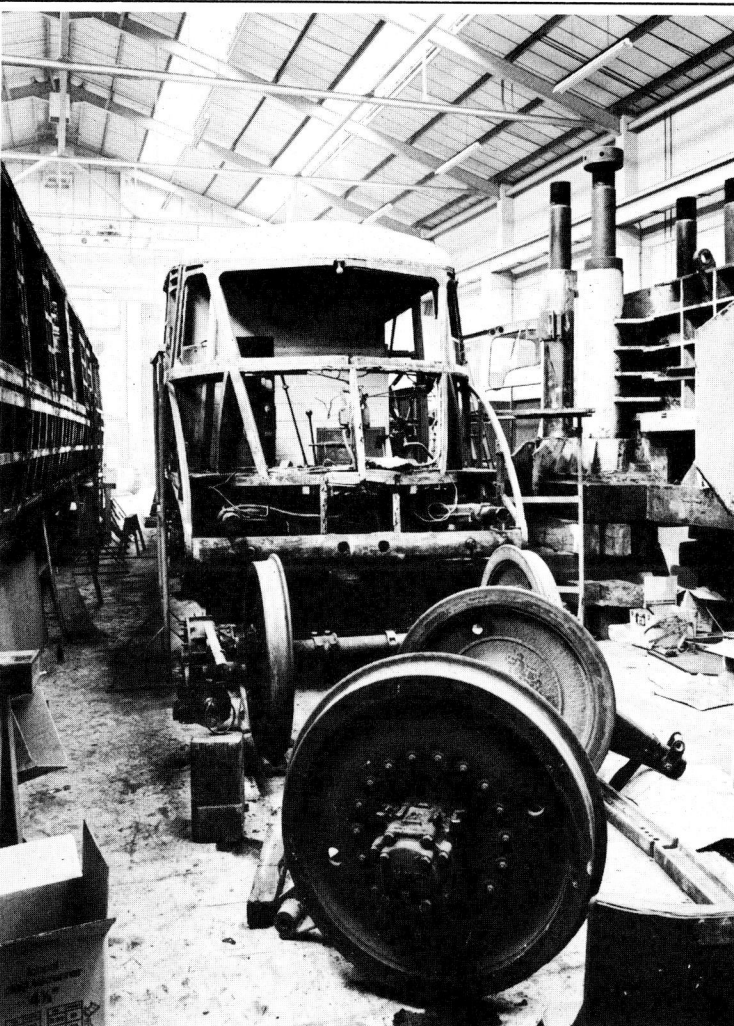

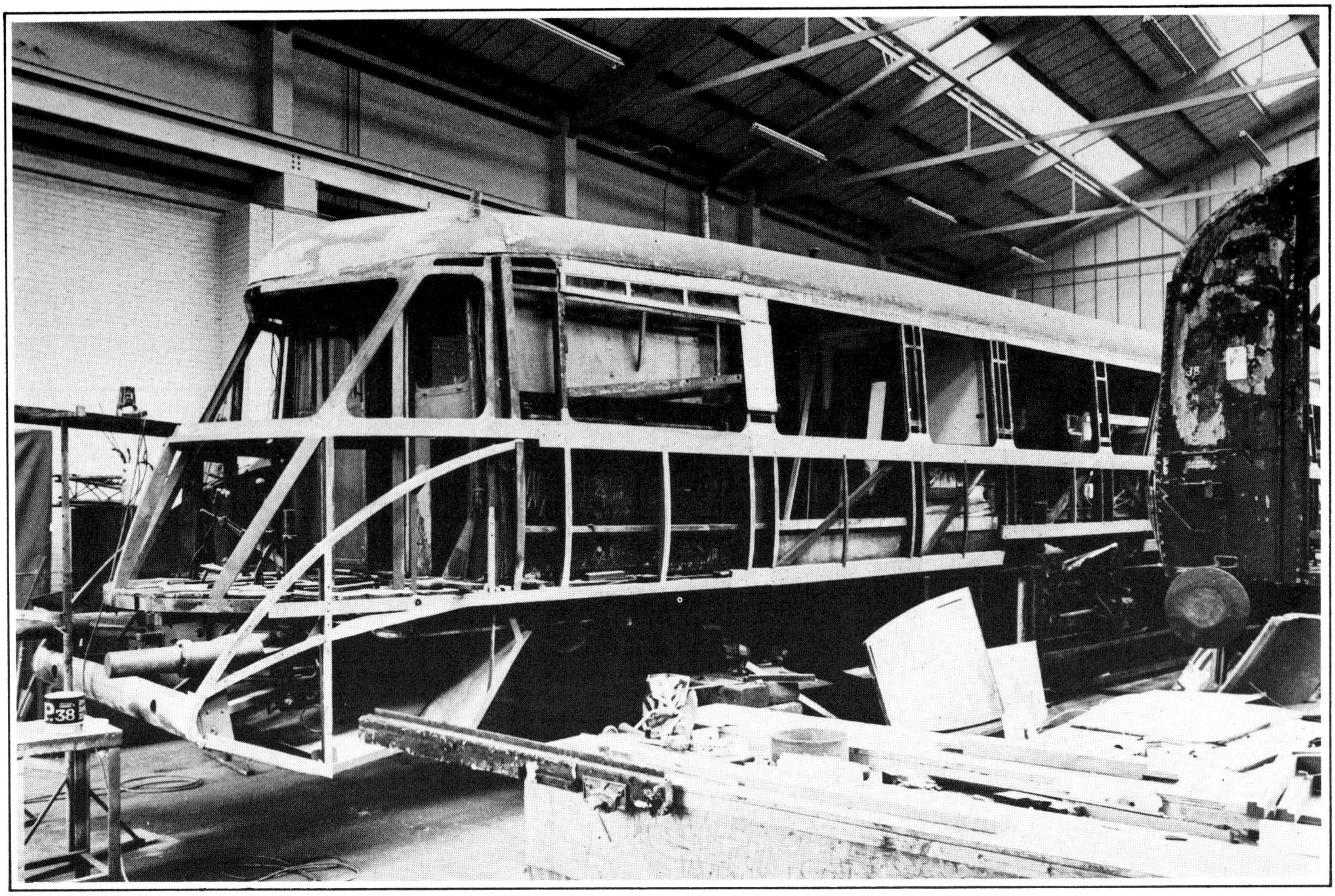
P.38

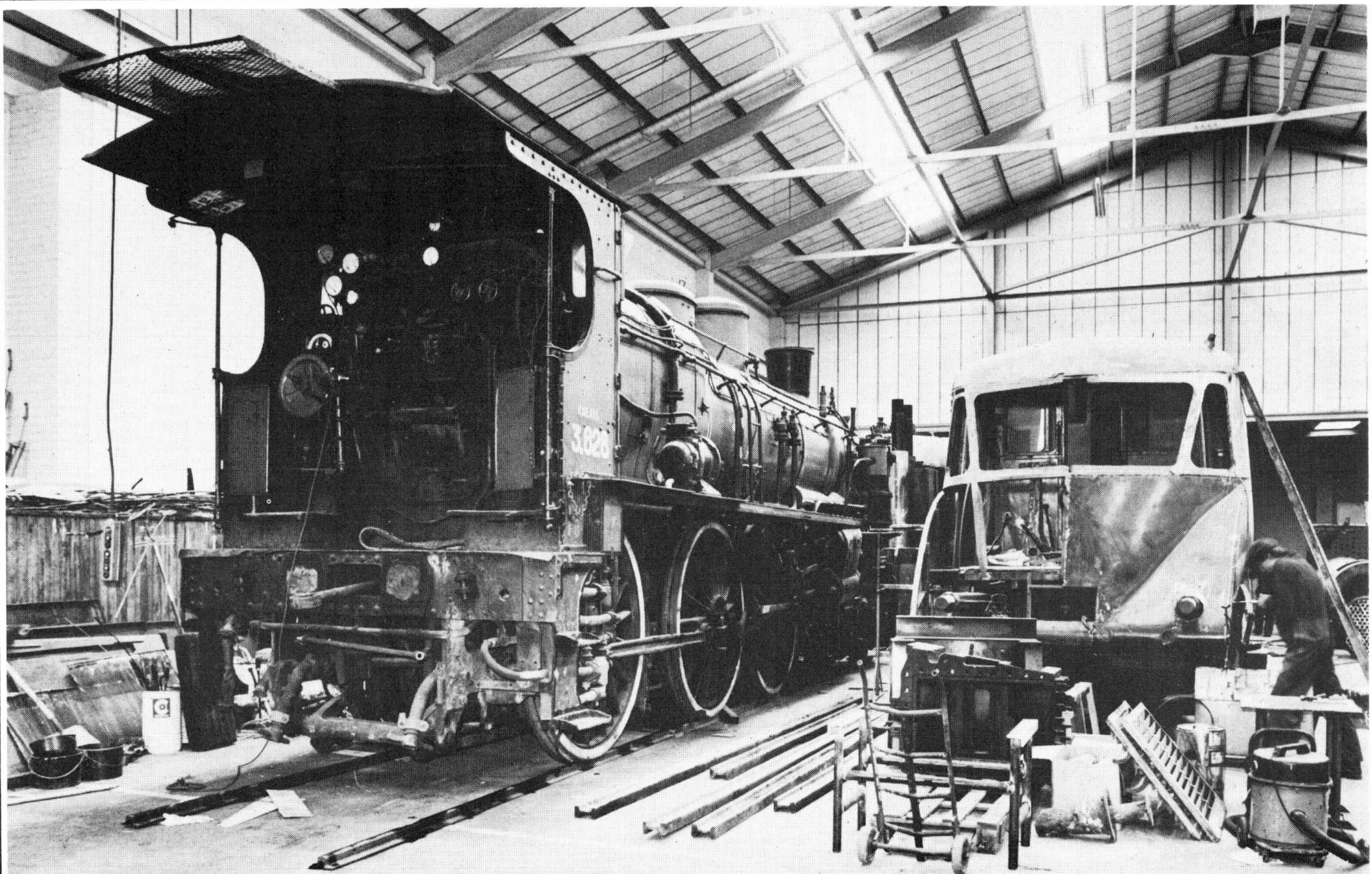
3.628

# Chapter Twelve: Railcar Workings, Timetables and a Pictorial Tribute

This chapter sets out to show the railcar workings of 25th September 1950 (in complete detail), with a pictorial tribute to these vehicles included. Firstly, the working of railcar No. 1 is set out below, from the working timetable of July 1934, to show that, from the start, these vehicles were worked hard. All the intermediate timings have been omitted, and there is no indication of refuelling, showing that No. 1 carried enough fuel for its whole day's working:

|  | Arrive a.m. | Depart a.m. | Miles | Chains |
|---|---|---|---|---|
| Southall | — | 8.33 RL to Didcot ML at Didcot | 44 | 4 |
| Didcot | 10.01 | 11.05 ML RL at Scours Lane | 34 | 54 |
|  | p.m. | p.m. |  |  |
| Slough | 12.11 | 12.15 RL | 17 | 42 |
| Reading | 12.46 | 12.55 (Bay) | 4 | 77 |
| Twyford | 1.03 | 1.05 | 4 | 48 |
| Henley on Thames | 1.16 | 1.34 | 4 | 48 |
| Twyford | 1.46 | 1.48 SO 2.24 SX RL | 4 | 77 |
| Reading | 1.56 SO 2.32 SX | East Bay 3.00 RL | 17 | 42 |
| Slough | 3.31 | 3.55 RL Bay | 2 | 64 |
| Windsor | 4.01 | 4.10 | 2 | 64 |
| Slough | 4.16 | 5.3 South Bay RL | 45 | 4 |
| Oxford | 6.29 | 6.42 RL to West Drayton ML West Drayton to Southall | 54 | 34 |
| Southall | 8.25 |  |  |  |
| (No Sunday workings shown for this vehicle) |  | Daily Total Weekly Total | 233 1,402 | 78 68 |

*Plate 226:* Diesel railcar No. W31W at Old Oak Common Shed on 21st September 1958.

*R. C. Riley*

*Plate 227:* Probably the first 'test passenger' run of diesel railcar No. 1 on 1st December 1933. It is seen at Paddington No. 2 platform alongside 4-6-0 'King' class locomotive No. 6001 King Edward VII.

*British Rail*

The following extract and timetables are taken from a report by British Railways in June 1951 on the expense of ex-GWR railcars.

**DIESEL RAILCAR ALLOCATION TO MOTIVE POWER DEPOTS ON SEPTEMBER 25th, 1950**

|  | Old Type Cars No. 1-17 |  |  | New Type Cars Nos. 18-38 |  |  |
|---|---|---|---|---|---|---|
| Motive Power Depot | Car No. | No. of Turns | Remarks | Car No. | No. of Turns | Remarks |
| Southall | 17 | 1 | Parcels Car | 34 | 1 | Parcels Car |
| Reading | 1 | 1 |  | 19 | 1 | Dual-ratio gearbox |
|  |  |  |  | 33/38 | 1 | Twin Set |
| Oxford | 2 | 2 |  |  |  |  |
|  | 15 |  |  |  |  |  |
|  | 16 |  |  |  |  |  |
| Bristol (St. Philip's M.) |  |  |  | 21 | 2 |  |
|  |  |  |  | 24 |  |  |
|  |  |  |  | 28 |  |  |
|  |  |  |  | 35/36 | 1 | Twin Set |
| Weymouth |  |  |  | 20 | 1 | Dual-ratio gearbox |
| Leamington |  |  |  | 26 | 2 |  |
|  |  |  |  | 29 |  |  |
| Stourbridge | 8 | 1 |  | 22 | 1 |  |
|  | 14 |  |  |  |  |  |
| Worcester | 5 | 2 |  | 27 | 2 |  |
|  | 6 |  |  | 31 |  |  |
|  | 7 |  |  | 32 |  |  |
| Cheltenham |  |  |  | 25 | 1 |  |
| Newport (Ebbw Jcn.) | 3 | 1 |  | 23 | 1 |  |
| Llantrisant |  |  |  | 18 | 1 |  |
| Pontypool Rd. |  |  |  | 30 | 1 |  |
| Swansea (Landore) | 4 | 3 |  |  |  |  |
|  | 10 |  |  |  |  |  |
|  | 11 |  |  |  |  |  |
|  | 12 |  |  |  |  |  |
| Carmarthen | 13 | 1 |  |  |  |  |
| Total | 16 units | 12 turns |  | 18 units | 16 turns |  |
| Grand Total |  | 34 units | — | 28 running turns |  |  |

Note: Car No. 9 damaged by fire 24th July 1945 and subsequently condemned
Car No. 37 damaged by fire 18th February 1947 and subsequently stored until scrapped in 1949
Cars No. 35 and 36 damaged at St. Anne's Park, Bristol by fire on 10th April 1956

*Plate 228:* Diesel railcar No. 1 stands at the 'up' platform at Wargrave, on the Henley branch, in the early 1950s.
*Lens of Sutton*

## Scheduled Working of Diesel Railcars:
## 25th September 1950

*SUMMARY*

**WEEKDAYS**

|  | Miles per day |  |
|---|---:|---:|
|  | M | C |
| Southall |  |  |
| (Parcels Car 'A' Working) | 78 | 2 |
| (Parcels Car 'B' Working) | 221 | 59 |
| Reading General |  |  |
| (Car 'A' Working) | 235 | 14 |
| (Car 'B' Working) | 169 | 14 |
| (Car 'C' Working) | 238 | 37 |
| Oxford |  |  |
| (Car 'A' Working) | 218 | 68 |
| (Car 'B' Working) | 84 | 20 |
| Weymouth | 245 | 12 |
| Bristol |  |  |
| (Car 'A' Working) | 265 | 40 |
| (Car 'C' Working) | 160 | 16 |
| (Car 'C' Working) | 245 | 47 |
| Cheltenham Spa | 226 | 18 |
| Pontypool Road | 145 | 28 |
| Newport | 246 | 46 |
| Newport Buffet Car | 162 | 50 |
| Llantrisant | 104 | 36 |
| Landore |  |  |
| (Car 'A' Working) | 221 | 74 |
| (Car 'B' Working) | 31 | 3 |
| (Car 'C' Working) | 41 | 14 |
| (Car 'D' Working) | 210 | 0 |
| (Car 'E' Working) | 5 | 42 |
| Carmarthen | 144 | 19 |
| Worcester |  |  |
| (Car 'A' Working) | 280 | 74 |
| (Car 'B' Working) | 233 | 50 |
| (Car 'C' Working) | 254 | 61 |
| (Car 'D' Working) | 239 | 66 |
| Leamington Spa |  |  |
| (Car 'A' Working) | 117 | 40 |
| (Car 'B' Working) | 173 | 19 |
| Stourbridge Junction |  |  |
| (Car 'A' Working) | 138 | 77 |
| (Car 'B' Working) | 156 | 0 |
| *Total* | 5,296 | 6 |

**SUNDAYS**

| | | |
|---|---:|---:|
| Bristol | 101 | 77 |
| Newport | 73 | 48 |
| Stourbridge Junction | 131 | 68 |
| Worcester | 117 | 66 |
| | 425 | 19 |
| One sixth = | 70 | 70 |
| *Grand Total* | 5,366 | 76 |

*Plate 229:* Railcar No. 11, near Frome, on 8th July 1938, showing roofing detail and also the change from the earlier white roof to black.

*H. C. Casserley*

*Plate 230:* This shows railcar No. 24 on the Weymouth service, seen here at Radipole Halt platform.

*D. K. Jones*

NOTE: The mileage shown against each trip in the Scheduled Working of Diesel Cars is the average daily mileage based on six-day working. Thus, where the trip is other than six-day, the mileage shown is the full mileage reduced in ratio to the frequency of the trip; i.e. 5/6th in the case of Monday to Friday working and 1/6th for Saturday only working.

In the present Winter Service Schedules, the Landore Car 'B' and 'E' Saturday only workings present an exception, in that the actual mileage is shown against each trip, and the average obtained by dividing the total miles by six.

**WEEKDAYS**

### Southall Car ('A' Working)

| Time | From | To | Arrive | Mileage M C | Remarks |
|---|---|---|---|---|---|
| Parcels Car No. 17 | | | | | |
| *10.00a.m. SX | Southall | West Ealing | *10.06a.m. | 2 11 | |
| 10.16a.m. SX | West Ealing | Paddington + | 10.32a.m. | 5 34 | |
| 11.42a.m. SX | Paddington + | Windsor & Eton Cen. | 1.08p.m. | 17 57 | |
| 1.25p.m. SX | Windsor & Eton Cen. | Paddington | 3.16p.m. | 17 57 | |
| * 3.30p.m. | Paddington | West Ealing | 3.58p.m. | 8 2 | Via P. Royal |
| 4.25p.m. SX | West Ealing | Greenford | 4.31p.m. | 2 17 | |
| 4.38p.m. SX | Greenford | Ruislip (for Ick.) | 4.48p.m. | 3 46 | |
| 5.00p.m. SX | Ruislip (for Ick.) | Greenford | 5.09p.m. | 3 46 | |
| 5.50p.m. SX | Greenford | Paddington | 6.05p.m. | 6 40 | Via P. Royal |
| * 6.50p.m. SX | Paddington | Acton Main Line | * 7.02p.m. | 3 44 | |
| 7.15p.m. SX | Acton Main Line | Greenford | 7.32p.m. | 4 7 | |
| * 7.25p.m. SX | Greenford | Southall | * 8.05p.m. | 3 41 | |

+ = Parcels Line     * = Empty

*MILEAGE = 78m. 2ch.*

### Southall Car ('B' Working)

| Time | From | To | Arrive | Mileage | Remarks |
|---|---|---|---|---|---|
| Parcels Car No. 34 | | | | | |
| * 3.26a.m. | Southall | Kensington (Olympia) | * 3.48a.m. | 8 47 | |
| 4.40a.m. | Kensington (Olympia) | Oxford | 6.28a.m. | 63 1 | |
| * 6.40a.m. | Oxford | Southall | * 7.52a.m. | 54 34 | |
| *10.00a.m. SO | Southall | West Ealing | *10.06a.m. | - 34 | |
| 10.16a.m. SO | West Ealing | Paddington + | 10.32a.m. | 1 17 | |
| *11.36a.m. SX | Southall | Paddington + | *11.52a.m. | 7 45 | |
| 11.42a.m. SO | Paddington + | Slough | 12.42p.m. | 3 6 | |
| 12.25p.m. SX | Paddington + | W. Ruislip (for Ick.) | 1.05p.m. | 11 16 | Via West Ealing |
| 12.55p.m. SO | Slough | Greenford | 1.33p.m. | 2 23 | |
| 1.30p.m. SX | W. Ruislip (for Ick.) | Paddington | 2.10p.m. | 10 6 | Via Park Royal |
| 2.05p.m. SO | Greenford | Paddington + | 2.24p.m. | 1 24 | Via Park Royal |
| 3.38p.m. | Paddington + | Slough | 4.54p.m. | 18 36 | |
| * 5.12p.m. SO | Slough | Southall | * 5.30p.m. | 1 45 | |
| 7.00p.m. SX | Slough | Paddington | 8.25p.m. | 15 30 | |
| 9.05p.m. SX | Paddington | Slough | 10.00p.m. | 15 30 | |
| *10.10p.m. SX | Slough | Southall | *10.22p.m. | 7 65 | |

+ = Parcels Line          *MILEAGE = 221m. 59ch.*          * = Empty

### Reading General Car ('A' Working)

| Time | From | To | Arrive | Mileage | Remarks |
|---|---|---|---|---|---|
| 3.15a.m. | Reading (General) | Basingstoke | 3.40a.m. | 15 39 | Mails |
| * 4.10a.m. | Basingstoke | Reading (General) | * 4.40a.m. | 15 39 | |
| 5.10a.m. | Reading (General) | Hungerford | 6.02a.m. | 25 45 | News & Parcels |
| * 6.06a.m. | Hungerford | Newbury | * 6.20a.m. | 8 36 | Parcels |
| 6.50a.m. | Newbury | Lambourn | 7.35a.m. | 12 33 | Parcels |
| 8.00a.m. | Lambourn | Newbury | 8.45a.m. | 12 33 | Mixed |
| 9.25a.m. | Newbury | Lambourn | 10.05a.m. | 12 33 | |
| 10.40a.m. | Lambourn | Newbury | 11.20a.m. | 12 33 | |
| 11.45a.m. | Newbury | Lambourn | 12.25p.m. | 12 33 | |
| 12.40p.m. | Lambourn | Newbury | 1.20p.m. | 12 33 | |
| 2.00p.m. | Newbury | Lambourn | 2.40p.m. | 12 33 | |
| 3.10p.m. | Lambourn | Newbury | 3.50p.m. | 12 33 | |
| 5.12p.m. | Newbury | Lambourn | 5.52p.m. | 12 33 | |
| 6.05p.m. | Lambourn | Newbury | 6.50p.m. | 12 33 | Mixed |
| 7.25p.m. | Newbury | Lambourn | 8.05p.m. | 12 33 | |
| * 8.15p.m. SX | Lambourn | Newbury | * 8.50p.m. | 10 28 | |
| * 9.15p.m. SX | Newbury | Reading (General) | * 9.50p.m. | 14 21 | (A) |
| 8.45p.m. SO | Lambourn | Newbury | 9.25p.m. | 2 5 | |
| 10.15p.m. SO | Newbury | Lambourn | 10.55p.m. | 2 5 | |
| *11.10p.m. SO | Lambourn | Newbury | *11.45p.m. | 2 5 | |
| *11.55p.m. SO | Newbury | Reading (General) | *12.25a.m. | 2 68 | |

A = *Works as a passenger trip when required*          * = Empty

*MILEAGE = 235m. 14ch.*

## Reading Car ('B' Working)

| Time | From | To | Arrive | Mileage | Remarks |
|---|---|---|---|---|---|
| 5.45a.m. | Reading (General) | Twyford | * 5.55a.m. | 4 77 | |
| 6.30a.m. | Twyford | Henley-on-Thames | 6.42a.m. | 4 49 | |
| 7.05a.m. SX | Henley-on-Thames | Twyford | 7.18a.m. | 3 68 | |
| 7.24a.m. SO | Henley-on-Thames | Twyford | 7.36a.m. | - 61 | |
| 7.28a.m. SX | Twyford | Henley-on-Thames | 7.40a.m. | 3 68 | |
| 7.57a.m. SO | Twyford | Henley-on-Thames | 8.09a.m. | - 61 | |
| 8.20a.m. | Henley-on-Thames | Twyford | 8.32a.m. | 4 49 | |
| 8.42a.m. | Twyford | Henley-on-Thames | 8.54a.m. | 4 49 | |
| 9.00a.m. | Henley-on-Thames | Twyford | 9.12a.m. | 4 49 | |
| * 9.22a.m. | Twyford | Maidenhead | * 9.34a.m. | 6 62 | |
| 9.43a.m. | Maidenhead | Didcot | 10.45a.m. | 28 71 | |
| 10.58a.m. | Didcot | Reading (General) | 11.33a.m. | 17 12 | |
| 1.05p.m. | Reading (General) | Twyford | 1.13p.m. | 4 77 | |
| 1.16p.m. | Twyford | Henley-on-Thames | 1.28p.m. | 4 49 | |
| 1.33p.m. | Henley-on-Thames | Twyford | 1.45p.m. | 4 49 | |
| 1.55p.m. | Twyford | Henley-on-Thames | 2.07p.m. | 4 49 | |
| 2.28p.m. | Henley-on-Thames | Twyford | 2.40p.m. | 4 49 | |
| 2.48p.m. SX | Twyford | Henley-on-Thames | 3.00p.m. | 3 68 | |
| 3.00p.m. SO | Twyford | Henley-on-Thames | 3.12p.m. | - 61 | |
| 3.35p.m. | Henley-on-Thames | Twyford | 3.47p.m. | 4 49 | |
| 3.54p.m. | Twyford | Henley-on-Thames | 4.06p.m. | 4 49 | |
| 4.24p.m. | Henley-on-Thames | Twyford | 4.36p.m. | 4 49 | |
| 4.45p.m. | Twyford | Henley-on-Thames | 4.57p.m. | 4 49 | |
| 5.12p.m. SO | Henley-on-Thames | Twyford | 5.24p.m. | - 61 | |
| 5.38p.m. SO | Twyford | Henley-on-Thames | 5.50p.m. | - 61 | |
| 6.12p.m. SO | Henley-on-Thames | Twyford | 6.27p.m. | - 61 | |
| 6.35p.m. SO | Twyford | Henley-on-Thames | 6.47p.m. | - 61 | |
| 7.15p.m. SO | Henley-on-Thames | Twyford | 7.27p.m. | - 61 | |
| 7.44p.m. SO | Twyford | Henley-on-Thames | 7.56p.m. | - 61 | |
| 5.40p.m. SX | Henley-on-Thames | Twyford | 5.52p.m. | 3 68 | |
| 6.21p.m. SX | Twyford | Henley-on-Thames | 6.33p.m. | 3 68 | |
| 6.45p.m. SX | Henley-on-Thames | Twyford | 6.57p.m. | 3 68 | |
| * 7.20p.m. SX | Twyford | Henley-on-Thames | * 7.32p.m. | 3 68 | (A) |
| 7.42p.m. SX | Henley-on-Thames | Twyford | 7.54p.m. | 3 68 | |
| 8.17p.m. SX | Twyford | Henley-on-Thames | 8.29p.m. | 3 68 | |
| 8.35p.m. | Henley-on-Thames | Twyford | 8.47p.m. | 4 49 | |
| 8.49p.m. | Twyford | Reading (General) | 8.57p.m. | 4 77 | |

A = Works as a passenger trip when required      * = Empty

*MILEAGE = 169m. 14ch.*

*Plate 231:* Twin car set, Nos. 33 and 38, (with intermediate coach) passes Oxford Road Junction, in 1954, just south of Reading en route to Reading (General) Station.

*National Railway Museum, M. Earley Collection*

## Reading Car ('C' Working)

**Two-car set (and extra Brake Third)**

| Time | From | To | Arrive | Mileage | Remarks |
|---|---|---|---|---|---|
| 6.55a.m. SX | Reading (General) | Slough | 7.22a.m. | 14 48 | |
| * 7.00a.m. SO | Reading (General) | Maidenhead | * 7.20a.m. | 1 76 | |
| * 7.30a.m. SX | Slough | Maidenhead | * 7.50a.m. | 4 66 | |
| 7.55a.m. | Maidenhead | Reading (General) | 8.18a.m. | 11 59 | |
| 8.26a.m. | Reading (General) | Newbury | 9.02a.m | 17 9 | |
| 9.32a.m. | Newbury | Reading (General) | 10.08a.m. | 17 9 | |
| 10.40a.m. | Reading (General) | Newbury | 11.12a.m. | 17 9 | |
| 12.05p.m. SX | Newbury | Reading (General) | 12.38p.m. | 14 21 | |
| 12.15p.m. SO | Newbury | Reading (General) | 12.48p.m. | 2 68 | |
| 12.55p.m. SO | Reading (General) | Newbury | 1.29p.m. | 2 68 | |
| 1.21p.m. SX | Reading (General) | Newbury | 1.54p.m. | 14 21 | |
| 2.03p.m. | Newbury | Reading (General) | 2.37p.m. | 17 9 | |
| 3.32p.m. | Reading (General) | Newbury | 4.07p.m. | 17 9 | |
| 4.20p.m. | Newbury | Reading (General) | 4.53p.m. | 17 9 | |
| 5.30p.m. | Reading (General) | Newbury | 6.04p.m. | 17 9 | |
| 6.10p.m. | Newbury | Reading (General) | 6.43p.m. | 17 9 | |
| 7.25p.m. | Reading (General) | Newbury | 8.00p.m. | 17 9 | |
| 8.15p.m. | Newbury | Reading (General) | 8.48p.m. | 17 9 | |

*MILEAGE = 238m. 37ch.*   * = Empty

*Plate 232:* A fine view of railcar No. W7W at Knightwick on 20th April 1957.

*Michael Hale*

## Oxford Car ('A' Working)

| Time | From | To | Arrive | Mileage | Remarks |
|---|---|---|---|---|---|
| * 5.30a.m. | Oxford | Kingham | * 6.05a.m. | 21 19 | |
| 6.40a.m. | Kingham | Oxford | 7.26a.m. | 21 19 | |
| 7.50a.m. | Oxford | Princes Risborough | 9.08a.m. | 21 5 | |
| 9.27a.m. | Princes Risborough | Oxford | 10.15a.m. | 21 5 | |
| 12.52p.m. SX | Oxford | Princes Risborough | 1.46p.m. | 18 24 | |
| 1.22p.m. SO | Oxford | Chipping Norton | 2.32p.m. | 4 23 | |
| 1.52p.m. SX | Princes Risborough | Oxford | 2.50p.m. | 18 24 | |
| 2.45p.m. SO | Chipping Norton | Oxford | 3.57p.m. | 4 23 | |
| 4.40p.m. | Oxford | Princes Risborough | 5.33p.m. | 21 5 | |
| 5.45p.m. | Princes Risborough | Thame | 5.58p.m. | 5 62 | |
| 6.15p.m. | Thame | Princes Risborough | 6.32p.m. | 5 62 | |
| 6.48p.m. | Princes Risborough | Oxford | 7.44p.m. | 21 5 | |
| 8.15p.m. SX | Oxford | Kingham | 9.01p.m. | 17 56 | |
| 9.10p.m. SX | Kingham | Oxford | 9.55p.m. | 17 56 | |

*MILEAGE = 218m. 68ch.*   * = Empty

### Oxford Car ('B' Working)

| Time | From | To | Arrive | Mileage | Remarks |
|------|------|-----|--------|---------|---------|
| 2.40p.m. | Oxford | Princes Risborough | 3.40p.m. | 21 5 | |
| 3.46p.m. | Princes Risborough | Oxford | 4.40p.m. | 21 5 | |
| 6.10p.m. | Oxford | Princes Risborough | 7.15p.m. | 21 5 | |
| 8.17p.m. | Princes Risborough | Oxford | 9.05p.m. | 21 5 | |

*MILEAGE = 84m. 20ch.*

### Weymouth Car

| Time | From | To | Arrive | Mileage | Remarks |
|------|------|-----|--------|---------|---------|
| * 4.20a.m. | Weymouth | Westbury | * 6.10a.m. | 58 78 | |
| 6.45a.m. | Westbury | Weymouth | 9.00a.m. | 58 78 | |
| 9.28a.m. | Weymouth | Yeovil (P.M.) | 10.39a.m. | 27 35 | |
| 10.50a.m. | Yeovil (P.M.) | Yeovil (Town) | 10.52a.m. | - 38 | |
| 11.24a.m. | Yeovil (Town) | Yeovil (P.M.) | 11.26a.m. | - 38 | |
| 11.50a.m. | Yeovil (P.M.) | Weymouth | 1.01p.m. | 27 35 | |
| 2.05p.m. WX | Weymouth | Dorchester West | 2.27p.m. | 5 66 | |
| 3.00p.m. WX | Dorchester West | Weymouth | 3.20p.m. | 5 66 | |
| 3.33p.m. WX | Weymouth | Maiden Newton | 4.13p.m. | 12 20 | |
| 4.30p.m. WX | Maiden Newton | Weymouth | 5.07p.m. | 12 20 | |
| 5.50p.m. WX | Weymouth | Maiden Newton | 6.30p.m. | 12 20 | |
| 6.39p.m. WX | Maiden Newton | Weymouth | 7.12p.m. | 12 20 | |
| 4.55p.m. WO | Weymouth | Abbotsbury | 5.21p.m | 1 32 | |
| 5.30p.m. WO | Abbotsbury | Weymouth | 5.59p.m. | 1 32 | |
| 6.20p.m. WO | Weymouth | Abbotsbury | 6.46p.m. | 1 32 | |
| 7.00p.m. WO | Abbotsbury | Weymouth | 7.28p.m. | 1 32 | |
| 8.25p.m. WO | Weymouth | Abbotsbury | 8.51p.m. | 1 32 | |
| 8.55p.m. WO | Abbotsbury | Weymouth | 9.20p.m. | 1 32 | |
| 9.30p.m. WO | Weymouth | Dorchester West | 9.54p.m. | 1 15 | |
| 11.13p.m. WO | Dorchester West | Weymouth | 11.38p.m. | 1 13 | |

*MILEAGE = 245m. 12ch.*

\* = Empty

*Plate 233:* Wyre Forest, on the Cleobury Mortimer to Bewdley line, alas now closed, with an unidentified railcar waiting to leave on 15th July 1961.
*C. Gammell*

### Bristol Car ('A' Working)

| Time | From | To | Arrive | Mileage | Remarks |
|---|---|---|---|---|---|
| * 6.18a.m. | St. Philip's Marsh | Bristol (T.M.) | * 6.25a.m. | - 77 | |
| 6.50a.m. | Bristol (T.M.) | Frome | 8.02a.m. | 24 14 | |
| 8.10a.m. | Frome | Bruton | 8.29a.m. | 10 42 | |
| 8.35a.m. | Bruton | Frome | 8.53a.m. | 10 42 | |
| 8.55a.m. WSO | Frome | Radstock West | 9.15a.m. | 2 60 | |
| 9.37a.m. WSO | Radstock West | Frome | 9.57a.m. | 2 60 | |
| 10.10a.m. | Frome | Wells (Tucker St.) | 10.55a.m. | 19 31 | |
| 11.10a.m. | Wells (Tucker St.) | Yatton | 11.50a.m. | 17 42 | |
| 11.52a.m. | Yatton | Bristol (T.M.) | 12.11p.m. | 12 - | |
| 1.05p.m. SX | Bristol (T.M.) | Yatton | 1.31p.m. ⎫ | 12 - | |
| 1.22p.m. SO | Bristol (T.M.) | Yatton | 1.46p.m. ⎭ | 12 - | |
| 2.05p.m. | Yatton | Clevedon | 2.12p.m. | 3 45 | |
| 2.20p.m. | Clevedon | Yatton | 2.27p.m. | 3 45 | |
| 2.47p.m. | Yatton | Frome | 4.53p.m. | 36 73 | Via Witham |
| 6.06p.m. | Frome | Bristol (T.M.) | 7.30p.m. | 24 14 | |
| 7.55p.m. | Bristol (T.M.) | Bath Spa | 8.20p.m. | 11 38 | |
| 9.08p.m. | Bath Spa | Bristol (T.M.) | 9.32p.m. | 11 38 | |
| 10.00p.m. | Bristol (T.M.) | Portishead | 10.35p.m. | 11 48 | |
| 10.52p.m. | Portishead | Bristol (T.M.) | 11.24p.m. | 11 48 | |
| 11.30p.m. | Bristol (T.M.) | Weston-super-Mare | 12.05a.m. | 19 7 | |
| *12.15a.m. | Weston-super-Mare | St. Philip's Marsh | *12.47a.m. | 19 36 | |

*MILEAGE = 265m. 40ch.*

\* = Empty

### Bristol Car ('B' Working)

| Time | From | To | Arrive | Mileage | Remarks |
|---|---|---|---|---|---|
| * 4.30a.m. | St. Philip's Marsh | Stapleton Road | * 4.40a.m. | 1 66 | |
| 5.10a.m. | Stapleton Road | Bristol (T.M.) | 5.17a.m. | 1 50 | |
| 5.27a.m. | Bristol (T.M.) | Portishead | 5.58a.m. | 11 48 | |
| 6.47a.m. | Portishead | Bristol (T.M.) | 7.19.am. | 11 48 | |
| 8.10.am. | Bristol (T.M.) | Portishead | 8.51a.m. | 11 48 | |
| 9.05a.m. | Portishead | Bristol (T.M.) | 9.38a.m. | 11 48 | |
| 9.42a.m. | Bristol (T.M.) | Severn Beach | 10.22a.m. | 11 67 | Via Pilning |
| 10.30a.m. SO | Severn Beach | Bristol (T.M.) | 11.11a.m. ⎫ | 11 67 | Via Pilning |
| 10.40a.m. SX | Severn Beach | Bristol (T.M.) | 11.21a.m. ⎭ | 11 67 | Via Pilning |
| 11.30a.m. SX | Bristol (T.M.) | Portishead | 12.05p.m. | 9 53 | |
| 12.12p.m. SX | Portishead | Bristol (T.M.) | 12.46p.m. | 9 53 | |
| 1.07p.m. | Bristol (T.M.) | Severn Beach | 1.47p.m. | 11 67 | Via Pilning |
| 2.05p.m. | Severn Beach | Bristol (T.M.) | 2.42p.m. | 11 67 | Via Pilning |
| 3.10p.m. | Bristol (T.M.) | Avonmouth Dock | 3.38p.m. | 9 3 | |
| 3.47p.m. | Avonmouth Dock | Bristol (T.M.) | 4.20p.m. | 9 3 | |
| 4.45p.m. | Bristol (T.M.) | Severn Beach | 5.28p.m. | 13 45 | |
| 5.32p.m. | Severn Beach | Lawrence Hill | 6.03p.m. | 10 63 | |
| * 6.04p.m. | Lawrence Hill | St. Philip's Marsh | * 6.07p.m. | - 20 | |

*MILEAGE = 160m. 16ch.*

\* = Empty

### Bristol Car ('C' Working)

| Time | From | To | Arrive | Mileage | Remarks |
|---|---|---|---|---|---|
| * 7.40a.m. | St. Philip's Marsh | Bristol (T.M.) | * 7.48a.m. | 1 22 | |
| 8.05a.m. | Bristol (T.M.) | Weymouth | 10.35a.m. | 87 16 | |
| 12.35p.m. | Weymouth | Bristol (T.M.) | 3.23p.m. | 87 16 | |
| * 3.28p.m. SO | Bristol (T.M.) | St. Philip's Marsh | * 3.35p.m. | - 13 | |
| 5.10p.m. SX | Bristol (T.M.) | Wells (Tucker St.) | 6.28p.m. | 24 48 | |
| 7.00p.m. SX | Wells (Tucker St.) | Bristol (T.M.) | 8.06p.m. | 24 48 | |
| 8.45p.m. SX | Bristol (T.M.) | Portishead | 9.22p.m. | 9 53 | |
| 9.42p.m. SX | Portishead | Bristol (T.M.) | 10.16p.m. | 9 53 | |
| *10.20p.m. SX | Bristol (T.M.) | St. Philip's Marsh | *10.29p.m. | 1 5 | |

*MILEAGE = 245m. 47ch.*

\* = Empty

### Cheltenham Spa Car

| Time | From | To | Arrive | Mileage | Remarks |
|---|---|---|---|---|---|
| 6.15a.m. | Cheltenham Spa (St. J.) | Gloucester | 6.31a.m. | 7 38 | |
| 6.42a.m. | Gloucester | Ledbury | 7.32a.m. | 19 0 | |
| 7.55a.m. | Ledbury | Gloucester | 8.42a.m. | 19 0 | |
| 9.20a.m. | Gloucester | Ledbury | 10.10a.m. | 19 0 | |
| 10.42a.m. | Ledbury | Gloucester | 11.34a.m. | 19 0 | |
| 12.02p.m. | Gloucester | Ledbury | 12.52p.m. | 19 0 | |
| 1.30p.m. | Ledbury | Gloucester | 2.17p.m. | 19 0 | |
| 2.30p.m. | Gloucester | Cheltenham Spa (St. J.) | 2.46p.m. | 7 38 | |
| 3.25p.m. | Cheltenham Spa (St. J.) | Gloucester | 3.42p.m. | 7 38 | |
| 4.05p.m. | Gloucester | Ledbury | 4.57p.m. | 19 0 | |
| 5.22p.m. | Ledbury | Gloucester | 6.21p.m. | 19 0 | |
| 6.25p.m. | Gloucester | Ledbury | 7.18p.m. | 19 0 | |
| 8.25p.m. | Ledbury | Gloucester | 9.13p.m. | 19 0 | |
| 9.25p.m. SO | Gloucester | Ledbury | 10.13p.m. | 3 13 | |
| 10.20p.m. SO | Ledbury | Gloucester | 11.07p.m. | 3 13 | |
| 10.00p.m. SX | Gloucester | Cheltenham Spa (St. J.) | 10.17p.m. | 7 38 | |
| 11.15p.m. SO | Gloucester | Cheltenham Spa (St. J.) | 11.31p.m. | 7 38 | |

*MILEAGE = 226m. 18ch.*

### Pontypool Road Car

| Time | From | To | Arrive | Mileage | Remarks |
|---|---|---|---|---|---|
| 7.46a.m. | Pontypool Road | Monmouth (May Hill) | 8.36a.m. | 18 43 | |
| 8.38a.m. | Monmouth (May Hill) | Pontypool Road | 9.57a.m. | 18 43 | |
| 11.00a.m. | Pontypool Road | Monmouth (Troy) | 11.43a.m. | 17 64 | |
| 12.00noon | Monmouth (Troy) | Pontypool Road | 12.46p.m. | 17 64 | |
| 2.30p.m. | Pontypool Road | Monmouth (May Hill) | 3.37p.m. | 18 43 | |
| 3.45p.m. | Monmouth (May Hill) | Pontypool Road | 4.26p.m. | 18 43 | |
| 6.10p.m. | Pontypool Road | Monmouth (Troy) | 6.52p.m. | 17 64 | |
| 7.05p.m. | Monmouth (Troy) | Pontypool Road | 7.51p.m. | 17 64 | |

*MILEAGE = 145m. 28ch.*

### Newport Car

| Time | From | To | Arrive | Mileage | Remarks |
|---|---|---|---|---|---|
| * 6.35a.m. | Ebbw Junction | Newport | * 6.40a.m. | 1 41 | |
| 7.05a.m. | Newport | Chepstow | 7.46a.m. | 17 10 | |
| 7.55a.m. | Chepstow | Monmouth (Troy) | 8.43a.m. | 14 46 | |
| 9.10a.m. | Monmouth (Troy) | Chepstow | 9.54a.m. | 14 46 | |
| 10.30a.m. | Chepstow | Monmouth (Troy) | 11.19a.m. | 14 46 | |
| 11.50a.m. | Monmouth (Troy) | Newport | 1.10p.m. | 31 56 | |
| 1.45p.m. | Newport | Monmouth (Troy) | 3.26p.m. | 31 56 | |
| 3.55p.m. | Monmouth (Troy) | Severn Tnl. Jcn. | 4.55p.m. | 21 72 | |
| 5.00p.m. | Severn Tnl. Jcn. | Monmouth (Troy) | 6.01p.m. | 21 72 | |
| 6.06p.m. | Monmouth (Troy) | Severn Tnl. Jcn. | 7.03p.m. | 21 72 | |
| 7.10p.m. | Severn Tnl. Jcn. | Monmouth (Troy) | 8.10p.m. | 21 72 | |
| 8.15p.m. | Monmouth (Troy) | Newport | 9.45p.m. | 31 56 | |
| * 9.50p.m. | Newport | Ebbw Junction | * 9.55p.m. | 1 41 | |

* = Empty    *MILEAGE = 246m. 46ch.*

### Newport Buffet Car

| Time | From | To | Arrive | Mileage | Remarks |
|---|---|---|---|---|---|
| * 5.50a.m. | Ebbw Junction | Newport | * 5.55a.m. | 1 41 | |
| 6.20a.m. | Newport | Bridgend | 7.18a.m. | 31 78 | |
| 7.35a.m. | Bridgend | Cardiff (Gen.) | 8.16a.m. | 20 17 | |
| 11.00a.m. | Cardiff (Gen.) | Newport | 11.20a.m. | 11 61 | |
| 1.30p.m. SX | Newport | Cardiff (Gen.) | 1.50p.m. | 9 64 | |
| 2.10p.m. SX | Cardiff (Gen.) | Swansea (H. St.) | 3.20p.m. | 38 12 | |
| 3.45p.m. | Swansea (H. St.) | Newport | 5.26p.m. | 47 76 | |
| * 5.35p.m. SX | Newport | Ebbw Junction | * 5.40p.m. | 1 21 | |

* = Empty    *MILEAGE = 162m. 50ch.*

*Plate 234:* A peaceful scene at Cleobury Mortimer with No. W28W awaiting departure on 15th July 1961.
*C. Gammell*

**Llantrisant Car**

| Time | From | To | Arrive | Mileage | Remarks |
|---|---|---|---|---|---|
| 6.45a.m. | Llantrisant | Cowbridge | 7.03a.m. | 5 56 | |
| 7.48a.m. | Cowbridge | Llantrisant | 8.06a.m. | 5 56 | |
| 8.20a.m. | Llantrisant | Cowbridge | 8.38a.m. | 5 56 | |
| 8.42a.m. | Cowbridge | Llantrisant | 9.00a.m. | 5 56 | |
| 9.20a.m. | Llantrisant | Cowbridge | 9.38a.m. | 5 56 | |
| 9.50a.m. | Cowbridge | Llantrisant | 10.08a.m. | 5 56 | |
| 11.15a.m. | Llantrisant | Cowbridge | 11.33a.m. | 5 56 | |
| 12.16p.m. | Cowbridge | Llantrisant | 12.34p.m. | 5 56 | |
| 1.45p.m. | Llantrisant | Cowbridge | 2.03p.m. | 5 56 | |
| 2.55p.m. | Cowbridge | Llantrisant | 3.13p.m. | 5 56 | |
| 4.00p.m. | Llantrisant | Cowbridge | 4.18p.m. | 5 56 | |
| 4.25p.m. | Cowbridge | Llantrisant | 4.43p.m. | 5 56 | |
| 5.32p.m. | Llantrisant | Cowbridge | 5.50p.m. | 5 56 | |
| 5.52p.m. | Cowbridge | Llantrisant | 6.10p.m. | 5 56 | |
| 6.18p.m. | Llantrisant | Cowbridge | 6.36p.m. | 5 56 | |
| 7.15p.m. | Cowbridge | Llantrisant | 7.33p.m. | 5 56 | |
| 7.50p.m. | Llantrisant | Cowbridge | 8.08p.m. | 5 56 | |
| 8.35p.m. | Cowbridge | Llantrisant | 8.53p.m. | 5 56 | |
| 9.05p.m. SO | Llantrisant | Cowbridge | 9.23p.m. | - 76 | |
| 9.28p.m. SO | Cowbridge | Llantrisant | 9.46p.m. | - 76 | |

*MILEAGE = 104m. 36ch.*

### Landore Car (Except Saturdays) ('A' Working)

| Time | From | To | Arrive | Mileage | Remarks |
|---|---|---|---|---|---|
| * 5.55a.m. | Landore | Swansea (High St.) | * 6.00a.m. | 1  7 | |
| 6.10a.m. | Swansea (High St.) | Porthcawl | 7.05a.m. | 19 40 | |
| 8.35a.m. | Porthcawl | Swansea (High St.) | 9.20a.m. | 19 40 | |
| 9.30a.m. | Swansea (High St.) | Carmarthen | 10.29a.m. | 26 35 | |
| 11.00a.m. | Carmarthen | Swansea (High St.) | 11.59a.m. | 26 35 | |
| 2.40p.m. | Swansea (High St.) | Carmarthen | 1.35p.m. | 26 35 | |
| 2.15p.m. | Carmarthen | Swansea (High St.) | 3.13p.m. | 26 35 | |
| 5.55p.m. | Swansea (High St.) | Port Talbot (Gen). | 6.36p.m. | 10 71 | Via Felin F. |
| 6.50p.m. | Port Talbot (Gen.) | Carmarthen | 8.24p.m. | 37 54 | |
| 8.45p.m. | Carmarthen | Swansea (High St.) | 9.45p.m. | 26 35 | |
| *10.00p.m. | Swansea (High St.) | Landore | *10.04p.m. | 1  7 | |

\* = Empty    MILEAGE = 221m. 74ch. (5/6th of daily mileage)

### Landore Car (Saturdays only) ('B' Working)

| Time | From | To | Arrive | Mileage + | Remarks |
|---|---|---|---|---|---|
| * 5.55a.m. | Landore | Swansea (High St.) | * 6.00a.m. | 1 25 | |
| 6.10a.m. | Swansea (High St.) | Porthcawl | 7.05a.m. | 23 32 | |
| 8.35a.m. | Porthcawl | Swansea (High St.) | 9.20a.m. | 23 32 | |
| 12.20p.m. | Swansea (High St.) | Porthcawl | 1.15p.m. | 23 32 | |
| 1.35p.m. | Porthcawl | Swansea (High St.) | 2.20p.m. | 23 32 | |
| 5.55p.m. | Swansea (High St.) | Port Talbot (Gen). | 6.36p.m. | 13  5 | Via Felin F. |
| 6.50p.m. | Port Talbot (Gen.) | Carmarthen | 8.24p.m. | 45 17 | |
| 8.45p.m. | Carmarthen | Swansea (High St.) | 9.45p.m. | 31 58 | |
| *10.00p.m. | Swansea (High St.) | Landore | *10.04p.m. | 1 25 | |

\* = Empty    + FULL MILEAGE = 186m. 18ch. Equivalent to daily mileage of 31m. 3ch.

### Landore Car (Except Saturdays) ('C' Working)

| Time | From | To | Arrive | Mileage | Remarks |
|---|---|---|---|---|---|
| * 4.30p.m. | Landore | Swansea (High St.) | * 4.35p.m. | 1  7 | |
| 5.05p.m. | Swansea (High St.) | Porthcawl | 5.56p.m. | 19 40 | |
| 7.40p.m. | Porthcawl | Swansea (High St.) | 8.30p.m. | 19 40 | |
| * 8.40p.m. | Swansea (High St.) | Landore | * 8.45p.m. | 1  7 | |

\* = Empty    MILEAGE = 41m. 14ch. (5/6th of daily mileage)

### Landore Car (Except Saturdays) ('D' Working)

| Time | From | To | Arrive | Mileage | Remarks |
|---|---|---|---|---|---|
| * 5.40a.m. | Landore | Swansea (High St.) | * 5.45a.m. | 1  7 | |
| 5.55a.m. | Swansea (High St.) | Pembrey & B. Port | 6.25a.m. | 12 56 | |
| 6.50a.m. | Pembrey & B. Port | Swansea (High St.) | 7.23a.m. | 12 56 | |
| 9.35a.m. | Swansea (High St.) | Gloucester | 12.18p.m. | 84 79 | |
| 1.10p.m. | Gloucester | Cheltenham Spa (St. J.) | 1.26p.m. | 6 18 | |
| 2.10p.m. | Cheltenham Spa (St. J.) | Swansea (High St.) | 5.15p.m. | 91 17 | |
| * 5.45p.m. | Swansea (High St.) | Landore | * 5.50p.m. | 1  7 | |

\* = Empty    MILEAGE = 210m. 0ch. (5/6th of daily mileage)

### Landore Car (Saturdays only) ('E' Working)

| Time | From | To | Arrive | Mileage + | Remarks |
|---|---|---|---|---|---|
| * 5.40a.m. | Landore | Swansea (High St.) | * 5.45a.m. | 1 25 | |
| 5.55a.m. | Swansea (High St.) | Pembrey & B. Port | 6.25a.m. | 15 20 | |
| 6.50a.m. | Pembrey & B. Port | Swansea (High St.) | 7.23a.m. | 15 20 | |
| * 7.35a.m. | Swansea (High St.) | Landore | * 7.39a.m. | 1 25 | |

\* = Empty    + FULL MILEAGE = 33m. 10ch. Equivalent to daily mileage of 5m. 42ch.

*Plate 235:* Railcars Nos. 35 and 36, running as a twin set, with an intermediate coach, seen near Reading West in 1944. Note the full GWR coat of arms on the front and side of the unit.

*National Railway Museum, M. Earley Collection*

*Plate 236:* Arriving at Leamington Spa on 25th August 1952 is railcar No. W26, towing an auto-coach for extra seating on the Leamington Spa to Stratford-upon-Avon service. A Class 56XX 0-6-2T shunts in the background.

*Brian Morrison*

## Carmarthen Car

| Time | From | To | Arrive | Mileage | Remarks |
|---|---|---|---|---|---|
| 6.35a.m. SX | Carmarthen | Lando Platform | 6.59a.m. | 12 41 | Workers' |
| 6.35a.m. SO | Carmarthen | Kidwelly | 6.51a.m. | 1 71 | Service |
| * 7.01a.m. | Lando Platform | Kidwelly | 7.26a.m. | 3 8 | (not |
| 7.26½a.m. | Kidwelly | Carmarthen | 7.45a.m. | 11 23 | advertised) |
| 7.55a.m. | Carmarthen | Haverfordwest | 8.44a.m. | 31 23 | |
| 9.00a.m. | Haverfordwest | Carmarthen | 10.17a.m. | 31 23 | |
| 1.20p.m. SX | Carmarthen | Swansea (High St.) | 2.20p.m. | 26 35 | |
| 2.25p.m. SX | Swansea (High St.) | Carmarthen | 3.23p.m. | 26 35 | |

\* = Empty                                                                 MILEAGE = 144m. 19ch.

*Plate 237:* Diesel railcar No. W17W (parcels car) at Stourbridge on 4th May 1958, in the British Railways crimson livery. *Philip J. Kelley*

## Worcester Car ('A' Working)

| Time | From | To | Arrive | Mileage | Remarks |
|---|---|---|---|---|---|
| * 4.55a.m. SX | Worcester (Tnl. Jcn.) | Highley | 5.51a.m. | 18 51 | |
| 6.07a.m. SX | Highley | Bewdley | 6.21a.m. | 4 74 | |
| * 5.35a.m. SO | Worcester (Tnl. Jcn.) | Bewdley | * 6.10a.m. | 2 65 | |
| 6.40a.m. | Bewdley | Hartlebury | 6.54a.m. | 5 40 | |
| * 7.06a.m. | Hartlebury | Kidderminster | * 7.12a.m. | 3 58 | |
| 7.22a.m. | Kidderminster | Henwick | 7.54a.m. | 16 8 | |
| * 8.04a.m. SO | Henwick | Worcester (S.H.) | * 8.13a.m. | - 18 | |
| 8.04a.m. SX | Henwick | Kidderminster | 8.38a.m. | 13 33 | |
| 8.55a.m. SX | Kidderminster | Worcester (F. St.) | 9.27a.m. | 12 67 | |
| * 9.30a.m. SX | Worcester (F. St.) | Worcester (S.H.) | * 9.34a.m. | - 43 | |
| 11.40a.m. SX | Worcester (S.H.) | Malvern Wells | 12.07p.m. | 7 78 | |
| 1.05p.m. SX | Malvern Wells | Worcester (S.H.) | 1.30p.m. | 7 78 | |
| 9.00a.m. SO | Worcester (S.H.) | Honeybourne | 9.44a.m. | 3 10 | |
| 9.50a.m. SO | Honeybourne | Worcester (F. St.) | 10.37a.m. | 3 18 | |
| *10.40a.m. SO | Worcester (F. St.) | Worcester (S.H.) | *10.44a.m. | - 8 | |
| 11.40a.m. SO | Worcester (S.H.) | Ledbury | 12.23p.m. | 2 48 | |
| 12.45p.m. SO | Ledbury | Worcester (S.H.) | 1.30p.m. | 2 48 | |
| 1.40p.m. | Worcester (S.H.) | Evesham | 2.12p.m. | 13 65 | |
| 2.40p.m. | Evesham | Stratford-on-Avon | 3.15p.m. | 13 77 | |
| 4.00p.m. | Stratford-on-Avon | Worcester (S.H.) | 5.10p.m. | 27 62 | |
| 5.45p.m. | Worcester (S.H.) | Stratford-on-Avon | 6.58p.m. | 27 62 | |
| 7.48p.m. | Stratford-on-Avon | Honeybourne | 8.08p.m. | 9 4 | |
| 8.25p.m. | Honeybourne | Moreton-in-Marsh | 8.48p.m. | 10 1 | |
| 9.00p.m. | Moreton-in-Marsh | Worcester (F. St.) | 9.57p.m. | 29 31 | |
| 10.20p.m. | Worcester (F. St.) | Droitwich Spa | 10.32p.m. | 5 75 | |
| *10.40p.m. | Droitwich Spa | Worcester (S.H.) | *10.50p.m. | 5 49 | |
| 11.15p.m. SX | Worcester (S.H.) | Honeybourne | 11.45p.m. | 15 48 | |
| *12.15a.m. MX | Honeybourne | Worcester (Tnl. Jcn.) | *12.45a.m. | 15 75 | |

\* = Empty                                         MILEAGE = 280m. 74ch.

### Worcester Car ('B' Working)

| Time | From | To | Arrive | Mileage | Remarks |
|---|---|---|---|---|---|
| * 5.10a.m. | Worcester (Tnl. Jcn.) | Kidderminster | * 5.34a.m. | 14 54 | |
| 5.53a.m. | Kidderminster | Alveley Halt | 6.25a.m. | 10 0 | |
| * 6.26a.m. | Alvley Halt | Hampton Loade | * 6.29a.m. | 1 52 | |
| 6.33a.m. | Hampton Loade | Alveley Halt | 6.36a.m. | 1 52 | Unadvertised |
| * 6.38a.m. | Alveley Halt | Hampton Loade | * 6.41a.m. | 1 52 | |
| 7.00a.m. | Hampton Loade | Bewdley | 7.21a.m. | 8 5 | |
| 7.42a.m. | Bewdley | Hartlebury | 7.57a.m. | 6 40 | |
| 8.15a.m. | Hartlebury | Northwood Halt | 8.34a.m. | 7 8 | |
| 8.36a.m. | Northwood Halt | Hartlebury | 8.55a.m. | 7 8 | |
| 9.22a.m. | Hartlebury | Kidderminster | 9.48a.m. | 9 7 | Via Bewdley |
| * 9.52a.m. | Kidderminster | Hartlebury | * 9.58a.m. | 3 58 | Direct |
| 10.10a.m. | Hartlebury | Bewdley | 10.24a.m. | 5 40 | |
| 11.10a.m. | Bewdley | Hartlebury | 11.26a.m. | 5 40 | |
| 12.10p.m. | Hartlebury | Bewdley | 12.24p.m. | 5 40 | |
| 12.27p.m. | Bewdley | Kidderminster | 12.36p.m. | 3 47 | |
| 1.45p.m. SX | Kidderminster | Bewdley | 1.54p.m. | 3 0 | |
| 2.25p.m. SX | Bewdley | Hartlebury | 2.40p.m. | 4 47 | |
| 12.40p.m. SO | Kidderminster | Highley | 1.13p.m. | 1 47 | |
| * 1.40p.m. SO | Highley | Alveley Halt | * 1.43p.m. | - 7 | |
| 1.45p.m. SO | Alveley Halt | Hampton Loade | 1.48p.m. | - 22 | Unadvertised |
| * 1.55p.m. SO | Hampton Loade | Alveley Halt | * 1.58p.m. | - 22 | |
| 2.00p.m. SO | Alveley Halt | Kidderminster | 2.30p.m. | 1 54 | |
| * 2.40p.m. SO | Kidderminster | Hartlbury | * 2.50p.m. | - 50 | |
| 3.16p.m. | Hartlebury | Bridgnorth | 4.07p.m. | 18 6 | |
| 4.20p.m. | Bridgnorth | Kidderminster | 5.10p.m. | 16 13 | |
| * 5.14p.m. | Kidderminster | Hartlebury | * 5.20p.m. | 3 58 | |
| 5.35p.m. | Hartlebury | Highley | 6.16p.m. | 11 33 | |
| 6.20p.m. | Highley | Bewdley | 6.34p.m. | 5 73 | |
| 7.12p.m. | Bewdley | Hartlebury | 7.27p.m. | 5 40 | |
| 8.10p.m. | Hartlebury | Buildwas | 9.24p.m. | 28 35 | |
| 9.30p.m. | Buildwas | Kidderminster | 10.45p.m. | 26 42 | |
| 10.50p.m. | Kidderminster | Worcester (S.H.) | 11.16p.m. | 15 6 | |
| *11.20p.m. | Worcester (S.H.) | Worcester (Tnl. Jcn.) | *11.25p.m. | - 32 | |

* = Empty          MILEAGE = 233m. 50ch.

### Worcester Car ('C' Working)

| Time | From | To | Arrive | Mileage |
|---|---|---|---|---|
| 6.40a.m. | Worcester (Tnl. Jcn.) | Malvern (Great) | * 6.58a.m. | 8 52 |
| 7.15a.m. | Malvern (Great) | Worcester (S.H.) | 7.35a.m. | 8 46 |
| 8.20a.m. | Worcester (S.H.) | Moreton-in-Marsh | 9.20a.m. | 28 59 |
| 9.50a.m. | Moreton-in-Marsh | Oxford | 10.41a.m. | 28 21 |
| 11.45a.m. SX | Oxford | Worcester (S.H.) | 1.50p.m. | 57 0 |
| 11.50a.m. SO | Oxford | Worcester (S.H.) | 1.55p.m. | 57 0 |
| 3.10p.m. | Worcester (S.H.) | Ledbury | 4.01p.m. | 15 49 |
| 4.20p.m. | Ledbury | Worcester (S.H.) | 5.05p.m. | 15 49 |
| 5.42p.m. | Worcester (S.H.) | Bromyard | 6.25p.m. | 14 41 |
| 6.50p.m. | Bromyard | Worcester (S.H.) | 7.31p.m. | 14 41 |
| 8.33p.m. | Worcester (S.H.) | Evesham | 9.00p.m. | 13 65 |
| 10.15p.m. ThSX | Evesham | Malvern (Great) | 11.07p.m. | 14 74 |
| *11.10p.m. ThSX | Malvern (Great) | Worcester (Tnl. Jcn.) | *11.30p.m. | 14 74 |
| 10.15p.m. ThSO | Evesham | Ledbury | 11.29p.m. | 9 65 |
| *11.32p.m. ThSO | Ledbury | Worcester (Tnl. Jcn.) | 12.05a.m. | 9 65 |

* = Empty          MILEAGE = 254m. 61ch.

### Worcester Car ('D' Working)

| Time | From | To | Arrive | Mileage | |
|---|---|---|---|---|---|
| * 5.35a.m. | Worcester (Tnl. Jcn.) | Shelwick Jcn. | * 6.20a.m. | 27 37 | |
| * 6.22a.m. | Shelwick Jcn. | Ludlow | * 7.01a.m. | 21 63 | |
| 7.25a.m. | Ludlow | Woofferton | 7.33a.m. | 4 48 | |
| 8.09a.m. | Woofferton | Kidderminster | 9.10a.m. | 24 9 | |
| 10.18a.m. | Kidderminster | Woofferton | 11.19a.m. | 24 9 | |
| 11.55a.m. | Woofferton | Kidderminster | 1.11p.m. | 24 9 | |
| 2.10p.m. | Kidderminster | Woofferton | 3.20p.m. | 24 9 | |
| 3.47p.m. | Woofferton | Kidderminster | 4.57p.m. | 24 9 | |
| 5.48p.m. | Kidderminster | Bewdley | 5.58p.m. | 3 47 | |
| 6.00p.m. | Bewdley | Kidderminster | 6.10p.m. | 3 47 | |
| 6.25p.m. | Kidderminster | Woofferton | 7.24p.m. | 24 9 | |
| 7.26p.m. | Woofferton | Leominster | 7.40p.m. | 6 25 | (A) |
| 7.45p.m. | Leominster | Worcester (S.H.) | 9.09p.m. | 27.33 | |
| * 0.00p.m. | Worcester (S.H.) | Worcester (Tnl. Jcn.) | * 0.00p.m. | - 32 | |

A = Conveys workpeople (not advertised)     MILEAGE = 239m. 66ch.     * = Empty

### Leamington Spa ('A' Working)

| Time | From | To | Arrive | Mileage | Remarks |
|---|---|---|---|---|---|
| * 6.00a.m. | Leamington Spa (Gen.) | Stratford-on-Avon | * 6.37a.m. | 12 64 | |
| 7.05a.m. | Stratford-on-Avon | Leamington Spa (Gen.) | 7.42a.m. | 12 64 | |
| 8.05.am. | Leamington Spa (Gen.) | Honeybourne | 9.09a.m. | 20 28 | |
| 9.50a.m. | Honeybourne | Leamington Spa (Gen.) | 10.52a.m. | 20 28 | |
| 1.20p.m. | Leamington Spa (Gen.) | Stratford-on-Avon | 1.53p.m. | 12 64 | |
| 5.14p.m. | Stratford-on-Avon | Leamington Spa (Gen.) | 5.48p.m. | 12 64 | |
| 6.30p.m. | Leamington Spa (Gen.) | Stratford-on-Avon | 7.08p.m. | 12 64 | |
| 7.35p.m. | Stratford-on-Avon | Leamington Spa (Gen.) | 8.07p.m. | 12 64 | |

* = Empty

*MILEAGE = 117m. 40ch.*

### Leamington Spa General ('B' Working)

| Time | From | To | Arrive | Mileage |
|---|---|---|---|---|
| 7.08a.m | Leamington Spa (Gen.) | Honeybourne | 8.25a.m. | 24 33 |
| 9.05a.m. | Honeybourne | Leamington Spa (Gen.) | 10.10a.m. | 24 33 |
| 10.25a.m. | Leamington Spa (Gen.) | Stratford-on-Avon | 11.04a.m. | 15 29 |
| 11.35a.m. | Stratford-on-Avon | Leamington Spa (Gen.) | 12.12p.m. | 15 29 |
| 2.22p.m. | Leamington Spa (Gen.) | Stratford-on-Avon | 3.02p.m. | 15 29 |
| 3.20p.m. SO | Stratford-on-Avon | Leamington Spa (Gen.) | 3.55p.m. | 2 45 |
| 3.57p.m. SX | Stratford-on-Avon | Hatton | 4.25p.m. | 9 20 |
| * 4.40p.m. SX | Hatton | Leamington Spa (Gen.) | * 4.53p.m. | 5 5 |
| 5.42p.m. | Leamington Spa (Gen.) | Stratford-on-Avon | 6.22p.m. | 15 29 |
| 6.50p.m. | Stratford-on-Avon | Leamington Spa (Gen.) | 7.25p.m. | 15 29 |
| 8.40p.m. | Leamington Spa (Gen.) | Stratford-on-Avon | 9.18p.m. | 15 29 |
| 10.30p.m. | Stratford-on-Avon | Leamington Spa (Gen.) | 11.10p.m. | 15 29 |

* = Empty

*MILEAGE = 173m. 19ch.*

### Stourbridge Junction Car ('A' Working) Except Saturdays

| Time | From | To | Arrive | Mileage + |
|---|---|---|---|---|
| * 6.00a.m. | Stourbridge Jcn. | Dudley | * 6.15a.m. | 5 0 |
| 6.28a.m. | Dudley | Old Hill | 6.42a.m. | 3 8 |
| 6.46a.m. | Old Hill | Dudley | 7.00a.m. | 3 8 |
| 7.10a.m. | Dudley | Old Hill | 7.27a.m. | 3 8 |
| 7.50a.m. | Old Hill | Dudley | 8.05a.m. | 3 8 |
| 8.38a.m. | Dudley | Old Hill | 8.52a.m. | 3 8 |
| 9.26a.m. | Old Hill | Dudley | 9.40a.m. | 3 8 |
| 9.55a.m. | Dudley | Birmingham | 10.20a.m. | 7 40 |
| 10.40a.m. | Birmingham | Dudley | 11.03a.m. | 7 40 |
| 11.48a.m. | Dudley | Old Hill | 12.02p.m. | 3 8 |
| 12.15p.m. | Old Hill | Dudley | 12.29p.m. | 3 8 |
| 12.45p.m. | Dudley | Old Hill | 12.59p.m. | 3 8 |
| 2.00p.m. | Old Hill | Dudley | 2.14p.m. | 3 8 |
| 2.30p.m. | Dudley | Old Hill | 2.44p.m. | 3 8 |
| 2.50p.m. | Old Hill | Dudley | 3.04p.m. | 3 8 |
| 3.27p.m. | Dudley | Old Hill | 3.41p.m. | 3 8 |
| 3.45p.m. | Old Hill | Dudley | 4.00p.m. | 3 8 |
| 4.20p.m. | Dudley | Old Hill | 4.34p.m. | 3 8 |
| 5.03p.m. | Old Hill | Dudley | 5.17p.m. | 3 8 |
| * 5.25p.m. | Dudley | Old Hill | * 5.37p.m. | 3 8 |
| 5.46p.m. | Old Hill | Dudley | 6.00p.m. | 3 8 |
| 6.05p.m. | Dudley | Birmingham | 6.31p.m. | 7 40 |
| 6.55p.m. | Birmingham | Dudley | 7.19p.m. | 7 40 |
| 7.45p.m. | Dudley | Old Hill | 7.59p.m. | 3 8 |
| 8.29p.m. | Old Hill | Dudley | 8.44p.m. | 3 8 |
| 9.15p.m. | Dudley | Old Hill | 9.29p.m. | 3 8 |
| 9.53p.m. | Old Hill | Dudley | 10.07p.m. | 3 8 |
| 10.25p.m. | Dudley | Old Hill | 10.39p.m. | 3 8 |
| 10.42p.m. | Old Hill | Dudley | 10.56p.m. | 3 8 |
| *11.05p.m. | Dudley | Stourbridge Jcn. | *11.20p.m. | 5 0 |

* = Empty

*MILEAGE = 114m. 32ch. (+5/6th of full mileage*

**Stourbridge Junction Car ('A' Working) Saturdays only**

| Time | From | To | Arrive | Mileage | Remarks |
|---|---|---|---|---|---|
| * 5.50a.m. | Stourbridge Jcn. | Old Hill | * 6.05a.m. | - 55 | |
| 6.20a.m. | Old Hill | Dudley | 6.35a.m. | - 50 | |
| 6.40a.m. | Dudley | Old Hill | 6.53a.m. | - 50 | |
| 7.02a.m. | Old Hill | Dudley | 7.16a.m. | - 50 | |
| 7.36a.m. | Dudley | Old Hill | 7.50a.m. | - 50 | |
| 7.55a.m. | Old Hill | Dudley | 8.09a.m. | - 50 | |
| 8.38a.m. | Dudley | Old Hill | 8.52a.m. | - 50 | |
| 9.26a.m. | Old Hill | Dudley | 9.40a.m. | - 50 | |
| 9.55a.m. | Dudley | Birmingham | 10.20a.m. | 1 40 | |
| 10.40a.m. | Birmingham | Dudley | 11.03a.m. | 1 40 | |
| 11.48a.m. | Dudley | Old Hill | 12.02p.m. | - 50 | |
| 12.15p.m. | Old Hill | Dudley | 12.29p.m. | - 50 | |
| 12.45p.m. | Dudley | Old Hill | 12.59p.m. | - 50 | |
| 1.07p.m. | Old Hill | Dudley | 1.21p.m. | - 50 | |
| 1.35p.m. | Dudley | Old Hill | 1.49p.m. | - 50 | |
| 2.00p.m. | Old Hill | Dudley | 2.14p.m. | - 50 | |
| 2.30p.m. | Dudley | Old Hill | 2.44p.m. | - 50 | |
| 2.50p.m. | Old Hill | Dudley | 3.04p.m. | - 50 | |
| 3.27p.m. | Dudley | Old Hill | 3.41p.m. | - 50 | |
| 3.49p.m. | Old Hill | Dudley | 4.03p.m. | - 50 | |
| 4.20p.m. | Dudley | Old Hill | 4.34p.m. | - 50 | |
| 5.03p.m. | Old Hill | Dudley | 5.17p.m. | - 50 | |
| 5.25p.m. | Dudley | Old Hill | 5.39p.m. | - 50 | |
| 5.46p.m. | Old Hill | Dudley | 6.00p.m. | - 50 | |
| 6.05p.m. | Dudley | Birmingham | 6.31p.m. | 1 40 | |
| 6.55p.m. | Birmingham | Dudley | 7.19p.m. | 1 40 | |
| 7.45p.m. | Dudley | Old Hill | 7.49p.m. | - 50 | |
| 8.29p.m. | Old Hill | Dudley | 8.44p.m. | - 50 | |
| 9.15p.m. | Dudley | Old Hill | 9.29p.m. | - 50 | |
| 9.53p.m. | Old Hill | Dudley | 10.07p.m. | - 50 | |
| 10.25p.m. | Dudley | Old Hill | 10.39p.m. | - 50 | |
| *10.45p.m. | Old Hill | Dudley | *10.56p.m. | - 50 | |
| *11.05p.m. | Dudley | Stourbridge Jcn. | *11.20p.m. | 1 0 | |

\* = Empty

*MILEAGE = 24m. 45ch. (1/6th of full mileage)*

*Plate 238:* Twin-coupled units, Nos. 35 and 36, are seen on the Brentford branch on a test run in 1939. They are passing under the unique 'Three Bridges', which consists of a road bridge (Windmill Lane) which runs over the Southall Canal Aqueduct.

*(A.E.C. Ltd.) Leyland Vehicles Ltd.*

**Stourbridge Junction Car ('B' Working) Except Saturdays**

| Time | From | To | Arrive | Mileage | Remarks |
|---|---|---|---|---|---|
| * 5.35a.m. | Stourbridge Jcn. | Dudley | * 5.50a.m. | 5 0 | |
| 5.58a.m. | Dudley | Old Hill | 6.12a.m. | 3 8 | |
| 6.20a.m. | Old Hill | Dudley | 6.35a.m. | 3 8 | |
| 6.58a.m. | Dudley | Old Hill | 7.12a.m. | 3 8 | |
| 7.21a.m. | Old Hill | Dudley | 7.36a.m. | 3 8 | |
| 8.01a.m. | Dudley | Old Hill | 8.15a.m. | 3 8 | |
| 8.22a.m. | Old Hill | Dudley | 8.36a.m. | 3 8 | |
| 9.00a.m. | Dudley | Birmingham (S.H.) | 9.25a.m. | 7 40 | |
| 9.55a.m. | Birmingham (S.H.) | Dudley | 10.19a.m. | 7 40 | |
| 11.15a.m. | Dudley | Birmingham (S.H.) | 11.40a.m. | 7 40 | |
| 12.30p.m. | Birmingham (S.H.) | Dudley | 12.53p.m. | 7 40 | |
| 2.00p.m. | Dudley | Birmingham (S.H.) | 2.23p.m. | 7 40 | |
| 2.35p.m. | Birmingham (S.H.) | Dudley | 2.59p.m. | 7 40 | |
| 3.10p.m. | Dudley | Birmingham (S.H.) | 3.33p.m. | 7 40 | |
| 4.35p.m. | Birmingham (S.H.) | Dudley | 4.58p.m. | 7 40 | |
| 5.17p.m. | Dudley | Old Hill | 5.31p.m. | 3 8 | |
| 5.36p.m. | Old Hill | Dudley | 5.50p.m. | 3 8 | |
| 5.56p.m. | Dudley | Old Hill | 6.10p.m. | 3 8 | |
| 6.21p.m. | Old Hill | Dudley | 6.38p.m. | 3 8 | |
| 6.45p.m. | Dudley | Birmingham (S.H.) | 7.10p.m. | 7 40 | |
| 7.30p.m. | Birmingham (S.H.) | Dudley | 7.53p.m. | 7 40 | |
| 9.25p.m. | Dudley | Birmingham (S.H.) | 9.48p.m. | 7 40 | |
| 10.15p.m. | Birmingham (S.H.) | Dudley | 10.39p.m. | 7 40 | |
| 10.45p.m. | Dudley | Stourbridge Jcn. | 11.05p.m. | 5 0 | |

* = Empty

MILEAGE = 131m. + (+ = 5/6ths of full mileage)

**Stourbridge Junction Car ('B' Working) Saturdays only**

| Time | From | To | Arrive | Mileage | Remarks |
|---|---|---|---|---|---|
| | | | | + + | |
| * 6.00a.m. | Stourbridge Jcn. | Dudley | * 6.15a.m. | 1 0 | |
| 6.23a.m. | Dudley | Old Hill | 6.42a.m. | - 50 | |
| 6.46a.m. | Old Hill | Dudley | 7.00a.m. | - 50 | |
| 7.10a.m. | Dudley | Old Hill | 7.27a.m. | - 50 | |
| 7.38a.m. | Old Hill | Dudley | 7.52a.m. | - 50 | |
| 8.01a.m. | Dudley | Old Hill | 8.15a.m. | - 50 | |
| 8.22a.m. | Old Hill | Dudley | 8.36a.m. | - 50 | |
| 8.55a.m. | Dudley | Birmingham (S.H.) | 9.20a.m. | 1 40 | |
| 9.55a.m. | Birmingham (S.H.) | Dudley | 10.19a.m. | 1 40 | |
| 11.15a.m. | Dudley | Birmingham (S.H.) | 11.40a.m. | 1 40 | |
| 12.45p.m. | Birmingham (S.H.) | Dudley | 1.08p.m. | 1 40 | |
| 2.00p.m. | Dudley | Birmingham (S.H.) | 2.23p.m. | 1 40 | |
| 2.35p.m. | Birmingham (S.H.) | Dudley | 2.59p.m. | 1 40 | |
| 3.10p.m. | Dudley | Birmingham (S.H.) | 3.33p.m. | 1 40 | |
| 4.35p.m. | Birmingham (S.H.) | Dudley | 4.58p.m. | 1 40 | |
| 5.56p.m. | Dudley | Old Hill | 6.10p.m. | - 50 | |
| 6.21p.m. | Old Hill | Dudley | 6.38p.m. | - 50 | |
| 6.45p.m. | Dudley | Birmingham (S.H.) | 7.10p.m. | 1 40 | |
| 7.30p.m. | Birmingham (S.H.) | Dudley | 7.53p.m. | 1 40 | |
| 9.25p.m. | Dudley | Birmingham (S.H.) | 9.48p.m. | 1 40 | |
| 10.15p.m. | Birmingham (S.H.) | Dudley | 10.39p.m. | 1 40 | |
| 10.45p.m. | Dudley | Stourbridge Jcn. | 11.05p.m. | 1 0 | |

* = Empty

MILEAGE = 25 miles + + (+ + = 1/6th of full mileage)

## SUNDAYS

**Bristol Car**

| Time | From | To | Arrive | Mileage | Remarks |
|---|---|---|---|---|---|
| * 8.00a.m. | St. Philip's Marsh | Bristol (T.M.) | * 8.07a.m. | 1 22 | |
| 8.20a.m. | Bristol (T.M.) | Weston-super-Mare | 8.56a.m. | 19 32 | |
| 9.15a.m. | Weston-super-Mare | Bristol (T.M.) | 9.52a.m. | 19 32 | |
| 10.15a.m. | Bristol (T.M.) | Avonmouth Dock | 10.43a.m. | 9 3 | Via Clifton |
| 11.10a.m. | Avonmouth Dock | Bristol (T.M.) | 11.41a.m. | 9 3 | Down |
| 11.55a.m. | Bristol (T.M.) | Bath Spa | 12.20p.m. | 11 38 | |
| 12.50p.m. | Bath Spa | Bristol (T.M.) | 1.15p.m. | 11 38 | |
| 2.02p.m. | Bristol (T.M.) | St. Andrews Rd. | 2.36p.m. | 9 76 | Via Clifton |
| 2.41p.m. | St. Andrews Rd. | Bristol (T.M.) | 3.14p.m. | 9 76 | Down |
| * 3.19p.m. | Bristol (T.M.) | St. Philip's Marsh | * 3.25p.m. | - 77 | |

* = Empty

MILEAGE = 101m. 77ch.

*Plate 239:* The intermediate design railcar No. 18, with two trailer cars, in an official photograph taken by the GWR.

*British Rail*

**Stourbridge Junction Car**

| Time | From | To | Arrive | Mileage | Remarks |
|---|---|---|---|---|---|
| 8.45a.m. | Stourbridge Jcn. | Dudley | 9.05a.m. | 6 0 | |
| 9.10a.m. | Dudley | Birmingham (S.H.) | 9.35a.m. | 8 79 | |
| 10.15a.m. | Birmingham (S.H.) | Dudley | 10.43a.m. | 8 79 | |
| 11.05a.m. | Dudley | Birmingham (S.H.) | 11.30a.m. | 8 79 | |
| 12.00noon | Birmingham (S.H.) | Dudley | 12.29p.m. | 8 79 | |
| *12.35p.m. | Dudley | Stourbridge Jcn. | *12.50p.m. | 6 0 | |
| * 1.35p.m. | Stourbridge Jcn. | Dudley | * 1.50p.m. | 6 0 | |
| 2.05p.m. | Dudley | Birmingham (S.H.) | 2.29p.m. | 8 79 | |
| 2.45p.m. | Birmingham (S.H.) | Dudley | 3.14p.m. | 8 79 | |
| 5.10p.m. | Dudley | Birmingham (S.H.) | 5.36p.m. | 8 79 | |
| 6.17p.m. | Birmingham (S.H.) | Dudley | 6.45p.m. | 8 79 | |
| 7.10p.m. | Dudley | Birmingham (S.H.) | 7.37p.m. | 8 79 | |
| 8.00p.m. | Birmingham (S.H.) | Dudley | 8.29p.m. | 8 79 | |
| 8.50p.m. | Dudley | Birmingham (S.H.) | 9.17p.m. | 8 79 | |
| 9.30p.m. | Birmingham (S.H.) | Dudley | 9.59p.m. | 8 79 | |
| *10.15p.m. | Dudley | Stourbridge Jcn. | *10.30p.m. | 6 0 | |

\* = Empty

*MILEAGE = 131m. 68ch.*

**Newport Car**

| Time | From | To | Arrive | Mileage | Remarks |
|---|---|---|---|---|---|
| * 8.45a.m. | Ebbw Junction | Newport | * 8.50a.m. | 1 41 | |
| 8.55a.m. | Newport | Cardiff (General) | 9.15a.m. | 11 61 | |
| 9.45a.m. | Cardiff (General) | Newport | 10.05a.m. | 11 61 | |
| +11.20a.m. | Newport | Cardiff (General) | +11.40a.m. | 11 61 | |
| 11.50a.m. | Cardiff (General) | Newport | 12.10p.m. | 11 61 | |
| §12.30p.m. | Newport | Cardiff (General) | §12.50p.m. | 11 61 | |
| 2.00p.m. | Cardiff (General) | Newport | 2.20p.m. | 11 61 | |
| * 2.30p.m. | Newport | Ebbw Junction | * 2.35p.m. | 1 41 | |

+ = *During Severn Tunnel occupation leaves Newport at 10.24a.m. and arrives Cardiff (General) 10.44a.m.*

§ = *During Severn Tunnel occupation leaves Newport at 1.00p.m. and arrives Cardiff (General) 1.17p.m.*

\* = Empty

*MILEAGE = 73m. 48ch.*

**Worcester Car**

| Time | From | To | Arrive | Mileage | Remarks |
|---|---|---|---|---|---|
| 6.30a.m. | Worcester (S.H.) | Honeybourne | 7.00a.m. | 18 58 | |
| 7.30a.m. | Honeybourne | Worcester (S.H.) | 8.00a.m. | 18 58 | |
| 8.50a.m. | Worcester (S.H.) | Malvern (Great) | 9.09a.m. | 8 46 | |
| 9.25a.m. | Malvern (Great) | Worcester (S.H.) | 9.45a.m. | 8 46 | |
| 10.25a.m. | Worcester (S.H.) | Malvern (Great) | 10.50a.m. | 8 46 | |
| 11.30a.m. | Malvern (Great) | Worcester (S.H.) | 11.55a.m. | 8 46 | |
| 12.30p.m. | Worcester (S.H.) | Malvern Wells | 12.59p.m. | 9 46 | |
| 2.05p.m. | Malvern Wells | Worcester (S.H.) | 2.30p.m. | 9 46 | |
| * 2.40p.m. | Worcester (S.H.) | Worcester (Tnl. Jcn.) | * 2.42p.m. | - 32 | |
| * 5.00p.m. | Worcester (Tnl. Jcn.) | Highley | * 5.41p.m. | 12 75 | (A) |
| 6.10p.m. | Highley | Bewdley | 6.25p.m. | 3 34 | (A) |
| * 6.38p.m. | Bewdley | Worcester (Tnl. Jcn.) | * 7.08p.m. | 10 13 | (A) Via Kidderminster Jcn. |

A = *Will not run 3rd December 1950 to 18th March 1951 inclusive*

\* = Empty

*MILEAGE = 117m. 66ch.*

## SPECIAL DIESEL RAIL CAR TRIPS, 1951

| Date of Trip 1951 | From | To | Route | Party | Guaranteed Number Passengers | Single Fare | Fare quoted | Total Receipts £ s. d. |
|---|---|---|---|---|---|---|---|---|
| Jan. 21st | Birmingham | Swindon | Return | Birmingham Loco. Club | 60 | 16/8d. | 20/0d. | 60 0 0 |
| May 14th | Llanharan | Oxford or Torquay | Return | Salem Young Peoples' Scty. | — | — | — | — |
| May 15th | Birmingham etc. | Swindon | Return | Birmingham Scty. Model Engineers | 70 | 16/8d. | 20/0d. | 70 0 0 |
| May 19th or 16th or June 2nd or 9th | Swansea | Bristol | Return | Steel Co. of Wales | 60 | 18/9d. | 22/0d. | 66 0 0 |
| May 20th | Wolverhampton | Swindon | Return | Wolverhampton Loco. Society | 40 | 19/3d. | 22/8d. | 45 6 8 |
| May 26th | Bridgend | Bristol | Return | Mrs J. G. Williams | 60 | 13/5d. | 16/0d. | 48 0 0 |
| June Open date | Birmingham | Birmingham | Leamington Spa Banbury Towcester Northampton Woodford Halse Stratford-on-Avon Broom Jcn. | Birmingham Loco. Club | — | — | — | — |
| June Open date | Birmingham | Port Talbot | Return | Institution of Civil Engineers | 60 | 26/0d. | 30/6d. | 91 10 0 |
| June 2nd | Birmingham | Birmingham | Kidderminster Bewdley Woofferton Craven Arms Much Wenlock Wellington | Birmingham Junior Chamber of Commerce | 60 | 11/4d. B'gham Craven Arms as Common Point | 14/0d. | 42 0 0 |
| June 10th | Llantwit Major | Weymouth | Return | Mr Davies, Kings Head Hotel | 80 | 28/10d. | 33/8d. | 134 13 4 |
| June 21st | Bristol | Swansea | Return | Railway Correspondence & Travel Society | 48 | 18/9d. | 22/0d. | 52 16 0 |
| June 23rd | Solihull | Solihull | 'A' Banbury Kingham Cheltenham Gloucester Newnham Chepstow Monmouth Ross Hereford Worcester Birmingham | Solihull Society of Arts | 70 | 41/10d. summation of single fares | 24/6d. | 85 15 0 |
| June 23rd | Tour 'B' as 'A' | to | Hereford *thence* Leominster Bromyard Worcester & Birmingham | | 70 | | 24/6d. | 85 15 0 |
| June 30th | Swansea | Bristol | Return | Millbrook Co. | 60 | 18/8d. | 22/0d. | 66 0 0 |
| Aug. 19th | Paddington | Westbury | Bath & Bristol | Railway Correspondence & Travel Society | 48 | 24/0d. | 28/6d. | 68 8 0 |

*Plate 240:* A GWR railcar in 'foreign' territory on 28th June 1952. It is seen at Tissington (famous for its well-dressing ceremonies) having travelled (via Barton and Ashbourne); it returned via Miller's Dale and Derby.
*R. H. G. Simpson*

*Plate 241:* Diesel railcar No. 8 at Wolverhampton, alongside GWR autocoach No. W70 in the early 1950s.
*R. C. Riley Collection*

*Plate 242:* Railcar No. W16W leaves Swindon on 24th April 1955 on the occasion of the Southall Railway Club's visit to the Works.
*Philip J. Kelley*

*Plate 243:* Southall Railway Club's railtour, again with railcar No. W16W, at Faringdon Station stop blocks. These vehicles were ideal for this type of railtour and society outing.
*Photomatic*

*Plates 244 & 245:* Two views of the burnt remains of railcar No. 9, seen here at Oxford Shed on 26th July 1945.

*R. H. G. Simpson*

*Plate 246:* Railcar No. W22W, in green livery, at Foley Park Halt on 4th July 1959, on the line between Kidderminster and Bewdley.

*Michael Hale*

*Plate 247:* A fine setting at Hartlebury (the junction for the Severn Valley line) with railcar No. W26W waiting for the 'road' on 4th July 1959.

*Michael Hale*

## THE HISTORY OF THE GREAT WESTERN A.E.C. DIESEL RAILCARS

**GREAT WESTERN RAILWAY**

Introduction of Additional Passenger Facilities
by means of a

**NEW STREAMLINED RAIL CAR**
(ONE CLASS ONLY)
Between

**SOUTHALL, SLOUGH
READING and DIDCOT**

on

MONDAY, FEBRUARY 5th, 1934 (and until further notice)

**WEEK DAYS ONLY**

| | | a.m. | a.m. | a.m. | p.m. | p.m. | p.m. | p.m. |
|---|---|---|---|---|---|---|---|---|
| SOUTHALL | dep. | 8 33 | | | | | | |
| Hayes and Harlington | ,, | | | | | | | |
| West Drayton and Yiewsley | ,, | 8 41 | | | | | | |
| Iver | ,, | 8 45 | | | | | | |
| Langley (Bucks) | ,, | 8 49 | | | | | 4 10 | 4¶47 |
| Windsor and Eton | dep. | 9·8 | 8¶47 | 11¶55 | *Saturdays only* | *Sats. excepted* | 4 16 | 5 3 |
| SLOUGH | dep. | 8 53 | 8 56 | 12 17 | | | | 5 9 |
| Burnham (Bucks) | ,, | | 9 1 | 12 22 | | | | 5 13 |
| Taplow | ,, | | 9 4 | 12 25 | | | | 5 17 |
| Maidenhead | ,, | | 9 9 | 12 30 | | 2 24 | | 5 27 |
| Twyford | ,, | | 9 19 | 12 40 | | | | 5¶43 |
| Henley-on-Thames | arr. | | | 1 16 | | | | |
| | dep. | | | 12†12 | 1 34 | 2† 5 | | |
| READING | arr. | | 9 28 | 12 48 | 1 56 | 2 32 | | 5 35 |
| | dep. | | 9 30 | | | | | 5 38 |
| Tilehurst | ,, | | 9 35 | | | | | 5 43 |
| Pangbourne | ,, | | 9 41 | | | | | 5 49 |
| Goring and Streatley | ,, | | 9 47 | | | | | 5 55 |
| Cholsey and Moulsford | ,, | | 9 53 | | | | | 6 1 |
| Wallingford | arr. | | | | | | | |
| | dep. | | | | | | | |
| DIDCOT | arr. | | 10 1 | | | | | 6 9 |

| | | a.m. | p.m. | p.m. | p.m. | | | |
|---|---|---|---|---|---|---|---|---|
| DIDCOT | dep. | 11 5 | | | 6 58 | | | |
| Wallingford | arr. | 12¶1 | | | 7¶35 | | | |
| | dep. | | | | | | | |
| Cholsey and Moulsford | dep. | 11 13 | | | 7 6 | | | |
| Goring and Streatley | ,, | 11 19 | | | 7 12 | | | |
| Pangbourne | ,, | 11 25 | | | 7 18 | | | |
| Tilehurst | ,, | 11 30 | | | 7 23 | | | |
| READING | arr. | 11 36 | | | 7 29 | | | |
| | dep. | 11 42 | 12 55 | 3 0 | 7 32 | | | |
| Henley-on-Thames | arr. | | 1 16 | | 8†G9 | | | |
| | dep. | 11¶34 | | | 7¶G5 | | | |
| Twyford | dep. | 11 50 | 1 5 | 3 8 | 7 40 | | | |
| Maidenhead | ,, | 12 0 | | 3 18 | 7 50 | | | |
| Taplow | ,, | 12 4 | | 3 22 | 7 54 | | | |
| Burnham (Bucks) | ,, | 12 8 | | 3 26 | 7 58 | | | |
| SLOUGH | arr. | 12 13 | | 3 31 | 8§ 4 | | | |
| Windsor and Eton | arr. | | | 4 1 | | | | |
| Langley (Bucks) | dep. | | | | 8 9 | | | |
| Iver | ,, | | | | 8 13 | | | |
| West Drayton and Yiewsley | ,, | | | | 8 17 | | | |
| Hayes and Harlington | ,, | | | | 8 22 | | | |
| SOUTHALL | arr. | | | | 8 26 | | | |

G *Saturdays excepted* · *Arrival time, by ordinary train.* § *Departure time Slough arrive 8.3 p.m.*
† *Ordinary train.* ¶ *Rail Motor Car, one class only.*

The following existing services will be worked by the new Streamlined Rail Car:
12.55 p.m. Reading to Twyford.
1. 5 p.m. Twyford to Henley-on-Thames and 1.34 p.m. Henley-on-Thames to Twyford.
2.24 p.m. (Saturdays excepted) Twyford to Reading.
3.55 p.m. Slough to Windsor and Eton and 4.10 p.m. Windsor and Eton to Slough.
5. 3 p.m. Slough to Maidenhead.

PADDINGTON STATION, February, 1934.     JAMES MILNE, General Manager.

MORTON, BURT & SONS, LTD., PRINTERS, BAYSWATER, W.2

*Figure 69:* The original leaflet reproduced above shows, in detail, in the first timetable of the railcar service introduced on Monday, 5th February 1934.

*Plate 248:* Ledbury Town Halt, on the now defunct line between Ledbury and Gloucester, with railcar No. W19W leaving on 9th May 1959.

*Michael Hale*

*Plates 249 & 250:* On 17th April 1938, an unidentified GWR railcar pulls out of Upwey Wishing Well Halt on the line to Weymouth. These two views show nicely the construction of this type of halt.

*R. W. Kidner*

# Appendix One: Shed Allocations and Changes

| A.E.C. Diesel Railcar No. | First Shed Allocated | Official Date into Service * | Shed at ‖ 8th Jan. 1938 | Shed at § 15th June 1947 | Shed at ★* 17th June 1950 | Official last British Rail Shed | Condemned Official Date |
|---|---|---|---|---|---|---|---|
| 1 | Southall | 5th Feb. 1934 ● | Southall | RDG | 81D | 81F | 13th Aug. 1955 |
| 2 | Tyseley | 9th July 1934 | Cardiff | LDR | 87E | 86A | 27th Feb. 1954 |
| 3 | Cardiff | 17th July 1934 | Tyseley | NPT | 86A | 81F | 26th Mar. 1955 |
| 4 | Tyseley | 22nd Sept. 1934 | Tyseley | LDR | 87E | 86A | 12th July 1958 |
| 5 | Oxford ★ | 8th July 1935 | Worcester | WOS | 85A | 85A | 28th Dec. 1957 |
| 6 | Worcester | 21st Sept. 1935 | Worcester | WOS | 85A | 85A | 19th Apr. 1958 |
| 7 | Worcester | 22nd July 1935 | Worcester | WOS | 85A | 84F | 3rd Jan. 1959 |
| 8 | Stourbridge ** | 5th Mar. 1936 | Bristol (SPM) | STB | 84F | 84F | 3rd Jan. 1959 |
| 9 | Oxford ★$ | 8th Feb. 1936 | Oxford | - | - | - | 18th May 1946 |
| 10 | Banbury | 14th Jan. 1936 | Bristol (SPM) | OXF | 81F | 81D | ★★ 21st May 1956 |
| 11 | Weymouth | 14th Jan. 1936 | Weymouth | OXF | 87E | 87E | 2nd Nov. 1957 |
| 12 | Oxford ★ | 11th Feb. 1936 | Oxford | RDG | 81D | 81F | 15th July 1957 |
| 13 | Neath × | 17th Feb. 1936 | Landore | LDR | 87E | 86A | 20th Aug. 1960 |
| 14 | Pontypool Road × | 28th Feb. 1936 | Pontypool Road | STB | 84F | 84E | 20th Aug. 1960 |
| 15 | Cheltenham | 18th Mar. 1936 | Bristol (SPM) | CARM | 87G | 84F | 3rd Jan. 1959 |
| 16 | Cardiff | 27th Apr. 1936 | Newport | CARM | 87G | 81D | 5th Oct. 1957 |
| 17 | Southall | 27th Apr. 1936 | Southall | SHL | 81C | 84D | 3rd Jan. 1959 |
| 18 | Reading | 4th Apr. 1937 | Reading | LTS | 86D | 81D | 18th May 1957 |
| 19 | Newport | 11th July 1940 | - | RDG | 81D | 85B | 27th Feb. 1960 |
| 20 | Newport | 4th June 1940 | - | WEY | 82F | 85A | Oct. 1962 |
| 21 | Bristol (SPM) | 11th July 1940 | - | SPM | 82B | 81C | Aug. 1962 |
| 22 | Newport | 18th Sept. 1940 | - | WOS | 81D | 85A | Oct. 1962 |
| 23 | Newport | 18th Sept. 1940 | - | NPT | 86A | 85A | Oct. 1962 |
| 24 | Bristol (SPM) | 18th Sept. 1940 | - | SPM | 82B | 85A | Oct. 1962 |
| 25 | Worcester | 18th Sept. 1940 | - | WOS | 85B | 82B | Aug. 1962 |
| 26 | Cheltenham | 18th Sept. 1940 | - | LMTN | 84D | 85A | Oct. 1962 |
| 27 | Newport | 6th Nov. 1940 | - | WOS | 85A | 81C | 17th Sept. 1960 |
| 28 | Newport | 16th Dec. 1940 | - | WOS | 82B | 82B | 17th Sept. 1960 |
| 29 | Newport | 6th Jan. 1941 | - | LMTN | 84D | 81D | Aug. 1962 |
| 30 | Newport | 13th Jan. 1941 | - | PPRD | 86G | 81C | Aug. 1962 |
| 31 | Llanelly | 3rd Feb. 1941 | - | LTS | 85A | 81C | Aug. 1962 |
| 32 | Llanelly | 3rd Feb. 1941 | - | GLD | 85A | 85A | Oct. 1962 |
| 33 | Worcester | 3rd Mar. 1941 | - | STB | 84F | 81D | Aug. 1962 |
| 34 | Southall | 15th Sept. 1941 | - | SHL | 81C | 81C | 17th Sept. 1960 |
| 35 | Stourbridge | 16th Nov. 1941 | - | RDG | 82B | 82B | 20th Apr. 1957 (b) |
| 36 | Stroubridge | 18th Nov. 1941 | - | RDG | 82B | 82B | 20th Apr. 1957 (b) |
| 37 | Stourbridge | 28th Feb. 1942 | - | SPM | - | 82B | 8th Sept. 1949 (a) |
| 38 | Stourbridge | 28th Feb. 1942 | - | SPM | 81D | 81D | Aug. 1962 |

\* Taken from official Joint Report of 1951 and checked against CME records at Kew

\*\* No. 8 fitted with experimental Vulcan Sinclair Coupling

★ Nos. 12, 9 and 5 were fitted with Single Line Automatic Train Control for Fairford Branch operation

★★ Damaged in crash and fire at Bridgnorth in March 1956

● No. 1 is shown to have been in 'service trials' with the GWR from 4th December 1933

$ Damaged and burnt out in July 1945 at Heyford

× Nos. 13 and 14 converted to parcel cars in 1959

‖ From *Railway Observer* Supplement No. 2, March 1938; information from GWR source

§ From *Railway Observer* Supplement No. 7, August 1947; not from any official source

★* From *Railway Observer* Supplement No. 9 August 1950; based on official BR source

a) Damaged by fire 18th February, stored until scrapped 1949

b) Destroyed at St. Anne's Park, Bristol by fire on 10th April 1956

(See list for shed code name following allocation)

## Shed Allocation Changes

These changes are taken from the GWR Stock Book records at the Public Record Office, Kew, *GWR Magazine*, *BR (WR) Magazine*, *SLS Journal* and *Railway Observer*, and record, where possible, the movement of these vehicles around the GWR. The early years produced many monthly changes for the same vehicle.

1934: Records in 1934 not available

1935:
No. 1 to OOC, 4th May but back to Southall on 21st Sept.
No. 4 into Swindon Works on 22nd Nov.
No. 5 into Swindon Works on 13th Nov.
No. 2 into Swindon Works on 23rd Nov.
No. 3 into Swindon Works on 13th Nov.
No. 8 to Gloucester Carriage on 22nd Dec.
No. 9 to Gloucester Carriage on 7th Nov., then to A.E.C. Southall on 2nd Dec.
No. 10 to Gloucester Carriage on 18th Nov., then to A.E.C. Southall on 20th Dec.
No. 11 to Gloucester Carriage on 25th Nov., then to A.E.C. Southall on 20th Dec.
No. 12 to Gloucester Carriage on 1st Nov., then to A.E.C. on 20th Dec.
No. 13 to Gloucester Carriage on 8th Nov.
No. 14 to Gloucester Carriage on 15th Nov.
No. 15 to Gloucester Carriage on 4th Dec.
No. 16 to Gloucester Carriage on 13th Dec.
No. 17 to Gloucester Carriage on 20th Dec.

Dates that follow are '4 weeks ending...'

1936:
| | | |
|---|---|---|
| 7th March. | No. 2 to Cardiff |
| 25th July. | No. 2 to Tyseley |
| | |
| 7th March. | No. 3 to Tyseley |
| 25th July. | No. 3 to Cardiff |
| 22nd Aug. | No. 3 to Tyseley |
| | |
| 8th Feb. | No. 4 to Cardiff |
| 2nd May | No. 4 to Tyseley |
| 19th Sept. | No. 4 to Cardiff |
| 17th Oct. | No. 4 to Tyseley |
| | |
| 7th March | No. 7 to Bristol |
| 2nd May | No. 7 to Worcester |
| 7th March | No. 8 to Stourbridge |
| 4th April | No. 8 to Worcester |
| 2nd May | No. 8 to Bristol |
| | |
| 8th Feb. | No. 9 to Oxford |
| | |
| 11th Jan. | No. 10 to Banbury |
| 8th Feb. | No. 10 to Bristol |
| | |
| 8th Feb. | No. 11 to Weymouth |
| | |
| 8th Feb. | No. 12 to Oxford |
| | |
| 7th March | No. 13 to Neath |
| | |
| 7th March | No. 14 to Pontypool |

| | | |
|---|---|---|
| 4th April | No. 15 to Cheltenham | |
| 17th Oct. | No. 15 to Bristol (SPM) | |
| 2nd May | No. 16 to Newport | |
| 25th July | No. 16 to Pontypool | |
| 22nd Aug. | No. 16 to Neath | |
| 19th Sept. | No. 16 to Stourbridge | |

**1937:**
| | |
|---|---|
| Sept. | No. 2 to Worcester |
| Oct. | No. 2 to Cardiff |
| May | No. 3 to Cardiff |
| Oct. | No. 3 to Tyseley |
| May | No. 4 to Swindon Works |
| Jan. | No. 5 to Worcester |
| April | No. 5 to Tyseley |
| May | No. 5 to Worcester |
| 3rd April | No. 6 to Worcester |
| March | No. 7 to Worcester |
| March | No. 8 to Bristol |
| July | No. 8 to Ebbw Vale |
| Oct. | No. 8 to Bristol |
| Feb. | No. 12 to Southall for accident repair, thence to Oxford |
| June | No. 13 to Ebbw Junction |
| Feb. | No. 14 to Bristol |
| March | No. 14 to Pontypool |
| Feb. | No. 15 to Bristol |
| April | No. 16 to Landore |
| May | No. 16 to Pontypool Road |
| June | No. 16 to Whitland |
| May | No. 18 to Reading |

**1938:**
| | |
|---|---|
| July | No. 2 to Tyseley |
| April | No. 4 to Tyseley |
| April | No. 4 to Cardiff |
| June | No. 4 to Cardiff |
| Aug. | No. 4 to Tyseley |
| May | No. 5 to Worcester |
| May | No. 6 to Worcester |
| May | No. 7 to Worcester |
| May | No. 8 to Bristol |
| May | No. 9 to Oxford |
| May | No. 10 to Bristol |
| May | No. 11 to Weymouth |
| May | No. 12 to Oxford |
| May | No. 13 to Landore |
| May | No. 14 to Pontypool |
| May | No. 15 to Bristol |
| Jan | No. 16 to Ebbw Vale |
| March | No. 16 to Pontypool |
| April | No. 16 to Ebbw Vale Junction |
| May | No. 16 to Newport |
| June | No. 16 to Neath |
| Sept. | No. 16 to Ebbw Vale Junction |
| Oct. | No. 16 to Neath |
| Dec. | No. 16 to Pontypool |
| May | No. 17 to Southall |
| May | No. 18 to Reading from Swindon Works |

**1939:** It was reported railcars ran 976,000 miles in 1938, an increase on 97,000 over 1937.

| | |
|---|---|
| Jan | No. 14 to Ebbw Junction. |
| Feb. | No. 16 to Pontypool Road. |
| Mar. | No. 3 to Cardiff. |
| | No. 14 to Pontypool Road. |
| Apr. | No. 10 to Oxford. |
| | No. 16 to Ebbw Junction. |
| May | No. 2 to Cardiff. |
| | No. 13 to Pontypool Road. |
| | No. 16 to Neath. |
| June | No. 2 to Worcester. |
| | No. 3 to Tyseley. |
| | No. 4 to Cardiff. |
| | No. 6 to Oxford. |
| July | No. 6 to Worcester. |
| Aug. | No. 2 to Cardiff. |
| | No. 4 to Tyseley. |
| | No. 12 to St. Philip's Marsh. |
| Oct. | No. 13 to St. Philip's Marsh. |
| 11th Nov. | No. 2 to Ebbw Junction. |
| | No. 10 to Reading. |
| | No. 12 to Tyseley. |
| | No. 13 to Pontypool Road. |

**1940:**
| | |
|---|---|
| 3rd Feb. | No. 1 to Reading. |
| | No. 11 to St. Philip's Marsh. |
| | No. 12 to Reading. |
| 30th March | No. 10 to Tyseley. |
| | No. 13 to Neath. |
| | No. 14 to Reading. |
| June | All transfer information was withdrawn until further notice due to wartime restrictions, but the following observations are interesting. |

**1941:**
| | |
|---|---|
| July | Railcars Nos. 6 and 33 re-appeared to take over steam auto-working in the Kidderminster area. Railcar No. 7 working in the Worcester area. All valance panels removed. |
| Sept. | Gloucester to Ledbury service changed to Railcar No. 29. Railcar No. 27 working Severn Tunnel to Chepstow and Monmouth service. |
| Dec. | No. 20 working around Newport. No. 34 working parcels around Acton. Nos. 35 and 36 seen around Southall. No. 24 in the Weymouth area. |

**1942:**
| | |
|---|---|
| Jan. | Railcars working the Worcester area; Nos. 5, 7, 19 and 25. |
| Feb. | Weymouth area records railcars Nos. 19, 20, 21, 24 and 25 working in. Railcars Nos. 35 and 36 left Southall and Nos. 37 and 38 arrived. No. 17 went in A.E.C. Works. Bridgnorth branch service included Nos. 19, 25 and 33. Worcester sees No. 19 arrive to work the Kidderminster to Woofferton and Bewdley to Bridgnorth services, and help Nos. 25 and 33. Apparently three other railcars, Nos. 5, 6, and 7, were allocated to Worcester at this time. |
| Mar. | Nos. 25 and 24 at Weymouth with No. 21 arriving on 24th February. |
| May | No. 26 arrives at Worcester. |
| Oct. | No. 22 working the Cowbridge to Llantrisant service. |

**1943:**
| | |
|---|---|
| Feb. | No. 6 seen outside Worcester Shed with one set of bogies removed. |
| June | Railcars Nos. 1, 9, 10 and 13 working Reading to Savernake local service. No. 18 working Lambourne branch. Nos. 37 and 38 on Stratford to Cheltenham service. |
| Aug. | Railcar No. 29 left Gloucester. Railcar No. 32 working Severn Tunnel Junction. |
| Sept. | No. 27 working Lambourn branch. |

**1944:**
| | |
|---|---|
| May | Railcar No. 19 was loaned to LNER on 18th April to work the Newcastle to North Wylam service. |
| June | Railcar No. 6 was loaned to LNER to work with No. 19. |
| July | Nos. 6 and 19 returned from LNER and allocated to Worcester. |
| Oct. | Railcar No. 32 working Lambourn branch. Nos. 37 and 38 working Reading to Hungerford service. |
| Nov. | No. 5 appeared dumped on Kidderminster Shed. Worcester sees No. 19 arrive to work the Kidderminster to Woofferton and Bewdley to Bridgnorth services, and help Nos. 25 and 33. Apparently three other railcars, Nos. 5, 6, and 7, were allocated to Worcester with No. 21 arriving on 24th February. |

**1945:**
| | |
|---|---|
| 26th Jan. | No. 6 to Worcester. |
| | No. 7 to Worcester. |
| 24th July | No. 9 destroyed by fire at Heyford in Oxfordshire. |
| 6th Oct. | No. 33 to Stourbridge. |
| 3rd Nov. | No. 20 to Reading. |
| | No. 23 to Pontypool Road. |
| | No. 31 to Llantrisant. |
| 1st Dec. | No. 11 to Reading. |
| | No. 20 to Weymouth. |
| | No. 21 to Reading. |
| 29th Dec. | No. 23 to Newport. |
| | No. 30 to Pontypool Road |

**1946:**
| | |
|---|---|
| 26th Jan. | No. 6 to Worcester. |
| | No. 7 to Worcester. |
| 18th May | No. 11 to Oxford. |
| 15th June | No. 5 to Worcester. |
| | No. 14 to Stourbridge. |
| | No. 19 to Oxford. |
| 13th July | No. 19 to Reading. |
| 10th Aug. | No. 8 to Stourbridge. |
| 7th Sept. | No. 35 to Reading. |
| | No. 36 to Reading. |
| 2nd Nov. | No. 2 to Newport. |
| | No. 3 to Landore. |
| | No. 14 to Worcester. |
| | No. 18 to Llantrisant. |
| 30th Nov. | No. 14 to Stourbridge. |
| | No. 21 to Bristol (SPM). |
| 28th Dec. | No. 37 to Bristol (SPM). |
| | No. 38 to Bristol (SPM). |

**1947:**
| | |
|---|---|
| 25th Jan. | No. 4 to Newport. |
| | No. 25 to Worcester. |
| 18th Feb. | No. 37 damaged by fire. |
| 22nd March | No. 3 to Newport. |
| | No. 4 to Landore. |
| | No. 32 to Worcester. |
| | No. 33 to Leamington. |
| 19th Apr. | No. 2 to Landore. |
| | No. 29 to Stourbridge. |
| 17th May | No. 16 to Carmarthen. |
| | No. 25 to Gloucester. |
| | No. 29 to Leamington. |
| | No. 33 to Stourbridge. |
| 14th June | No. 25 to Worcester. |
| | No. 32 to Gloucester. |
| 12th July | No. 2 to Newport. |
| | No. 13 to Carmarthen. |
| | No. 28 to Bristol (SPM). |
| 9th Aug. | No. 16 to Landore. |
| | No. 25 to Gloucester. |
| | No. 28 to Bristol (SPM). |
| | No. 32 to Worcester. |
| 6th Sept. | No. 2 to Newport. |
| | No. 3 to Landore. |
| | No. 13 to Carmarthen. |
| 4th Oct. | No. 3 to Newport. |
| | No. 14 to Worcester. |
| | No. 20 to Bristol (SPM). |
| | No. 21 to Weymouth. |
| 1st Nov. | No. 3 to Landore. |
| | No. 31 to Worcester. |

**1948:**
| | |
|---|---|
| 24th Jan. | No. 14 to Stourbridge. |
| | No. 16 to Carmarthen. |
| 21st Feb. | No. 5 to Landore. |
| | No. 14 to Stourbridge. |
| | No. 32 to Gloucester. |

|  | |  |
|---|---|---|
| 20th March | | No. 13 to Landore. |
| | | No. 32 to Worcester. |
| 17th April | | No. 2 to Landore. |
| 15th May | | No. 14 to Worcester. |
| | | No. 22 to Bristol (SPM). |
| 10th July | | No. 3 to Newport. |
| 7th Aug. | | No. 20 to Weymouth. |
| | | No. 21 to Newport. |
| 4th Sept. | | No. 2 to Newport. |
| | | No. 23 to Gloucester. |
| 2nd Oct. | | No. 5 to Worcester. |
| Nov. | | No. 14 to Stourbridge. |
| | | No. 22 to Reading. |
| | | No. 23 to Newport. |
| | | No. 35 to Bristol (SPM). |
| | | No. 36 to Bristol (SPM). |
| | | No. 38 to Reading. |

**1949:**
- Jan. — No. 24 into Swindon Works.
- 26th Feb. — No. 21 to Bristol (SPM).
- 23rd April — No. 2 to Oxford.
  - No. 3 to Landore.
  - No. 4 to Newport.
  - No. 11 to Landore.
  - No. 28 to Weymouth.
- 21st May — No. 3 to Newport.
  - No. 4 to Landore.
  - No. 13 to Carmarthen.
- 16th July — No. 12 to Oxford.
- Aug. — No. 16 to Landore.
  - No. 31 to Gloucester.
- 5th Nov. — No. 10 to Reading.
  - No. 28 to Bristol (SPM).
- 3rd Dec. — No. 10 to Oxford.
  - No. 31 to Worcester.
- 31st Dec. — No. 3 to Landore.
  - No. 4 to Newport.
  - No. 12 to Reading.

**1950:\***
- 25th March — No. 3 to 86A.
  - No. 4 to 87E.
- 20th May — No. 12 to 81F.
  - No. 28 to 82F.
- 17th June — No. 28 to 82B.
- 15th July — No. 12 to 87E.
  - No. 28 to 85B.
- 4th Nov. — No. 4 to 86B.
  - No. 28 to 82B.
  - No. 29 to 84F.
- 2nd Dec. — No. 10 to 87E.
  - No. 16 to 81F.
- 30th Dec. — No. 29 to 84D.

*(See list following allocations for shed code names)*

1951: No records available from any source.

**1952:**
- March — No. 18 to 81D.
- 14th June — No. 13 to 81C.
- 4th Oct. — No. 21 to 86A.
  - No. 23 to 82B.
- 1st Nov. — No. 20 to 82F.

**1953:**
- 24th Jan. — No. 36 to 81D.
- 21st Feb. — No. 11 to 87E.
- 18th April — No. 13 to 81D.
  - No. 17 to 81F.
  - No. 18 to 81D.
  - No. 33 to 81C.
  - No. 36 to 81C.
- 5th Sept. — No. 20 to 85B.
  - No. 25 to 82F.
- 3rd Oct. — No. 2 to 86A.
  - No. 10 to 81D.
  - No. 12 to 81F.
  - No. 19 to 85A.
  - No. 27 to 81D.
- 31st Oct. — No. 38 to 81C.
- 28th Nov. — No. 3 to 81F.
  - No. 36 to 82B.

**1954:**
- 27th Feb. — Two railcars transferred back from London Midland Region (from trials).
  - No. 27 to 81C.
- 17th July — No. 10 to 85A.
  - No. 16 to 81D.
- 11th Sept. — No. 31 to 86G.
- 9th Oct. — No. 13 to 86A.
  - No. 17 to 84D.
  - No. 31 to 81C.
  - No. 33 to 81D.
  - No. 38 to 81D.

**1955:**
- 24th Feb. — No. 18 was reported in Swindon Works awaiting major modifications.
- 23rd April — No. 21 to 81C.
  - No. 30 to 81C.
- 16th July — No. 1 to 81F.
  - No. 25 to 82B.
  - No. 28 to 82F.
- 5th Nov. — No. 19 to 85B.
  - No. 20 to 85A.

**1956:**
- 24th Mar. — No. 11 to 85A.
- 19th May — No. 19 to 85B.
- 3rd Nov. — No. 28 to 82B.

**1957:**
- 26th Jan. — No. 12 to 81D.
  - No. 16 to 81F.
- 30th Nov. — No. 7 to 84F.
  - No. 15 to 84F.
  - No. 22 to 85A.
  - No. 26 to 85A.
  - No. 29 to 81D.

**1958:**
- 25th Jan. — No. 7 to 85A.
  - No. 13 to 84F.
- 14th June — No. 23 to 85A.
- 1st Nov. — No. 20 to 85B.
  - No. 29 to 85A.
  - No. 30 to 81D.
  - No. 31 to 81D.
- 27th Dec. — No. 20 to 85A.
  - No. 31 to 81C.

**1959:**
- 16th May — No. 13 to 84D.
  - No. 14 to 84D.
- 11th July — No. 25 to 81C.

1960: No changes recorded in the records at Kew or BR (WR) Magazine.

1961: An article in the October issue of *BR (WR) Magazine* stated that: 'recently the remaining diesel railcars have been concentrated on the diesel depots at Southall and Worcester from where they operate the branch lines in these area'.
No. 4 was also recorded as being earmarked for preservation.

1962: Nothing recorded on the diesel railcar fleet that still existed.

To help identify the various shed codes, the following table has been included:

| Code | Depot | Code | Depot | Code | Depot |
|---|---|---|---|---|---|
| 81A | Old Oak Common | 84A | Wolverhampton (Stafford Rd.) | 87A | Neath<br>Glyn Neath<br>Neath (N. & B.) |
| 81B | Slough<br>Marlow<br>Watlington | 84B | Oxley | 87B | Duffryn Yard |
| 81C | Southall | 84C | Banbury | 87C | Danygraig |
| 81D | Reading<br>Henley-on-Thames | 84D | Leamington Spa | 87D | Swansea East Dock |
| | | 84E | Tyseley<br>Stratford-on-Avon | 87E | Landore |
| 81E | Didcot<br>Wallingford | 84F | Stourbridge Junc. | 87F | Llanelly<br>Burry Port<br>Pantyffynnon |
| 81F | Oxford<br>Fairford | 84G | Shrewsbury<br>Builth Road<br>Clee Hill<br>Craven Arms<br>Knighton | 87G | Carmarthen |
| 82A | Bristol (Bath Road)<br>Bath<br>Wells<br>Weston-super-Mare<br>Yatton | 84H | Wellington (Salop) | 87H | Neyland<br>Cardigan<br>Milford Haven<br>Pembroke Dock<br>Whitland |
| | | 84I | Croes Newydd<br>Bala<br>Penmaenpool<br>Trawsfynydd | 87J | Goodwick |
| 82B | Bristol (S.P.M.)<br>Chippenham | 84K | Chester | 87K | Swansea (Victoria)<br>Gurnos<br>Llandovery<br>Upper Bank |
| 82C | Swindon | 85A | Worcester<br>Evesham<br>Kingham | | |
| 82D | Westbury<br>Frome | 85B | Gloucester<br>Brimscombe<br>Cheltenham<br>Cirencester<br>Lydney<br>Tetbury | 88A | Cardiff (Cathays)<br>Radyr |
| 82E | Yeovil | | | 88B | Cardiff East Dock |
| 82F | Weymouth<br>Bridport | | | 88C | Barry |
| 83A | Newton Abbot<br>Ashburton<br>Kingsbridge | 85C | Hereford<br>Ledbury<br>Leominster<br>Ross | 88D | Merthyr<br>Cae Harris<br>Dowlais Central<br>Rhymney |
| 83B | Taunton<br>Bridgwater<br>Minehead | 85D | Kidderminster | 88E | Abercynon |
| 83C | Exeter<br>Tiverton Junc. | 86A | Newport (Ebbw Jc.) | 88F | Treherbert<br>Ferndale |
| | | 86B | Newport (Pill) | 89A | Oswestry<br>Llanidloes<br>Moat Lane<br>Welshpool (W & L) |
| 83D | Laira (Plymouth)<br>Launceston<br>Princetown | 86C | Cardiff (Canton) | | |
| | | 86D | Llantrisant | | |
| 83E | St. Blazey<br>Bodmin<br>Moorswater | 86E | Severn Tunnel Junc. | 89B | Brecon<br>Builth Wells |
| | | 86F | Tondu | | |
| | | 86G | Pontypool Road | 89C | Machynlleth<br>Aberayron<br>Aberystwyth<br>Aberystwyth (V. of R.)<br>Portmadoc<br>Pwllheli |
| 83F | Truro | 86H | Abergeeg | | |
| 83G | Penzance<br>Helston<br>St. Ives | 86J | Aberdare | | |
| | | 86K | Abergavenny<br>Tredegar | | |

*Plate 251*: On Sunday, 20th July 1952, the Reading Society of Model Engineers had a tour of the Berkshire, Buckinghamshire and Oxfordshire railways, and railcar No. W15W was used. A picnic tea was enjoyed at Thame Station, and this photograph was taken at a special stop in a cutting near Speen on the Lambourn Valley line. The railcar was twice pushed up to speeds of 70m.p.h. during this exciting railtour.
*National Railway Museum, Maurice Earley Collection*

# Appendix Two: Lot Numbers, Miles and Hours, Dates into Service, Mileage and Costs

## DIESEL RAIL CARS — MILES and HOURS 1934 to 1950

| Year | Cars | Train (Miles) | Shunting (Miles) | Other (Miles) | Deptl. (Miles) | Total (Miles) | Train (Hours) | Shunting (Hours) | Other (Hours) | Deptl. (Hours) | Total (Hours) | Fuel Gallons | m.p.g. | Lub. Oil Pints | Pts. per 100 miles | Train Miles per Train Hour | Train Miles per Engine Hour |
|---|---|---|---|---|---|---|---|---|---|---|---|---|---|---|---|---|---|
| 1934 | 1 to 18 | 90,224 | - | - | 1,232 | 91,456 | 3,911 | - | - | 62 | 3,973 | | | | | 23.07 | 22.71 |
| 1935 | | 256,279 | - | - | 6,006 | 262,285 | 10,600 | - | - | 285 | 10,885 | | | | | 24.18 | 23.54 |
| 1936 | | 866,873 | - | - | 25,527 | 892,400 | 42,989 | - | - | 1,301 | 44,290 | | | | | 20.16 | 19.57 |
| 1937 | | 864,931 | 1,984 | - | 12,884 | 879,799 | 45,720 | 396 | - | 841 | 46,957 | | | | | 18.92 | 18.42 |
| 1938 | | 972,130 | 2,689 | - | 8,656 | 983,475 | 53,690 | 532 | - | 485 | 54,707 | | | | | 18.11 | 17.77 |
| 1939 | | 724,881 | 2,706 | - | 7,056 | 734,643 | 42,016 | 544 | - | 367 | 42,927 | + | 5.86 | + | 6.28 | 17.25 | 16.89 |
| 1940 | | 421,172 | 1,453 | - | 2,806 | 425,431 | 29,144 | 290 | - | 186 | 29,620 | | 5.44 | | 6.80 | 14.45 | 14.22 |
| 1941 | | 626,993 | 2,704 | 2,196 | 76,666 | 639,559 | 48,785 | 539 | 119 | 538 | 49,981 | | 4.99 | | 7.30 | 12.85 | 12.54 |
| 1942 | | 891,272 | 3,109 | 4,464 | 13,525 | 912,370 | 75,676 | 608 | 240 | 762 | 77,286 | | 4.74 | | 7.91 | 11.78 | 11.53 |
| 1943 | All Cars | 908,181 | 2,298 | 3,792 | 14,549 | 928,820 | 79,019 | 449 | 198 | 815 | 80,481 | 216,779 | 4.63 | 83,025 | 8.28 | 11.49 | 11.28 |
| 1944 | | 887,589 | 2,221 | 3,549 | 13,850 | 907,209 | 77,159 | 435 | 181 | 760 | 78,535 | 221,810 | 4.62 | 84,035 | 8.20 | 11.50 | 11.30 |
| 1945 | | 827,629 | 2,256 | 3,375 | 25,858 | 859,118 | 71,201 | 450 | 167 | 1,578 | 73,396 | 201,932 | 4.59 | 75,738 | 8.16 | 11.62 | 11.28 |
| 1946 | | 1,040,286 | 1,115 | 2,588 | 22,159 | 1,066,148 | 85,102 | 224 | 171 | 1,326 | 86,823 | 260,190 | 4.76 | 101,721 | 8.21 | 12.22 | 11.98 |
| 1947 | | 1,216,135 | 282 | 407 | 24,575 | 1,241,399 | 94,574 | 52 | 33 | 1,389 | 96,048 | 263,051 | 4.97 | 107,263 | 8.20 | 12.86 | 12.66 |
| 1948 | | 1,233,698 | 309 | - | 22,546 | 1,256,553 | 97,016 | 65 | - | 1,262 | 98,343 | 265,276 | 4.98 | 103,633 | 7.85 | 12.72 | 12.54 |
| 1949 | | 1,352,999 | 142 | - | 19,028 | 1,372,169 | 104,077 | 31 | - | 1,124 | 105,232 | 307,299 | 4.85 | 100,050 | 6.71 | 13.00 | 12.86 |
| 1950 | | 1,342,187 | 264 | - | 21,729 | 1,364,180 | 102,172 | 53 | - | 1,246 | 103,471 | 303,833 | 4.81 | 99,888 | 6.84 | 13.14 | 12.97 |

## LOT NUMBERS

| Railcar | Lot No. | Railcar | Lot No. |
|---|---|---|---|
| No. 1 | 1516 | No. 20 | 1635 |
| No. 2 | 1522 | No. 21 | 1635 |
| No. 3 | 1522 | No. 22 | 1635 |
| No. 4 | 1522 | No. 23 | 1635 |
| No. 5 | 1522 | No. 24 | 1635 |
| No. 6 | 1522 | No. 25 | 1635 |
| No. 7 | 1522 | No. 26 | 1635 |
| No. 8 | 1547 | No. 27 | 1635 |
| No. 9 | 1546 | No. 28 | 1635 |
| No. 10 | 1547 | No. 29 | 1635 |
| No. 11 | 1547 | No. 30 | 1635 |
| No. 12 | 1547 | No. 31 | 1635 |
| No. 13 | 1546 | No. 32 | 1635 |
| No. 14 | 1546 | No. 33 | 1635 |
| No. 15 | 1546 | No. 34 | 1636 |
| No. 16 | 1546 | No. 35 | 1637 |
| No. 17 | 1547 | No. 36 | 1637 |
| No. 18 | 1635 | No. 38 | 1637 |

## TOTAL MILES RUN

| Car No. | Date to Service | | Aggregate miles to 30/12/50 | Car No. | Date to Service | | Aggregate miles to 30/12/50 |
|---|---|---|---|---|---|---|---|
| 1 | February | 1934 | 551,516 | 20 | June | 1940 | 378,513 |
| 2 | July | 1934 | 342,427 | 21 | July | 1940 | 357,927 |
| 3 | July | 1934 | 360,558 | 22 | September | 1940 | 309,256 |
| 4 | September | 1934 | 391,276 | 23 | September | 1940 | 308,012 |
| 5 | July | 1935 | 469,612 | 24 | September | 1940 | 349,859 |
| 6 | August | 1935 | 474,937 | 25 | September | 1940 | 420,123 |
| 7 | July | 1935 | 568,457 | 26 | September | 1940 | 335,592 |
| 8 | March | 1936 | 438,976 | 27 | November | 1940 | 398,676 |
| 9 | February | 1936 | 388,018 | 28 | December | 1940 | 393,489 |
| 10 | February | 1936 | 616,574 | 29 | January | 1941 | 298,637 |
| 11 | February | 1936 | 539,500 | 30 | January | 1941 | 278,077 |
| 12 | February | 1936 | 564,064 | 31 | February | 1941 | 353,510 |
| 13 | March | 1936 | 499,601 | 32 | February | 1941 | 390,194 |
| 14 | March | 1936 | 505,228 | 33 | March | 1941 | 325,029 |
| 15 | April | 1936 | 507,442 | 34 | September | 1941 | 313,130 |
| 16 | April | 1936 | 412,810 | 35 | November | 1941 | 470,143 |
| 17 | April | 1936 | 525,531 | 36 | November | 1941 | 470,141 |
| 18 | April | 1937 | 354,362 | 37 | February | 1942 | 184,470 |
| 19 | July | 1940 | 449,251 | 38 | February | 1942 | 316,383 |

## Details of Cost of Diesel Railcars

| Description | Date of Contract | Year Built | Car Nos. | No. of Cars | + G.W. Cost £ | A.E.C. Cost £ | Total Cost £ |
|---|---|---|---|---|---|---|---|
| Diesel Railcars, single engine | 4/12/1933 | 1934 | 1 | 1 | 249 | 3,000 | 3,249 |
| Diesel Railcars, with Buffet and Lavatory | exchange of of letters | 1935 | 2-4 | 3 | 250 | 6,291 | 6,541 |
| Diesel Railcars without Buffet and Lavatory | April 1934 | 1935 | 5-7 | 3 | 265 | 4,766 | 5,031 |
| Diesel Railcars, without Buffet and Lavatory | 28/1/1935 | 1936 | 8-10 | 3 | 278 | 4,816 | 5,094 |
| | | | | | 278 | 4816 | 5,094 |
| | | | | | 278 | 4,886 | 5,164 |
| Diesel Railcars, without Buffet and Lavatory | 28/1/1935 | 1936 | 11-13 | 3 | 278 | 4,886 | 5,164 |
| | | | | | 278 | 4,886 | 5,164 |
| | | | | | 277 | 4,816 | 5,093 |
| Diesel Railcars, without Buffet but with Lavatories | 28/1/1935 | 1936 | 14-16 | 3 | 277 | 4,816 | 5,093 |
| | | | | | 278 | 4,816 | 5,094 |
| | | | | | 278 | 4,816 | 5,094 |
| Diesel Railcars, Parcel Van Body | 28/1/1935 | 1936 | 17 | 1 | 279 | 4,572 | 4,851 |
| Diesel Railcars, New Model Car | 11/10/1935 | 1937 | 18 | 1 | 244 | 5,577 | 5,821 |
| Diesel Railcars, New Model Car | 31/3/1939 | 1940 | 19-28 | 10 | 3,102 | 3,138 | 6,240 |
| | | 1941 | 29-33 | 5 | 3,102 | 3,138 | 6,240 |
| Diesel Railcars, Parcel Car | 31/3/1939 | 1941 | 34 | 1 | 2,412 | 3,340 | 5,752 |
| Diesel Railcars, Twin Car Sets | 31/3/1939 | 1941 | 35-36 | 2 | 3,507 | 3,030 | 6,537 |
| Diesel Railcars, Twin Car Sets | 31/3/1939 | 1942 | 37-38 | 2 | 3,507 | 3,030 | 6,537 |

+ NB: GW Co.'s Costs were Departmental costs including Workshop Expenses and Superintendence.
No addition made to cover Head Office charges, Maintenance of Buildings, National Insurance, etc.
The first 18 cars were supplied by the A.E. Company as complete vehicles. GWR expenditure represents cost of fitting ATC apparatus and warning horns. The expenditure on cars 19 to 38 was the cost of constructing the bodies also fitting ATC apparatus and warning horns only.

# Appendix Three: Lubrication

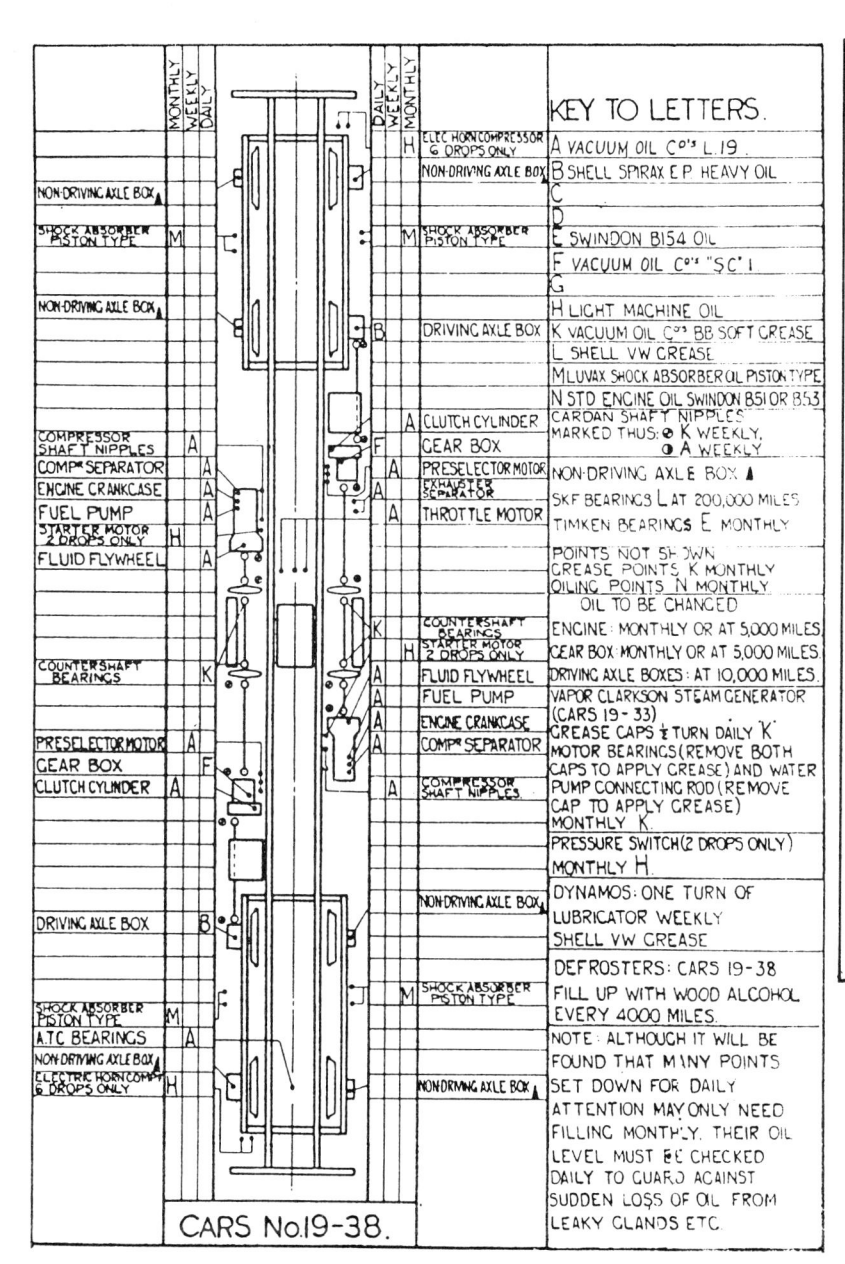

**Lubrication Chart for 1950, British Railways**

KEY TO LETTERS.
- A VACUUM OIL Co's L.19
- B SHELL SPIRAX E.P. HEAVY OIL
- C
- D
- E SWINDON B154 OIL
- F VACUUM OIL Co's "SC" 1
- G
- H LIGHT MACHINE OIL
- K VACUUM OIL Co's BB SOFT GREASE
- L SHELL VW GREASE
- M LUVAX SHOCK ABSORBER OIL PISTON TYPE
- N STD ENGINE OIL SWINDON B51 OR B53

CARDAN SHAFT NIPPLES MARKED THUS: ⊙ K WEEKLY, ⊙ A WEEKLY

NON-DRIVING AXLE BOX ▲

SKF BEARINGS L AT 200,000 MILES
TIMKEN BEARINGS E MONTHLY

POINTS NOT SHOWN
GREASE POINTS K MONTHLY
OILING POINTS N MONTHLY

OIL TO BE CHANGED
- ENGINE: MONTHLY OR AT 5,000 MILES.
- GEAR BOX: MONTHLY OR AT 5,000 MILES.
- DRIVING AXLE BOXES: AT 10,000 MILES.

VAPOR CLARKSON STEAM GENERATOR (CARS 19-33)
GREASE CAPS ½ TURN DAILY 'K'
MOTOR BEARINGS (REMOVE BOTH CAPS TO APPLY GREASE) AND WATER PUMP CONNECTING ROD (REMOVE CAP TO APPLY GREASE) MONTHLY K.
PRESSURE SWITCH (2 DROPS ONLY) MONTHLY H.

DYNAMOS: ONE TURN OF LUBRICATOR WEEKLY SHELL VW GREASE

DEFROSTERS: CARS 19-38 FILL UP WITH WOOD ALCOHOL EVERY 4000 MILES.

NOTE: ALTHOUGH IT WILL BE FOUND THAT MANY POINTS SET DOWN FOR DAILY ATTENTION MAY ONLY NEED FILLING MONTHLY, THEIR OIL LEVEL MUST BE CHECKED DAILY TO GUARD AGAINST SUDDEN LOSS OF OIL FROM LEAKY GLANDS ETC.

CARS No. 19-38.

*Plate 252*: The special body lifting rig to raise the body from the chassis. Here railcar No. 10 is being used for this official A.E.C. picture.
*(A.E.C. Ltd.)*
*Leyland Vehicles Ltd.*

# Appendix Four: Wheel Profiles

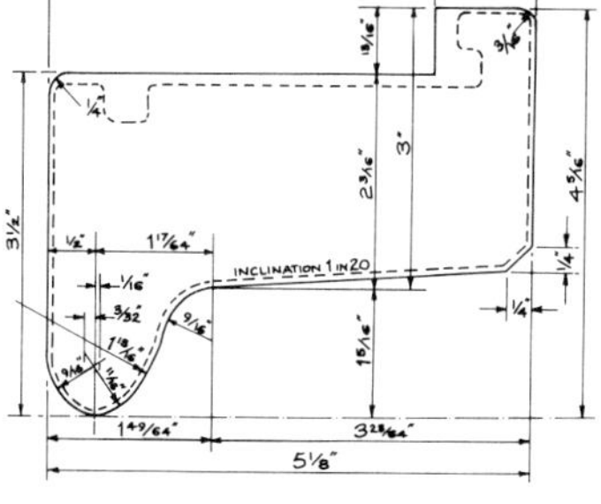

STANDARD TYRE SECTION FOR AEC DIESEL RAIL CAR Nos. 1-18

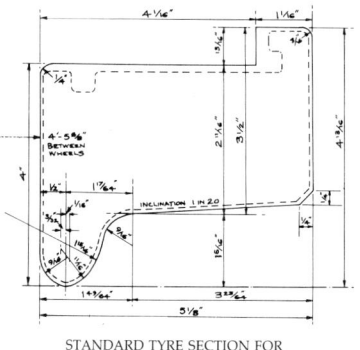

STANDARD TYRE SECTION FOR DIESEL RAIL CAR No. 19 & UPWARDS

# Appendix Five: Railcar Driving Instructions for GWR Cars Nos. 19 to 38

## ENGINES.

### Before starting up:—

1. Close main control and lighting switches
2. See that radiators are full.
3. See that the oil level in the sump is up to the "full" mark on the dipstick.
4. See that gears are in neutral, i.e., preselector lever should point to "N," and to be sure it is engaged the engaging lever should be pulled over to right and released.

### To start engines when cold (at beginning of day's work):—

5. Remove small panels in valance just ahead of engines.
6. Pull throttle lever just ahead of engine over to right as far as it will go.
7. Press starter button and release it immediately the engine picks up.
8. Repeat (5) and (6) for second engine.
9. Keep both engines running without racing, for five minutes before moving car.
   Note.—The engine throttle is held open by compressed pressed air, and if there is no air pressure in the reservoir, it will be necessary to hold first engine throttle open for a few seconds while pressure is built up, or it will not idle.

### To start engines when warm:—

10. Carry out (6), (7) and (8) from driver's seat, but instead of using throttle lever, press down accelerator pedal fully.
    Note.—If car has been standing for some time and the air pressure has fallen, it will be necessary to start first engine from side of car as above.

## TO MOVE THE CAR.

11. Wait until the gauges show 25in. of vacuum, and 75lbs. of air.
12. See that A.T.C. flag is "down" at driving end of car and "up" at other end.
13. Insert key in lock on top of table and turn it a quarter turn to the right.
14. Pull engaging lever over to right and hold it there while key is given another turn to the right.
15. Move reversing lever over to forward or reverse position as required (forward to left, reverse to right).
    Note.—The reverse and engaging levers are interlocked and the latter must be held over to the right while moving the former.
16. On cars 19 and 20, move gear ratio lever over to high or low position according to the tail load to be hauled.
    Note.—This is also interlocked with the engaging lever and needs same operation as reverse.
17. See that brake handle is put in "running" position as soon as necessary vacuum shows on gauge.
18. Place preselector lever with pointer opposite to figure "1" thereby preselecting first gear.
19. Pull engaging lever over to right, pause for a second and let go, at the same time pressing the accelerator pedal down gently.
20. Move preselector lever over to second gear position.
21. When speedometer needles are opposite the "change up" position, allow accelerator pedal to come up, pull engaging lever over to right, pause a second and let go and at the same time press down accelerator pedal gently.
22. Repeat (20) and (21) for third, fourth and fifth gears. If, due to gradients, checks or for any similar reason, the car speed drops until the speedometer needle falls until opposite the "change down" position, gear should be changed down to fourth gear as explained in (20) and (21) except that the accelerator pedal is kept down all the time. Similarly, gear may be changed down if required to third or lower.

## BRAKE APPLICATION.

23. When slowing down for a station stop or for a signal check, neutral must be selected and engaged before coming to rest. Where practicable neutral should be engaged at not less than 10 m.p.h. if the brakes have already been applied.
24. When applying brakes on a "down" grade, release the accelerator but do not select or engage neutral unless the car is to be brought to rest.
25. To release brakes, place handle in "release" position and move it over to "running" when vacuum is restored on gauge. If a quick release is required—especially when hauling trailers—the accelerator may be pressed down slightly and engine speeded up for a few seconds, with gear in neutral.
26. To release brakes when car is "dead," pull cords under valance where marked with a star.

## TO STOP ENGINES.

27. Release accelerator pedal and press down engine stop button until engines stop.

## TO REVERSE CAR OR TO CHANGE RATIO.

28. See Notes (15) and (16).
    Keep foot off accelerator when doing this and *never* try to reverse or change ratio when the car is moving.

## CHANGING FROM ONE END OF CAR TO THE OTHER.

29. Place preselector, reverse and gear ratio levers (where fitted) in neutral.
30. Hold over engaging lever and give locking key a quarter turn to left.
31. Release engaging lever, give key another quarter turn and remove it.
32. Stop engines (see 27).
33. Apply vacuum brake and place it in "lap" position without releasing, and release hand brake if necessary.
34. Place A.T.C. flag in "up" position.
35. Proceed to other end of car, unlock controls and start up engines as previously instructed.

## BEFORE LEAVING CAR.

36. Stop engines.
37. Apply hand brake.
38. At end of day only. Select first gear and pull over engaging lever and release it smartly six times. Repeat for all other gears. This must only be done with engine stopped. If there is not sufficient air to complete these operations, select and engage neutral, start engines and run up air pressure. Stop engines before continuing.
    The object of these operations is to take up by a self-adjusting device any wear on the gear bands that has taken place during the day.
39. Place all gear levers in neutral, lock up as in paragraphs (29), (30) and (31).
40. Switch off Main Control and Lighting Switches (at end of day only).

## CONNECTING TWO CARS.

When required, two cars may be coupled together and driven as one.

41. Lock up all control tables and when coupled up only unlock the one at the leading end of the cars. The key of the second (non-driving) car should be withdrawn and locked up.
42. Two coupling "receptacles" are fitted under each headstock, one at either side, but only one is used at a time and opposite ones are connected without cross coupling. The receptacle cover is raised and the "jumper" head pushed in, care being taken that it is in the right position, as indicated by the slot and key. Be sure the jumper is pushed right in so that the catch inside the receptacle cover engages with that on the jumper.
43. Having coupled up (including screw coupling, brake, steam, etc.), the engines may be started up and the two cars driven from one control position.
44. To start the engines of the trailer car, press down accelerator and press the lower starter buttons marked "trailer" until the corresponding oil pressure lights show up.
45. To the right of the instrument board is a lamp marked "trailer air pressure," and the cars must not be moved until this lights up and shows that air is available in the trailer for working the controls.
46. When car is running alone, the jumper coupling must be carried in its correct position in the Guard's compartment.

## SHUNTING.

If required, the car may be driven from the rear end by leaning out of the side window and using one of the special shunting lever fitted at either side of the window.

47. Release left hand lever by withdrawing bolt on front face of table.
48. Pre-select first or second gear according to whether car is running with trailers or alone.
49. On cars 19 and 20, place gear ratio in "low."
50. To move car, raise shunting lever when the gear will be engaged and further upward movement will open throttle.
51. To stop car, pull down lever to engage neutral and press down further to apply brake.
    Note.—A series of notches will be felt in moving the shunting lever, and it should be moved slowly with a slight pause at each notch.
52. When shunting is completed, bolt lever in neutral position, return pre-selector to neutral and pull over and release engaging lever.

## IN CASE OF CAR FAILURE.

53. Stop engines immediately.
54. Place all controls in neutral and lock them.
55. Find out on which side of car the failure has occurred.
56. Remove the set screws holding the air connections of the driving axle box on the side of the car that has failed.
57. Screw in the "neutral" set screws carried on the car in place of those removed.
    Note.—All set screws are numbered and must be replaced by those carrying corresponding numbers. See that set screws are tight home.
58. Carry on driving the car by one engine only.
59. Take great care not to accidentally press the starter button of the engine on the side of the car that has failed.
    Note.—The car side numbers are painted on the sides of the car just above the engine cover plates and these numbers correspond with those marking the starter buttons.
60. Should it be necessary to tow the car, both axle boxes must be placed in neutral as in (56) and (57) above.

**THE ASSOCIATED EQUIPMENT CO. LTD**
SOUTHALL, MIDDX.

TELEPHONE:
SOUTHALL 2424
(17 Lines)

TELEGRAMS:
"ANGASTOW PHONE
SOUTHALL"

*Plate 253: W3, one of the first design series of streamlined railcars.*
*British Rail.*

# Appendix Six:                                              Heating of Railcars

The heating of railcars Nos. 1-18 (which were not constructed by the GWR) was by engine cooling water. Problems arose as this system depended on the correct functioning of a thermostat, which was incorporated in the system, to restrict the flow of water direct from the engine to the heater tank, and caused the water to circulate through the heating pipes. From the time A.E.C. railcar No. 18 was built, and the subsequent units were designed to haul tail-loads of steam-heated rolling stock, this restricting heating system, employed in the early cars, had to be abandoned. Accordingly, all the new cars delivered to the GWR were provided with Vapor Clarkson steam generators, which supplied steam to the standard heating equipment of the trailing vehicles, and to the cars which now embodied similar equipment.

This generator was manufactured by Gresham & Craven Ltd., of Salford, under licence from the Vapor Car Co., of Chicago. Oil-fired and fully automatic in action, the generator incorporated a special coil which split the combustion gases into very narrow films flowing in reverse direction to that of the water in the coils. The result was a heat release of more than 1,000,000 BTUs per cubic foot of combustion space — an exceptionally large output for a set which occupied a floor area of only 24in. x 36in. The generator had a capacity of 300lb. of steam per hour, and an evaporation of from 10 to 12lbs. of steam per lb. of fuel oil. This oil was the same as that used in the engines, and was carried in a separate 45 gallon tank, which held more than enough for a normal day's working.

A ½hp electric motor drove the water and fuel pumps, ignition and blower, the fuel supply to the burner being automatically regulated according to the quantity of water circulating through the coil and the amount of air being delivered for combustion. By running the motor at three different speeds, the approximate steam supply needed for the car alone, or for the car with one or two trailer vehicles, could be readily obtained. The pressure of the steam supply could also be controlled up to a maximum of 200p.s.i. by means of a pressure switch. This shut down the set when the pre-determined pressure was reached, and restarted it automatically when the pressure fell below this figure. Automatic control of superheat up to a maximum of 600 degrees Fahrenheit was also a feature of the unit.

Complete protection was given by automatic safety devices which immediately stopped the set working in the event of the water or fuel supply failing, breakdown of the ignition, overheating, or from any other cause.

As the illustrations (*Plates 254 and 255*) show, the boiler was mounted on an open frame stand. This was enclosed in a small cupboard in the luggage compartment of the car to which access was easily obtained. A 90 gallon water tank, with a filler on the outside of the car, was installed alongside the boiler. As the coil assembly was an independent unit capable of being easily removed from the frame, the periodic cleaning of the coils was reasonably easy.

The technical specification of the generator No. V4930 was as follows:

Max. Water Consumption             16 gallons per hour
Max. Fuel Consumption              1.6 gallons per hour
Capacity of Water Tank = 100 gallons = 6.25 hours working at full output
Capacity of Fuel Tank = 50 gallons = 31.25 hours working at full output
Working pressure of steam supply = 45lb. per sq. in.
Temperature of steam approx. 300 degrees Fahrenheit
Capacity 300lb. per hour

Many reports were prepared on the subject of 'Railcar Heating' and an extract from one such letter shows a typical problem.

*Drawing Office 5th Dec. 1944, Swindon*

Diesel cars Nos. 19 to 38 were built by Great Western, and with the exception of the parcels car No. 34 and the twin units, all were fitted with Vapor-Clarkson Steam Generators for heating the saloons and drivers' compartments. Owing to the frequent failures of the Steam Generators when they were first fitted, it was decided to modify the arrangement so that the drivers' compartments should be heated by engine cooling water which at that time was considered to be satisfactory on cars Nos. 1 to 18. Cars Nos. 26, 27, 29 and 33 were so altered but, as complaints were immediately received regarding these vehicles, the matter was further investigated, and it was found that with the exception of the twin units, the thermostats had been removed from all cars by the A.E.C., and without the thermostats the heating of all cars using the engine cooling water was unsatisfactory. When it became known that the thermostats had been removed, no further cars were modified.

Since the introduction of the Vapor-Clarkson Steam Generators various modifications have been made to improve their performance and, when correctly maintained, their operation is now generally satisfactory. This fact is proved by the performance of the cars stationed at Bristol to which the Swindon fitter was not called during the whole of the winter of 1943/4. When these units are operating correctly, satisfactory heating is provided both in the saloons and drivers' compartments. At the end of the 1943/4 winter, the thermostats in the engine cooling water circuit of the twin units were still fitted and it is significant that, during this winter, no complaints were made to the Drawing Office regarding the heating of the drivers' compartments of these cars, though some troubles were experienced with the Vapor-Clarkson Generators used for heating the additional car running with these units.

When it was ascertained that the thermostats had been removed from most of the cars to which they had been fitted, the matter was taken up with the A.E.C., who stated that difficulty had been experienced in maintaining the thermostats and obtaining spare parts, and they recommended that an electrically-driven pump be fitted in the heating pipe circuit to maintain an adequate flow of water through that part of the system. It was agreed to fit one car experimentally in this manner and a pump has been obtained, but, up to the present, the Carriage & Wagon Dept. have been unable to obtain delivery of a suitable motor.

With regard to the suggestion that an electric plate warmer be fitted in the drivers' compartments, it is not considered that the existing electrical equipment would be able to maintain the additional electrical load which would be approximately 26 amps., and an additional dynamo would be required to be driven from the main engine shaft. From the above it will be seen that satisfactory heating on all cars fitted with Vapor-Clarkson Boilers can be obtained if adequate maintenance is given to the generators. For cars not so fitted, and obtaining heat from the engine water, the restoration of the thermostats will produce a marked improvement.

In the meantime, the Carriage & Wagon Dept. have been asked to try to expedite the delivery of a pump motor so that the alternative scheme may be tried.

Another extract shows the effort being put into the problem.

Cars Nos. 19-38 were originally heated by Vapor-Clarkson steam generators, but owing to frequent failures originally experienced with these units, four cars Nos. 26, 27, 28 and 29 were modified so that the drivers' compartments were heated by the radiator cooling water. This did not prove satisfactory and application has been made from the Wolverhampton Division for these cars to be reconverted to the original layout. The Vapor-Clarkson steam generators are giving less trouble than formerly, but the water pumps on these units are the main cause of failure and car No. 22 is now fitted with a slow-acting pump which appears to be giving better service. Parcel cars Nos. 17 and 34 have the drivers' compartments heated by radiator cooling water and are heated most efficiently when thermostats are fitted. Car No. 18 is also heated by radiator cooling water, but also has a thimble-tube boiler to heat trailer cars which may be attached. Twin cars Nos. 35 and 38 are also heated by radiator cooling water and the same remarks apply regarding the thermostats. Steam generators are fitted to Nos. 35 and 37, but only heat the additional car when three car sets are formed.

From various sources, it appears that the heating on these vehicles was never totally satisfactory, and late in the 1950s, modifications were still being carried out and reports written.

*Plates 254 & 255:* Two views of the Vapor Clarkson steam generator.
*(A.E.C. Ltd.) Leyland Vehicles Ltd.*

# Appendix Seven:

# General Appendix to the Rule Book Extracts

### Extracts from the 1936 GWR General Appendix

**WORKING OF STREAMLINED RAIL CARS.**

In connection with the running of Streamlined Rail Cars the instructions for Auto Car Services shewn on pages 128 to 131 must be observed except as varied below:—

**Clause 1** (fifth paragraph).
Guards must in all cases give the signal to the Driver to start by means of the electric bell communication provided for the purpose, and not by hand signal. In case of failure of the bell communication, the Guard must give a verbal message and must report to his Station Master that the bell communication has failed, the Station Master to notify the Telegraph Lineman immediately.

**Clause 3** (second paragraph).
This paragraph will not apply to streamlined cars.

**Clause 4.**
A Guard or other man to act as Guard must always be provided for Streamlined Rail Cars.

**Clause 21.**
When any movement with passengers in the car is required, the Driver must always be at the leading end.

When there are no passengers in the car and bell signals can be given in the rear driving compartment by the Guard or Shunter from the leading end, the shunting movement may be performed with the Driver at the rear end, but the Guard or Shunter must ride at the leading end, keep a sharp look-out and be prepared to signal to the Driver by means of the bell push provided for the purpose.

The bell codes to be used are:—

"Go ahead" .. 1 ring.
"Set back" .. 2 rings.
"Stop" .. 3 rings.

In the event of the bell communication failing the Driver must ride at the leading end.

**Rule 55.**
Streamlined Rail Cars must not be relied upon to operate track circuits, and the Guard will always be held responsible for carrying out the provisions of Rule 55 in regard to reminding the Signalman of the presence of the car when it is stopped at signals.

At those places where difficulty is likely to arise if the car is allowed to draw up to Advanced Starting signals or Starting signals in advanced position in consequence of the distance which the Guard would have to walk in going to and from the signal box, the car must be brought to a stand opposite the signal box, and kept there until permission is received from the box in advance to allow it to proceed.

This, however, will not relieve the Guard from the responsibility of going to the signal box for the purpose of carrying out the provisions of Rule 55.

**Clause (c).**
The duty of going to the Signal Box must be performed by the Guard or Shunter, and to enable this to be done a Guard or Shunter must always accompany the Car.

**Use of "Vehicle on Line" Switch.**
In the event of the Streamlined Car having to stand on a platform line where a "Vehicle on Line" switch is provided, it must be protected by means of the switch, and the Station Master concerned will be responsible for seeing that this is done.

**Instructions to Signalmen.**
Streamlined Cars must be brought within the protection of the Home signal as soon as possible. At Signal Boxes where an additional Home signal is provided, the Signalman must not acknowledge the "Is Line Clear?" signal for the Streamlined Car until permission can be given for the car to proceed to the Inner Home signal. Streamlined Cars must not be detained at the outermost Home signal except in case of emergency.

Where intermediate Block signals controlled from the Signal Box in rear are provided, the Car must not be allowed to leave the Signal Box in rear until the "Is Line Clear?" signal has been accepted by the Signalman at the Box in advance, nor must any train be allowed to follow the Car towards the intermediate Block signal until the "Train Out of Section" signal has been received for it.

**Trains stopped by Accident, Failure or Obstruction or other exceptional cause. Rules 179 to 181.**
The Guard must act in accordance with the Rule, and where necessary the protection usually performed by the Fireman must be carried out by the Driver. Clauses (g) and (h) of Rule 179 and (h) of Rule 181 will apply to Streamlined Rail Cars.

Should it be necessary for the Guard or Driver to leave the Streamlined Rail Car unattended the Driver, before leaving the Car, must apply both hand brakes and place the engine in reverse on falling gradients. The gear change lever must be locked up by the Driver in the tool box. All doors giving access to the Driver's compartments must be locked before the Driver leaves the Car to carry out the provisions of these Rules.

**No Additional Vehicles can be attached to the Car.**
A special coupling is carried in the car for use in emergency only, by means of which the Car can be pulled or propelled by an engine. Whenever the Car has to be pulled or propelled the special coupling must be used.

When the special coupling is used the Streamlined Car may be drawn by any type of engine, tender or coach, and where the line is straight this may be done at normal speeds. On sharp curves the speed must not exceed 5 m.p.h. Propelling movements must be made very carefully and must not in any case exceed 5 m.p.h.

**Head and Tail Lamps.**
The Car will not carry the standard G.W. head or tail lamps.

After sunset, or during fog or falling snow, or when proceeding through a tunnel, a red light must be exhibited at the rear to act as tail light, and the two white lights (horizontally at platform level) must be exhibited at the leading end as "A" headlights.

When "B" headlights are required, one white light (at top—centre) will be used.

The switching on of Head and Tail lights after sunset, during fog or falling snow, or before passing through tunnels, must be performed by the Driver.

A spare oil lamp is to be carried on each car for use in emergency or when standing in sidings. A bracket is provided to enable this lamp to be used when necessary.

**Instructions to Guards.**
The "right-away" signal must invariably be given by means of the vestibule bell and must not be given until all doors are closed and securely fastened.

The doors next to the adjoining running line must not be used except under unavoidable circumstances, and in such cases special care must be exercised to see that no other train is approaching.

The number of passengers in and out of each station must be recorded on the Guard's journal. Guards will be responsible for keeping the two clocks in the car at correct time.

**Warning of the approach of Car.**
These cars are fitted with a whistle at each end, operated from the engine exhaust, also an electric horn for use when stationary or moving slowly, and Station Masters, Depot Masters, Permanent Way Inspectors and Gangers must specially warn their men of the latter in order that the signal may not be confused with that given by a road vehicle. Men must also be prepared for the car to approach them quietly and at high speed.

It is most important that men engaged on permanent way work, etc., shall move promptly to a point of safety upon sighting or receiving audible warning of the approach of the Car.

**Automatic Train Control Apparatus.**
Streamlined Rail Cars are equipped with A.T.C. apparatus at each end. After a Car has been standing for a considerable time the vacuum in the reservoir may be destroyed, thus opening both the A.T.C. brake valves. Before the Car is moved, both brake valves must be closed to enable the Driver to create the necessary vacuum, and the Driver must ask the Guard to raise the brake-restoring handle on the apparatus at the rear end of the Car until five inches of vacuum has been created.

**Gas and Water.**
Gas will be required for the Buffet Car and a supply of water for lavatories and buffet where provided.